Managing Dynamic Networks

Lieber Jörg,

eine Dublin-Münsteraner

(oder sogar europäische)

Co-Produktion.

Hoffentlich auch im

ERCIS-Kontext hilfreich.

Viele Grüße

[illegible]

Stefan Klein
Angeliki Poulymenakou
Editors

Managing Dynamic Networks

Organizational Perspectives of Technology Enabled Inter-firm Collaboration

With 26 Figures
and 23 Tables

Springer

Professor Stefan Klein
University College Dublin
Belfield
Dublin 4
Ireland
E-mail: stefan.klein@ucd.ie

Dr. Angeliki Poulymenakou
Athens University of Economics and Business
Patission 76
10334 Athens
Greece
E-mail: akp@aueb.gr

Cataloging-in-Publication Data
Library of Congress Control Number: 2005937526

ISBN-10 3-540-25367-X Springer Berlin Heidelberg New York
ISBN-13 978-3-540-25367-9 Springer Berlin Heidelberg New York

Springer is a part of Springer Science+Business Media
springeronline.com

Printed in Germany

Cover design: Erich Kirchner
Production: Helmut Petri
Printing: Strauss Offsetdruck

SPIN 11408673 Printed on acid-free paper – 42/3153 – 5 4 3 2 1 0

Preface

In the current business environment, collaboration and networking seem to be promising strategic options. As an outbound maneuver they are used by firms to extend their control over a complex and distributed environment and to achieve an advantageous position. As an inbound maneuver they are targeted at extending and augmenting the firm's capabilities.

The proliferation of information and communication technology has been a major driver for increased networking. Technology itself follows a networked model. It facilitates and enables networking by providing an information and communication infrastructure and by leveraging positive network effects.

Networks appear in a multiplicity of arrangements and have become ubiquitous forms of organising. Networks emerge across all parts of society; from neighbourhood networks and the Mafia to international political or military alliances. Medieval examples of far flung trade networks like the Hanseatic League underscore, that networks are by no means a new phenomenon. Combining different firms, inter-firm networks manifest themselves in highly diverse, criss-crossing and overlapping forms and shapes. However, despite their benefits networks are precarious organisational arrangements. They are inherently unstable, hybrid and underorganised.

As a response, the contributions in this book emphasize the salience of dedicated and diligent network management. Network management is not just an extension to classical management but requires a profound reorientation and acknowledgement of network-specific requirements. Looking at European examples of ICT enabled inter-firm networks in different industries – education, construction, automotive, grocery retailing, pharmaceutical and bio-technology industry, telecommunication and mobile technology, IT and financial services –, the chapters reflect the diversity of network forms across sectors and countries. Employing quantitative as well qualitative methods embed in rich and diverse theoretical traditions, they provide a contextualized account of network management practices and challenges. Specifically the chapters elaborate on:

- network strategy and identity,
- network governance,
- the management of a portfolio of network relations,
- social capital and control,
- power and identification,
- performance measurement and benchmarking, and
- the role of information, knowledge and communication infrastructures.

The life-cycle view of network management reflects the changing managerial requirements as networks emerge and are transformed. At the same time, it provides a framework to position and link the various contributions.

The contributions in this book are based on research, which was funded by the European Commission through the 5th Framework Programme in a project on Dynamic Organisational Management for Interfirm Network Orchestrations (DOMINO, IST-2000-29545).

Table 1. The DOMINO consortium

Participating Organisation	Representative
Athens University of Economics and Business, Greece (co-ordinating partner)	Professor Angeliki Poulymenakou
Copenhagen Business School (CBS), Denmark	Professor Kenneth Husted
University of Muenster, Germany	Professor Stefan Klein
University of St.Gallen (HSG),Switzerland	Professor Daniel Corsten
DIOS A/S - Danish Institute for Organization, Denmark	Kim Pedersen
Exodus S.A., Greece	Anastasia Garbi
Namics AG, Switzerland & Germany	Dr. Dorian Selz
Project Online S.A., Greece	Anastasia Garbi
ECR - Efficient Consumer Response Association, Switzerland	Valentin K. Wepfer

Our thanks go to Athanassios Chrissafis, who provided helpful feedback and guidance in his role as project officer on behalf of the Commission of the European Communities and Dr. Kostas Samiotis who was the DOMINIO project manager.

Professor Andrew Deegan, Dean of the School of Business, UCD, provided generous support for the book project. Elpida Prassopoulou has been instrumental as our editorial research assistant. Our colleagues Harry Bouwman, Torsten Brodt, Daniel Corsten, Ulrich Frank, Marcel Gogolin, Martijn Hoogeweegen, Robert Johnston, Bernhard Katzy, Kate Kenny, Elpida Prasopoulou, Kai Reimers, Dorian Selz, Pascal Sieber, Alexander Teubner, Theresia Theurl and Rolf Wigand reviewed the chapters and provided critical feedback. Kai Wehmeyer put the book into its proper shape. Finally, Dr. Werner Müller and Manuela Ebert, Springer, provided guidance and critical support during the editing and publication process.

Angeliki Poulymenakou
Stefan Klein

Contents

Part I
Framing Inter-firm Network Management

Chapter 1

Networks as Orchestrations: Management in IT-enabled Inter-firm Collaborations

Angeliki Poulymenakou and Stefan Klein
Athens University of Economics and Business; University College Dublin

Abstract: In which way does network management display the characteristics of networked modes of organising? Based on a brief digest of the history, motives and alleged benefits of network arrangements, the chapter elaborates on modes of managing networks. It does so by reflecting in particular the role of information and communication technology for and in networks. As conclusion a balanced view of networks is articulated.

Key words: Motives and benefits of networking, definition and characteristics of networks, IOIS, modes of network management

1. Introduction

> *„The impulse to set-up a co-operative venture is almost always the insight that co-operation is the only way to achieve strategic opportunities beyond the individual companies' capabilities. This justifies the price of a not sufficiently predictable and manageable, precarious co-operative relationship." (Bleicher, 1999:546, own translation)*

Co-operative arrangements have a long tradition (Granovetter, 1994). Medieval examples like the Hanseatic League, a trade network among cities in the Baltic region, show already elaborated and advanced inter-organisational networks. In the literature the concept of inter-organisational networks has been first coined during the 1930's in the field of organisational behaviour (Roethlisberger and Dickson, 1939) in order to describe patterns of human behaviour. Ever since then, the idea of a network-like pattern characterizing the behaviour of various actors (e.g. humans, organizations, states) has infiltrated various field of research like sociology, organization theory and even molecular biology.

In recent years, the concept of inter-firm networks reached a new momentum especially in organization theory and information systems literatures as a result of vast technical innovations that took place in the early 1990's. The wide proliferation of ever more advanced information and communication technologies (ICTs) coupled with intense and rapid changes in economic activity (Doz and Hamel, 1998) shaped a highly complex and rapidly changing environment where organizations needed a profoundly different set of characteristics in order to successfully pursue their activities (Miles and Snow, 1986). One of the prevailing visions in both industry and academia, regarding the new organizing principles for firms, was that of "an electronic network, which [...] enables a fluid, flexible and dense pattern of interconnections that cut across various intra- and inter-organizational boundaries" (Nohria and Eccles, 1992: 289).

Inter-firm networks are a model for organizing people and resources (Ebers, 1999) which is fundamentally different to the logic of bureaucratic organizations. More specifically, networks are complex actor constellations with the purpose of "organizing economic activities through inter-firm coordination and cooperation" (Ebers, 1999). The central issue in the structuring of such arrangements is the precarious balance between competitive advantages and efficiency gains on the one side and coordination costs on the other (Grandori and Soda, 1995). McGuire (1988) posits that the existence of contradictory elements forming the network and the need for synthesis in order to achieve a form of stability leads to a dialectical process where actors negotiate their interdependence (Grandori and Soda, 1995). This combination of diverging and converging forces among the network actors typically yields a high level of organisational dynamics (Benson, 1975) which is different from the aggregation of the partners' attributes.

The potential of high benefits and increased efficiency (Oliver, 1990) explain the recent propensity of firms to enter into inter-organizational arrangements (Vyas, Shelburn, and Rogers, 1995). Yet, despite the growing acceptance of such inter-firm arrangements as the appropriate strategic and organisational choice for the new economic landscape, their success is far from guaranteed (Madhok and Tallman, 1998). Inter-organizational networks are unstable arrangements in the sense that major changes might occur in the composition without being planned by one or more of the partners (Das and Teng, 2000). The reason for such instabilities can be attributed to the fact that networks are under-determined organizational forms: they lack the clear rules of market exchanges and do not feature management structures like companies. It is the premise of this book that a dedicated network management function (Ireland, Hitt, and Vaidyanath, 2002) that enables partners to *handle the inherent complexity of inter-firm relationships* can mitigate these difficulties.

There are a number of reasons justifying the need for a dedicated network management function spanning from governance choices to innovation processes and technological investments among the partners. Inter-firm networks are powerful instruments not only to recruit superior resources and competencies but also to develop competencies in a cooperative manner (Browning and Beyer, 1995). However, there is a huge challenge to manage and balance incentives among the participants (Buono, 1997) in order to be able to create and maintain a seminal mix of competencies and not slip into exacerbated conflicts among the network members (Alter, 1990).

Innovation is one of the primary reasons for the formation of inter-organizational networks (Hagedoorn, 1993). Recently matured or emerging technologies favour a collaborative mode of research and development since the necessary resources are harboured by a web of firms (Ouchi and Bolton, 1988). To stay on track of technological innovation, firms are obliged to team up with each other in order to gain access to the necessary expertise in a fast and flexible way (Dyer, Kale, and Singh, 2001). However, the knowledge produced through inter-firm collaboration needs to be carefully managed for all the partners to reap the benefits of their collaborative efforts (Inkpen, 2000). As Simonin (1999) explains the process of knowledge transfer in inter-organizational environments is quite ambiguous. Therefore *managing an inter-firm collaboration as a knowledge pool* is not only intellectually challenging but poses also numerous challenges in terms of intellectual property rights management.

Network management focuses on benefiting from the open-endedness of networks in terms of flexibility and at the same time tries to compensate for some of the challenges or deficits that emerge from the lack of strict organizational rules and routines. Moreover, network management provides the concepts and methods that organizations engaged in inter-firm arrangements need in order to make sense of the more complex yet inherently more focused situation in which they are involved. Dyer et al. (2001) define the role of network management as to "coordinate all [network] related activity within the organization". However, network management is not only about setting up the collaboration. It is also about sustaining it over time. As Doz and Hamel (1998:vi) state "managing the [network] relationship over time is usually more important than crafting the initial formal design". Unlike what most managers think, once the deal is done the work is not over (Isabella, 2002). On the contrary, it is precisely at this point that network management is even more important since *managers need to infuse a collaborative mindset on the partners* in order to ensure success.

2. Network characteristics

Inter-firm networking has been examined by a large number of theoretical strands (Monge and Contractor, 2003), which provide rich insights in various managerial and organizational issues linked to this type of collaboration among firms (Powell and Smith-Doer, 1992). Since the early 1970s when the concept of network drew significant interest, various perspectives have been developed on what exactly the term entails.[1] This is illustrated by the great variety of inter-organizational arrangements like strategic alliances, consortia, joint ventures, geographical areas or social networks that have been examined under the prism of networks (Ebers, 1999). A basic reason for this variety is the fact that the term network according to Ebers (1999) is sufficiently abstract since it refers to "the structure of ties among the actors of a social system" (Nohria and Eccles, 1992) where actors can be individuals, organizations or even states while ties among them can be based on anything that can form the basis of a relation such as kinship, friendship, economic or information exchange (Nohria and Eccles, 1992).

A definition is supposed to draw boundaries and to delineate a construct (and the related phenomena) from other constructs. By doing this, a definition defines what is within its scope and thereby providing some clarity about the diversity of phenomena subsumed under one phrase. In order to define inter-firm networks, we will on the one side identify constituting elements of networks and on the other contextualize them into their environment. While we are trying to present an integrated perspective, we are drawing upon three underlying perspectives, (institutional) economics, (strategic) management and social sciences. We view the influence of information technology and technological artefacts such as interorganizational information systems as embedded in the three mentioned perspectives.

As the wide range of network names and concepts already indicates, networks appear in different forms and shapes. The common denominator is a very simple formal description as a collection of nodes and links. Whereby the nodes are organizations, typically independent firms, and the links are relationships between them, typically covering business transactions or a part thereof, governed in a collaborative or co-opetitive mode. Following from this abstract definition we can relate to network theorists who have studied structural properties of the topology of networks (e.g. Burt, 1980).

---

[1] The notion of networks is applied across a multitude of disciplines such as sociology, political science, communication and computer science, to name just a few. However, while we are not agnostic about the discussion in other disciplines, we confine our analysis to the network discourse in management and information systems.

In line with authors like Williamson (1991) we regard networks from an analytical point of view as distinct form of organizing economic activities. In particular they are regarded as distinct from individual companies, i.e. hierarchical forms of governance, and from markets. From an empirical point of view, networks are regularly described as hybrid organizational arrangements, which combine properties of hierarchical and market coordination. Hence, the boundaries between hierarchies, networks and markets are sometimes seen as blurred or indeed increasingly blurring.

Just as firms, networks can be described and characterized by myriad dimensions. We propose to characterize networks by their actors (number, types, roles etc.), by the linkages between the actors (different types of dependencies, economic, contractual and social relations, shared values) and by their environment.

Actors

Firms or companies are the main *actors* in networks. The reasons to initiate or join one or several networks typically reflect specific strategic rationales. These strategic rationales might reflect certain stages in the life cycle of a firm (Bleicher, 1999), an assessment of a firm's competencies or an analysis of the (market) environment. While we can take the whole range of dimensions the management literature has developed to characterize companies, we pay specific attention to issues such as collaborative experiences, competencies, and indeed reputation. In order to characterize networks we study roles and linkages (Kambil and Short, 1994). Roles denote the, i.e. the relative position to each other in the market (competitor, supplier- buyer, complementor, service provider etc.).

Linkages

Linkages express the type of economic dependence (Kumar and van Dissel, 1999), formal, contractual *relationships* (relational contracts) and governance structures including power relations as well as the quality of the social relationships. *Exchanges* of resources (e.g. financial, goods or services, technology, learning etc) are the economic basis of the inter-firm relationship. Compared to markets, the nature of the exchanged resources require a closer relationship, e.g. knowledge exchange, or a level of commitment and responsiveness, which can not be covered by standardized contracts. Business transactions constitute economic exchange. Williamson (1991) suggests four attributes (transaction frequency, uncertainty, information asymmetry, asset specificity) to characterize transactions and bases his analysis of comparative advantages of different *governance* structures on combinations of those attributes. Accordingly, network forms of governance are chosen, when the transaction attributes are in a middle range, i.e. when hierarchies are not sufficient to deal with the dynamics of the transactions and markets do not provide sufficient stability to deal with medium-range commitments or non-contractible issues (Bakos and Brynjolfsson, 1993).

Networks require higher levels of *social integration*, such as social capital or trust (Riemer in this volume), mutual loyalty, identification with the network and commitment, to compensate for incomplete contracts and administrative controls.

In contrast to markets, which facilitate the efficient pursuit of the participants' self interests, networks are characterized by some form a common purpose, which may be based on *shared values* or aligned strategies (Klein and Mangan, 2005) and identification with the network (Corsten et al., in this volume). While some networks show a high level of homogeneity among the linkages others are depict profoundly different linkages, some of them reflecting the prior history of relationships among individual members, different capabilities or preferences, or different roles among the members. The dynamic alignment of particular interests and common interests and the search for incentive compatible solutions is therefore characteristic for networks.

Networks are characterized by a dual boundary setting dynamics: Internally the members are defining and redefining the boundaries of what is *us* (the members) and what is *them* (the scope of the specific network). Externally the boundaries have to be defined in terms of membership or even differentiated types or levels of membership, such as core or associated. The external boundaries can be undermined or blurred by relationships members of one network have to one or more other networks (for examples see Overby and Mahnke, in this volume).

Environment

Inter-firm networks are in manifold ways linked to their *environment*, be it the competitive environment of other networks (group vs. group: Gomes Casseres 1994) or other governance forms, be it the broader view of a business ecosystem. Moreover, economic activities are embedded into a wider range of social, political and legal environments.

In *summary*: inter-firm networks are seen as distinct forms of organizing economic activities. They are governed by relational contracts, which are – compared to contracts used in markets or in a firm setting – underspecified. This makes networks very flexible but at the same time precarious organizational arrangements. Networks are highly heterogeneous organizational arrangements which do not only capture the heterogeneity of their member organizations but add their own level of heterogeneity and dynamics. While networks have boundaries of variable clarity and precision, many of them are non-exclusive, which yield situations of criss-crossing and overlapping networks (Thorelli, 1986) and calls for network portfolio management as task for the network members (Overby and Mahnke, in this volume).

3. The technology perspective

As information and communication technology (ICT) has become salient within companies, it is increasingly also shaping inter-firm networks. Networks as communication and coordination rich environments are likely to gain advantages from the implementation of inter-organizational information systems (IOIS). Given the characteristics of networks, information and communication technology (ICT) plays a pivotal role in many networks:

- By providing information and communication channels ICT enables the joint activities among separate and often distributed firms.
- Many networks are actually established to create information or communication infrastructures (Clemons, 1990) or to use information resources jointly, i.e. information partnerships (Konsynski and McFarlan, 1990).
- The recent advances in ICT infrastructures have created a situation in which companies are forming networks specifically to create innovative forms of business. While even large firms realise that they can no longer capture the dynamics of technologically driven markets alone (see Overby and Mahnke in this volume), many small and medium sized companies have identified value propositions, which are based on technologically facilitated network effects (see Riemer, in this volume for examples). Moreover, ICT facilitates changing roles and linkages within networks (Kambil and Short, 1994).

Information technology is not triggering networking only through the rational realization of its benefits for management. The role of ICT in networking has its roots in deeper institutional changes characterizing contemporary organizations. Avgerou (2002:31) argues that the perception of ICT applications "as taken-for-granted fixtures of contemporary organizations" and the subsequent pressure to exploit all the possibilities offered by new technologies is triggering to a great extend the formation of inter-firm ties that could not exist but through advanced information technology. Moreover, recent trends for restructuring and reengineering the large underperforming organizations into more efficient and agile ones is turning firms towards information technology as the infrastructure for multi-party organizational arrangements. It is therefore evident that technology is deeply implicated in the formation of inter-firm networks (Fulk, 2001). Fulk and DeSanctis (1999) point out that the increased capacity for long-distance communication among organizations has led to the proliferation of smaller firms focusing primarily on their core activities while collaborating in the form of electronically mediated networks. While Murray and Willmott (1997) stress the fact that the role of information technology in product innovation and faster production cycles is leading to the emergence of more agile and technology-intensive firms.

However, managing the organizational dimension of IOIS in networks is more challenging than within companies: the requirements on joint standards on multiple levels (e.g. semantics or infrastructure) are high, dynamics is high but resources to invest into accompanying organizational measures are typically relatively low, consensus building and performance measurement are difficult.

It has become obvious that technology alone is not a panacea to create successful networks (see e.g. Nikas and Poulymenakou; Prasopoulou et al., in this volume). Hence this volume addresses the challenges of managing networks by looking at strategic, organisational and technical issues.

4. Network management mode

The reflection on the nature and characteristics of networked forms of organising inform our understanding about the mode of managing networks and indeed in a networked environment. While network management in its core applies to managerial tasks on the network level itself, it clearly needs to be extended into related managerial tasks in and throughout the participating organisations.

Sydow (1992) has claimed that networks require profoundly different approaches and philosophies towards networking. This reflects the underlying dialectics of extending a firms influence and scope of what it can do ("virtual size") without being able to extend organizational structures, power and control to the same level. As a result, the network mode of management emphasizes notions of orchestration and *improvisation*, i.e. indirect ways of influencing, shaping and guiding the development of the joint activities. The conductor is aware of the need to rehearse, to communicate a vision and to facilitate a dynamics within the orchestra, while the means of prescription, power and control are limited.

Balancing scope of action and responsibility

Networks face a structural risk of increasing responsibilities in the extended realm of the network without extending the scope of influence and action accordingly. As the influence and scope of action cannot single-handedly be extended in a network setting, a common sense of support for those who take responsibility needs to be developed.

Mobilizing support

We see networks as widely dispersed multi-layer arrangements. This implies that support for the network needs to be extended beyond the immediately affected members of the participating organisations, typically management and the boundary spanners. Throughout the ranks and files of the organisations, uncertainties about the network and its impact on daily routines as well as on the future of the company may prevail and need to be addressed. To convey a balanced sense of collaboration opportunities and challenges is certainly one of the most difficult parts of network management.

Identity

One way of mobilizing support is to create a strong sense of identity, e.g. to build on shared values and to provide a platform for identification. However, in most cases the firms' identities will be stronger than the network's identity. Throughout the network, the scope of cultural diversity is higher and hence the risk of misunderstanding and conflict. An obvious need emerges to create a sense of tolerance and indeed appreciation of the diversity as a source for learning and innovation. And yet, as the notion of social capital illustrates (see Riemer, in this volume), there is a clear risk of overinvestment in the network.

Embedded technology

As networks are communication rich environments. In order to succeed as a distributed and under-organised arrangement, extensive forms of communication are needed to stabilize the network. Recent advances of technology have particularly focused on facilitating the virtual presence of individuals and thereby lowering communication thresholds. Information infrastructures have been developed to increase the level of informatization (Zuboff, 1988) and transparency throughout the network. However, organizational embedding and processes of sense making and critically reflecting the informational models and representations of the network (Lilley et al., 2004) appear to be prerequisites of network success.

Network lock-in

As networks are stabilized they create exit barriers. Exchanges throughout the network, network specific assets, inter-organisational information systems and the reputation of the network all create barriers for those who want to leave the network. Given the complexity of trade-offs of network membership, no simple guideline can be provided. However, network members should critically and openly review their social, intellectual, human, technological and financial investments and returns, as well as network strategy and governance in order to avoid a creeping deterioration of the network.

5. Towards a balanced view of networks

While the Arthur D. Little (2001) study gives evidence of an impressive acknowledgement of the virtues of partnering throughout all industries, it raises at the same time concerns that partnering (and for that matter networking) might be viewed as opportunistic or idealistic business behaviour. Opportunistic in the sense that during the late phase of the Dot.com boom stock markets typically paid a premium for even announced partnership agreements. Idealistic in the sense that benefits were rated higher than the related risks and the awareness of the challenges of network management had not been well developed. Neither of these views, we argue, informs in an appropriate manner the content of network management.

In this volume we propose a balanced view of network management in the sense that opportunities and expectations of firms engaged in networking arrangements need to be moderated by adequate reflection upon and action on issues that transcend the boundaries of the firm and can only be resolved in a consensus mode. A fundamental element of inter-firm networking is the dynamic and evolving nature of these arrangements. We explicitly address this notion by proposing a *life cycle* view for network management. Management challenges and ensuing decisions to be made change significantly in nature according to the stage in the network 'life' we are considering.

The life cycle model for network management is presented in chapter 2 of this volume. Subsequent chapters comprise an in-depth exploration of issues highlighted in the framework. Our approach is selective rather than exhaustive. However, we have taken care to include works that will address is a balanced manner issues of strategy, organisation and technology which are core elements of the management framework we are proposing. The method of research is case studies comprising both quantitative and qualitative elements of analysis. This book is predominantly focused on a European perspective for inter-firm networks and this is reflected in the industrial contexts and specific networking examples discussed.

The chapters in this volume reflect this balanced view, they report about pitfalls and failures of networks as much as they reflect upon their potentials and benefits. The concluding chapter in this volume synthesises experiences and insights gained through this body of work into a set of organising principles for inter-firm network management. We strongly believe that the ability to work and thrive in networks has become one of the most essential and crucial competences for individuals and organisations alike. We hope that this book will underscore this believe and illustrate challenges and possible responses alike.

References

Alter, C., 1990, An exploratory study of conflict and coordination in interorganizational service delivery systems, *Academy of Management Journal.* **33**(3):478-502.

Avgerou, C., 2002, *Information systems and global diversity,* Oxford University Press, New York.

Bakos, J. Y., and Brynjolfsson, E., 1993, Information Technology, Incentives, and the Optimal Number of Suppliers, *Journal of Management Information Systems.* **10**(2):37-53.

Benson, J. K., 1975, The interorganizational network as a political economy, *Administrative Science Quarterly.* **20**(2):229-249.

Bleicher, K., 1999, *Das Konzept Integriertes Management,* 5th ed., Campus, Frankfurt/M.; New York.

Browning, L. D., and Beyer, J. M.,1995, Building cooperation in a competitive industry: Sematech and the semiconductor industry, *Academy of Management Journal.* **38**(1):113-151.

Buono, A. F., 1997, Enhancing strategic partnerships: Intervening in network organizations, *Journal of Organizational Change Management.* **10**(3):251-266.

Burt, R. S., 1980, Models of network structure, *Annnual Review of Sociology.* **6**:79-141.

Clemons, E. K., 1990, MAC - Philadelphia National Bank's Strategic Venture in Shared ATM Networks, *Journal of Management Information Systems.* **7**(1):5-25.

Das, T. K., and Teng, B.-S., 2000, Instabilities of strategic alliances: An internal tensions perspective, *Organization Science.* **11**(1):77-101.

Doz, Y. L., and Hamel, G., 1998, *Alliance advantage: The art of creating value through partnering,* Harvard Business School Press, Boston, MA.

Dyer, J. H., Kale, P., and Singh, H., 2001, How to make strategic alliances work, *Sloan Management Review.* **42**(4):37-43.

Ebers, M., 1999, Explaining inter-organizational network formation, in: *The formation of inter-organizational networks,* M. Ebers, ed., Oxford University Press, New York, pp. 3-40.

Fulk, J., 2001, Global network organizations: Emergence and future prospects, *Human Relations.* **54**(1):91-99.

Fulk, J., and DeSanctis, G., 1999, Articulation of communication technology and organizational form, in: *Shaping organization form: Communication, connection and community,* G. DeSanctis and J. Fulk, eds., Sage Publications, Thousand Oaks, CA, pp. 5-32.

Gomes-Casseres, B., 1994, Group versus group: How alliance networks compete, *Harvard Business Review.* **72**(1):62-74.

Grandori, A., and Soda, G., 1995, Inter-firm networks: Antecedents, mechanisms and forms, *Organization Studies.* **16**(2):183-214.

Granovetter, M., 1994, Business Groups, in: *Handbook of Economic Sociology,* N. Smelser and R. Swedberg, eds., Princeton, NJ, pp. 453-475.

Hagedoorn, J., 1993, Understanding the rationale of strategic technology partnering: Interorganizational modes of cooperation and sectoral differences, *Strategic Management Journal.* **14**(5):371-385.

Inkpen, A. C., 2000, Learning through joint ventures: A framework of knowledge acquisition, *Journal of Management Studies.* **37**(7):1019-1043.

Ireland, R. D., Hitt, M. A., and Vaidyanath, D., 2002, Alliance management as a source of competitive advantage, *Journal of Management.* **28**(3):413-446.

Isabella, L. A., 2002, Managing an alliance is nothing like business as usual, *Organizational Dynamics.* **31**(1):47-59.

Kambil, A., and Short, J. E., 1994, Electronic integration and business network redesign: A roles-linkage perspective, *Journal of Management Information Systems.* **10**(4):59-84.

Klein, S., and Mangan, A., 2005, Stability in Times of Change: A Strength of Co-operatives, in: *Economics of Inter-Firm Networks,* T. Theurl, ed., Mohr Siebeck, Tübingen, pp. 89-117.

Konsynski, Benn R.; McFarlan, Warren E., 1990, Information Partnerships - Shared Data, Shared Scale, *Harvard Business Review.* **68**(5):114-120.

Kumar, K., and van Dissel, H. G., 1996, Sustainable Collaboration: Managing Conflict and Cooperation in Interorganizational Systems. *MIS Quarterly.* **20**(3):279-300.

Lilley, S, Lighfoot, G. and Amaral, P., 2004, *Representing Organization - Knowledge, Management, and the Information Age,* Oxford University Press, Oxford.

Madhok, A., and Tallman, S. B., 1998, Resources, transactions and rents: Managing value through inter-firm collaborative relationships, *Organization Science.* **9**(3):326-339.

McGuire, J. B., 1988, A dialectical analysis of interorganizational networks, *Journal of Management.* **14**(1):109-124.

Miles, R. E., and Snow, C. C., 1986, Organizations: New concepts for new forms, *California Management Review.* **28**(3):62-73.

Monge, P. R., and Contractor, N. S., 2003, *Theories of Communication Networks,* Oxford University Press, Oxford.

Murray, F., and Willmott, H., 1997, Putting information technology in its place: Towards flexible integration in the network age?, in: *Information technology and organizations: Strategies, networks and integration,* B. P. Bloomfield, R. Coombs, D. Knights, and D. Littler, eds., Oxford University Press, Oxford, pp. 160-180.

Nohria, N., and Eccles, R. G., 1992, Face-to-face: Making network organizations work, in: *Networks and organizations: Structure, form, and action,* N. Nohria and R. G. Eccles, eds. ,Harvard Business School Press, Boston, MA.

Oliver, C., 1990, Determinants of interorganizational relationships: Integration and future directions, *Academy of Management Review.* **15**(2):241-265.

Ouchi, W. G., and Bolton, M. K., 1988, The logic of joint research and development, *California Management Review.* **30**(3):9-33.

Powell, W. W., and Smith-Doer, L., 1992, Networks and economic life, in: *Networks and organizations: Structure, form, and action,* N. Nohria and R. G. Eccles, eds., Harvard Business School Press, Boston, MA, pp. 368-402.

Roethlisberger, F., and Dickson, W., 1939, *Management and the worker,* Cambridge University Press, Cambridge.

Simonin, B. L., 1999, Ambiguity and the process of knowledge transfer in strategic alliances, *Strategic Management Journal.* **20**(7):595-623.

Sydow, J., 1992, On the Management of Strategic Networks, in: *Regional Development and Contemporary Industrial Response: Extending Flexible Specialisation,* H. Ernste and V. Meier, eds., Belhaven Press, London, New York, pp. 114-129.

Vyas, N. M., Shelburn, W. L., and Rogers, D. C., 1995, An analysis of strategic alliances: Forms, functions and framework, *Journal of Business & Industrial Marketing.* **10**(3):47-60.

Williamson, O. E., 1991, Comparative economic organization: The analysis of discrete structural alternatives, *Administrative Science Quarterly.* **36**(2):269-296.

Zuboff, S., 1988, *In the age of the smart machine: The future of work and power,* Basic Books, New York.

Chapter 2

Network Management Framework

Kai Riemer and Stefan Klein
University of Münster; University College Dublin

Abstract: The chapter identifies and highlights network specific management issues. It does so by presenting a walk-through of the DOMINO network management framework. The different views and building blocks are introduced and respective management challenges are elaborated.

Key words: Network management issues, network life cycle, network and firm view, network environment.

1. Introduction

To develop a comprehensive treatise on network management is a task beyond the scope of this book. And yet, given the breadth and diversity of contributions on network management, we will introduce a framework for network management, as a frame of reference for the discussion of management tasks and approaches. The framework takes the perspective of a network manager, i.e. a governing authority or collective actor which represents the focal organisation or the network members. The framework will make our assumptions and perspectives explicit and we will use it to provide links to the book chapters. Eventually it is meant as an aid to provide points of orientation for the reader in the web of criss-crossing and overlapping network relations.

Generally, network management can be seen as the coordination of activities between companies (Konsynski and McFarlan, 1990). The managerial actions that are necessary from a network perspective are more selective and focused than general management of single firms, because a network typically serves a specific purpose for its member organisations (Castells, 1996; Riggins, Kriebel, and Mukhopadhyay, 1994). Consequently, networks rarely demand the coverage of the whole range of issues that a single firm has to address. Nevertheless, network management is not simpler nor easier. It has to deal with the collection, combination and allocation of labour and tasks, knowledge and resources, as well as benefits and profits among network members. Reflecting the precarious nature of networks, Sydow (2005:225) posits that network management itself is precarious: "the development of networks [...] is a process full of frictions, resistances, surprises and self-momentum, and therefore not steadily controllable."

Network management aims to establish structures and mechanisms that are needed to sustain ongoing coordination efforts among network members (Johnston and Vitale, 1988). Hence, management within a network environment faces a series of complexities: coordinating different actors with different knowledge and backgrounds, creating an environment where collaborative action can evolve and take place, and dynamically aligning different strategic, organisational and technological perspectives and systems.

Our network management framework does not aim at providing a recipe for network management as it cannot adequately reflect the variety of network types and the inherent complexities of networks. Rather, the framework distinguishes typical perspectives on network management and provides an orientation over network management issues. It is thus a collection and conceptualisation of network management areas that have to be taken into account by network managers and network participants. The components of the framework can be read as a checklist of potentially relevant management aspects.

We will introduce our network management framework step-by-step, explaining the different views and components in detail before we present the model in its entirety. The model consists of three distinct layers representing the different perspectives one can take in discussing networks and network management. Firstly, the network layer focuses on the network itself. Here, management can take a life cycle-oriented view or focus on the building blocks or areas in which management decisions have to be made. Secondly, networks can be dealt with from the perspective of a single firm (the firm view); single firms are the players in networks; they initiate and manage networks or they simply participate in networks. Finally, the environmental perspective captures the market and industry view on networks. Networks, their initiation and proliferation, are shaped by their surroundings but they also influence their environment. We will start by introducing the network view, followed by the firm view and the environmental view of network management.

2. Network view – the core management layer

In line with Dyer and Singh's comment "changing one's mindset from the firm to the dyad/network as a key unit of analysis may be uncomfortable because the firm is the 'unit of accrual' for performance" (1999:186), we do start with the network level as the key unit of analysis. Comparable to the management of a firm, network management is contingent on the environment, the type of network and its development stage. We will start by exploring the dynamics and challenges of network management along a model of development stages before reflecting on the role of environmental factors. A range of different types of networks will be reflected throughout the following chapters of the book. Implicitly we refer primarily to heterarchical and dynamic forms of networks (Sydow, 2005).

2.1 Life cycle view of network management

Management literature uses life cycle models of the firm to explain changing tasks and leadership requirements as firms grow and develop (Bleicher, 1999). More specifically, the outsourcing literature uses process models (e.g. Lever, 1997) to characterise the initiation and set-up of this particular type of network relations (see Prasopoulou and Poulymenakou in this volume for a theoretical reflection on the life cycle view). For networks, which are characterised as transient forms of organising, i.e. they would typically have a much shorter life span than firms, the life cycle view is salient as it emphasises the ongoing dynamics of network development: initiation, growth, transformation and eventually dissolution. The life cycle shown in Figure 1 is an ideal type to distinguish and explain generic development stages, along a plan – build – run logic, with a particular emphasis on design issues. It is, however, not meant to suggest a normative model of phases.

The life cycle view assumes network development as a result of deliberate design. While we recognize the salience of uncontrolled, indeed uncontrollable, dynamics in the development of networks, we do not focus on examples of spontaneously emerging networks. As management tasks and challenges vary across the different life cycle phases, the life cycle provides the internal context for management.

2.1.1 Initiation

Initiation is the entrepreneurial stage of networks. It is about finding an (business) idea that might work as a common purpose to link independent firms together. During this phase, a first definition of the scale and scope of the network's activities is developed as well as a first rough concept of the network members' roles and linkages. Moreover, the reasons to go for a network rather than alternative forms of organising need to be clarified.

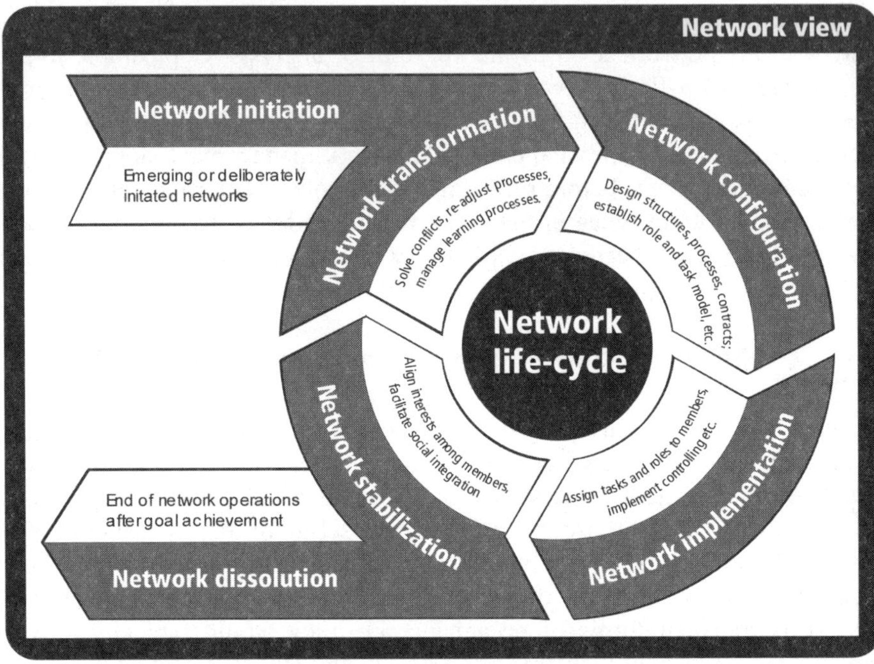

Figure 1. The network life cycle model

By bringing firms together, network initiation is the first step of community building. A core part of which is to select, screen and mobilize potential partners and thereby to define – however loosely – the boundaries of the network. The selection of partners requires special attention, as consensus about the purpose of the network and shared strategic goals is crucial for defining a joint set of activities and responses to emerging challenges. Specific (task-related), social, psychological, organisational and technical competencies are needed to be able to collaborate in an inter-firm network. While the strategic and formal fit of the companies is important, the social chemistry needs to be in balance, too. Or, as Moss Kanter (1994:96) puts it:"Yet, too often, top executives devote more time to screening potential partners in financial terms than to managing the partnership in human terms." The challenge is to find a good fit of partners who show common goals and the right fit in terms of their ability to cooperate. Alt et al. (2000) have captured some of these competencies in the notion of networkability.

A certain level of competition among the network members is almost inevitable and necessary, and yet network management has to ensure that competition is contained and does not turn into destructing force. Different types of network arrangements, alternative forms such as collaborative marketplaces or even mixed-mode arrangements (Holland and Lockett, 1997) might be considered.

While over time a good understanding of drivers and motives of networking has been developed, we still know very little about the processes leading to the initiation of networks, especially how collective actors emerge or how they are formed. Many examples suggest that typically a small group of individuals, who have developed mutual understanding and respect, forms the core of a network.

Typical management issues in the initiation phase[2]

- What is the business idea for the network?
- What is the aim, what the scope of the network? How are the boundaries of the network defined? What are the relationships towards other networks?
- What are the criteria for member selection? Which capabilities are expected? What is the targeted level of diversity or complementarity among the network members?
- What are the comparative advantages of a network arrangement compared to internal solutions, a merger or market relations?
- Would mixed-mode arrangements be beneficial?

2.1.2 Configuration

Configuration is like blueprinting the network. Miller and Friesen (1984:XIII) use the notion of configuration to describe complex organisational patterns: "... Specifically, structural, environmental, and strategic variables seem to cluster tightly to produce common 'gestalts,' 'quantum states,' or 'configurations' which reflect integral interdependencies among their elements." (see also Miller, 1996). The process of configuration is thus a complex and reflexive balancing act between the core elements of inter-firm networks (for an example see (Klein and Mangan, 2005)):

- During the configuration the network business model is further shaped. In particular the *exchange relations*, including communication, information and knowledge, among the partners and with the network environment have to be structured. The underlying operating model including the

---

[2] For a list of issues in alliance strategy see Bamford et al. (2003, 3-4).

role of technical infrastructures and systems needs to be specified as well. Expected outcomes and related property rights need to be defined in order to get the incentives among the partners right (Wolff, 1996). "For the configuration of any particular network, the flows of power and information may be actually more important than those of money and utilities." (Thorelli, 1986:39)

- A choice has to be made about the underlying organisational or *governance model* (a few options are discussed by Jorgensen and Vintergaard in this volume, see also (Riemer, Klein, and Selz, 2001)), the rules of the game need to be defined. The institutional rules, in particular the constitutional contract and the governance mechanisms and structures as well as the member roles are formulated. There are plenty of contractual and governance options from joint ventures (e.g. Kogut, 1988) to cooperatives (e.g. Theurl and Schweinsberg, 2004). However, there are few comparative studies about the underlying decision criteria for when to choose a certain governance model.
- The – typically underorganised – governance model needs to be complemented by *social* mechanisms of *integration*. The social capital among the initiators and early members of the network needs to be extended across and into the participating firms.
- The common purpose as well as shared values are articulated more clearly or even modified as a result of an ongoing specification of network design parameters. A sense of *network identity* develops and becomes articulated in terms of symbols, such as name, logo etc. The emerging identity forms a basis for increasing identification with the network (see Corsten et al. in this volume)

The configuration will be typically the result of negotiations among the network partners. This formative stage defines the identity of the network and sets the tone and the expectations for the subsequent collaboration. In their guide for mastering alliance strategy, Bamford et al. (2003) subsume initiation and configuration under the heading of "design of an alliance".

Typical management issues in the configuration phase

- What are the exchanges among the network members? What are the exchanges of the network with the wider environment?
- What are the incentives of the network members? How is an incentive compatible solution achieved? How are (intellectual) property rights resulting from joined activities assigned to or divided among the network partners?
- What is the governance model? How are institutional rules selected and communicated?

- What tasks have to be fulfilled, what roles have to be established for governance purposes?
- What is the joint strategic purpose of the network? Have shared values been identified and articulated? What is the network's identity and what are its symbols?
- Who is in charge of the negotiations?

2.1.3 Implementation and operation

During the implementation phase, the design is enacted and specific roles are assigned to the network members. Thus, it is very important to be clear about the division of tasks and roles and to facilitate members' understanding of the governance structures of the network. Moreover, structures and processes have to be put into practice and technical infrastructures and systems (inter-organisational information systems - IOIS) have to be implemented.

One major challenge is the ability to align the network strategy with the daily business operations. This involves the extension of network operations from a managerial level into the participating organisations. In operational terms numerous adjustments between the members and the network operation will then take place in order to ensure that the collaboration benefits (relational rents) exceed the coordination and adjustment costs. To this end, network managers need to guide workers and staff to incorporate the new practices in their daily routines. This type of assistance is crucial since a potential rejection of the network practice by its members will destabilise the network. Moreover, management has to learn to handle incongruities between (limited) formal authority and (extended) de facto responsibility (Sydow, 1992).

Also important is the management of communication processes, in particular if a new information systems infrastructure is established for network-wide communication. People have to adapt to the ways in which communication takes place on the network level (using new collaboration platforms), especially since the mentality of information exchange (e.g. who reports to whom, in which format etc.) at the network level might be different from the one at the firm level.

In order to be able to monitor progress along the network specific aims, e.g. learning and knowledge development within the network, performance goals and metrics for performance measurement have to be developed and agreed upon (see Papakiriakopoulos in this volume). If network rents have been accumulated, rules for the division of these rents also have to be developed and agreed upon. This might not be an easy task as Riggins and Mukhopadhyay (1994:875) observed for inter-organisational systems (here:

IOS):"The fact that IOS are shared by separate trading partners means that the benefits from IOS are both unequal and interdependent."

Typical management issues in the implementation and operation phase

- Which roles have been established? How will they be assigned to network members?
- How is the role of technology for the network determined? How will the shared systems and infrastructures and those of the network members be linked?
- What has to be done to ensure effective (IS-based) communication on the network level? In what ways do network communication processes differ from communication within the partnering firms?
- How are network strategy and daily operations aligned? What practices have been established to extend the networking operations into the participating organisations?
- Which metrics are used for performance measurement? How is performance monitoring institutionalized? How are network rents divided among the network members?

2.1.4 (Internal) Stabilization

Relational contracts[3], on which networks are typically based, are inevitably incomplete. Moreover, in comparison to firms, networks are underorganised. Hence, in addition to the design of the structural properties of the network, the social integration among the involved organisations, groups and individuals needs to be facilitated. The void which is left by the formal organisation needs to be – at least partly – offset or compensated by informal mechanisms on the inter-personal level.

Effective collaboration within the network can only be assured by aligning the different interests among the partners in the network and by facilitating the social integration among the involved people. The establishment of social ties among people improves the flow of information, facilitates the emergence of trust and helps to avoid misunderstandings and conflicts. Thus, besides configuring the organisational structure of the network, the social structure has to be taken care of to stabilize collaboration among the partners and to ensure smooth network operations.

Especially when collaboration in joint tasks in the network is complex and innovative, people need to build social relationships with each other to

---

[3] MacNeil (1985) has theoretically developed the concept of relational contracts, emphasising the embeddedness of all exchanges in relations. See also Williamson (1985:71-72).

be able to collaborate (Riemer, 2004; Riemer and Klein, 2004). Relationships provide people with trust and more importantly with a shared understanding of the tasks at hand (Riemer and Klein, 2004:278). Two individuals or a group cannot begin to coordinate complex tasks "without assuming a vast amount of shared information or common ground – that is mutual knowledge, mutual beliefs, and mutual assumptions" (Clark and Brennan, 1991). The more mutual knowledge exists between individuals, the less interaction is required to understand the situation and to deal with the task (Olson and Olson, 2000). These aspects of social relationships are covered by the concept of social capital; network managers have to take care of social capital investments to ensure effective collaboration in the rather underorganised network environment (Riemer and Klein, 2004:288). Social capital as a necessary group-level complement to individual capabilities provides the conditions that are necessary for knowledge creation processes (Nahapiet and Ghoshal, 1998).

As part of the stabilization process, the primary relations among network members need to be extended beyond the management team and the individuals directly involved with the network. For relevant units and departments, the members of the participating organisations need to be made aware of the network and given opportunities (and incentives) to establish relations with their peers in other organisations. And yet, too much embeddedness can lead to sclerotic structures and might limit the network's capabilities to respond to external changes and to innovate (Monge and Contractor, 2003).

The social texture of the network is reflected and partly complemented by a power structure, i.e. the ability of different actors to influence the action of others or the network as a whole (Forsgren and Johanson, 1992). Power may be used in a very subtle or covert way, but it can also be used explicitly (Corsten et al. in this volume).

While a basic set of collaborative capabilities are a precondition for the network initiation, those capabilities have to be further developed and extended across the participating organisations as the network develops. Hence, this phase is crucial for the social integration of the network partners and the development of social capital (see Riemer in this volume). The sense of identity is further developed – or indeed lost – during the operations (see Corsten et al. in this volume). The development of these informal mechanisms takes place throughout the existence of the network and is not bound to a specific phase in the life cycle.

Stabilization takes place as a combination of informal and formal mechanisms and can be depicted as an ongoing balancing act between the inherent contradictions of network arrangements, such as trust and control, flexibility and stability, autonomy and mutual dependence. Processes of reflexive monitoring (Sydow, 2005) need to be established as part of the ongoing learning and stabilization.

Typical management issues in the stabilization phase

- Who is responsible for the stabilization of the network?
- Which practices have emerged or have been established in the network to extend collaborative capabilities and social capital?
- Where can people meet and engage in social interactions to get to know each other and build social capital?
- How will collaborative capabilities be developed across the network members?
- How are conflicts among network members managed or contained? Have the network members developed a voice strategy (Monge and Contractor, 2003:152) to articulate dissent?
- How is the network communicated internally within the network members? How is networking within the participating organisations encouraged?
- Are there any controls for too much embeddedness?
- What does the power structure look like? How is power used?
- What is the identity of the network? What are its symbols for identification?
- Have processes of reflexive monitoring been established?

2.1.5 Transformation

Networks have been heralded as particularly dynamic and flexible organisational arrangements. Transformations of networks may be required for various reasons from external pressure to internal development at any stage in the network life cycle.

As networks develop and grow, they undergo a transformation of what initially often was a small group of companies, even a dyad, to an increasing number of participants. With an increasing number of participants but also increasing complexity or centrality of transactions and opportunism risks, formal mechanisms of rule setting and controls have to be intensified (Grandori, 1993). As this change happens, what initially is typically a personal relationship turns into an institutionalised relationship with the need to more formally define formal processes and structures. Moreover, as the individual member's influence and incentives are affected and indeed often diluted during the expansion of a network, while the network as a whole might get stronger, rules have to be defined for growth and network expansion.

Borys and Jemison (1989)address the need to constantly adjust the strategic focus of the network in order to be able to respond to changing exogenous requirements, such as market pressure or a changing network environment with increasing competition from other groups (see Gomes-Casseres, 1994). Bresser (1989) then takes up the point of realigning the individual network members' strategies with the collective strategy without eroding the individual competitive position or losing strategic flexibility individually and indeed as a network.

Bleicher (1989) emphasises the evolutionary character of networks, whose success depends on continuous joint learning and conflict management, which takes the members strategic and cultural interests into account. Successful networks are able to learn from past experiences and to re-adapt to changing needs and requirements coming from network partners and the surrounding network environment.

And yet there is a delicate balance between the need for adaptation and the need for stabilization to preserve the cohesion and identity of the network (Klein and Mangan, 2005).

Typical management issues in the transformation phase

- Are the institutionalized rules of the network regularly reviewed?
- Have rules been defined for growth and network extension, including necessary adjustments of the governance structure?
- Is the network strategy reviewed including the strategic alignment between the network members?
- Which mechanisms of environmental screening and competitive (network) analysis are used?
- How is network learning facilitated? Has the collaboration been organised as a learning process (Sydow, 1992)

2.1.6 Dissolution

Networks are flexible arrangements that often serve a specific purpose, e.g. the development of a product, and are thus established only to last for a certain period of time. Hence, a network might not only change and reinvent itself, it might also be terminated after its mission is accomplished. In this case, the partners go about there own business again; they might also participate in or initiate other networks with new (or a group of the same) partners. Another reason for network dissolution is the termination in case of serious conflicts or diverging strategic orientations, when the partners do not see any solution but the termination of network operations. Since networks and alliances are often set up between competitors, the latter case is not unlikely.

Either way, the process of terminating operations and dissolving the network has to be managed. Central to this phase is the management of the existing assets of the network and to distribute existing network rents among the members. Existing assets might have to be sold and network benefits will have to be split between network partners. From the single firm point of view, the protection of firm knowledge might be of particular interest. Firms might feel exploited by the network partners due to the uneven distribution of network benefits. Some alliances have been characterized as learning competitions, where the partners try to reap as much information and knowledge as possible from the other network members in a limited period of time (Badaracco, 1991). For opportunistic partners, collaboration might be a vehicle to internalize the skills of the other partners; Hamel (1991) observed this type of behaviour in cross-cultural alliances between Western and Asian firms. Once the individual goals have been achieved or the incentives for additional learning have diminished, the collaborative arrangement is dissolved. In these cases the benefits of one partner outweigh the common benefits of the alliance (Inkpen, 2000; Khanna, Gulati, and Nohria, 1998). Opportunistic behaviour might lead to conflict and the subsequent dissolution of the network, without fulfilling its purpose. In such situations of serious conflict, the appointment of an external third party as a mediator might help to solve the problems without having to exert legal actions.

Typical management issues in the dissolution phase

- How do firms in the network protect their knowledge assets against exploitation or uncontrolled proliferation?
- What mechanisms are in place to deal with partner exploitation and generally with conflict?
- How are assets and rents distributed in the end?
- In case of conflict, who is able to mediate between the parties in order to balance out interests?

2.2 Building blocks of network management

The network life cycle view was used to structure network management according to the typical phases a network might go through from initiation to transformation or its final dissolution. It highlighted the challenges of an ongoing transformation and the balancing between facets of management as well as the inherent contradictions of network arrangements. The next step is to focus on the building blocks or areas of network management. In this view, the same issues are of interest, but they are organised in a different way, namely according to decision areas.

Throughout the discussion of the network life cycle, three underlying themes have dominated: strategy, organisation and the technological infrastructure of networks. Hence, management aspects will be organised along these themes.

2.2.1 Network strategy

The strategy domain comprises the network mission, network resources, market positioning and the network business model (see Figure 2). Generally, there are two approaches to the formulation of corporate strategy: the market-based view, which takes an outside-in look on strategy starting from the market environment and the resource-based view, which views strategy inside-out focusing on the resource portfolio. Both approaches can be applied to networks, with the positioning of the network in the market and the definition of the network resource portfolio being the two main strategy aspects. To formulate a more detailed network strategy, the network business model is specified. Particularly since new Internet-based information systems have dramatically impacted the way firms are able to operate, scholars and practitioners have paid a great deal of attention to the discussion of the business model concept (e.g. Riemer, Klein, and Gogolin, 2002; e.g. Timmers, 1998).

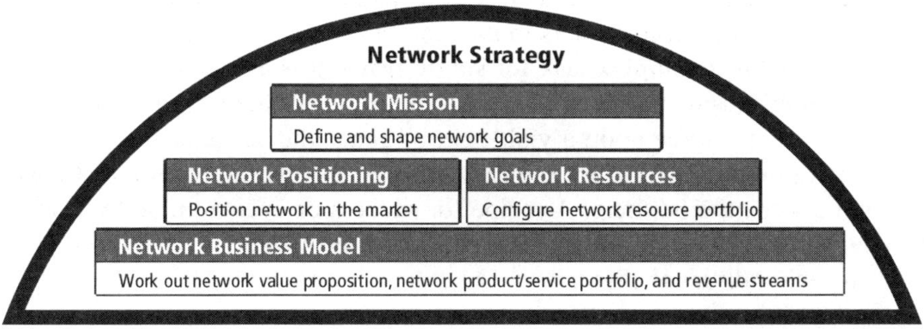

Figure 2. Network Strategy Layer

Network mission

The initiation of a network normally starts from an idea for a joint product, service, or any other project. The formulation of the network purpose and more specifically its goals lead to the creation of a network mission. A mission statement is the most top level document to describe the network. While the network mission might change throughout the life cycle of the network (see transformation above) it is important as a reference point for the network members and is the starting point to form a network identity. The mission statement however is rather unspecific and not suitable for strategic guidance. The network strategy is defined as the interplay between the internal resources and structures of the network and the external market situation and the network environment.

Network positioning

The proliferation of networks is supposed to impact entire industries by shifting competition from a firm level to a group or network level (Gomes-Casseres, 1994). In this scenario, entire supply chains or networks of firms compete with each other making it necessary for networks to position themselves and to build out a competitive advantage.

The market-based view (MBV) on strategy assumes that economic success is determined by both the structure of the market in which a firm (or network) operates and by its behaviour in relation to the five market forces: rivalry among competitors, power of customers, power of suppliers, new entrants and substitutes (exemplarily see Porter, 1997). Competitive advantages thus derive from a strategic fit of behaviour and environment and thus are determined by a unique market positioning. This view takes an outside-in perspective: A strategic advantage is achieved by positioning the network in the market and then adjusting the network operations to the external requirements. The network as a whole plays the role of and strives to be perceived as a single player within the market and stands in competition with other networks and firms. It thus has to differentiate itself from its competitors in the eyes of the customers in the market.

While this is a complex task for single firms, it is even more complex in multi-partner arrangements with the single players having their own goals and agendas. To agree upon a viable set of goals and subsequently a unique network value proposition for the network is a task that needs a lot of negotiation between the partners. A recipe for success or even a guide for how to achieve such a strategic positioning cannot be provided and has to be dealt with in each individual case.

Network resources

The resource-based view (RBV) on strategy concentrates on the development, maintenance and – importantly – the exploitation of (core) resources (see Prahalad and Hamel, 1990). Competitive advantage therefore derives from unique (core) resources and the ability (capabilities) to develop products which provide a unique selling proposition as an outcome of these resources. Ergo, an inside-out perspective is taken, by concentrating on (internal) resources and their exploitation to create marketable outcomes for the external market. While RBV initially focused on the single firm as the locus of control over resources and their development, it has subsequently been expanded to the network level, where resources are developed jointly in order compete with larger companies or other networks (Klein and Kronen, 1995). Similar to the differentiation in the single-firm case, the network has to work out its core competencies and resources to ensure the delivery of unique value to the market in terms of products and services. This requires planning and monitoring of the network resource pool and the development of products and services based on these resources.

In doing so, one of the biggest challenges is the integration of partner contributions to a functioning whole. Resources contributed to the network by the partners have to be (virtually) aggregated to a network resource pool or allocated on a project basis (Göransson and Schuh, 1997). A network wide planning and a common understanding of value creation processes are necessary. A certain level of compatibility of partner contributions has to be assured, e.g. by standardization activities and documentation of partner competencies, processes and interfaces, products, services, etc.

While in some networks, the understanding of required competencies is clearly defined and secured within the boundaries of the network, in others, network members function as boundary spanners into other networks in order to learn and to get access to required resources (see Mahnke et al. in this volume).

Network business model

While network position and resource portfolio define the network strategy in terms of the "what, why, and for whom", the network business model is necessary to spell out the strategy in terms of "how to" achieve the network goals. Following the well-known definition by Timmers (1998), a business model is:

1. "An architecture for the product, service and information flows, including a description of the various business actors and their roles; and
2. a description of the potential benefits for the various business actors; and
3. a description of the sources of revenues."

Ergo, a network business model can be characterized using the three elements (1) value proposition, (2) revenue streams and (3) architecture. While the notion of business model originally has been focused on a single firm, it has been expanded to reflect specific requirements in networks (Bouwman and Van den Ham, 2003; Riemer et al., 2002). The configuration of networked business models has to focus on the value creation network, its structure and the roles of the players involved in network value creation. More specifically, in the network context the balancing of value propositions and revenue streams between partners is a crucial task in order to achieve an incentive compatible solution for the participating players. The network business model thus specifies the group of actors, their roles in terms of value creation activities ("who does what"), the interplay between the actors ("how does it work together") and the value flow between the partners. The network business model is the starting point for the definition of the network organisation which will be discussed in the next paragraphs.

Typical management issues for network strategy

- What are the network specific mission and core value propositions?
- How can the network be positioned in the market? What is the basis for collaborative competitive advantage?
- What is the unique competence portfolio that provides the network with competitive advantage?
- Who are the network members? By what means are resources of the member firms combined to achieve collaborative advantages?
- How is the dynamic alignment of firms' strategies and the network strategy achieved?
- What is the business model of the network? Specifically, how are relational rents (network benefits, positive network effects) generated and distributed among the partners?

2.2.2 Network organisation

Drawing on the general definition of a network as "a specific set of linkages among a defined set of actors, with the additional property that the characteristics of these linkages as a whole may be used to interpret the social behaviour of the actors involved" (Mitchell, 1969; cited from Sydow and Windeler, 2000), a network comprises a structural dimension with linkages among actors and a behavioural dimension with interactions that take place between the people within the structure of the network. This definition implies not only a structural but also a behavioural understanding of a network, defining network organisation by the relations between a set of autonomous, yet interdependent organisations (the network structure) and their interactions within that structure (the network behaviour). Besides this, network policies and governance mechanisms are necessary to govern the network operations within the network structures (see Figure 3).

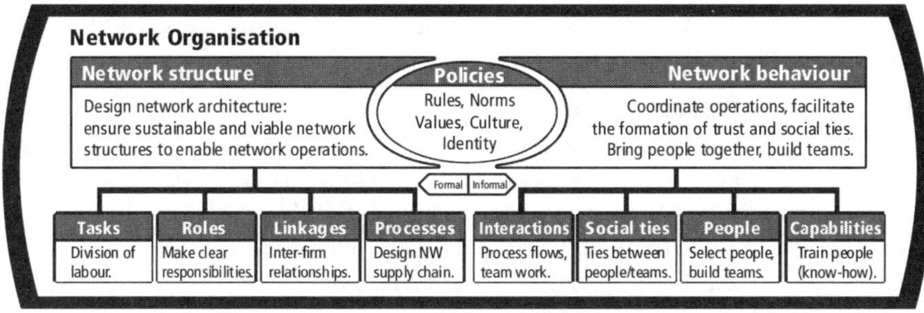

Figure 3. Network Organisation Layer

Network structure

Designing sustainable and viable network structures is a crucial management task to enable the intended network operations. For this purpose, network tasks have to be identified and assigned to appropriate roles fulfilled by the participating firms. The linkages (dyads) between the partners have to be spelled out and network-wide (inter-firm) processes have to be specified and agreed upon:

- **Tasks:** Task definition is concerned with the division of labour among partners of the network. It describes the procedure by which network members at the configuration stage decide what precisely each participating firm is obliged to do to contribute to the network. Tasks within a network can be allocated to specific partners or they can be commonly carried out by all partners.
- **Roles:** The partnering firms within a network fulfil different roles according to their size, position and competencies: e.g. initiator and adopter roles and various coordination/management roles that can be used to assign responsibilities to single actors in the network (see Table 1).
- **Linkages:** The type and structure of linkages between the network members characterizes the network. Kumar and van Dissel (1996) distinguish types of inter-organisational systems based on the linkages: sequential, pooled or reciprocal. The management of network linkages entails issues such as the type of exchange, (a)symmetries of power relations and relation specific investments (lost after the dissolution of the network), as well as the resulting lock-in issues.
- **Processes:** Organisational networks have to design their processes to ensure frictionless operations. More specifically partners have to agree on tasks allocation and network procedures in a way that will reduce complexity and heterogeneity in the network.

Table 1. Typical network management roles adapted from Göransson and Schuh (1997) and Riemer et al. (2002; 2001)

Role	Role description
Network facilitator	The facilitator fosters the initial configuration of the network by bringing together partners, consulting in establishing the necessary linkages and balancing out the incentives and contribution.
Network coach	The network coach is responsible for the entry management, the infrastructure development and settlement of the relationships between the partners of the network.
Network broker	The broker takes care of external customer relationship management, the order acquisition and other market specific tasks.
Performance manager	The performance manager configures project-specific sub-networks or value chains to fulfil a specific customer order (e.g. in a manufacturing network). He takes care of monitoring and project controlling issues.
Order manager	The order manager is responsible for the order transaction, the process management and if necessary the project planning and management.
Auditor or mediator	The auditor or mediator is responsible for a balanced allocation of resources and tasks. In the case of conflicts this role mediates between partners in order to (re-)stabilise the relationship.
Standards manager	The standards manager takes care of interconnection issues on the process and technology level between the network partners.

Network behaviour

Managing network behaviour means taking care of people, team building and the establishment of social ties among those who are working in and for the network. This means coordinating (informal) interactions, which take place within the formal organisational structure of the network. Besides, managers have to deal with the capabilities of the cooperating people:

- **People:** Firms are the institutional actors forming the network, but members (employees) of the participating firms are the ones who carry out the actual work. It is important to select the right ("network-savvy") individuals to represent the firm within the network and to work with others in the network.
- **Social ties:** The development of good social ties within the network facilitates joint understanding, information flows and efficient communication. Social ties (relationships) are necessary to build stable inter-personal trust, to avoid conflicts and to support sense making among the people as a prerequisite of effective collaboration on the inter-personal level. The formation of social ties can thus be viewed as investments in social capital (Riemer and Klein, 2004). Management has to review the emerging level of embeddedness in order to

avoid too much or too little embeddeness (Monge and Contractor, 2003).

- **Interactions:** Interactions are the exchange actions, transactions and inter-personal interactions, which take place within the formal structure of the organisational network. Network management has to coordinate interactions and to take care of informal communication among people to ensure efficient and effective information flows and process executions. Informal interactions often have the advantage of being fast and efficient, but they have significant disadvantages in terms of documenting what has happened. Thus, a good mixture of formal process execution and informal interaction has to be found. Informal interactions are important to build social relationships and thus social capital.
- **Capabilities:** Besides physical assets and formally established resources, network management has to consider peoples' capabilities in terms of knowledge and behavioural skills (cooperativeness, communicational skills etc.). Management has to develop and train people and to take care of qualifications to ensure that people are able to fulfil network goals. This is both related to the direct task-related capabilities as well as the cooperative competencies in terms of the above mentioned networkability aspect.

Policies: Network governance

Network governance comprises formal rules and norms as well as informal aspects such as culture and identity. Institutional arrangements and governance structures are needed to deal with the complexity of the network relations and to ensure the implementation of strategies. Normally, a separate umbrella organisation is established to deal with the issues of network management. However, these structural arrangements have to reflect the network strategy and the constraints resulting from the fact that the network participants are autonomous organisations. They have to combine flexible institutional arrangements, limited power, and medium-term commitment of the participants. As the participating organisations relinquish some of their managerial sovereignty and some control over their own organisational boundaries, they are particularly concerned about the development of the network boundaries and very sensitive about emerging governance structures.

Sabel's (1993) concept of networks as constitutional orders puts strong emphasis on the rule-setting function, which is institutionalized in the role of a superintendent. But at the same time, the execution of power is embedded in social processes of consultation, trust-building and re-interpretation of the situation. By these means the decentralized knowledge of the network parties is acknowledged and the adaptability of the institutional arrangement is ensured.

Network culture and identity sustain the network as a whole (the network will be perceived as an organisational entity by network participants). Appropriate network policies encourage network participants to work together. In order to enable the coordinating effect of network policies, content as well as interpretation of rules and values have to be communicated clearly. Network managers have to consider in which way norms, values etc. can be communicated to all network participants and how to ensure the internalization of these values.

Typical management issues for network organisation

- What are the general tasks, operational and management-wise, which have to be fulfilled by the network partners to ensure effective network operations?
- To whom will the tasks be assigned? What are the operational and managerial roles and who is capable of fulfilling these roles? Have all roles been assigned?
- Are the linkages between the partners clearly specified in terms of knowledge, materials, product, and financial exchanges?
- What relational investments have the partners to make to participate in the networks and in order to be able to engage in joint activities (e.g. investments in IT and systems)?
- Have network processes been specified? Do the partners know how network operations work?
- Which people will work in the network processes, e.g. have "network savvy" people with collaboration experience been selected? Have all tasks been assigned to people?
- Do the people have enough opportunities to build social relationships? Are events being planned for people to meet outside the work settings (in informal social settings)?
- Will there be mentors to guide people regarding cooperative behaviour with people from other organisational and cultural backgrounds?
- Have formal rules and policies been established to guide people in their network interactions?
- Who is in charge of network governance? Is there a governing body/entity, a management role, or certain people been appointed to take care of coordination, governance, and controlling?
- Do network managers display authentic cooperative behaviour to encourage cooperation and the development of a culture of cooperation?

2.2.3 Network Information Management

Network management deals with the coordination of the activities and resource sharing between the network participants (Konsynski, 1993). Normally network management addresses organisational and strategic concerns. Nevertheless the role of ICT as enabler of inter-organisational relationships creates a link between information management and network management (English, 1996). Regional and international organisations, across different sectors utilize capabilities of ICT to more efficiently organise their supply chains (observed in the grocery retail industry) (Holland, 1995); knowledge and learning networks exploits mediation platforms for disseminating knowledge and announce research results (observed in the biotechnology industry) (Barley and Hybels, 1992); organisations operating with many suppliers introduced collaborating platforms to monitor activities and restructure the existing relationships (observed in the construction and automotive industries) (Korezynski, 1994). In all these instances network information management acquires different roles and provides manifold contributions to network management.

Network Information Management (NIM) comprises the information and ICT issues and extends the notion of information management to inter-firm networks. From a systemic point of view, the focus of NIM is to improve the management of information flows in the network (Klein, 1993); from a strategic and relational point of view the focus is on enabling information partnerships between the participating firms (Konsynski and McFarlan, 1990). The goal of NIM is to make sure – by managing information infrastructures, systems and resources – that information can be deployed throughout the network efficiently and effectively. This encompasses the management of intellectual property rights throughout the network. In sum, NIM addresses the network's (structural, institutional and human) capabilities to process information (Teubner, 2003; Wigand, Picot, and Reichwald, 1997), the information metabolism (Brynjolfsson, 2003). However, this is not a goal in itself but has to contribute to the performance of the network.

The distinction of Information management tasks is based on Wollnik's (1988) framework, which analytically divides three domains of management tasks: (1) information deployment or information resource management (IRM), (2) information and communication systems management (ISM) and (3) information infrastructure management (IIM) (see Figure 4).

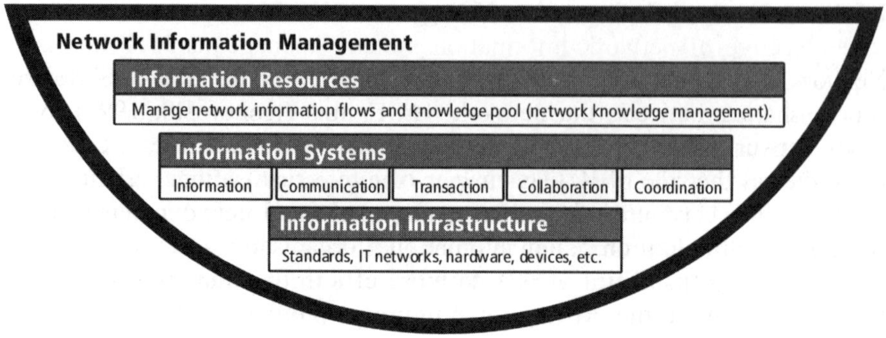

Figure 4. Network Information Management Layer

Network Information Resource Management (NIRM)

The role of network information resource management (NIRM) depends on whether information and knowledge creation are core goals of the network (Badaracco, 1991) and hence a core part of the exchange processes or whether information is primarily used to facilitate the coordination and operation of the network. In the first case, a specific information and knowledge asset management needs to be established; in the second case the main challenge is to secure the provision of information throughout the network in an economic manner. NIRM has to identify information requirements, to design network information and communication flows, to facilitate the deployment of information, and to assess the value of information. It has to support the distribution of information as well as its integration based on common semantic references (e.g. ontologies) and collaborative processes of sense making, e.g. in the area of forecasting or trend analysis.

The information value and payoff depend on the purpose of information deployment (Wollnik, 1988). Information may be a product or service in itself or an increasingly important part of products and services in the network. The latter aspect has been addressed by Porter and Millar's notion of information intensity of products and services (1985).

Information sharing increases transparency across the network and stimulates the inter-organisational cooperation and collaboration, facilitates partnerships and trust among the network members. It thus potentially improves the overall success of the participating organisations (Dawes, 1996; Kumar and van Dissel, 1996). NIRM has to identify the range of aims, tasks, and processes that are addressed in a given network and has to cater for the related information needs.

Network Information Systems Management (NISM)

The objective of network information systems management (NISM) is to support NIRM and specifically to ensure the appropriate usage of information and communication technology (ICT) for the completion of inter-organisational tasks and in particular the inter-organisational information flows (Riggins et al., 1994). This implies the selection (with a particular emphasis on the relevant functional scope), implementation and maintenance of inter-organisational information systems (IOIS).

Typically, IOIS facilitate information access throughout the network and contribute to the design of inter-organisational processes. They enable new forms of collaboration (Garbe, 1998). As a result the organisational boundaries of the network members will become blurred and opened towards the network. The technical design of IOIS, specifically different modes of coupling or integration, is related to the organisational linkages among the network members. IOIS can be designed and implemented as instruments of power or collaboration (Webster, 1995).

Depending on the information requirements and the strategic intent of the IOIS, managers have to design the functionality of the IOIS. Since various organisations exist in the context of IOIS, the offered functionality depends on the individual needs of each organisation. IOIS in networks might generally enable or facilitate, among others, the development of new sources of information, the establishment of closer links with other companies, the exchange of product characteristics between network partners, or the monitoring of the network supply chain etc. Typical generic functions of IOIS are:

- **Information:** The IOIS is the carrier of information sources, which enables new ways of decision making, increases the transparency in a supply network, smoothes the production processes etc. Examples are FAQs, electronic catalogues or enterprise portals that allow the sharing of corporate information (e.g. inventory data).
- **Communication:** The IOIS brings together geographically dispersed units and enables formal communication and the establishment of standards. A whole portfolio of communication applications such as e-mail, structured message exchange (EDI) or video conferencing and virtual meeting rooms is available to support dispersed working. Real time communication applications such as Skype™ or Siemens HiPath Openscape™ integrate different communication modes and channels and support virtual presence throughout the network.
- **Collaboration:** In order to support geographically dispersed teams and projects, IOIS are needed to support typical collaboration tasks such as joint work on documents, joint planning and coordination, and the management of information and knowledge. Here, CSCW, groupware, and

knowledge management systems enable the sharing of documents, calendars, and workspaces.

- **Transaction:** The exchange of structured transaction data is also carried through the IOIS. These data support the inter-organisational business processes of the organisations, e.g. through planning and execution of inter-company processes.
- **Coordination:** In order to facilitate an efficient allocation of resources across the network, IOIS are used to coordinate and manage resource flows and the related inter-firm processes. Especially production networks need systems to coordinate information and materials flows throughout the network between the partners; furthermore joint decision making has to be supported. Examples are workflow management systems (WFMS), supply chain management systems (SCMS), and process portals (Alt and Österle, 2004).

Potentials and benefits of IOIS can only be attained if the IOIS design is well integrated into existing systems and co-evolves with the inter-organisational processes in the network (Ives and Jarvenpaa, 1991) and the organisational routines of the participating organisations. Thus the NISM is not an isolated domain, but interacts with the information resources and the dynamic nature of the underlying information infrastructure. In particular, the existing information infrastructure has a great impact on the design of the technical architecture of an IOIS.

Network Information Infrastructure Management (NIIM)

The information infrastructure is the technical basis for the IOIS within a network. Ciborra (2002) has introduced the metaphor of "Gestell", something like a skeleton or scaffolding, to highlight the specific challenges of managing information infrastructures: while it provides a basic set of structures, the payoff is largely determined by network effects and externalities. Moreover, the infrastructure is difficult to control and can provide (or inhibit) a significant dynamics in the network. The notion of infrastructure or platform addresses those elements or aspects of ICT, which do not have a single, dedicated functional scope and owner, but which provide a broad range of support for network information systems (IOIS), i.e. numerous applications and users. The information infrastructure provides the basis for systems development, transformation and adaptation to future needs. Hanseth (2000) points out that information infrastructures are larger and more complex systems, involving significant numbers of independent actors as developers as well as users.

Information Infrastructures increasingly become the platform on which network arrangements are being built. From the early cases of a shared ATM network (Clemons, 1990), to various forms of process portals (Alt and Österle, 2004) or collaboration marketplaces (Gogolin and Klein in this volume), which enable efficient inter-organisational process support and flexible out-tasking. Despite progressing standardization and increasing availability of technologies, such as Web services, which promise flexible integration of independent organisations, the benefits of network members and of the network as a whole typically depend on the adjustment of organisational routines and practices (for an example see Nikas and Poulymenakou in this volume) and, consequently, partner and network specific investments. While partners' investments into the information infrastructure might function as trust-building credible commitments towards the common cause (Laat, 1993), a lock-in situation needs to be avoided, whereby firms remain in the network only to avoid a loss of these investments.

An important task and a great challenge for NIIM is to concatenate various information infrastructures that exist within the participating organisations (e.g. in order to couple existing IS such as ERP systems). Enterprise Application Integration (EAI) is already a serious concern within firms, but on a network level it is not only more important but also more complex. Basically, there are two strategies for providing a network-wide information infrastructure. An infrastructure can be constructed from scratch, although this is not very likely for most networks due to cost and complexity reasons. Therefore, it is necessary to link existing infrastructures and establishing a (virtual) network structure. This process takes place in two stages. Firstly, a common set of standards, protocols, interfaces etc. has to be negotiated. Secondly, existing infrastructures have to be coupled using these standards in order to create a (virtual) network infrastructure (e.g. by introducing a clearing centre). During this process, networks can either rely on common data standards (e.g. UN/EDIFACT, ebXML, etc.) and infrastructures (e.g. ENX) or they might instead develop proprietary formats for data exchange, interfaces, and applications. Finally, NIIM also has to monitor and to evaluate recent and future developments in ICT in order to identify future application areas.

Organisational and technical linkage

In most networks, ICT is an integral and embedded part of the network and its operation. However, given the diversity of technology and the multiplicity of the forms of its use, ICT may be governed in a different way than the network itself. The core axis in Figure 5 of Electronic Market, Electronic Network and Electronic Hierarchy describe the cases in which network relations and IOIS customization fit. The upper left corner of the matrix describes cases of close coupling among network members without similar technical support. This might reflect cases of efficient organizational arrangements supported by commodity ICT infrastructures and solutions. The lower right corner refers to a situation where a high level of technical integration based on customized solutions has been achieved, and still the network members operate quite independently from each other. A possible scenario could be highly standardized transactions conducted efficiently over an electronic platform, which would also provide facilities for back-end integration. The level of customization is expected to have an influence on partner-specific investments (asset specificity). If a central hub (e.g. a marketplace provider, see Gogolin and Klein in this volume) provides governance structures which are sufficient for the participants, additional investments in closer organisational linkages seem not be necessary.

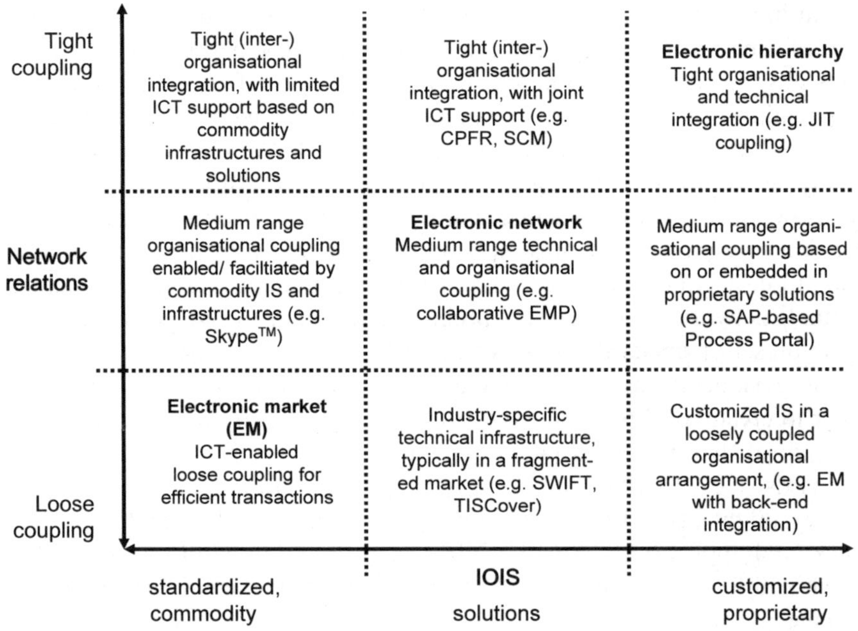

Figure 5. Network relations and IOIS customization

Typical management issues regarding network information management

- What role does information and ICT play for the particular type of network? Is the network build around an information system (e.g. an Internet business model) or is ICT only supporting network operations?
- For what specific purposes do the network partners have to share or jointly use information? What is the current or targeted information intensity of products and processes?

- How do the firms go about information sharing? Is there enough trust to ensure open information exchange? How are intellectual property rights and confidentiality protected?
- What types of joint IOIS are needed in the network and for what reason?
- Who is in charge of IOIS selection, adaptation, or development? Do the partners feature a participatory requirements analysis that involves all partners?
- Which modes of integration and technical coupling of internal systems are used? Will an integration of the partner systems be necessary or is a loose coupling enough?
- Does the network need to invest in IOIS and joint infrastructures? By what means is the distribution of cost managed?

3. Firm view on network management

So far, the emphasis has been on the network layer. We have discussed network management assuming that there is a management entity, a manager or governing body, who takes care of network-wide management. The discussion has underscored the critical and precarious balancing act among and between the network members and the network as a whole. The relationship between the network members and the network is reciprocal: the network shapes and confines the actions, policies and identity of its members as it is shaped by them. Firms establish networks, act in networks and are influenced by the participation in networks. The results and quality of network operations are often attributed to both the individual firm and to the network as a whole.

> *„The impulse to set-up a co-operative venture is almost always the insight that co-operation is the only way to achieve strategic opportunities beyond the individual companies' capabilities. This justifies the price of a not sufficiently predictable and manageable, precarious co-operative relationship." (Bleicher, 1999:546, own translation)*

The Bleicher quote underscores that not only the management of networks is challenging and precarious but that challenges are mirrored on the firm level. We are taking a firm view to complement the analysis of network-level management and to elaborate on the linkages between the two views.

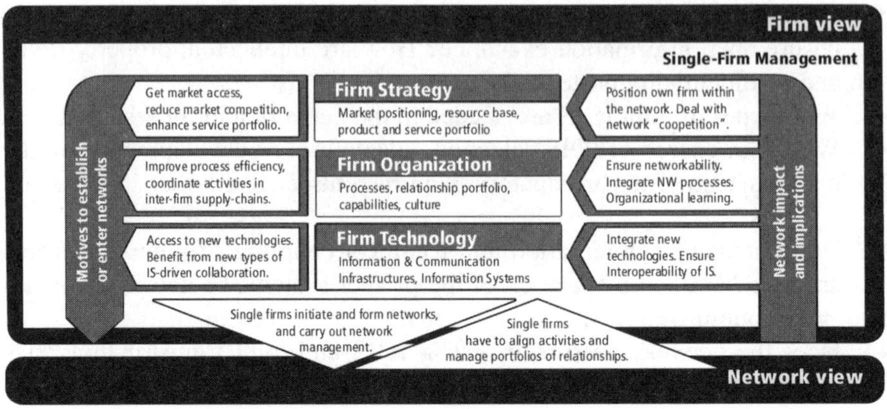

Figure 6. Firm view of network management

The firm view addresses the perspective of firms in their roles as network members or network initiators. Firms are the actors within organisational networks. Firms pursue specific goals by participating in networks and are on the other hand affected by their participation (see Figure 6).
Network achievements have to be internally exploited and intra-firm structures have to be aligned to external network requirements. Like network management, management at the single-firm level can also be discussed in the three domains strategy, organisation and technology:

1. Generally, a firm has to position itself strategically in the market in a way that ensures an advantageous competitive position. It must gain access to a superior resource base in order to be able to set-up a unique service portfolio (Hagedoorn, 1993; Johnston and Vitale, 1988). Setting-up or joining a network becomes a strategic option to extend the reach of a company's activities and still retain a high level of autonomy. It is at the same time an "outbound manoeuvre: controlling the complexity of the environment … [and] an inbound manoeuvre: augmenting the organisational capabilities." (Ciborra, 1992:96) In doing so, the establishment of organisational networks might be a suitable approach.
2. The firm has to design appropriate organisational structures that ensure efficiency, flexibility and sustainability (Zuboff, 1996). Networks often promise efficiency improvements and access to new (external) organisational capabilities (learning, benchmarking).
3. The technology (or information management) perspective highlights the increasing relevance of ICT infrastructures and information systems (IOIS) for conducting business (Hanseth and Braa, 1998; Ives and Jarvenpaa, 1991). Consequently, IOIS adoption often means network participation.

3.1 Strategy

While firms join or initiate networks for strategic reasons, their strategy and strategic thinking is at the same affected by the participation in networks.

3.1.1 Strategic motivation to form or join network

Network initiatives can be motivated either from a market-based or resource-based view. From a market-based perspective reasons for network participation might be to enter or develop new markets, to overcome barriers to market entry by collaborating with incumbent players, to collaboratively offer services/products, to reduce competition within the market or to extend control over the market environment. Well-known examples are strategic alliances in the airline industry (e.g. Star Alliance), virtual organisations of small and medium-sized companies (e.g. Virtual Factory Bodensee), which collaborate to produce joint products or distribution partnerships of so-called mega-brands (e.g. SonyEricsson).

Resource-based network initiatives (collaborative sourcing) focus on the collaborative development or the sharing of different types of resources like knowledge, technology, human resources, infrastructure etc. Well-known examples are R&D and innovation partnerships, collaborative procurement initiatives and information partnerships. For smaller firms it might be strategically interesting to cooperate in order to achieve virtual size. This is done by establishing a network-wide resource pool, where each company brings in its core competencies. The combined competencies have then to be positioned in the market.

3.1.2 Strategic implications of network participation

Entry into a network raises new strategic questions – again from a market-based and a resource-based view.

The enterprise has to position itself in the market and in the network at the same time. Networks often are complex arrangements with many different players and it is crucial for firms to search for an appropriate position or role within the network. Each company strives for a superior or at least equal position to assure its participation in the distribution of the positive effects of the network, either in terms of revenue streams, collaborative knowledge or other. Moreover, a good and powerful position allows the company to influence the network strategy to assure the achievement of its own goals, which may differ from the other participants' goals. Especially in networks where companies cooperate with their competitors ("co-opetition"), strategic positioning remains very important (Hamel, Doz, and Prahalad, 1989). The presence of cooperative and competitive behaviour is highly demanding for managers at the firm and the network level.

To be part of the overall network, the enterprise has to link its resources and activities into the overall value creation of the network. Integration in this sense means to carefully design process interfaces and to contribute to the network resource pool. On the one hand the own resources (e.g. production processes, knowledge, services) have to be adjusted and documented, so that it becomes transparent for the other network partners, what resources are available and furthermore how the firm resources may be used by the other partners. On the other hand, the company has to ensure the integration of network benefits and of external resources offered by other partners into the internal operations. Here, organisational learning is very important in that the firm learns from the network partners in terms of innovation, product design, process competence, and other strategic capabilities (Håkansson, Havila, and Pedersen, 1999; Hamel, 1991; Kale, Singh, and Perlmutter, 2000).

Increasingly firms are members not just in one but in a portfolio of criss-crossing and overlapping networks (Thorelli, 1986). While a portfolio of relationships offers access to a broader range of resources and a reduced dependency on a single network, it makes the managing and balancing of the various network relations even more demanding (see Mahnke et al. in this volume).

Typical issues for firm strategy in a network setting

- What is the strategic rationale to join the network? How is the balance between individual autonomy and inter-firm interdependence managed?
- How does the firm deal with competition in the network? How can the individual goals be pursued without sacrificing the cooperative solution?
- How are the firm and its representatives positioned in the network?
- What are the mechanisms for collaborative resource development? How are the firm's benefits secured in this?
- What are the mechanisms to learn from network participation? How can the firm make best use of external resources?
- How can the firm learn and at the same time protect strategic resources from external partners?
- How is the portfolio of network relations managed by the firm?

3.2 Organisation

Organisational motives might lead to the formation of networks, while the network participation requires organisational adaptations from the single firm.

3.2.1 Organisational motivation to form or join network

Networks are often initiated with the intent to improve the coordination of activities along the value chain between different partners in the market. In doing so, inter-firm business processes have to be aligned and integrated. Driven by efficiency concerns these networks aim at decreasing cost and improving process cycle times within the supply chain. In addition, they might aim at offering new services to the end customer (e.g. the Efficient Consumer Response (ECR) initiatives in the grocery industry). Here, network participation is less strategic but motivated by operational and efficiency concerns. Such efficiency oriented cooperation concentrates on synergies, on transactional benefits or increasing economies of scale. Examples are procurement partnerships or supply chain collaborations, which concentrate on gaining advantages within the market by jointly decreasing their costs (Alt and Österle, 2004).

3.2.2 Organisational implications of network participation

Firms have to integrate network processes and to align internal processes to external requirements of the network. More specifically, firms have to develop their own networkability, the ability to cooperate and to participate in networks. Networkability covers not only the process issues, but also the networkability of products and services, employees, the organisational structure, and a cooperative culture. Firms in this sense have to be able to learn how to collaborate and to create inter-firm interfaces for their processes and products (Alt et al., 2000).

Besides this, the firm has to staff its network teams and to decide who will work in various network-related roles or on the network level itself. A crucial role play the so called boundary spanners, who link firm and network level operations. The boundary spanner role embodies the promises of the extended enterprise as well as the tensions between firm and network. Boundary spanners are often torn in their loyalty between their own firm and the network (Lütz, 1993). A related role is that of a relationship promoter. According to Walter (1999), "relationship promoters are persons who intensively shape and advance inter-organisational exchange processes; they do this on the basis of their network of good personal relationships with significant actors of the partner organisations (…) as well as their ability to develop and use new network relationships.” These people typically build up a high level of social capital that the firm can capitalize on in governing and influencing the partner network. Hutt et al. further argue that boundary spanners also contribute to producing a shared interpretation of common goals within the inter-firm network (Hutt et al., 2000).

The question from the firm perspective is who to select to play such boundary spanning roles. Gomes-Casseres (1994) describes a few options which companies have chosen: ”Some companies have put a top executive in charge of external strategic relations. ... other companies allocate alliance responsibility along functional lines, such as marketing alliances under marketing executives or technology alliances under R&D departments. Still others require business units to manage their own relationships. Particularly critical alliance networks are sometimes managed by specific senior-executive 'champions' ... Collective governance structures (…) may help maintain network cohesion.”

Another challenge for the firm management related to increasing network collaboration is the management of psychological boundaries. With people working in an inter-firm context in various collaborative arrangements the sense of organisational identity might get blurred. As Hirschhorn and Gilmore (1992:105) note: ”Indeed, once traditional boundaries of hierarchy, function, and geography disappear, a new set of boundaries becomes important. These new boundaries are more psychological than organisational. ... And instead of being reflected in a company's structure, they must be 'enacted' over and over again in a manager's relationships with bosses, subordinates, and peers.” Managers thus have to deal with the phenomenon of blurring boundaries and at the same time with the management challenge of heterogeneous teams with people from different organisations (Riemer and Klein, 2004).

Typical issues for firm organisation in a network setting

- How can operational efficiency goals be achieved by setting up collaborative arrangements with supply chain partners?
- What are suitable value creation processes that benefit from closer coordination with other actors in the supply chain?
- How can the firm build cooperative capabilities (networkability) in terms of processes, people, and organisational culture?
- What internal structures do have to be set up to manage network participation? Who will act as boundary spanners and firms’ representatives in the network?
- What operational adjustments on the process level do have to be made (logistics, manufacturing etc.)?

- How will the increased network participation be managed on the team level? How can psychological boundaries be managed to preserve the organisational identity of the firm without creating a harmful "us vs. them" attitude in the network at the same time?

3.3 Technology

Driven by new Information Systems opportunities, firms set up new network business models, flexibly integrating (electronic) services from different partners. Furthermore, firms collaborate to get access or develop new technologies through collaboration in networks. On the other side, participation in networks also has implications on the technology level.

3.3.1 Technological motivation to form or join a network

The increasing role of ICT within companies is reflected in the set-up of ICT-focused network arrangements. Firms are keen to expand their technological resource base and to pool or share information, information systems or infrastructures with other firms. Outsourcing of IT services is one particular way to achieve this goal. While outsourcing is often chosen by firms who do not see technology as their own core competence, it requires not only relationship management capabilities in order to achieve a productive working relationship with the service provider (Lee et al., 2003) but also information management capabilities in order to be able to evaluate the business value of ICT and in particular the strategic potential of ICT innovations.

The diffusion of new and ubiquitous communication technologies like the Internet has yielded new opportunities to efficiently integrate services and information from different market players in order to set-up innovative services for consumers. This value creation principle, known as "syndication" (Werbach, 2000), has led to the formation of new network organisations that integrate services and information assets from different players. The example of a financial service provider may illustrate the idea of a network business model: by establishing a Web-based platform integrating several banking, brokering and insurance services an all-in-one service can be provided. In doing so, the provider has to integrate external services and thus establish a partner network.

Another reason for networking is to get access to or jointly develop new technologies that are necessary for the firm's business. UMTS partnerships for example have been established to jointly set up new mobile services based on the new technology of UMTS and also to reduce the financial risks regarding the immense investments for UMTS licenses. Besides, certain direct effects to enhance the service portfolios of the collaborative firms were achieved by immediately setting up new services based on the interim standard GPRS.

3.3.2 Technological implications of network participation

Network information resource, systems and infrastructure management need to be mirrored on the firm level. Network relevant information assets need to be identified and policies for sharing, pooling, developing or protecting need to be devised. The above mentioned concept of networkability does also refer to the interoperability of information systems and infrastructures as another factor to ensure the ability to cooperate. Firms have to develop the ability to connect Information Systems that contribute to collaborative processes in the network (e.g. to exchange order data, product development sketches, or to couple manufacturing and inventory (ERP) systems). This aspect is similar to the networkability of products; to make IS "networkable" one needs to describe the software interfaces, exchange formats, and increase systems interoperability by using common standards.

From a systems architecture point of view, different tightly or loosely coupled models of linking or integrating the firm's systems into the network systems need to be evaluated. This includes an assessment of the dependency on network systems or infrastructures and the related risks as well as planning of systems development in light of network resources and their development. Firms have to be able to integrate new technologies that are developed in the network into their businesses. This aspect is not only related to information technology but also to product and production technology (e.g. a new manufacturing procedure or a product prototype).

Typical issues for firm information management in a network setting

- How can information management in all its facets be extended to the network?
- What technologies can be built in house and which part of the technology portfolio lends itself to inter-firm cooperation?
- What IT/IS services are suitable for outsourcing? What is the risk of outsourcing strategically relevant technology?
- What are the requirements of technical networkability and how can it be achieved?
- What are the risks of networked based infrastructures?
- How can firm and network based IS planning be aligned?

3.4 Aligning firm view and network view

Our network management framework presents structural similarities between the firm and the network level. While alignment processes take place among the strategic, organisational and technical domains on the firm as well as on the network level, these alignment processes have to be linked to each other (see Figure 7).

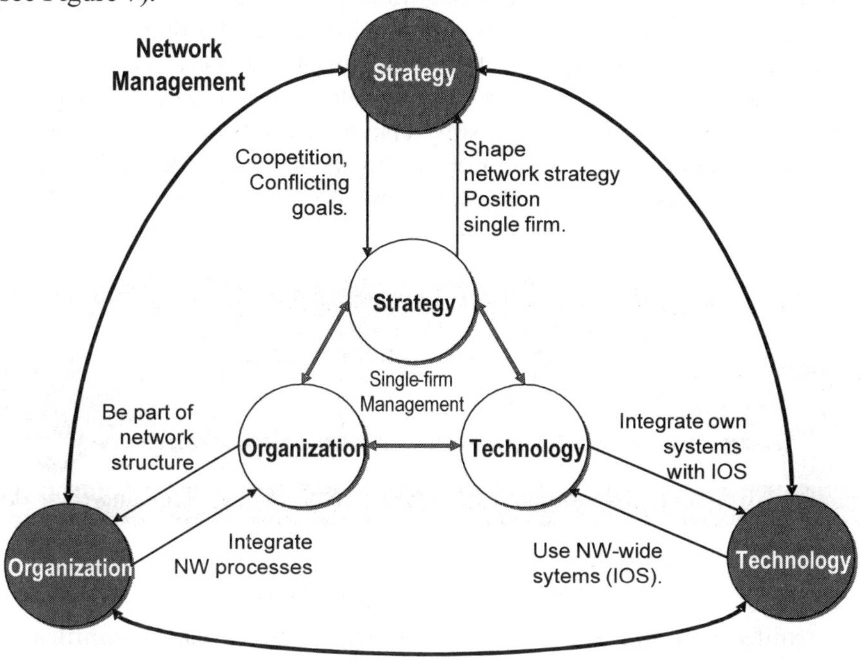

Figure 7. Management Interdependencies

Prasopoulou et al. (in this volume) illustrate the needs and pitfalls of aligning technology and organization on a firm (i.e. university) and network level. This creates an ongoing dynamics and tensions within the network, but is at the same time a protection against sclerotic structures within the network. The strategic dimension is always also outward looking to respond to ongoing changes in the environment (see next section).

4. The network environment

"... why it is that in every known capitalist economy, firms do not conduct business as isolated units, but rather form cooperative relations with other firms, with social boundaries of variable clarity around such relations." Granovetter (1994:453)

Co-operative arrangements have a long tradition. Medieval examples like the Hanseatic League, a trade network among cities in the Baltic regions, show already elaborated and advanced inter-organisational networks. In recent years, networks have proliferated more widely as firms are extending their scale and scope of activities, probably also as a result of technical innovation. Some authors (e.g. Tapscott et al., 2000) claim that networks are the paradigm for value creation in the New Economy.

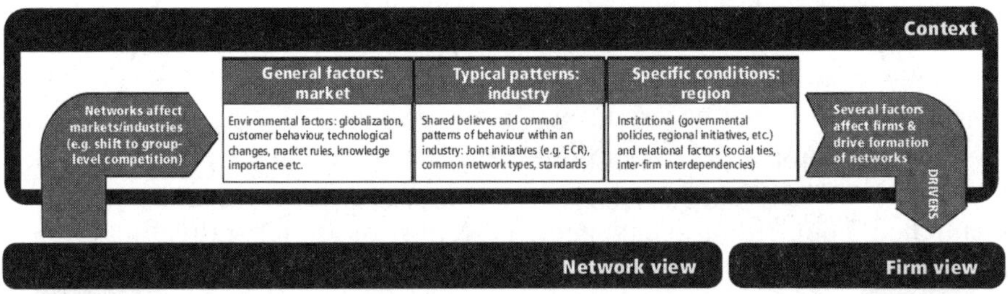

Figure 8. The network environment

The proliferation and design of network arrangements varies significantly across industries (Reimers et al., 2004). The environment or context of the firm and the network provides explanations for the initiation of networks (collaborative advantages, level of fragmentation), the existence of specific types or configurations (dominant patterns, business logic, standards) as well as the micro conditions that might lead a firm to initiate a new network. At the same time the formation of networks affects and shapes markets, industries and geographical regions and might spur further changes in the organisational patterns and lead to more network activity then before (see Figure 8).

4.1 General market drivers for network formation

There are general macro-level market conditions that favour the formation of organisational networks and can account for the increase in cooperation among firms in the last decades. These drivers, single-handedly or in combination, affect the strategic design of modern firms and prompt them into joining alliances, relationships, and networks. The following list introduces some of the drivers that can influence firms to enter or form network arrangements:

Technological changes: New ways of communication and information processing technology, specially based on the Internet, allow new forms of organising and value creation: The significantly lower costs of obtaining, processing, and transmitting information allow new efficient (electronic) information links between firms. In economic terms, the new information infrastructure may redefine the roles and relationships between buyer, seller, and middleman, allowing new ways of accessing and tapping information and price arrangements. On the one hand, new opportunities arise, giving enterprises the chance to enter new markets, to set-up new services or to organise their value creation in a more efficient manner, e.g. by concentration on core competencies. On the other hand enterprises need to heavily invest into new product and process related technologies facing the challenge of an arising technology-based competition with shorter product lifecycles and a speed-up regarding time-to-market. This leads companies to collaborate to share risks and to get access to new technologies. Thus the drivers for network formation are new opportunities of an increasingly efficient way of inter-firm coordination based on IT, as well as the reaction to the above mentioned competition challenges in terms of collaborative investment strategies or joint R&D projects in terms of risk reduction and acceleration of time-to-market.

Globalization: The phenomenon of globalization – driven by technological changes like the emergence of the Internet, deregulation and opening of national markets, global reporting in mass media, and changes in people's minds – causes eroding of market structures confronting companies with the entrance of new competitors and an increasing competition within the market leading to shifting market boundaries. The turbulent business environment is forcing organisations to re-evaluate their processes and structures, indicating an increasing need for networking and cooperative arrangements. On the other hand globalization opens the opportunity to get access to new markets. To face competition challenges, to overcome barriers of distance, and to become global players, network collaboration promises to be a sound solution for enterprises. Strategic alliances in the airline industry are only one example of this phenomenon.

Changing customer needs and fragmented markets: The trend towards individualisation and customization of products and services has led to increasingly fragmented markets and the emergence of micro segments. This fragmentation forces companies to likewise increase their amount of product variants, to increase the specificity of their products to better meet customer needs and to develop new mass customization strategies. This leads to business approaches which are meant to be better applied in a collaborative manner. The real potential of mass customization strategies for example derives from inter-firm linkages within the value chain which allow for an efficient processing of customer specific and production related information between retailer and manufacturer. Furthermore, companies try to expand their service offerings and to increase customer retention through partnering.

Increasing information intensity and importance of knowledge: The fourth major trend evolves from the increasing information richness of products and services and the rising importance of knowledge in terms of innovation and technological complexity. Today, even big companies are not able to access and control all necessary information and knowledge available in the market (Ciborra, 1992). Ergo, collaboration seems to be a practical way to integrate external knowledge and business know how by engaging in learning alliances or joint development initiatives in networks.

In addition to these market and technological trends, national and even regional factors drive the development of network arrangements. On a national level a wide range of policies and regulation have influences on the proliferation of networking arrangements (specifically on the diffusion of Electronic Commerce: see Gibbs, Kraemer, and Dedrick, 2003). Despite the prevalence of electronic forms of communication, regional proximity and a rich ecosystem of educational institutions, as well as attractive working and living conditions and a critical mass of companies are some of the factors which drive the development of regional clusters (Best, 1990).

4.2 Typical industry patterns favour network formation

The propensity of firms to form inter-organisational networks is triggered not only by general market forces but also by the specific types of organising that are prevalent in a specific industry or a market segment (see Prasopoulou and Poulymenakou in this volume for a discussion of industry characteristics and their impact on network types). DiMaggio and Powell (1983) have studied different forms of isomorphism, i.e. a push towards homogenization of organisational arrangements, in organisational fields. The existence of specific patterns within industries such as trends to outsource activities or to form vertical partnerships with suppliers (e.g. the automotive industry), horizontal partnerships with competitors (e.g. the airline industry), or cross-sectional partnerships with technology companies (e.g. consumer electronics – SonyEricsson) puts pressure on the firm to also engage in collaborative arrangements. A few typical patterns are:

Outsourcing: In many industries companies are increasingly seeing the necessity to focus on their core competencies and to collaborate with other firms for the fulfilment of the rest of the activities necessary for the delivery of their product. Up until the 1990s companies tried to accomplish all processes necessary for their operation by themselves. However, this tactic resulted in the creation of large bureaucratic companies that were perceived to be unable to flexibly react to shifts in customer demand. For this reason companies started to re-evaluate their processes, to focus on value adding activities, and to outsource peripheral activities to companies with superior expertise in these areas. This practice gradually led to networks of companies collaborating closely for the delivery of specific products. This trend is quite evident in the construction industry where the complexity of the task demands close collaboration among a variety of companies that cannot undergo the project by themselves. Close collaboration during the construction period forges stable relationships and leads to more or less fix collaboration schemes. The same practices are employed in the automotive industry. The large OEMs (Original Equipment Manufacturer) use specific systemic suppliers for each product line and therefore a network of companies is gradually formed to design and manufacture certain car models.

Standardization initiatives: In various industrial sectors initiatives that aim to establish standard procedures for collaboration between industry actors become the precursor of industry-wide networking activity. These initiatives do not explicitly intend to form inter-organisational networks but rather focus on the standardization of common activities that are performed on a frequent basis. Since standardization usually imposes a rearrangement of firm-specific processes towards common processes among value chain partners the transition from single units to a network of firms is easier. In the retail industry for example the ECR movement aimed to bring about the close collaboration between retailers and suppliers for the alignment of the entire value chain. This initiative led to the creation of supply chain hubs around the major retailers world-wide. In this particular industry the notion of networking was the natural outcome of an initiative that made major players aware of the benefits of collaborative processes and thus facilitated the formation of networks. Similarly, in the automotive industry the notion of Just-in-Time production led to the formation of networks around the major OEMs. Since JIT demanded highly coordinated processes, the firms became so forcefully affiliated that in some cases they even rearranged their location in order to reside in proximity and thus even more facilitate collaboration. For these firms the idea of networking was the final stage of a collaborative process that originated in the adoption of a process redesign initiative.

Co-opetition: The notion of co-opetion is the final stage of a trend towards collaboration that emerged 10 years ago (Brandenburger and Nalebuff, 1996;

Moore, 1996). The outsourcing of firm-specific activities and the close co-operation with other firms for the accomplishment of common goals paved the road for more audacious collaborations. Co-opetition describes cooperation among competitors. It is often linked to the metaphor of a business eco-system, which emphasises the coexistence of competition and collaboration as a prerequisite for a dynamic and innovative industry. An example is the biotechnology industry. The need for constant innovation in combination with the small size of many of the biotechnology companies led to collaboration among competitors for the sake of risk sharing and achieving virtual size. The fluid character of operations within specific industries and the rapid rearrangements of activities force companies to enhance their portfolio of partnerships even with companies with the same product offerings in order to stay competitive.

4.3 Specific micro conditions lead to network formation

While macro-level conditions generally describe the trend towards networking and meso level factors explain the emergence of certain types of networks in an industry, it is the micro-level conditions in the regional or relational environment between single firms and even single managers that explain the formation of collaborative initiatives. These factors might specify why a specific set of companies teams up and competes with other groups of partners later on:

Existence of a business opportunity: The main antecedent for network creation is the existence of a concrete business opportunity. Networks occur among companies that join their forces in order to jointly develop their business or to deliver new value to their customers through joint actions where each partner can bring in their expertise and resources to jointly serve the customer. Existing complementarity and interdependence between companies contribute to the formation of networks, but it is the actual opportunity to do business together that ultimately triggers network formation.

Taking the initiative: In many industries organisational networks emerge because a dominant player incorporates networking in its strategy and forces suppliers and customers to cooperate and adopt certain procedures and ways of doing business. This approach triggers a wave of collaborative agreements with the dominant player in the epicentre. Therefore, the commitment of a dominant player can greatly enable networking within a specific market since the initiative is usually supported by heavy investments both in technological and social capital.

Existing social networks: While one of the prime factors for the creation of networks is the need of firms to address the environmental uncertainty of a competitive environment, the actual action of setting up collaborations entails severe risks in terms of partner selection. Not all opportunities for collaboration between two organisational units materialize in networks. Firms need sufficient information regarding their prospective partners in order to avoid opportunistic behaviour. More specifically, they need to know the true capabilities, needs and performance of potential partners in order to minimize decision risk and guarantee future performance. Existing social networks and trusting relationships with partners in the marketplace might thus be the trigger for certain partner constellation. An existing social relationship between two management executives might also be the agars for collaboration ideas and lead to the discovery or creation of joint business opportunities and thus the formation of a network.

5. The comprehensive view

In the last sections we gave explanations for the networking phenomenon, we introduced different perspectives on network management and discussed levels and areas of network decision making. We also showed the linkages between the network management areas and listed typical management questions in each of those areas. We now integrate these findings in one comprehensive network management framework and discuss our findings by summarising the core management modes that characterise the management of business networks.

5.1 The framework

Figure 9 provides a synopsis of the building blocks of the network management framework and illustrates their interdependencies. The network view is at the centre, encompassing the network life cycle as context for a dynamic network management. The linkages to the firm view illustrate the duality of network management from a firm and from the network perspective. The context captures contingency factors of network formation and development.

5.2 The network management model

Across the network life cycle we have identified four interdependent functional domains of network management: designing governance structures, coordinating exchanges, fostering social integration and facilitating shared visions and values.

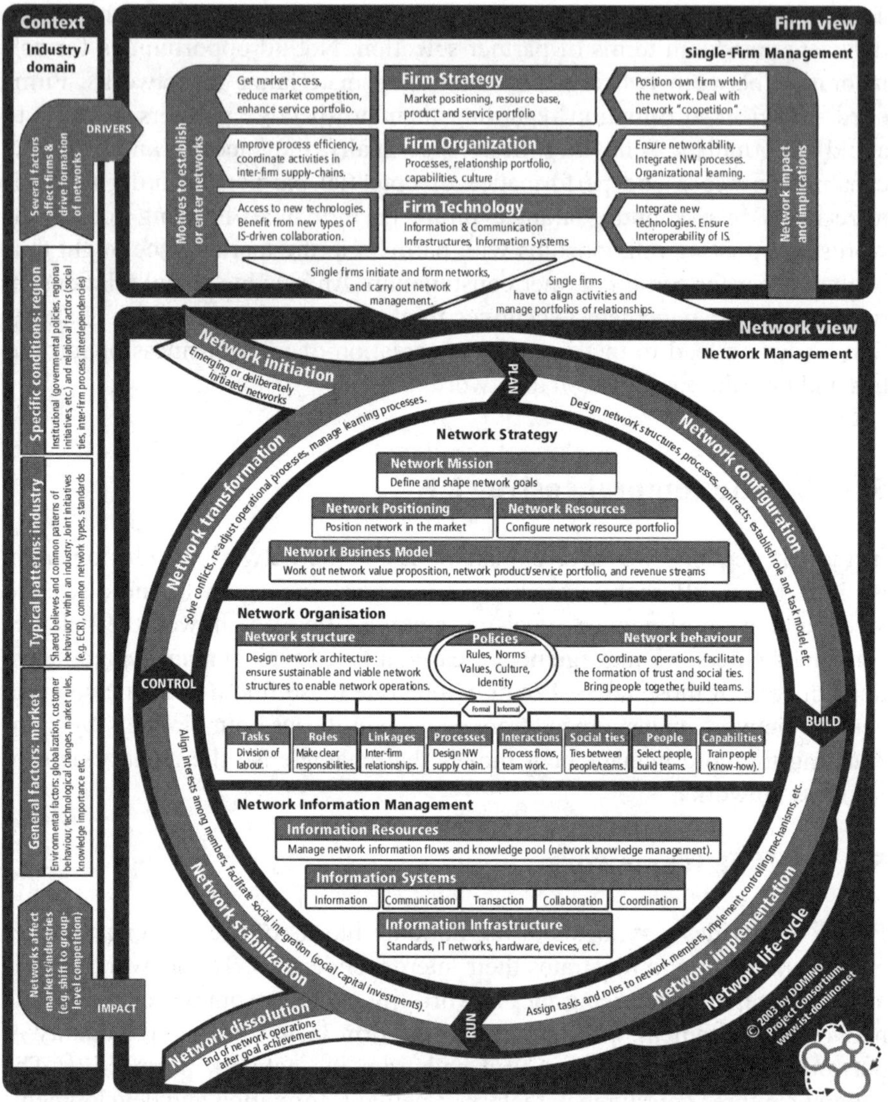

Figure 9. The comprehensive network management framework

Designing governance structures

The governance structure provides the 'rules for the game': it defines roles and responsibilities, mechanisms for conflict resolution as well as for the protection of property rights. As Gogolin and Klein (in this volume) show, the governance structure provides a framework within which the network members can conduct their business; they help to manage the expectations of the network members. While the network governance is underorganised compared to hierarchies, it provides richer and more complex rules than the governance structures of markets. In particular it takes care of a situation of multiple games, i.e. recurrent exchanges and ongoing relationships. Trust and social capital among the network members as well as shared values support the enactment of the governance structures.

Coordinating exchanges

The exchanges among the network members and across the boundaries of the network can be described as 'plays of the game'. Networks can be characterized as medium to long-term recurrent exchanges, which create interdependencies "that rest on the entangling of obligations, expectations, reputations, and mutual interests. The initial economic transactions become embedded, not only in a larger set of economic exchanges but also in a rich and active network of social relationships that couple the organisations strategically and administratively." (Larson, 1992:98). Network management has to provide a proper balance of incentives, a balance of contributions and returns and generally a sense of fairness even when contributions of partners are asymmetric.

Fostering social integration

The quote by Larson (1992) emphasizes the social embedding of exchange relationships. A dense and rich communication environment supports the development of social relationships and the emergence of trust. While the influence of management in this area is clearly limited (see also Riemer in this volume), the structure of the exchange relations and institutional rules within the network can nevertheless help to foster social capital. Professional governance structures and professional conduct among the network members help to build trust. In return, the developed trust helps to contain conflicts and to operate in an environment of incomplete contracts.

Developing and articulating shared visions and values

The network identity, expressed across a range of themes – from a shared strategy right up to shared values (see Klein and Mangan, 2005) – stabilizes the network and reinforces the exchange and social relations. Management can play a role in articulating and nurturing a common identity, which has to be reflected in the governance structures. A clear network identity facilitates the identification of the members with the network.

Throughout the network life cycle, the four areas are enacted in three core themes, which highlight at the same time the underlying dynamics of networks as well as the limits of managerial control: boundary management, creating potentials and improvisation.

The metaphor of orchestration captures the challenge of network management to create a coherent and outstanding unity (the performance) by bringing together specialist with assigned roles (the musicians) and conducting their efforts based on a joined, but underspecified strategy (the selected piece of music). The process of joined learning is repeated over time and across multiple projects. The musicians depend on each other and have to learn to act together.

Boundary management

Networks are organisational arrangements with boundaries of variable clarity. Boundaries define the range of the governance structures, different types of roles and – in the form of boundary spanners – the linkage between what is inside the firms (and not part of the network) and what is part of the network. Whatever network members do (and do not do) is attributed in a dual way, to the network member and to the network. While on the positive side, the network and its members clearly want to benefit from positive reputation effects and reputation spill over, the same mechanisms work also in case of conflicts and negative reputation.

Externally, the boundaries define access rules as well as relationships to other networks. As network members can be expected to maintain a portfolio of network linkages (see Mahnke et al. in this volume) conflicts among different networks might not be limited to the network members but might extend to the network itself.

Creating potentials

A network provides multiple linkages among the network members, it engenders rich opportunities. These linkages extend beyond what is intentionally designed or actively managed. The linkages provide opportunities to explore and extend beyond the official purpose of the network.

Metcalfe's law formally states that the value of a network equals approximately the square of the number of users of the system. It refers to positive network externalities, which extend beyond what is planned. The rich communication environment of the network, the social embedding and emerging social capital provide a productive setting for learning and innovation, reciprocal exchanges or even inspiration.

The art of management is to facilitate or contribute to positive network dynamics and community building without actually being part of it. Network management is about empowering decentralized structures while maintaining a rich communication environment.

Improvisation

The dynamics within the network, among its members as well as in relationship to its environment, continually creates unforeseen situations and challenges, which require a high level of improvisation. The art of network management lies in the balance between reifying the (governance) structure and identity while fostering – within the limits of the structures – flexibility on the process level. The governance structures provide the requisite structure and predictability in order to be able to extend beyond them. The life cycle model has underscored that this is a reflexive process, whereby the structures are adjusted over time.

Trust among the network members is a prerequisite to adjust existing structures and to allow for flexibility which extends beyond the defined boundaries of the network.

6. Conclusions

The network management framework is not an empirical account of how networks work, but rather a landscape of network management areas. It is a result of empirically informed sense making and network practice. It is meant to guide and structure further research; to guide practitioners in setting up and carrying out network projects or even as a checklist for network management initiatives.

The framework and its elaboration have been shaped by the view that networks are promising but inherently precarious organisational arrangements. Networks are characterized by dialectic tensions between autonomy and interdependency, trust and control, cooperation and competition, flexibility and the need for stabilisation, openness and the need to build out a network identity. This is reflected in the management of networks, which is precarious as well. Confronted with an underorganised ensemble of actors, structures have to be provided to facilitate collaboration, (social) integration, flexibility, innovation and productivity.

References

Alt, R., Fleisch, E., and Werle, O., 2000, The Concept of Networkability - How to Make Companies Competitive in Business Networks, in: *Proceedings of the 8th European Conference on Information Systems*, H. R. Hansen, M. Bichler and H. Mahrer, eds., Wien, pp. 405-411.

Alt, R., and Österle, H., 2004, *Real-time Business: Lösungen, Bausteine und Potenziale des Business Networking*, Springer, Berlin etc.

Badaracco, J. L., 1991, *The Knowledge Link - How Firms Compete Through Strategic Alliances*, Harvard Business School Press, Boston, MA.

Bamford, J. D., Gomes-Casseres, B., and Robinson, M. S., 2003, *Mastering Strategic Alliance Strategy - A Comprehensive Guide to Design, Management, and Organization*, Jossey Bass, San Francisco, CA.

Barley, S. R., J., F., and Hybels, R. C., 1992, Strategic alliances in commercial biotechnology, in: *Networks and organizations: Structure, form and action*, N. Nohria and R. G. Eccles, eds., Harvard Business School Press, Boston, pp. 311-347.

Best, M., 1990, *The New Competition: Institutions of Industrial Restructuring*, Harvard University Press, Cambridge, MA.

Bleicher, K., 1989, Zum Management zwischenbetrieblicher Kooperation - Vom Joint Venture zur strategischen Allianz, in: *Führungsorganisation und Technologiemanagement*, R. Bühner, ed., Duncker & Humblot, Berlin, pp. 77-89.

Bleicher, K., 1999, *Das Konzept Integriertes Management* 5th ed., Campus, Frankfurt/M.; New York.

Borys, B., and Jemison, D. B., 1989, Hybrid Arrangements as Strategic Alliances - Theoretical Issues in Organizational Combinations, *Academy of Management Review.* **14**(2):234-249.

Bouwman, H., and Van den Ham, E., 2003, Business models and eMetrics, a state of the art, in: *Elife after the Dot.com bust*, B. Preissl, H. Bouwman, and C. Steinfield, eds., Springer, Berlin, pp. 83-101.

Brandenburger, A. M., and Nalebuff, B. J., 1996, *Co-opetition*, Doubleday, New York.

Bresser, R. K. F., 1989, Kollektive Unternehmensstrategien, *ZfB,* **59**(5):545-564.

Brynjolfsson, E., 2003, The IT Productivity Gap, *Optimize*:21.

Castells, M., 1996, *The rise of the network society*, Blackwell Publishers, Cambridge, MA.

Ciborra, C., 2002, *The Labyrinths of Information - Challenging the Wisdom of Systems*, Oxford University Press, Oxford.

Ciborra, C. U., 1992, Innovation, Networks and Organizational Learning, in: *The Economics of Information Networks*, C. Antonelli, ed., Amsterdam, pp. 91-102.

Clark, H. H., and Brennan, S. E., 1991, Grounding in Communication, in: *Perspectives on Socially Shared Cognition*, L. B. Resnick, J. M. Levine and S. D. Teasley, eds., American Psychological Association, Washington D.C., pp. 127-149.

Clemons, E. K., 1990, MAC - Philadelphia National Bank's Strategic Venture in Shared ATM Networks, *Journal of MIS.* **7**(1):5-15.

Dawes, S. S., 1996, Interagency information sharing: Expected benefits, manageable risks, *Journal of Policy Analysis and Management.* **15**(3):377-394.

DiMaggio, P. J., and Powell, W. W., 1983, The Iron Cage Revisited: Institutional Isomorphism and Collective Rationality in Organizational Fields, *American Sociological Review.* **48**(2):147-160.

Dyer, J., and Singh, H., 1999, Response to relational view commentary, *Academy of Management Review.* **24**(2):184-186.

English, L., 1996, Redefining information management: IM as an effective business enabler. *Information Systems Management.* **13**(1):65-67.

Forsgren, M., and Johanson, J., 1992, Managing Internationalization in Business Networks, in: *Managing Networks in International Business*, M. Forsgren and J. Johanson, eds., Gordon&Breach Publishing Group, Philadelphia, et al., pp. 1-18.

Garbe, M., 1998, *The impact of information technology on the boundaries of the firm,* Paper presented at the Twelfth Biennial Conference of the International Telecommunications Society, Stockholm, Sweden.

Gibbs, J., Kraemer, K. L., and Dedrick, J., 2003, Environment and Policy Factors Shaping Global E-Commerce Diffusion: A Cross-Country Comparison, *Information Society,* **19**(1):5-18.

Gomes-Casseres, B., 1994, Group Versus Group - How Alliance Networks Compete, *Harvard Business Review.* **72**(4):62-74.

Göransson, A., and Schuh, G., 1997, Das Netzwerkmanagement in der virtuellen Fabrik, in: *Virtualisierung von Organisationen*, G. Müller-Stewens, ed., Schäffer-Poeschel, Stuttgart, pp. 61-82.

Grandori, A. 1993. *A Comparative Assessment of Interfirm Coordination Modes.*Unpublished manuscript, Milan.

Granovetter, M., 1994, Business Groups, in: *Handbook of Economic Sociology*, N. Smelser and R. Swedberg, eds., Princeton, NJ, pp. 453-475.

Hagedoorn, J., 1993, Understanding the rationale of strategic technology partnering: Interorganizational modes of cooperation and sectoral differences, *Strategic Management Journal.* **14**(2):371-385.

Håkansson, H., Havila, V., and Pedersen, A.-C., 1999, Learning in Networks, *Industrial Marketing Management.* **28**(5):443-452.

Hamel, G., 1991, Competition for Competence and Inter-Partner Learning within International Strategic Alliances, *Strategic Management Journal.* **12**(4):83-103.

Hamel, G., Doz, Y. L., and Prahalad, C. K., 1989, Collaborate with your Competitors - and win, *Harvard Business Review.* **67**(1):133-139.

Hanseth, O., 2000, The economics of standards, in: *From control to drift*, C. U. Ciborra, ed., Oxford University Press, New York, pp. 56-70.

Hanseth, O., and Braa, K., 1998, *Technology as traitor: Emergent SAP infrastructure in a global organization,* Paper presented at the 19th International Conference on Information Systems, Helsinki, Finland.

Hirschhorn, L., and Gilmore, T., 1992, The New Boundaries of the "Boundaryless" Company, *Harvard Business Review.* **70**(3):104-115.

Holland, C., and Lockett, G., 1997, Mixed Mode Network Structures: The Strategic Use of Electronic Communication by Organizations, *Organization Science.* **8**(5):475-488.

Holland, C. P., 1995, Cooperative supply chain management: the impact of interorganizational information systems, *Journal of Strategic Information Systems.* **4**(2):117-133.

Hutt, M. D., Stafford, E. R., Walker, B. A., and Reingen, P. H., 2000, Case study: Defining the social network of a strategic alliance, *Sloan Management Review.* **41**(2):51-62.

Inkpen, A. C., 2000, A note on the Dynamics of Learning Alliances: Competition, Cooperation and relative Scope, *Strategic Management Journal.* **21**(7):775-779.

Ives, B., and Jarvenpaa, S., 1991, Applications of global information technology: Key issues for management, *MIS Quarterly.* **15**(1):33-47.

Johnston, H. R., and Vitale, M. A., 1988, Creating Competitive Advantage With Interorganizational Information Systems, *MIS Quarterly.* **12**(2):153-165.

Kale, P., Singh, H., and Perlmutter, H., 2000, Learning and protection of proprietary assets in strategic alliances: building relational capital, *Strategic Management Journal.* **21**(3):217-237.

Khanna, T., Gulati, R., and Nohria, N., 1998, The Dynamics of Learning Alliances: Competition, Cooperation, and relative Scope, *Strategic Management Journal.* **19**(3):193-210.

Klein, S., 1993, Information logistics, *Electronic Markets.* **3**(3):11-12.

Klein, S., and Kronen, J., 1995, IT-Enabled Cooperations: A Resource-Based Approach, in: *Proceedings of the 3rd ECIS*, G. Doukidis, T. Jelassi, H. Krcmar, and F. Land, eds., Athens, pp. 43-56.

Klein, S., and Mangan, A., 2005, Stability in Times of Change: A Strength of Co-operatives, in: *Economics of Inter-Firm Networks*, T. Theurl, ed., Mohr Siebeck, Tübingen, pp. 89-117.

Kogut, B., 1988, Joint Ventures: Theoretical and Empirical Perspectives, *Strategic Management Journal.* **9**(4):319-332.

Konsynski, B., 1993, Strategic control in the extended enterprise, *IBM Systems Journal.* **32**(1):111-142.

Konsynski, B. R., and McFarlan, W. E., 1990, Information partnerships - Shared data, shared scale, *Harvard Business Review.* **68**(6):114-120.

Korezynski, M., 1994, Low trust and opportunism in action: Evidence on inter-firm relations from the British engineering construction industry, *Journal of Industrial Studies.* **1**(2):43-63.

Kumar, K., and van Dissel, H. G., 1996, Sustainable Collaboration: Managing Conflict and Cooperation in Interorganizational Systems, *MIS Quarterly.* **20**(3):279-300.

Laat, P. d., 1993, 435-464, *Technological Alliances - Securing Trust by Mutual Commitments,* Paper presented at the ESF-Conference: Forms of Inter-Organizational Networks: Structures and Processes, Berlin.

Larson, A., 1992, Network Dyads in Entrepeneurial Settings - A Study of the Governance of Exchange Relationships, *Administrative Science Quarterly.* **37**(1):76-104.

Lee, J.-N., Huynh, M. Q., Kwok, R. C., and Pi, S.-M., 2003, IT outsourcing evolution - Past, present, and future, *Communications of the ACM.* **46**(5):84-89.

Lever, S., 1997, An analysis of managerial motivations behind outsourcing practices in human resources, *Human Resource Planning.* **20**(2):37-48.

Lütz, S., 1993, *Network Contingencies in Interfirm Research Collaborations,* Paper presented at the ESF-Conference: Forms of Inter-Organizational Networks: Structures and Processes, Berlin.

MacNeil, I. R., 1985, Reflections on Relational Contracts, *Journal of Institutional and Theoretical Economics.* **141**:541-546.

Miller, D., 1996, Configurations Revisited, *Strategic Management Journal.* **17**(7):505-512.

Miller, D., and Friesen, P. H., 1984, *Organizations - a Quantum View*, Prentice Hall, Englewood Cliffs, NJ.

Mitchell, J. C., 1969, *Social Networks in Urban Situations*, University Press, Manchester.

Monge, P. R., and Contractor, N. S., 2003, *Theories of Communication Networks*, Oxford University Press, Oxford.

Moore, J., 1996, *The Death of Competition*, Harper Business, New York.

Moss Kanter, R., 1994, Collaborative Advantage - The Art of Alliance, *Harvard Business Review.* **72**(4):96-108.

Nahapiet, J., and Ghoshal, S., 1998, Social capital, intellectual capital, and the organizational advantage, *Academy of Management Review.* **23**:242-266.

Olson, G. M., and Olson, J. S., 2000, Distance Matters, *Human Computer Interaction.* **15**(2):139-178.

Porter, M. E., 1997, How Competitive Forces Shape Strategy (HBS Reprint), in: *Competitive Strategy*, H. B. School, HBS Publishing, pp. 1-10.

Porter, M. E., and Millar, V., 1985, How information gives you a competitive advantage, *Harvard Business Review.* **63**(4):149-160.

Prahalad, C. L., and Hamel, G., 1990, The core competence of the corporation, *Harvard Business Review.* **90**(3):79-91.

Reimers, K., Johnston, R., and Klein, S., 2004, The Shaping of Inter-organisational Information Systems: Main Design Considerations of an International Comparative Research Project, in: *Proceedings of the 17th Bled Electronic Commerce Conference*, Y.-H. Tan, D. R. Vogel, J. Gricar and G. Lenart, eds., Moderna Organizacija, Kranj.

Riemer, K., 2004, *The role of social capital in managing relationships with E-Commerce suppliers,* Paper presented at the 17th Bled eCommerce Conference, Bled, Slovenia, June 21-23.

Riemer, K., and Klein, S., 2004, How can Virtual Organizations deliver? Promises, challenges and potential remedies., in: *E-Learning: Modelle, Instrumente und Erfahrungen - Software Produktlinien - Communities in E-Business*, H. H. Adelsberger, S. Eicker, H. Krcmar, J. M. Pawlowski, K. Pohl, D. Rombach and V. Wulf, eds., Akademische V.-G. Aka, Berlin, pp. 275-291.

Riemer, K., Klein, S., and Gogolin, M., 2002, Network Business Model Configuration - New Roles for Dynamic Network Arrangements, in: *Challenges and Achievements in E-business and E-work - Proceedings of e2002 Conference*, B. Stanford-Smith, E. Chiozza and M. Edin, eds., IOS Press, Amsterdam et al., pp. 892-899.

Riemer, K., Klein, S., and Selz, D., 2001, Classification of dynamic organizational forms and coordination roles, in: *E-work and E-commerce (Proceedings of the e2001 Conference on E-work and E-business, Venice 2001)*, B. Stanford-Smith and E. Chiozza, eds., IOS Press, Amsterdam et al., pp. 825-831.

Riggins, F. J., Kriebel, C. H., and Mukhopadhyay, T., 1994, The growth on inter-organisational systems in the presence of network externalities, *Management Science.* **40**(8):984-998.

Sabel, C. F., 1993, Constitutional Ordering in Historical Context, in: *Games in Hierarchies and Networks*, F. W. Scharpf, ed., Campus, Frankfurt/M., pp. 65-123.

Sydow, J., 1992, On the Management of Strategic Networks, in: *Regional Development and Contemporary Industrial Response: Extending Flexible Specialisation*, H. Ernste and V. Meier, eds., Belhaven Press, London; New York, pp. 114-129.

Sydow, J., 2005, Managing Interfirm Networks, in: *Economics of Interfirm Networks*, T. Theurl, ed., Mohr Siebeck, Tübingen.

Sydow, J., and Windeler, A., 2000, Steuerung von und in Netzwerken - Perspektiven, Konzepte, vor allem offene Fragen, in: *Steuerung von Netzwerken*, J. Sydow and A. Windeler, eds., Westdeutscher Verlag und Gabler, Opladen, pp. 1-24.

Tapscott, D., Ticoll, D., and Lowy, A., 2000, *Digital Capital - Harnessing the Power of Business Webs*, Harvard Business School Press, Boston, MA.

Teubner, R. A. 2003. *Grundlegung Informationsmanagement.*Unpublished manuscript, Münster.

Theurl, T., and Schweinsberg, A., 2004, *Neue kooperative Ökonomie*, Mohr Siebeck, Tübingen.

Thorelli, H. B., 1986, Networks - Between Markets and Hierarchies, *Strategic Management Journal.* **7**(1):37-51.

Timmers, P., 1998, Business Models for Electronic Markets, *Electronic Markets.* **8**(2):3-8.

Walter, A., 1999, Relationship Promoters: Driving Forces for Successful Customer Relationships, *Industrial Marketing Management.* **28**(5):537.

Webster, J., 1995, Networks of collaboration or conflict? Electronic data interchange and power in the supply chain, *Journal of Strategic Information Systems.* **4**(1):31-42.

Werbach, K., 2000, Syndication: The Emerging Model for Business in the Internet Era, *Harvard Business Review.* **78**(3):84-93.

Wigand, R. T., Picot, A., and Reichwald, R., 1997, *Information, organization and management: Expanding markets and corporate boundaries*, John Wiley, New York.

Williamson, O. E., 1985, *The Economic Institutions of Capitalism*, Free Press, New York.

Wolff, B., 1996, Constitutional Contracting and Corporate Constitution, in: *Perspectives on Contract Theory*, A. Picot and E. Schlicht, eds., Springer, Berlin et al., pp. 95-108.

Wollnick, M., 1988, Ein Referenzmodell des Informations-Managements, *Information Management.* **3**(3):34-43.

Zuboff, S., 1996, Foreword, in: *Groupware and teamwork: Invisible aid or technical hindrance?,* C. U. Ciborra, ed., Wiley, Chichester.

Part II
Elaboration on Network Management – Core Themes in Select Industry Settings

Chapter 3

Connecting Company Strategy and Network Identity

Heidi Jørgensen and Christian Vintergaard
Copenhagen Business School

Abstract: Current literature has explained how strategic interorganisational relations can be of concern for management. However when it comes to explain the causalities between theses relations and corporate strategies, it is less elaborated. As companies today more than ever operate in networks of relations it is of crucial importance to understand how these networks should be dealt with in relation to corporate strategy. The aim of this empirical study is thus to conceptualize how strategic relations are managed in accordance with the overall corporate strategy. Thus it tries to answer: Are there important connections between a firm's network strategy and its corporate strategy?

Key words: Strategy, network, relational embeddedness, redundant and non-redundant relations network identity, defenders, analysers, prospectors and reactors

1. Introduction

Are there important connections between a firm's network strategy and its corporate strategy? Over the years, a considerable amount of resources have been spent on studying the making of corporate strategy. The main focus has been on analysing single companies in isolation in order to understand how they behave and perform. Today, however, managers increasingly stress the importance of engaging in strategic relations beyond the isolated firm. Since the expected benefits of engaging in a network of strategic relations are high, the concept of networks or networking has gained increasing momentum. As a result, previous measures of effective strategy, i.e., those that focus on the position of a company within an industry (Porter, 1980) or the internal resources and capabilities of a company (Wernerfelt, 1984; Barney, 1991), have become inadequate for predicting the effect and effectiveness of corporate strategies. The concept of networking is well suited to explain how networks of strategic relations can be a concern of management. But it lacks insight when it comes to explaining the relation of strategic networks to corporate strategies. It is this relation that we will shed light on here.

Common sense suggests that companies that differ as to corporate strategies would also differ as to the management of their strategic relations. At present, research enables us neither to verify nor disprove this assertion as the focus has been on the issues such as explaining the factors that have lead to focus on inter-firm cooperation (Gulati et al., 2000), determining what constitutes a network and how to maintain and/or develop a company's network relations (Holm et al., 1996; Håkansson and Johanson, 1993; Miles and Snow, 1992; Ritter, 1999), and determining how to develop a network perspective (Gulati et al., 2000; Dyer and Singh, 1998). While the literature on strategic alliances (e.g., Bresser, 1989) strives to connect network behaviour with business strategy, the link between corporate strategy and network strategy still calls for further theoretical investigation and empirical exemplification. Hence this paper strives to conceptualise the processes by which strategic relations are managed in accordance with the overall corporate strategy.

To this end, the paper applies the well-known framework from organisational behaviour developed by Miles and Snow (1978) to provide distinct categories of firm level or corporate strategies. We do acknowledge the shortcomings of the model (Zahra and Pearce, 1990, 753; Namiki, 1989). However, as pointed out by Torres and Murray (2002) in contrast to Porter, Ansoff and others, Miles and Snow's framework "characterises entire organisations as an integrated and dynamic whole, taking into account the interrelationships of strategy, structure and process" (Torres and Murray, 2002, 2). Another question concerning the applicability of the framework is the strong categorization of each business typology's behaviour. Shortell and Zajac (1990) studied the reliability and validity of Miles and Snow's business typology. They concluded: "researches can use the typology with increased confidence in future work on organizations and their strategies" (Shortell and Zajac, 1990, 829-830). Zahra and Pearce (1990) assessed the status of prior research on the Miles and Snow typology. They concluded that, overall, the predictions put forward by Miles and Snow in regard to the typology relating to the three different element of the adaptive cycle are supported.

To sum up, questions can be raised regarding the validity of some of the elements of Miles and Snow's typology or framework for organisational behavior in general. However, most studies support the validity of Miles and Snow's typology and argue for the wide applicability of the framework. As stated by Torres and Murray (2002) "The Miles and Snow (1978) model has been a robust, integrated, contingency framework for exploring diversity. It sheds light on the nature of diversity in strategy and form by illuminating the simple underlying order." (Torres and Murray, 2002, 2). Despite the shortcomings and the significant developments in the field of strategic management since the 1970s, the original framework provides very workable groupings that clearly illustrate the point of this paper.

Three case studies from the Danish biotech industry will be drawn into the analysis to exemplify and illustrate how a company's corporate strategy is directly correlated to how it manages its strategic network identity. The following section will provide a theoretical overview which includes an introduction to Miles and Snow's (1978) framework as well as descriptions of each case company. Furthermore, the methodology and a review of existing network literature will be presented. Section three will contain the analysis where theory will be linked to the findings from the cases. Finally, due to the linkage between the business typology of a company, its patterns of network behaviour and subsequent network identity, the importance for company strategy is to know how to manage these relations. We will present the linkage between these issues in a framework.

2. Theoretical overview

Strategic models such as Porter's (1980) three generic strategies and Ansoff's (1965) theory of strategic direction both provide useful tools for analysing company positioning in relation to strategy. Miles and Snow's (1978) strategy-structure configuration (compared to the other two) has the additional advantage of incorporating the interrelationship between company strategy, structure and processes. This makes it a more illustrative framework when categorizing network strategies.

A focal premise of Miles and Snow's (1978) typology are patterns of competitive behaviour. Their framework provides four business typologies: *Defenders, Prospectors, Analysers* and *Reactors*. The business typology of a company is illustrated by the way a company relates to the "adaptive cycle" which consists of three intricately interwoven problems that affect organisational behaviour: 1) the entrepreneurial, 2) the engineering, and 3) the administrative problem (Miles and Snow, 1978). It is often said that managers have to relate to a range of different problems; nevertheless, according to Miles and Snow, they can be categorised into those three main problem areas (Torres and Murray, 2002). The entrepreneurial problem concerns the choice of product and market domain. A company has to decide whether to focus on a wide or narrow product/market domain. The second problem is related to the company's use of technology, i.e., processes that favour scales of economies or effectiveness and flexibility (engineering problems). A correlation exists between the choice of production process (as an enabler) and the company's choice of product/market domain. Lastly, the administrative problem deals with the organisational structure of the company (centralised versus decentralised). Inherently, a company has to deal with all three problems simultaneously but depending on the business typology of the company, the problems will be prioritised differently. A short introduction to the four business typologies as well as a description of the corresponding case company will be given below. It is however important to keep in mind that when using typologies, a variety of companies are dichotomised into narrow categories. Consequently, corresponding case companies were chosen to illustrate and exemplify the main characteristics of the typologies in this new field (Glaser and Strauss, 1967; Eisenhardt, 1999).

The cases are all drawn from the Danish medical industry. By limiting the analysis to a particular country and industry, the paper tries to overcome some of the possible biases of identifying changes in network behaviour based on different industry contexts. The framework for network behaviour in this paper will not be country- or industry-specific.

The cases were identified (Yin, 1984) based on the characteristics of business typologies developed by Miles and Snow (1978). Each case was selected on the basis of how well it exemplified the relation between the three different parameters of product/market domain, organisational structure and production processes. For this purpose, secondary data (corporate communication such as annual reports, press briefings, etc.) was used to single out a number of qualified companies. The primary data was gathered through several rounds of semi-structured interviews with these companies in 2003/2004. The first round of interviews was conducted to verify what typology the company belonged to. This was done by presenting a list of questions that reflected how the companies are related to the three dimensions of the adaptive cycle. The next round of interviews was constructed so that insight was obtained as to how each case company relates to issues of networking. All interviews were tape-recorded and transcribed in order to assure a more accurate interpretation. Based on the information from the interviews, the data was analysed by linking the various answers to the parameters identified as important for network behaviour in the theoretical part of the paper. This provided a comprehensive picture of patterns of network behaviour. By incorporating the data from the case studies, the individual typologies were linked to specific network behaviour; providing for the identification of each business typology's network identity. In the paper, the identity of each case company and the names of the respective interviewees will be kept anonymously. The companies' names will be replaced with synonyms, reflecting their identity.

2.1 The defender

Defenders want stability. Stability is achieved by reducing the organisation's vulnerability to changes in the environment as well as uncertainty through a series of decisions and actions. Stability and reduced uncertainty is crucial for the defender's entrepreneurial problem (Shortell and Zajac, 1990). A defender's success depends on its ability to stay competitive within its chosen domain, which is defined by price and/or quality, i.e., by relying on high efficiency. As a consequence, the engineering focus of a defender tends to be on efficient production processes (Torres and Murray, 2002; Shortell and Zajac, 1990). However, to ensure the success of this operating process, a defender must maintain a high level of internal control through a highly centralised organisational structure (Tuominen, 1997; Torres and Murray, 2002). It can be argued that defenders tend to ignore developments outside their core market, consequently achieving growth through market penetration in their current domain (Miles and Snow, 1978). A defender's strategy could thus be characterised as the most stable of the business typologies.

Case 1: Respiratory A/S

Respiratory A/S provides a rich illustration and exemplification of a defender. The company is a leading pharmaceutical company in the field of allergy diagnosis and treatment. Respiratory A/S was founded in 1923 and has approximately 1000 employees. What characterizes this defender company is its perusal in centralising its organisational structure with the main focus on streamlining production processes in order to obtain efficiency gains. Secondly, Respiratory A/S's core product portfolio is relatively focused around products to cure allergies from diagnosis to treatment. To support this strategy, their Director of Strategic Marketing & Sales explains, "Our aim is to have a limited number of product lines out of which two are focused on tablets and one on injections". Another clear example of the company's defender strategy is its focus on quality. As the Director of Strategic Marketing & Sales argues, "We seek to differentiate ourselves on quality – meaning that we aim at setting the standard within the industry". As can be seen, many of the central strategic issues for Respiratory A/S fit well into the characteristics of a defender.

Respiratory A/S's current external relationships centre around four big established companies. Each relationship has a specific objective but seen as a whole, all four serve to improve or maintain the company's leading position within the field of allergy diagnosis and treatment. The relationships are long-term and based on close personal ties. Respiratory A/S also governs a range of relationships of minor importance. These are based on weak connections. The Director of Strategic Sales & Marketing explains, “We do have some minor relations with smaller companies but they are not presented as much as other more important strategic relations”.

2.2 The prospector

Contrary to the defender, a prospector interacts dynamically with its environment and is continuously on the look out for new business opportunities (Miles and Snow, 1978). A prospector’s solution to the entrepreneurial problem focuses on a relatively wide product/market domain (Morgan et al., 2000). The strategy of a prospector is often associated with innovation, and companies that pursue this strategy are often trying to promote change (Miles and Snow, 1984). The engineering problem is to increase effectiveness. This allows for more flexible production processes. Correspondingly, the solution to a prospector’s administrative problem is a decentralised organisational structure (Torres and Murray, 2002). Compared to the reactive posture of a defender, a prospector can thus be characterised as being very pro-active.

Case 2: Innovator A/S

The strategy of Innovator A/S unmistakably exemplifies the basic ideas of a prospector. Innovator A/S is a biotech-based company, which has become the world leader in industrial enzymes. The company was recently spun off from another major pharmaceutical company and has approximately 3.700 employees. The organisational structure gives a first indication that Innovator A/S is a prospector. Senior Director of Innovator A/S explains, “There is a very short distance between top management and lower levels. Our focus is on easy flow of communication between all employees and levels”. Secondly, the target market and the product portfolio are very broad as the company is represented within 120 countries and carries over 700 different products. Thirdly, and very typical for a prospector, Innovator A/S is dedicated to a strategy of continued innovation of new products as well as development of new business areas. The Senior Director of Innovator A/S explains the strategy, “At the outset, we were only into enzymes. But we have to continue developing new areas such as bio-polymers and bio-pharmaceuticals. It is our vision to keep building new areas”. These are not based on enzymes but they do provide synergy when combined with the enzyme business. As is typical for the prospector, the focus is thus not specifically on efficiency but instead on effectiveness.

Innovator A/S has a different perspective on strategic relationships, which also serve many different functions. That is, many of Innovator A/S's strategic relations are with the company's biggest clients. Coupled with the long development process of new products in this industry, these strategic relationships are generally long-term and personal. The reason for this strategy, according to the Senior Director of the company, is that "You have to make it work on the personal level. Otherwise it cannot function on the commercial level". If an opportunity arises or other changes make current relationships obsolete, Innovator A/S will have to eliminate existing long-term relations. The Senior Director of Innovator A/S explains the necessity of this in relation to its strategy: "When changing business focus we sometimes have to change our strategic partners". Innovator A/S also has an array of informal relationships with smaller companies or organisations. These types of relations often serve the purpose of accessing information that currently lay outside Innovator A/S's core business areas.

2.3 The analyser

Defenders and prospectors represent the two ends of a continuum, i.e., the two extremes. The analyser typology can be found between the two (Miles and Snow, 1978; Hougaard and Bjerre, 2002). The analyser's entrepreneurial focus aims at positioning itself within a domain defined by both change and stability. As a consequence, focus is both on innovation as well as maintaining its more traditional markets (Torres and Murray, 2002). This duality is also reflected in its solution to its engineering problem. A balance is found between technological flexibility and stability (Touminen, 1997). Correspondingly, an analyser has to accommodate its organisational structure to encompass both the stable and dynamic domains of its operations. A common example of this type of strategy is found in corporate venture companies (Burgleman, 1983; Vintergaard, 2005; Husted and Vintergaard, 2004).

Case 3: Derma A/S

The research- and development-based pharmaceutical company Derma A/S aptly illustrates the business typology of the analyser. Derma A/S was established in 1908 and employs roughly 3200 people today. The company's area of expertise is in dermatology and critical care of humans. It is the vision of Derma A/S to become a global leader in the field of dermatology. The first indication of Derma A/S's analyser strategy is that Derma A/S is currently searching for a new area of expertise while simultaneously retaining its present business focus. Explaining this strategy, Executive Vice President of Marketing & Sale explains, "For our company it is very important to have access to innovation. We are therefore looking for a third leg to stand on which does not have to be directly related to our existing business areas". The company's product domain is thus a blend of its core focus within dermatology and critical care and those derived from research in new areas of business – clearly a perfect example of an analyser strategy. Secondly, the company is committed to a decision making process that is quick and founded on sound principles. This is supported by a relatively flat organisational structure. Explaining this structure, Executive Vice President of Marketing & Sales argues, "You have to keep the finger on the pulse in order to make some qualified decisions. It is therefore important to have a flat organisational structure". Due to Derma A/S's unique position between a defender and prospector strategy (i.e. analyser) it can sometimes be hard to pinpoint any specific characteristics of its production processes. The standpoint is however that efficient production is important.

At present, Derma A/S has very few strategic relations of any importance. Each relation is only to provide Derma A/S with access to resources necessary for the development of a specific product. Supporting this strategic move, Executive Vice President of Marketing & Sales explains, "It is important to have all the experts in-house. In that way we are able to explain to others what we want them to do for us. The final product is however always entirely developed inside the company". Derma A/S's network relations are in general long-term and personal. The reasons for relationships being long-term are that the R&D process in general is very time consuming. In addition to its more stable strategic relationships, Derma A/S is recognised as a venture capital investor in small companies and consequently has several more informal relationships with minor companies.

2.4 The reactor

Reactors have often been described as being positioned in-between the other typologies. Companies belonging to this typology fail to respond reliably to changes in the environment as no consistency exists between the choice of domain, organisational structure, and processes (Torres and Murray, 2002). Reactors perceive changes and opportunities in its external environment but, owing to a lack of internal focus and coordination, it becomes impossible to respond successfully (Touminen, 1997).

Touminen (1997) proposes that a reactor should not be seen as a unique type but rather an illustration of defenders, prospectors and analysers that find themselves "stuck in the middle". Supporting this argument is the fact that other researchers have refrained from working with this business type (Hambrick, 1993; Touminen, 1997). Furthermore, Miles and Snow's study of the Electronics and Food Processing industries found that only 2 out of 27 companies analysed could be characterised as reactors (Miles and Snow,

1978, 193). As a consequence, this paper will not include this business typology in the analysis and only three cases will be presented to exemplify the business typologies.

Based on the three dimensions of the adaptive cycle, the business types can each be fitted into the framework below hereby illustrating how each of them is situated compared the others.

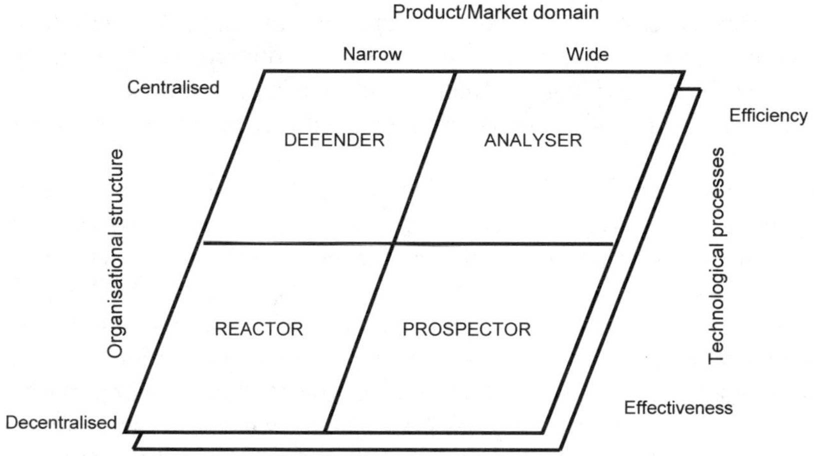

Figure 1: Miles and Snow's framework, Adapted from Touminen (1997)

2.5 A new strategic strand: networks

A central question in strategy research has been why companies behave and perform differently. Until recently, the focus has mostly been on the company's internal resources and capabilities (i.e. the resource-based view of the firm) (Wernerfelt, 1984; Barney, 1991; Hamel and Prahalad, 1996) and how they position themselves within a market, i.e., the industry structure view (Porter, 1980). What characterises both views is that they tend to see companies as single entities. A trend towards inter-firm cooperation has become apparent (Gulati et al., 2000) whereas the company and its network have become intertwined and cannot be separated.

2.6 Networks representing relations

No clear definition of strategic networks exists. However, the majority of research focuses on the kinds of relationships that bind these network structures together (Gulati et al., 2000). As defined by Anderson et al. (1994), business networks should be seen as connected relationships. The focal company can through its own relations be connected to third parties. Thus, the network does not consist exclusively of dyadic relations but relations established among various companies. Håkansson and Johanson (1993) and Håkansson and Snehota (1997a, 1997b) identify the companies within a network as actors which are bound together by dependencies. Accordingly, actors are the various organisations or individuals represented within the network, whereas resources are the elements that are central for performing the activities, hereby forming activity chains and structures (Håkansson and Snehota, 1997a). According to Blau (1968) business relations, in many cases, can be compared to social relations with different levels of embeddedness.

Rowley et al. (2000) defines the level of relational embeddedness as being dependent on the use of either weak or strong ties. Strong ties facilitate the exchange of important information and tacit knowledge since strong ties are built on a high level of trust and insight (Granovetter, 1992). This coincides with Blau's (1968) ideas. Companies bound together by strong ties often mutually adapt their processes and therefore often become very dependent on each other (Rowley et al., 2000). Nonetheless, it is important to emphasise that the adaptation process between the two actors can be related to various areas (Johanson and Mattsson, 1994). How much the actors have to adapt to each other thus varies depending on the area of interest. Hence, little adaptation is needed if the objective is to access information as opposed to knowledge. High level of relational embeddedness, i.e. the use of strong ties, can exist while still having a low level of dependency. Weak ties, on the other hand, do not facilitate the same type of information exchange and for that reason do not involve the same degree of dependency. Their function is to provide novel information by functioning as "gatekeepers" to other companies (Granovetter, 1973). Whether or not strong or weak ties enhance performance is contingent on the environment (Rowley et al., 2000). Strong ties are more efficient in settings with low uncertainty and high demand for exploitation of existing product/processes. Where uncertainty is high and exploration is crucial, relationships bound together through weak ties are the best solution (Rowley et al., 2000). Nevertheless, Rowley et al. (2000) argue that a mix of the two types would be beneficial. This argument is supported by Burt (1992) who states that a company's possibilities within its strategic network are maximised by incorporating what he refers to as "structural holes". Non-redundant network ties (e.g., network ties with little overlap) can therefore also be seen to provide a company with innovative possibilities if it wants to expand into new areas. In other words, by adding loosely coupled relations represented by weak tie binding mechanisms, a company can avoid getting stuck in an unwanted position (Ibarra, 1992). Hence, it becomes interesting to analyse how much the level of relational embeddedness influences a company's strategic relations. Secondly, the mixture of redundant and non-redundant relations also seems to play an important part in how a company chooses to design its strategic relations.

2.7 Network identity

What still seems to be an open-ended question in the discussion of strategic networks is the formation and development of relationships that constitute the network structures (Ahuja, 2000). One explanation for networks to occur, according to Ahuja (2000), is systematically related to inducement and opportunities. Dyer and Singh (1998) support this argument by stating that a company's critical resources may span company boundaries. Opportunities on the other hand relate to a company's prior patterns of relationships. According to Ahuja (1998) the position held in prior network structures influences a company's opportunity to form new relationships. Granovetter (1992) likewise emphasises that a company's history of relations and actions will play a part in shaping the present situation (Granovetter, 1992; Mattson, 1986). It follows that a company must not only be willing to establish relationships but also has to be an attractive partner (Ahuja, 1998).

Anderson et al. (1994) also emphasise the importance of "opportunities". Each company has a certain network identity. Network identity refers to how the focal company sees itself in a network, and how other actors within the business network perceive it. The opportunities open to the company as well as the inducements are thus often dependent on the company's network identity. As argued by Ahuja (1998) as well as Granovetter (1992), it is not only the present but also the past that influences a company's network identity (Anderson et al., 1994; Ford et al., 1986). Network identity can thus have a considerable influence on a company's strategic options in the future, making it of fundamental importance.

Now, several specific elements can be identified to influence companies' strategic options when engaging in strategic relations. What seems to be the most important of all, however, is the issue of network behaviour and hereby network identity. Company behaviour is defined by the internal construction of the company, i.e., strategy, structure and processes. It is thus argued that company network behaviour is defined by these three elements. A company's network identity is naturally mirrored by its network behaviour but other elements also affect network identity. Issues such as past and present network relations, how the company is linked to the partner's resources, the type of relations established also have a great influence on the network identity. Network behaviour is thus dependent on the individual business typology. This is based on the fact that network identity is dependent on a company's relations with other actors and links to their activities as well as resources.

Consequently is becomes necessary to determine how the company relates to elements that are found to have an influence on network behaviour. The level of relational embeddedness, i.e., the development of weak/strong ties and level/area of adaptation as well as the issue of redundant/non-redundant relations have to be established. Furthermore, the importance of what incentives drive the respective business typology to engage in strategic relations as well as its prior history of relations should not be overlooked as they are often mirrored by the company's network identity.

3. Analysis

We will use Miles and Snow's (1978) framework to categorize network identity and link it to business strategy. Each of the business strategies and examples will be linked with the literature on networks and discussed separately. Thus the individual domains (technology: effectiveness vs. efficiency, product/market: wide vs. narrow, structure: centralised vs. decentralised) of the strategies will be related to how they influence network management.

3.1 The defender

3.1.1 Product/market domain

Respiratory A/S produces medication for patients with allergies and asthma, which constitutes a minor part of the bigger group of respiratory diseases. According to the Director of Strategic Marketing & Business Planning, Respiratory A/S is in a market, which can be characterised as fairly stable, allowing the company to focus on the exploitation of its opportunities. According to the Director of Strategic Marketing & Business Planning, Respiratory A/S's business strategy is based on, "What we try to do with our research and development strategies is to bring new life to existing products" and "We are very focused on the respiratory area". When reviewing the network literature, a company following this type of business strategy is said to be strongly relationally embedded, thus making use of strong tie binding. In the case of Respiratory A/S, the Director of Strategic Marketing & Business Planning argues that personal relations become of crucial importance for the partnership to work, "We have established strong relations in particular with our partners Bayer and Maxygen. It is a question of setting up a personal relation of some kind". This is closely linked with the general nature of the company's relationships. These are sought on the basis of the future partner's core competencies that should complement those of Respiratory A/S. The company creates a strong chain of relations with its strategic partners. This is illustrated by the strategic relation established with Maxygen - a leading company in the field of gene manipulation. The background for the strategic relation is the co-development of a new gene manipulated allergy vaccine. Strategic relations are often established with organisations that complement Respiratory A/S in areas that lie outside its own focus. Interdependency arises because Respiratory A/S relies on access to certain activities provided by its strategic relationship partners. Strong ties therefore have to be established to create the level of trust necessary to make the transfer of resources possible. When analysing Respiratory A/S's choice of its product/market domain from a network point of view, strong connections exist between its business strategy and its relationship to partners. Contracts could very well be used to protect these relations.

3.1.2 Production process

Companies such as Respiratory A/S need to focus on efficiency. As pointed out by the company's Director of Strategic Marketing & Business Planning, "We would like to drive the development away from the use of a wide area of vaccines and instead develop a minor set of vaccines. That would give us some sure production gains". Respiratory A/S needs to establish strategic relationships with organisations, which can somehow ensure that efficiency is maintained or improved within the company's existing product/market domain. By having a targeted product portfolio that covers the domain, therefore, efficiency can be obtained in terms of economies of scale. Respiratory A/S has established strategic relationships with companies within each of the areas they cover, i.e., diagnosing, prevention and treatment of allergies. Efficiency gains are obtained through its strategic relationships in that the quality of its products is ensured so as its sales volume.

3.1.3 Organisational structure

Respiratory A/S is currently striving to streamline its organisational structure. According to their Director of Strategic Marketing & Business Planning, "We are working on streamlining the organisation so that it becomes more centralised". This indicates that it will be difficult for a company like Respiratory A/S to maintain relations that are based on different levels of relational embeddedness and types of ties. The reason for these types of relations is that defenders are often highly dependent on access to activities performed by its strategic relationship partners. As a consequence, a considerable amount of resources have to be spent on each relationship. A consequence of a centralised organisational structure where decision-making is slow and where time and resources are strained can make it difficult to maintain the company's strategic relationships. Relationships built on a high level of trust involve mutuality, which forces defenders, in most cases, to form strategic relationships with organisations with similar characteristics. Respiratory A/S holds some relationships, which are based on weaker ties: the Director of Strategic Marketing and Business Planning states, "We do run some business relationships of minor character with small bio-tech companies. They are however only related to projects of little significance". These relationships may function as non-redundant relationships or as structural holes. This will provide Respiratory A/S access to information outside its established strategic network and a safety net in case of crises in the established strategic relationships. In sum, a general alignment exists between the organisational structure of a defender and the indications of network behaviour.

3.1.4 Network identity

As has been shown, Respiratory A/S depends on access to resources outside its internal boundaries. Strong incentives exist for it to establish business relationships with organisations possessing the needed resources. However, the opportunities available to the company depend on its prior history of relationships as well as the present situation of the company (Ahuja, 1998; Anderson et al., 1994). Due to Respiratory A/S's leading position within its field, we presume it has had a considerable level of success. Furthermore, the fact that the company paid attention to the issue of prior relationships indicates that it is aware of the dangers of being negatively influenced by less successful relations. The Director of Strategic Marketing & Business Planning, Respiratory A/S argues, "You do take into account who the company has been working with before and the outcome of it". Consequently, Respiratory A/S benefits from a positive network identity. A defender furthermore has access to a considerable amount of resources and information through their business relationships as they have a high degree of relational embeddedness making them attractive as partners and thus enlarge its opportunity set. The majority of the business relations established by Respiratory A/S are based on strong ties, which exhaust a considerable amount of resources. This can have a negative influence on its network identity and hereby limit its set of opportunities.

3.2 The prospector

3.2.1 Product/market domain

Innovator A/S is situated within one specific business environment. The Senior Director of Innovator A/S however states, “It is an industry that keeps on changing. New applications and opportunities are constantly arising and our clients (are) constantly pushing for new products”. Innovator A/S has to continually introduce new innovative products and seek to develop new markets. The Senior Director of Innovator A/S, says that “This is our living (introducing new products). Within all areas - also totally new products”. In order to successfully follow its explorative strategy, it is important for Innovator A/S to have the resources needed to follow up on new opportunities. Therefore, strategic relationships will in most cases be based on a relatively low degree of relational embeddedness and weak tie binding. This avoids locking resources into permanent relations. The Senior Director of the company refers to the strategic relationships established by Innovator A/S as strategic accounts rather than as relationship partners. Innovator A/S puts a great deal of effort into maintaining its clients and therefore seeks to develop personal relations between the companies. As the clients in some cases also represent strategic relationships, these relations naturally become long-term and based on personal understanding. The Senior Director of Innovator A/S states, “You have to have a personal understanding to make things work. Building personal relations takes time”. Nevertheless, personal relations are not only developed because the strategic relationship partner is a client. Personal relations also serve the purpose of enhancing the success of the relationship itself.

Using the strategic relations established with Procter & Gamble (P&G) as an example, it becomes clear that Innovator A/S is searching for strategic relationship partners that provide access to knowledge about the future demands of the industry. Hence, as the area of interest for the strategic relationship is built on exchange of information, the level of adaptation and hereby also interdependency in the relationship is limited. The Senior Director explains this by arguing as follows: “Some of our customers (strategic relationship partners) will be the same but as we move away form technical applications over to medical devices and the pharmaceutical business, the customers (strategic relationship partners) will become new ones”. Hence, the level of relational embeddedness may be high in accordance with the level of personal involvement. However, interdependencies in terms of production are not created since the main purpose of the strategic relations established is to access information. It is therefore fair to argue that from a network point of view, alignment exists between Innovator A/S's choice of product/market domain and established types of strategic relationships.

3.2.2 Production process

For organisations dedicated to a wide exploration of new products, it is of crucial importance to have a production system that allows for flexibility. For Innovator A/S this means that focus is on the ability to use the same facilities for various purposes, e.g., enzymes and micro-organisms can be grown in the same tanks etc. Hence, synergy exits between all of Innovator A/S businesses as stated by their Senior Director, "Synergies between new businesses and back to what we do today will always be present". Innovator A/S has therefore established strategic relations with some of the biggest customers in the various markets. E.g., in the market for animal food, Innovator A/S has developed a strong strategic relationship with Roche, which is one of the most dominant producers. It is thus reasonable to argue that according to indications from the network literature as well as empirical data, prospectors will mainly engage with organisations providing access to information on new developments both inside and outside their current business areas.

3.2.3 Organisational structure

Prospectors need an organisational structure that can help support the dynamic nature of their business. The organisational structure of Innovator A/S provides a good example. As stated by the Senior Director of Innovator A/S, "Even though it looks like our organisation is very hierarchical it is actually very flat. There is a very short distance to the top. You can discuss with all people and management as well". The flexible structure of Innovator A/S should thus enable it to handle a number of different strategic relationships to access a wide area of information. Furthermore, Innovator A/S seeks to avoid tying up resources with a specific relationship. As stated by the Senior Director, "When we change business focus we have to change partners". It is therefore unlikely that business relationships will be established with defenders as this typology often invests a considerable amount of resources in its relations. Nevertheless, even the most capable organisation has its limits in terms of resources available. Having non-redundant relationships is therefore wise as they demand less attention while at the same time providing access to unavailable information. Coupled with a decentralised organisational structure, the strain on resources diminishes, thus facilitating the handling of a larger number of strategic relationships.

3.2.4 Network identity

A company's network identity is a question of the incentives it offers and the opportunities available to it. In relation to its current situation, Innovator A/S benefits from being positively known as a leader within its field. Furthermore, the fact that Innovator A/S cooperates with some of the biggest companies within various industries adds positively to its network identity. Innovator A/S nonetheless have to be careful not to overstretch its engagement in too many areas as this will drain resources and hereby have a negative effect on its network identity. However, as Innovator A/S emphasises the existence of synergy between all areas of business as well as a satisfactory level of personal understanding and involvement (i.e. medium level of relational embeddedness) the danger of damaging its network identity is diminished.

3.3 The analyser

3.3.1 Product/market domain

Currently Derma A/S is trying to explore new business areas but it has not yet decided which area to target. Derma A/S Executive Vice President of Marketing & Sales explains, "We are searching for a third leg to stand on. It's somewhat a matter of what falls into our hands". The company is thus following a dual strategy of exploitation and exploration. Within existing areas, the goal of Derma A/S is, according to Executive Vice President of Marketing & Sales, "To become the absolute leading company within dermatology. It demands new products but it does not necessarily mean that we have to be the biggest". Henceforth, the company is securing its position within current markets primarily by introducing new products while still improving existing ones. As can be seen from the previous sections, strategic relationships established by companies following a strategy of exploitation often have a higher degree of relational embeddedness than the ones established by companies focused on exploration. As Derma A/S follows a dual strategy, it engages in strategic relations of different characteristics. The strategic relation with, e.g., GlaxoSmithKlein (GSK) is long-term and based on Derma A/S having access to GSK's databank of products of interest for dermatological research. The Executive Vice President of Marketing & Sales explains that strategic relationships often become long-term solely due to the fact that the basis for these relationships (R&D) is a time-consuming process. It therefore becomes important to establish personal relations and hereby to develop a certain level of relational embeddedness. Still, Derma A/S makes sure that they do not suddenly get locked into a relation they cannot get out of. It is important to notice that contrary to Respiratory A/S, Derma

A/S does not engage in joint development of a specific product. As the example with GSK illustrates, Derma A/S however establishes strategic relations with the purpose of accessing resources that are vital for the further development of its own products. Interdependencies are thus created, as Derma A/S does not posses the competencies necessary for the development of these activities internally. The fact that Derma A/S also functions as a venture capital investor in minor companies illustrates the more explorative side of its dual strategy. The level of relational embeddedness here is much lower as these relations have often been built on weak ties. These business relations are thus not established with the intent to access certain resources or activities. Derma A/S holds a range of informal contacts. Consistency exists between the product/market domain of Derma A/S and established strategic relationships.

3.3.2 Production processes

Companies that are focused on the exploitation as well as explorative side of business need to apply a production system that can follow up on this dual strategy. Derma A/S illustrates this point well as the strategic relationship with the company Halas Pharma is based purely on the development of new production methods. As mentioned by the Executive Vice President of Marketing & Sales: "we aim to be just as efficient as a generic producer. We are therefore constantly optimising on all fronts". In addition, effectiveness is sought in the way that existing production facilities can be used for various purposes: "Our newest product will be produced on our two fabrics using existing production systems".

It is important to remember that an analyser has to strike a balance between exploitation and exploration and that the production system is merely a means to an end. The previously mentioned relation with Halas Pharma is however a direct example of one that is intended to improve efficiency. Overall Derma A/S seems to establish strategic relations, which can enhance efficiency. However, as the company is searching for a new area of business, the issue of effectiveness is likewise considered.

3.3.3 Organisational structure

The organisational structure of an analyser often becomes a centralised and decentralised structure. In the case of Derma A/S, the organisational structure is according to the Executive Vice President of Marketing & Sales: "a very flat organisational structure with little distance from the lower levels of the organisation to the top". When following a dual strategy like Derma A/S's, it is important that the organisation is capable of working with different types of organisations. Prospectors are organized to make quick decisions. If relationship partners are not organized accordingly, decision-making processes will become slow and problems may arise. On the other hand, defenders are characterised by slower processes and if working with a strategic partner who makes quick decisions, the defender might interpret the partner as superficial. Therefore, the organisational structure of an analyser is created to make room for working with both types. The Executive Vice President of Marketing & Sales explains: "It is a question of having some effective decision making processes and making sure that you have the time you need to make qualified decision". In order not to put the organisation under too heavy pressure from having to deal with different types of strategic relations it is of vital importance that the analyser has the correct mixture of redundant and non-redundant relations. Since Derma A/S engages in more stable relations while functioning at the same time as a venture capital investor, it seems to illustrate this point well.

3.3.4 Network identity

The two major incentives driving Derma A/S to establish strategic relationships are: its need for complementary resources and access to information outside its more stable area of business. As analysers in general have a good reputation among defenders, prospectors as well as other analysers, they have abundant opportunities available. Based on the age of Derma A/S and its current position, it can be argued that the company has had success with its prior relationships. Further supporting this is the fact that Derma A/S takes the question of network identity seriously. As commented by the Executive Vice President of Marketing & Sales: "What we are looking at is their (future partner's) prior relationships, the size of the company, how flexible they are and if they seem to be on the same wave length as us". In addition, the company's ability to engage in different types of strategic relationships as well as its current position within its more stable area of business indicates that the company has a rather positive identity. It can however have a negative influence that the analyser has to allocate its resources among strategic relationships requiring different levels of relational embeddedness. As the analyser uses its activities within the more stable environment to secure its activities within the less stable ones, it can be difficult for it to free up resources needed to "nurse" its strategic relationships within minor areas. Derma A/S does however cope well with this problem as non-redundant relations are used to obtain information on new business opportunities, which require few resources. It hereby secures that the sufficient amount of resources available to handle the strategic relationships requires a higher level of relational embeddedness.

4. Framework and discussion

The illustration below highlights how different typologies are linked to the network dimensions.

Table 1. Findings linking business typologies with network behaviour

	Level of relational embeddedness		**Incentives to establish strategic relations**		**No. of redundant relations**	**No. of non-redundant relations**	**Strategic relationship partners**
	Weak ties	**Strong ties**	**Complementary resources**	**Market information**			
Defender	Few	Many	High	Low	Many	Few	Mostly defenders
Prospector	Many	Few	Low	High	Few	Many	Mostly analysers or prospectors
Analyser	Some	Some	High	High	Some	Some	Defenders, analysers and prospectors

As can be seen from the findings above some main differences exist as to how each business type relates to networking. Defenders have a tendency to get more engaged and create a higher level of interdependency with their strategic relationship partners than analysers or prospectors do. This is due to a focus on exploitation of existing products/markets. The main incentive for establishing strategic relations is thus access to complementary resources that can help secure the company's position. Non-redundant relations therefore become less important as their main purpose often is to provide information from outside the existing area of business. Prospectors, on the other hand, get less relationally embedded because they focus on the exploration of new products/markets. Access to information thus becomes the driving force for establishing strategic relations that can secure its position. A low level of interdependency is thus created, as the prospector is not dependent on certain activities/resources. It hereby follows that non-redundant relations are preferred over redundant relations as they provide the needed type of information. Finally analysers seek to find a balance between levels of relational embeddedness as well as levels of interdependency that stem from its activity/resource chains, as they are dedicated to the exploitation as well as exploration of products/markets. It thus follows that access to complementary resources as well as information drives the company to establish business relations. Consequently non-redundant relations become just as important as redundant relations.

This paper has made a first attempt to link business typologies with network behaviour and identity. Evidence has been provided that a clear systematic connection in fact exists. It has been shown that defenders, prospectors and analysers each relate differently to the various elements defined as parameters of network behaviour. From the analysis, support has thus been provided to show that patterns of network relations can be established on the basis of the business typology of a company. The results of the analysis make clear that the relation between business typologies and network identity and behaviour is an important element, which should not be overlooked when pursuing company strategy.

Based on the present paper, insight has been gained as to how the relations between the business typology of a company and patterns of network behaviour can become of importance for a company's network relations. Hence a first attempt has been made to link a company's strategy, structure and processes with indicators of network behaviour. This offers the strategy field a conceptualisation that affords an understanding of how to manage networks and it offers the network literature a better understanding of who links with whom and why. An attempt has been made to link the field of organisational behaviour to the literature on networks, and subsequently to contribute to the understanding of how different types of companies best make use of their network relations.

References

Ahuja, G., 2000, The Duality of Collaboration, *Strategic Management Journal.* **21**(3): 317–343.

Anderson, J. C., Håkansson, H., and Johanson, J., 1994, Dyadic Business Relationships within a Business Network Context, *Journal of Marketing.* **58**(4):1-15.

Ansoff, H., 1965, *Corporate Strategy,* Penguin Books, London.

Barney, J., 1991, Firm Resources and Sustained Competitive Advantage, *Journal of Management.* **17**(1):99–120.

Bresser, R. K. F., 1989, Kollektive Unternehmensstrategien, *Zeitschrift für Betriebswirtschaft.* **59**:545-564.

Blau, P. M., 1968, The Hierarchy of Authority in Organizations, *American Journal of Sociology.* **73**:453-467.

Burgelman, R. A., 1983, A Process Model of Internal Corporate Venturing in the Diversified Major Firm, *Administrative Science Quarterly.* **28**(2):223-244.

Burt, R. S., 1992, The Social Structure of Competition, in: *Networks and Organisations: Structure, Form and Action,* N. Nohria, G. E. Eccles, eds., Harvard Business School Press, Boston, pp. 57-91.

Dyer, J. H., and Singh, H., 1998, The Relational View: Cooperative Strategy and Sources of Interorganisational Competitive Advantage, *The Academy of Management Review.* **23**(4):660–679.

Eisenhardt, K., 1999, Building theories from case study research, *Academy of Management Review.* **14**(4):532-550.

Ford, D., Håkansson, H., and Johanson, J., 1986, How Do Companies Interact?, in: *Understanding Business Markets,* D. Ford, ed., The Dryden Press, pp. 55–67.

Glasser, B., and Strauss, A., 1967, *The discovery of grounded theory, Strategies of qualitative research,* Wiedenfeld and Nicholson, London.

Granovetter, M., 1992, Problems of Explanation in Economic Sociology, in: *Networks and Organisations: Structure, Form and Action,* E. Nohria, and G. E. Eccles, eds., Harvard Business School Press, Boston, pp. 25-56.

Gulati, R., Nohria, N., and Zaheer, A., 2000, Strategic Networks, *Strategic Management Journal.* **21**(3):203–215.

Hambrick, D. C., 1993, Some Tests of the Effectiveness and Functional Attributes of Miles and Snow's Strategic Types, The Academy of Management Journal. **26**(1):5–26.

Hamel, G., and Prahalad, C. K., 1996, The Core Competence of the Corporation, in: *Managing the Multibusiness Company – strategic issues for diversified groups,* M. Goold, and K. L. Sommers, eds., Routledge, London, pp. 218-239.

Holm, D. B., Eriksson, K., and Johanson, J., 1996, Business Networks and Cooperation in International Business Relationships, *Journal of International Business Strategies.* **27**(5):1033-1053.

Hougaard, S., and Bjerre, M., 2002, *Strategic Relationships Marketing,* Samfundslitteratur.

Husted, K., and Vintergaard, C., 2004, Stimulating innovation through corporate venture bases, *Journal of World Business.* **39**(2):296-306.

Håkansson, H., and Johanson, J., 1993, The network as a Governance Structure: Interfirm Cooperation beyond Markets and Hierachies, in: *The embedded Firm,* G. Grabher, ed., Routledge, London, pp. 35-51.

Håkansson, H., and Snehota, I., 1997a, No business is an Island: The Network Concept of Business Strategy, in: *Understanding Business Markets,* D. Ford, ed., 3rd ed., Thomson Learning, 2002, pp. 150-161.

Håkansson, H., and Snehota, I., 1997b, Analysing Business Relationships, in: *Understanding Business Markets,* D. Ford, ed., 2. ed., The Dryden Press, pp. 151-175.

Ibarra, H., 1992, Structural Alignments, Individual Strategies, and Managerial Action: Elements Toward a Network Theory of Getting Things Done, in: *Networks and Organisations: Structure, Form and Action,* N. Nohria, and G. E. Eccles, eds., Harvard Business School Press, Boston, pp. 165-188.

Johanson, J., and Associates, 1994, *Internationalisation, Relationships and Networks,* Uppsala University.

Johanson, J., and Mattsson, L. G., 1994, Interorganisational Relations in Industrial System, in: *Internationalisation, Relationships and Networks,* J. Johanson, and Associates, eds., Uppsala University, pp. 171-181.

Mattson, L. G., 1986, A "Markets-as-Networks" Perspective, in: *The Management of Strategic Change,* A. Pettegrew, ed., Basil Blackwell, Oxford, pp. 234–256.

Miles, R. E., and Snow, C. C., 1978, *Organizational strategy, structure and process,* McGraw-Hill Book Company, New York.

Miles, R. E, and Snow, C. C., 1984, Fit, Failure and the Hall of Fame, *California Management Review.* **26**(3):10–28.

Miles, R. E, and Snow, C. C., 1992, Causes of Failure in Network Organisations, *California Management Review.* **34**(4):53-72.

Morgan, R, Strong, C and McGuinness, T., 2000, *Prospector strategy & competitive attributes – a multiattribute analysis of strategy,* Research Paper No. 01-12.

Namiki, N., 1989, The impact of competitive strategy on export sales performance: an exploratory study, *The Mid-Atlantic Journal of Business.* **25**:21-37.

Porter, M., 1980, *Competitive Advantage,* The Free Press, New York.

Ritter, T., 1999, The Networking Company – Antecedents for Coping with Relationships and Networking Effectively, *Industrial Marketing Management.* **28**(5):467-479.

Rowley, T., Behrens, D., and Krackhardt, D., 2000, Redundant Governance Structures, *Strategic Management Journal.* **21**(3):369-386.

Shortell, S. M., and Zajac, E. J., 1990, Perceptual and archival measures of Miles and Snow's strategic types: a comprehensive assessment of reliability and validity, *Academy of Management Journal.* **33**(4):817-832.

Torres, AM, and Murray, JA., 2002, Diversity, marketing practice and organisational evolution: Implications for the management of productive evolution, *Journal of Change Management.* **2**(3):229-243.

Touminen, M., 1997, *Marketing Capability and Marketing Orientation in Strategy Interface,* Helsinginkauppakorkeakaulum.

Vintergaard, C., 2005, Opportunities in Corporate Venturing – Actors Creating Passageways, *International Journal of Innovation Management.* **9**(1):215-239.

Wernerfelt, B., 1984, A Resource-based View of the Firm, *Strategic Management Journal.* **5**(2):171-80.

Yin R., 1984, *Case study research,* Sage Publications, Beverly Hills, CA.

Zahra, S. A., and Pearce, J. A., 1990, Research Evidence on the Miles-Snow Typology, *Journal of Management.* **16**(4):751-768.

Chapter 4

Institutional Design of Mixed-mode Electronic Marketplaces

Marcel Gogolin and Stefan Klein
University of Münster; University College Dublin

Abstract: Based on a critical reflection of transaction cost economics, the chapter elaborates the notion of institutional design and distinguishes different layers of design. Moreover the notion of governance structures – and subsequently the design framework – is expanded to reflect the specifics of multilevel forms of coordination, in particular mixed-mode electronic marketplaces. Mixed-mode marketplaces encompass different modes of coordination, including network coordination, under the institutional framework of a market. The notion of mixed-mode governance structures will be elaborated as it runs contrary to Williamson's distinct forms of governance, namely hierarchies, networks (or hybrids), and markets. The chapter concludes with suggestions for institutional design which reflect the competition among markets and other forms of governance.

Key words: Electronic Marketplaces, Institutions, Marketplace Design

1. Introduction

Although organizations conduct their businesses in different ways, all are engaged in external, inter-organizational exchange relations or transactions. Organizations face the challenge to adopt an appropriate institutional arrangement that mitigates potential coordination and motivation problems. Transaction cost economics is a well-known approach to analyze and assess the organization of transactions. Unfortunately, transaction cost economics merely offers a static framework focusing on comparative efficiencies, while it says little about the emergence and change of institutional arrangements. The chapter addresses this void and attempts to shed some light on the notion of institutional arrangements or, to use Williamson's terminology, governance structures.

In recent years a novel institutional arrangement has emerged: the electronic marketplace. Although the concept of electronic marketplaces seemed to be promising from a theoretical perspective (Malone et al., 1987), numerous implementations of electronic marketplaces have failed for various reasons (Day et al., 2003; Wise and Morrison, 2000). Nevertheless, in contrast to the public perception, electronic marketplaces have flourished in several industries, and the use of – specialized forms of – electronic marketplaces (e.g., e-procurement applications or business integration hubs) has gained momentum (B2B Expert Group, 2003). This chapter focuses on a specific type of electronic marketplaces, so called mixed-mode electronic marketplaces, which combine network and market coordination mechanisms.

A main function of electronic marketplaces is the provision of an institutional infrastructure (Bakos, 1998). The marketplace institution aims at facilitating and safeguarding the efficient execution of business transactions (Clark and Lee, 1999). This includes transactions which take place within the context of collaborative or network relationships. However, despite its importance, electronic marketplace research has widely neglected the institutional structure, with only a few exceptions (Clark and Lee, 1999; Kambil and van Heck, 2002; Reimers, 1996). Therefore, this chapter explores the institutional structure and the process of institutionalization of electronic marketplaces. Our research questions are:

- What are the building blocks of the institutional structure of an electronic marketplace?
- Which external factors influence the design and implementation of the institutional structure?

The remainder of this chapter is structured as follows. Starting with a brief review of transaction cost economics, the institutional arrangement electronic marketplace will be elaborated in greater detail. The institutional structure of SupplyOn, a mixed mode electronic marketplace for the automotive industry, will be introduced. Afterwards, the opportunities and threats of designing an institutional structure will be discussed. Concluding remarks will follow.

2. Transaction cost economics and the organization of inter-organizational transactions

Specialization and division of labour are the main characteristics of western economies (Milgrom and Roberts, 1992). Economic actors are specializing in their product activities and transact with other parties. On the one hand, they acquire resources, tools etc. from suppliers, and on the other hand, they distribute their products to customers. However, relying on other actors might result in a loss of sovereignty leading to dependencies between transacting actors.

In order to achieve efficient and effective outcomes, economic actors are coordinating their activities and are defining incentive mechanisms for overcoming the motivation problem. That is, the actors attempt to organize their transactions. Institutions (contracts, organizational rules, laws, etc.) are commonly recognised as mechanisms to mitigate the organization problem (Khalil, 1995; Picot et al., 2005). North (1991; 1992) defines institutions as "humanly devised constraints that structure political, economic, and social interaction. They consists of both informal constraints (sanctions, taboos, customs, traditions, and codes of conduct), and formal rules (constitutions, laws, property rights)" (North, 1991:97).

The analysis and assessment of various institutional arrangements is the core of transaction cost economics (cf. Williamson, 1985; 1991). Starting from Coase's initial question "Why do firms exist?" (Coase, 1937), transaction cost economics has evolved into a major organizational theory. The unit of analysis is the transaction which occurs "when a good or service is transferred across a technologically separable interface" (Williamson, 1994:103). The execution of transactions causes transaction costs. The level of transaction costs depends on the independent variables asset specificity, uncertainty and frequency, two behavioural assumptions (bounded rationality and opportunism), and the underlying institutional arrangement or governance structure.

Transaction cost economics provides a "comparative-efficiency framework" with which the transaction costs of one institutional arrangement can be compared with a set of alternatives (Roberts and Greenwood, 1997). It is assumed that the most efficient institutional arrangement, i.e., the one with the relatively lowest transaction costs, will be adopted by an organization. Transaction cost reasoning has been applied to a number of institutional arrangements, for example, markets, hybrids, hierarchies (Williamson, 1985), networks (Jarillo, 1988; Thorelli, 1986), bureaucracies, and clans (Ouchi, 1980).

According to a strict application of transaction cost reasoning, actors have to select the most efficient institutional arrangement for each transaction, otherwise they underperform and are driven out of business in the long run (Roberts and Greenwood, 1997). However, organizations will experience difficulties when selecting the optimal institutional arrangement (Figure 1). There are at least two reasons why it is difficult or even unrealistic to employ the strict form of transaction cost economics.

Firstly, organizations have to deal with trade-offs when selecting an institutional arrangement: "whereas more decentralized forms of organizations (e.g. markets) support high powered incentives and display outstanding adaptive properties to disturbances of an autonomous kind, they are poorly suited in cooperative adaptation respects" (Williamson, 1994:90). That is, there is no institutional arrangement that is optimal for all transactional settings.

Secondly, actors act with bounded rationality; they are influenced by technical and institutional constraints, and do not possess all relevant information. Hence, we cannot take it as given that they are able to select the most efficient institutional arrangement. Moreover, following Alchian (1950) and Meyer/Rowan (1991), it is not the most efficient organization that will survive but the one that can gain legitimacy and resources needed to survive. One way to achieve this is to imitate the behaviour of successful others. Therefore, organizations will adopt those institutional arrangements that are commonly perceived as efficient. Hence, it is assumed that actors tend to adopt a "satisficing design" (Roberts and Greenwood, 1997) , one that is acceptable but not necessarily optimal.

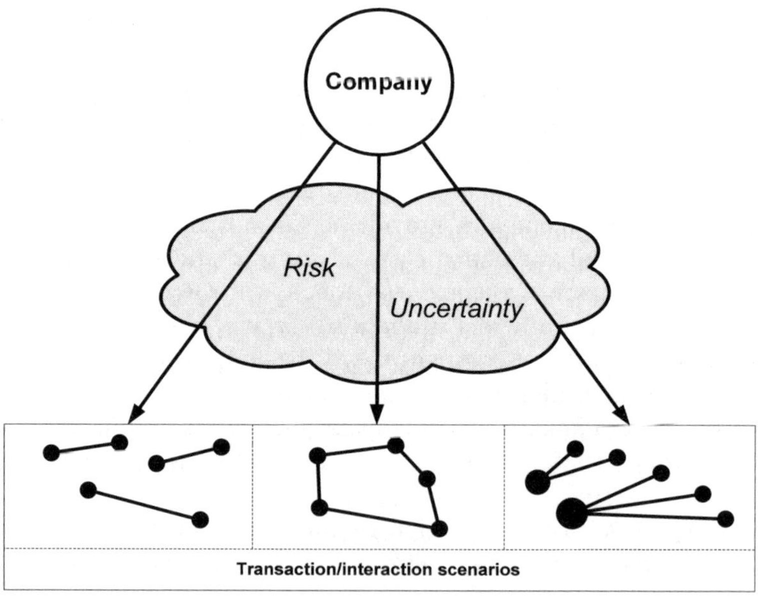

Figure 1. Selection of institutional arrangements

In sum, transaction cost economics while a useful analytical instrument, is not as suitable as basis for normative or predictive statements on a company level. Transaction cost economics focuses on the comparison of stylized institutional arrangements, but it does not account for specific implementations of these arrangements such as different electronic marketplaces, which execute their institutional regimes with varying strictness. Moreover, transaction cost economics does not take into account the cost of switching institutional arrangements.

Another crucial aspect of transaction cost economics lies in its static nature (Roberts and Greenwood, 1997). Transaction cost economics neither can explain the dynamics of institutions nor the emergence of novel forms of institutional arrangements. A certain set of institutional arrangements is given ex ante. Actors assess the alternatives and select the most appropriate ones. However, institutional arrangements need resources to operate and have to be organized. Thus, this chapter deals with the nature of institutional arrangements in greater details. The next section will explore one specific type of institutional arrangements: electronic marketplaces.

3. Electronic marketplaces

3.1 Mixed-mode electronic marketplaces

It is commonly acknowledged that the Internet has the potential to significantly reduce the coordination and motivation costs compared to traditional transactions (Garicano and Kaplan, 2001; Malone et al., 1987). However, the impact of the Internet on the relative transaction cost advantage of certain institutional arrangements (markets, networks and hierarchies) has been disputed intensely. Meanwhile, empirical evidence suggests that neither the predictions of the "move-to-the-market" (Malone et al., 1987) nor of the "move-to-the-middle" hypothesis (Clemons et al., 1993) has been fulfilled. Rather most companies organize their external relationships and transactions in various "mixed mode operations" ranging from arm's length to almost hierarchical arrangements (Holland and Lockett, 1997).

This is reflected by recent marketplace developments. A number of electronic marketplaces are not limited to exchanges any more, but have transformed into "all-in-one markets" (Kambil et al., 1999) or "collaboration electronic marketplaces" (Markus and Christiaanse, 2003). Besides pure allocation mechanisms, these marketplaces also offer coordination (e.g., electronic data interchange, vendor managed inventory, etc.) and collaboration services (e.g., joint research and development, project management, etc.). Since they resemble the "mixed mode operations" mentioned before, we use the term mixed-mode electronic marketplace in order to characterize their value proposition.

3.2 The institutional arrangement "Electronic marketplace"

Transaction cost economics differentiates various levels of institutions and denotes that institutions are accommodated in a hierarchical way (Dietl, 1993; Williamson, 2000). On the top level there are fundamental, informal institutions such as human rights, traditions or religion. Secondary institutions are derived and constrained by their superordinate counterparts. They refine the goals and purposes of the institutions for specific settings. For example, the definition and enforcement of property rights and contract laws take place on a high institutional level.

The (collective) institutional arrangement electronic marketplace resides on an intermediate institutional level between inter-individual or inter-organizational governance structures and the institutional environment (Brousseau, 2000). Usually, a private institutional organization operates the electronic marketplace. It defines and enforces a certain set of regulatory rules for marketplace-typical exchange processes and provides one or more coordination services. Marketplace participants can execute their transactions more efficiently, since they do not have to negotiate every transaction separately. Similar to general terms and conditions, the institutional arrangement simplifies, expedites and standardizes market transactions which might lead to economies of scale in contrast to individually negotiated inter-organizational governance structures.

Following several theorists (Brousseau, 2000; Ménard, 1995; Reimers, 2000) we differentiate between the institutional arrangement (e.g., market, network, and firm) and underlying coordination and/or allocation mechanisms (e.g., price system, mutual agreements, and authority; see Figure 1). In a similar way, Scharpf discusses multilevel forms of coordination as not only widespread but also advantageous: "Networks [...] often exist in the shadow of the market, majority rule, or hierarchical authority - and there is reason to think that these hybrids or multilevel forms of coordination may have particularly attractive welfare implications." (Scharpf, 1993:9) Williamson's stylized governance structures market and hierarchy reflect the combinations market/price system and firm/authority, respectively. The gray area represents the "swollen middle" of hybrid arrangements (cf. Hennart, 1993; Ménard, 1995).

Accordingly, a mixed-mode electronic marketplace is a market(place) that encompasses multiple coordination and allocation mechanisms (Figure 3). Furthermore, it is very likely that several coordination and allocation mechanisms require their own "rules of the game". That is, the mixed-mode electronic marketplace incorporates several governance structures.[4] The sum of multiple coordination mechanisms including their governance structures is what we term institutional structure.

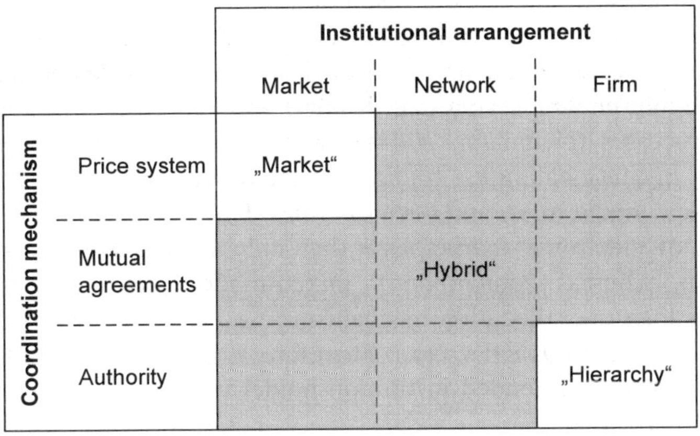

Figure 2. A comparison of institutional arrangements and coordination mechanisms

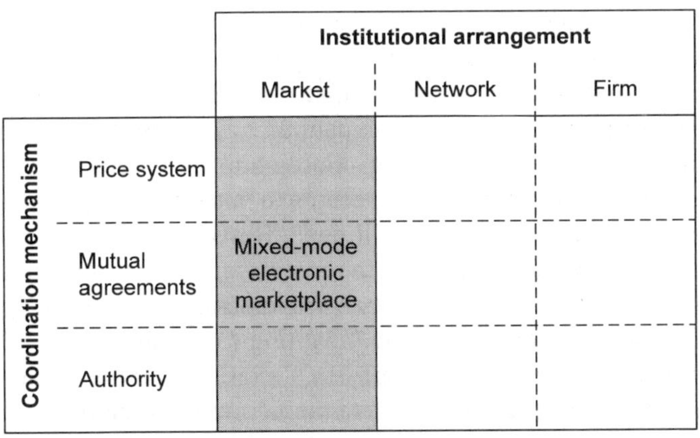

Figure 3. Coordination mechanisms of mixed-mode electronic marketplaces

Although many researchers have stressed the importance of the institutional structure of electronic marketplaces, a comprehensive analysis of the rele-

---

4 For reasons of simplicity it is assumed that every coordination/allocation mechanism necessitates its own governance structure which might be derived from a certain set of general institutional rules.

vant elements of the regulatory rules and enforcement mechanisms is still outstanding. Kambil and van Heck (2002), for example, differentiate between basic trade processes and trade context processes. However, their notion of trade context processes (product representation, regulation, risk management, influence, and dispute resolution), which are somehow related to the institutional structure, seems to be quite sketchy and selective.

Neumann's concept of the extended institution of an electronic market system is more encompassing than Kambil and van Heck's notion of trade context processes (Neumann, 2004). Neumann differentiates between five classes of institutional rules: trading object definition, participation rules, trading rules, media rules, and business rules. However, Neumann's concept presumes an electronic marketplace that only provides one coordination mechanism, whereas contemporary mixed-mode electronic marketplaces offer more than one allocation mechanism (e.g., auctions, reverse auctions, catalogue buying, RfQs/RfPs, etc.). Therefore, it is necessary to adapt and to expand Neumann's extended institution model with respect to mixed-mode electronic marketplaces.

3.3 Building blocks of the institutional structure

Figure 4 shows a more comprehensive view of the institutional structure of electronic marketplaces. The conceptual model is strongly related to Brousseau's (2000) conceptualization. It incorporates the mentioned considerations of the institutional structure (regulatory rules, transaction type-specific coordination mechanisms) which is expanded by a business perspective.

The *institutional organization* of an electronic marketplace normally is a profit-oriented organization which attempts to exploit business opportunities, for example, by bridging institutional gaps. Based on the marketplace strategy and cost-benefit considerations the institutional organization has to find a trade-off between the universality (implementing solutions for a large community) and the appropriateness (adapting to specific needs of users) of the institutional structure which results in a more or less incomplete solution (Brousseau, 2000). In order to increase the adoption probability by potential users, participatory structures might be advisable. By doing so, marketplace users can propose amendments or changes of the business model or the institutional structure.

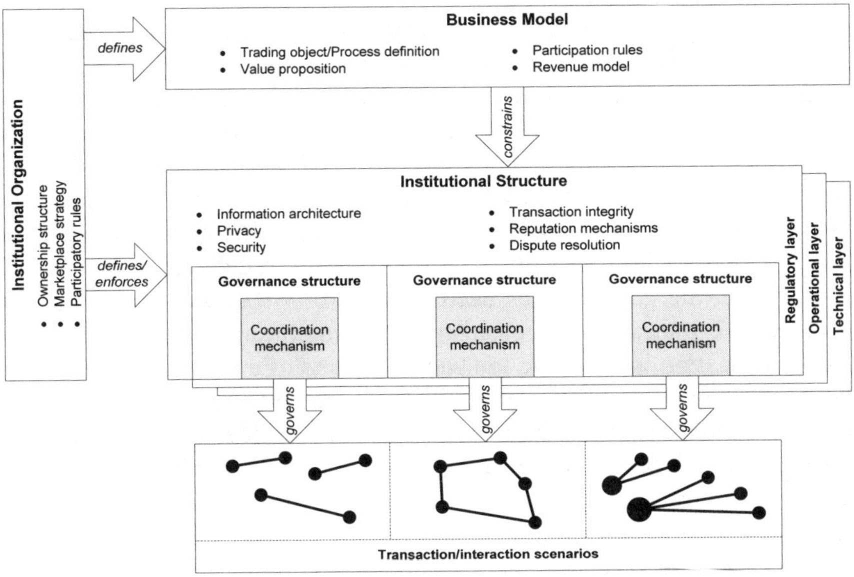

Figure 4. A conceptual model of the institutional structure

Moreover, the transactional behaviour of the marketplace users is indicative of the perceived effectiveness of the institutional structures. A high number of discontent marketplace users indicated by a decreasing number of transactions, and/or an increasing number of passive marketplace participants might drive the marketplace organization to adapt the institutional structure.

Depending on certain design considerations, the institutional organization determines the business model and the institutional structure. The *business model* encompasses fundamental design parameters of the marketplace such as supported trading objects (direct/indirect products, MROs, etc.) and processes (strategic sourcing, spot buying, etc.) as well as respective marketplace services (e.g., business directories, product catalogues, auction mechanisms, etc.). Moreover, the business model defines who is allowed to participate in the marketplace (open/closed marketplace, membership rules) and the revenue model (transaction fees, membership fees, etc.). The business model encompasses the different governance structures and coordination mechanisms, which are defined in the institutional structure and provides differentiated rules where appropriate.

In contrast to Neumann's model, the *institutional structure* suggested here is two-fold. It resembles to the institutional hierarchy discussed before. On the one hand, we propose an overarching regulatory level where the general regulatory structure is defined. The general institutional structure defines rules that are valid for the whole marketplace. It encompasses regulative rules regarding the information architecture (Koppius, 2002), privacy and security issues, transaction-integrity and monitoring services, trust-building and dispute resolution mechanisms.

Besides the fundamental institutional structure, we emphasize the necessity of transaction type-specific adaptations and amendments of the institutional structure, since mixed-mode electronic marketplaces are designed to support various, heterogeneous transaction scenarios. Different transaction types and their respective coordination mechanisms (auctions, reverse auctions, RfQ/RfP, VMI, etc.) often require specific regulatory measures. On the one hand, the general rules need to be further specified and adapted to the respective transaction mechanism. For example, it should be specified which information is available to the participants of a bidding process. Usually, there is an information asymmetry between the buyer who can see and compare all bids and the bidders who can only see their own bids and eventually the current best bid and/or their rank. On the other hand, transaction type-specific "rules of the game" and sometimes even the "plays of the game" (e.g., particular process steps are "hard coded" in the institutional structure) are defined accordingly.

The institutional structure consists of a regulatory structure and respective monitoring and enforcement mechanisms. The monitoring and enforcement mechanisms can be either implemented in the marketplace system (technical layer), executed by marketplace employees (operational layer), or a combination of both.

3.4 An illustrative example

In this section, we apply our conceptual model to the institutional arrangement of SupplyOn[5], a mixed-mode electronic marketplace for the automotive industry. We briefly discuss the elements of the institutional arrangement, namely the institutional organization, the business model, and institutional structure.

Institutional organization
SupplyOn, headquartered in Hallbergmoos near Munich, was founded by Bosch, Continental, INA, SAP and ZF Friedrichshafen in August 2000. The common objective was the development of e-business applications for procurement, engineering and supply chain management. In November 2001 Siemens VDO joined SupplyOn as a new shareholder. In the beginning of 2004, about 4,600 customers from 30 countries with more than 16,500 active users were registed on the marketplace. Around 1,200 electronic inquiry processes are transacted and 110,000 WebEDI messages are sent per month.

---

[5] http://www.supplyon.com

SupplyOn's current shareholder structure indicates a strong buy side bias. Nevertheless, SupplyOn attempts to position itself as a neutral intermediary. This is mainly done by the set up of participatory arrangements. During the early days of SupplyOn, for example, the founding members were supported by 14 associate members (e.g., Siemens VDO, Degussa, Hella, Karmann, Knorr Bremse, Mann & Hummel, Phoenix, and Sachs Automotive). The associate members have shaped the functionality of the marketplace by their participation in working groups.

During a workshop with medium-sized suppliers in July 2005, a working committee for suppliers was set up. The committee defines the requirements of the processes executed via the marketplace from the supplier's point of view. SupplyOn promised to incorporate the suggestions into the further development of the marketplace.

Business model

SupplyOn operates an electronic marketplace "by suppliers for suppliers" and develops standardized solutions for all processes of the automotive industry. The current service portfolio follows a product life cycle covering the stages collaborative engineering, sourcing, logistics/supply chain management, and quality management (Figure 5). Every life cycle stage contains one or more coordination mechanisms (Table 2). Besides, SupplyOn also offers consultancy and training services.

SupplyOn's trading object focus is on direct and indirect material used in production (so called A- and B-parts). The marketplace processes are designed accordingly. For example, since most products traded on the marketplace are complex, highly transaction specific, and have a low degree of commoditization, the sourcing stage provides dynamic (RfQ and reverse auction) rather than fixed price mechanisms (e.g., electronic catalogues).

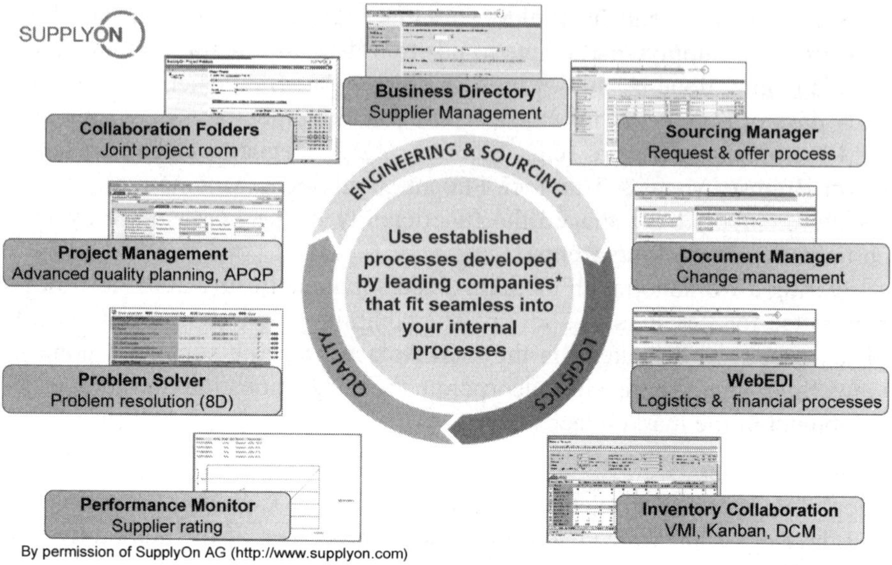

Figure 5. SupplyOn's service portfolio

SupplyOn is a closed marketplace. Only automotive and related-industry suppliers are allowed to participate in the marketplace. In August 2002 SupplyOn introduced a new pricing model that depends on the annual turn over of the participating companies. Instead of around € 667 per month (€ 8,000 per year) a direct material supplier has to pay € 220 (with less than € 5 million turn over), € 440 (with up to €10 million turn over) and 660 €, respectively. For companies offering indirect materials or services only, the annual cost – irrespective of company size or turn over – is € 220. Buying companies have to pay a fixed annual price ranging from € 10.000 up to more than € 1 million depending on their annual turn over and the number of applications used.

Institutional structure

SupplyOn's institutional structure is shown in Table 1 (general rules) and in Table 2 (transaction type-specific rules).

Table 1. Fundamental institutional structure

	Regulatory rule	Implementation
General level	Information architecture	• Business directory: questionnaire on specific material groups, private data (e.g., performance data; limited visibility) • Material groups (SupplyOn standard) • Code of Conduct (e.g., avoidance of prohibited information exchange, no coordination of supply and demand behavior)
	Privacy Security Transaction-integrity	• BS 7799 certificate (security and operating concept, monthly internal audit, annual audit) • Fairness according to SupplyOn (e.g., confidentiality and security) in cooperation with Arbeitsgemeinschaft der Zulieferindustrie (ArGeZ) • Support of "User & Access Management" (UAM) by Odette
	Reputation mechanism	• Registration process for new users • Supplier's performance data (private)
	Dispute resolution	• SupplyOn as an arbitrator (on request)

As mentioned before, SupplyOn emphasizes its neutral role. SupplyOn's "code of conduct", for example, defines several rules in accordance with antitrust regulations (e.g., avoidance of prohibited information exchange and the prohibition of coordinated supplier or demand behaviour such as demand bundling). Moreover, in May 2003 SupplyOn announced an agreement with the supplier industry association "Arbeitsgemeinschaft Zulieferindustrie (ArGeZ)"[6] on clear-cut rules of engagement for electronic purchasing (with a special emphasis on electronic auctions). The agreement defines rules for trustworthy and constructive cooperation among marketplace participants.

Another crucial aspect is the maintenance of a high security standard of the marketplace. In January 2004 SupplyOn received the BS 7799 certificate which confirms the implementation of a comprehensive management system guaranteeing secure information storage and exchange in the marketplace. A central aspect of the BS 7799 certification is a continuous improvement process of the security management system. In addition to a monthly internal audit of all safety relevant aspects, an annual monitoring audit is integral part of the process. In December 2004 the certificate was confirmed within the scope of the annual monitoring audit.

---

[6] The ArGeZ (Working Committee of the Supplier Industry) is a consortium of German trade associations. It represents approx. 8,000 mostly medium-sized supplier companies, and its task is to assert the interests of the supplier firms against the public, politics and buyer industries as well.

Table 2. Transaction type-specific institutional structure

		Coordination mechanism	Functionalities/Governance structure
Transaction type-specific level	Engineering	**Document Manager**	• Provision and distribution of internal documents • Management of access rights for own employees, suppliers and partners
		Collaboration Folders	• Virtual project rooms (bi-directional document exchange) • Document author manages access rights
	Sourcing	**Sourcing manager (RfQ)**	• Quotation form for every material group • Standardized request structure
		Bidding (Reverse auction)	• Configuration of auction design (auction strategy, placing criteria, extra time, etc.) • Fairness according to SupplyOn (e.g., transparency and clear rules for auctions) in cooperation with Arbeitsgemeinschaft der Zulieferindustrie (ArGeZ) • Qualification process possible (e.g., RfQ)
	SCM	**WebEDI**	• Processes: order, delivery, and settlement (based on recommendations of VDA, Odette)
		Vendor Managed Inventory	• Current stock levels and future customer demands • Warning in advance of possible bottlenecks
	QM	**Performance Monitor**	• Transfer of evaluation and quality data to supplier • Data is presented in a standardized and unified structure • Recommended by Fachverband Metallwaren- und verwandte Industrien e.V. (FMI)
		Project Management	• Standardized APQP method

The transaction type-specific institutional structure follows the mentioned product life cycle (engineering, sourcing, logistics/supply chain management/, and quality management). The regulatory rules of sourcing applications are mainly designed to ensure fairness and to safeguard transactions, whereas the rules of coordination and collaboration applications mostly focus on an efficient flow and execution of transactions by standardizing processes, i.e. by defining the “plays of the game”. In order to be able to play the game, the participating companies have to adjust their own processes, in other words they make marketplace specific organizational investments. Furthermore, SupplyOn attempts to implement industry standards, where applicable (e.g., SupplyOn’s WebEDI messages are based on recommendations of VDA and Odette).

In sum, SupplyOn is a good example of a mixed-mode electronic marketplace, which encompasses network and market coordination mechanisms. SupplyOn’s institutional structure indicates that scope and purpose of institutional rules differ across different coordination mechanisms. Institutional rules can be designed for safeguarding transactions as well as for ensuring transaction efficiency. The relation between both aspects depends on the nature of the underlying coordination mechanism. Basically, for exchange- or price-oriented mechanisms it is more likely that they are governed by safeguards and trust building structures; coordination and collaboration mechanisms are rather governed by efficiency-oriented structures.

4. Designing the institutional structure

Electronic marketplace rules and regulations do not simply emerge, but are deliberately designed, maintained and enforced by the institutional organization. Obviously, the institutional structure provides a broad range of design alternatives, and offers institutional organizations numerous business opportunities (Zwass, 2003). With respect to the entrepreneurial nature of the definition of the business (model), we use the term "institutional entrepreneur" (Garud et al., 2002). The institutional entrepreneur is continuously looking for new business opportunities and institutional gaps in order to enhance the business. However, sometimes the institutional entrepreneur does not have the free choice to design the institutional structure in his or her own sense. This is due to two reasons. Firstly, as we already mentioned before, the direct (participatory rules) and indirect (transactional and strategic behaviour) influence of marketplace users has to be taken into consideration. Secondly, the institutional entrepreneur acts boundedly rational and is restricted and constrained by external institutional and technological factors. Thus, based on design ideas of the institutional organization but also as a result of cognitive, institutional and technical constraints, the institutional structure of a mixed-mode electronic marketplace evolves (Figure 6).

Surrounding institutions shape and constrain the institutional structure in multiple ways. On the one hand, the institutional structure is unilaterally shaped by formal and informal remote institutions (general, contract and antitrust law, customs of trade, codes of conduct, etc.). They can hardly be influenced by deliberate actions and design considerations of the institutional organization. On the other hand, there are several institutions that have strong interdependencies with the institutional structure of the marketplace (immediate institutions). These institutions are normally situated in the "organizational field" (DiMaggio, 1991) of the electronic marketplace. They can be antecedents or results of design considerations of the institutional organization. For example, if an industry standard for the electronic interchange of documents exists, it is likely that the marketplace provider adopts this standard (e.g., SupplyOn's implementation of VDA/Odettes's WebEDI recommendations). On the other hand, it is also likely that a successful and widely accepted marketplace standard can become an industry standard in the long run (e.g., SupplyOn's business directory is becoming a quasi-standard in the automotive supplier industry).

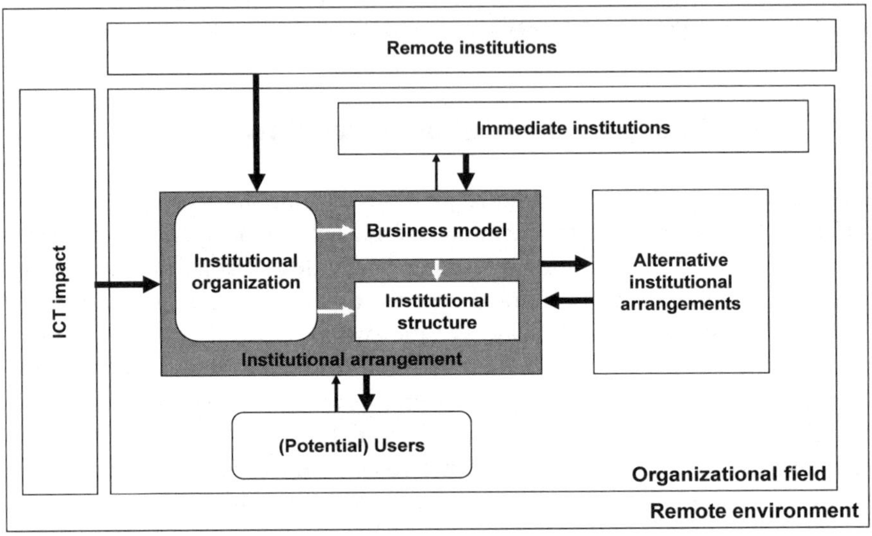

Figure 6. Environmental constraints

Several theorists assume that actors and organizations comply with exogenous institutions (Dietl, 1993; DiMaggio and Powell, 1983; Granovetter, 1992; Williamson, 2000). However, organizational and individual actors usually are not passive, but, as Oliver (1991) suggests, act strategically depending on the implementation of the institutional structure. According to Oliver, potential marketplace users – at least partly – have the choice to adopt the institutional structure of one certain electronic marketplace or of an alternative (e.g., a competitor or a totally different institutional arrangement).

Institutional change is not only induced by changes of superordinate institutions and by strategic actions of individual actors, but my also the result of the emergence of new technologies (Pelikan, 2003). Advances in Internet technologies, for example, enable companies to exchange data electronically rather than by traditional communication means. New technologies sometimes necessitate amendments of established institutional arrangement and sometimes even the creation of novel ones.

In sum, the institutional organization develops and implements the institutional structure of an electronic marketplace in accordance with its business strategy and its business model. Thus, the design of the institutional structure can be regarded as an entrepreneurial task. Nevertheless, the institutional structure is also shaped and constrained by the institutional and technical environment as well as the demands of participating users.

5. Conclusion

Despite their important role for the organization of inter-organizational transactions, theoretical and conceptual models of institutional arrangements and respective institutional structures are underdeveloped. Williamson's analysis of governance structures serves as a good starting point, but needs to be refined in several dimensions:

- Dynamics of institutional arrangements, e.g., lock-in and cost of changes among governance structures,
- Consideration of mixed mode institutional arrangements,
- Genesis and change of institutional arrangements, i.e., institutional arrangements are not given, but result of deliberate design by the institutional entrepreneur within the confines of regulatory structures etc.

Based on Brousseau's (2000) conceptual work on institutional arrangements, we developed a more comprehensive model of a specific institutional arrangement, the mixed mode electronic marketplace. Besides the institutional structure comprising fundamental institutional rules and transaction type-specific coordination mechanisms, the proposed model also integrates a business (model) perspective.

Future work is suggested in two directions. Firstly, the conceptual model has to be validated and refined empirically. In this chapter, we just sketched the institutional arrangement of one mixed-mode electronic marketplace. In particular, the design alternatives of the fundamental and transaction type-specific regulatory system as well as the interplay between the various coordination mechanisms have to be examined in more detail.

Secondly, the evolution of the institutional arrangement is still an open question. In particular, the role of the institutional entrepreneur and institutional design processes need further theoretical and empirical attention. For example, the analysis of the proportion of self-determination (conscious and deliberate design) versus heteronomy (institutional and technological forces) might be of great importance for understanding the evolving nature of institutional arrangements. Existing economic approaches of market design or market engineering often incorporate game theoretical reasoning and rely on rational actors. In fact, the rational actor does not exist in reality. Instead, it might be more appropriate to model economic actors as boundedly rational, influenced or even constrained by institutional forces.

References

Alchian, A. A., 1950, Uncertainty, Evolution and Economic Theory, *Journal of Political Economy.* **58**(3):211-221.

B2B Expert Group, 2003, *Report of the Expert Group on B2B Internet Trading platforms: Final Report,* http://europa.eu.int/comm/enterprise/ict/policy/b2b/wshop/fin-report.pdf, Download 2005-01-29.

Bakos, Y., 1998, The emerging Role of Electronic Marketplaces on the Internet, *Communications of the ACM.* **41**(8):35-42.

Brousseau, E., 2000, What institutions to organize electronic commerce? Private institutions and the organization of markets. *Economics of Innovation & New Technology.* **9**(3):245-273.

Clark, T. H., and Lee, H. G., 1999, Electronic Intermediaries: Trust building and market differentiation. in: *Proceedings of the 32nd Annual Hawaii International Conference on System Sciences,* Bd. V, IEEE Computer Society Press, Los Alamitos, CA, pp. 5038.

Clemons, E. K., Reddi, S. P., and Row, M. C., 1993, The impact of information technology on the organization of economic activity: The "move to the middle" hypothesis, *Journal of Management Information Systems.* **10**(2):9-35.

Coase, R. H., 1937, The Nature of the Firm, *Economica.* **4**(13-16):386-405.

Day, G. S., Fein, A. J., and Ruppersberger, G., 2003, Shakeouts in Digital Markets: Lessons from B2B Exchanges, *California Management Review.* **45**(2):131-150.

Dietl, H., 1993, *Institutionen und Zeit,* Mohr: Tübingen.

DiMaggio, P. J., 1991, Constructing an Organizational Field as a Professional Project: U.S. Art Museums, 1920-1940, in: *The New Institutionalism in Organizational Analysis,* W. W. Powell, and P. J. DiMaggio, eds., University of Chicago Press, Chicago/London, pp. 267-292.

DiMaggio, P. J., and Powell, W. W., 1983, The iron cage revisited: Institutional isomorphism and collective rationality in organizational fields, *American Sociological Review.* **48**:147-160.

Garicano, L., and Kaplan, S. N., 2001, The Effects of Business-to-Business E-Commerce on Transaction Costs, *Journal of Industrial Economics.* **49**(4):463-485.

Garud, R., Jain, S., and Kumaraswamy, A., 2002, Institutional entrepreneurship in the sponsorship of common technological standards: The case of Sun Microsystems and Java, *Academy of Management Journal.* **45**(1):196-214.

Granovetter, M., 1992, Economic institutions as social constructions: A framework for analysis, *Acta Sociologica.* **35**(2):3-11.

Hennart, J.-F., 1993, Explaining the swollen middle: Why most transactions are a mix of "market" and "hierarchy", *Organization Science.* **4**(4):529-547.

Holland, C. P., and Lockett, G. A., 1997, Mixed Mode Operation of Electronic Markets and Hierarchies, in: *The Formation of Inter-Organizational Networks,* M. Ebers, ed., Oxford University Press, New York, pp. 238-261.

Jarillo, J. C., 1988, On Strategic Networks, *Strategic Management Journal.* **9**(1):31-41.

Kambil, A., Nunes, P. F., and Wilson, D., 1999, Transforming the marketspace with all-in-one markets, *International Journal of Electronic Commerce.* **3**(4):11-28.

Kambil, A., and van Heck, E., 2002, *Making markets: How firms can design and profit from online auctions and exchanges,* Harvard Business School Press, Boston, MA.

Khalil, E. L., 1995, Organizations versus institutions, *Journal of Institutional and Theoretical Economics.* **151**(3):445-466.

Malone, T. W., Yates, J., and Benjamin, R., 1987, Electronic Markets and Electronic Hierarchies, *Communications of the ACM.* **30**(6):484-467.

Markus, M. L., Christiaanse, E., 2003, Adoption and impact of collaboration electronic marketplaces, *Information Systems and e-Business Management.* **1**(2):139-155.

Ménard, C., 1995, Markets as institutions versus organizations as markets? Disentangling some fundamental concepts, *Journal of Economic Behavior & Organization.* **28**(2):161-182.

Meyer, J. W., and Rowan, B., 1991, Institutionalized Organizations: Formal Structure as Myth and Ceremony, in: *The New Institutionalism in Organizational Analysis,* W. W. Powell, and P. J. DiMaggio, eds., The University of Chicago Press, Chicago, pp. 41-62.

Milgrom, P., and Roberts, J., 1992, *Economics, organization and management,* Prentice-Hall International, London.

Neumann, D., 2004, *Market Engineering: A structured design process for electronic markets,* Department of Economics and Business Engineering, University of Karlsruhe, Karlsruhe.

North, D. C., 1991, Institutions, *Journal of Economic Perspectives.* **5**(1):97-112.

North, D. C., 1992, *Institutionen, institutioneller Wandel und Wirtschaftsleistung,* Mohr, Tübingen, 1992.

Oliver, C., 1991, Strategic responses to institutional processes, *Academy of Management Review.* **16**(1):145-179.

Ouchi, W. G., 1980, Markets, Bureaucracies, and Clans, *Administrative Science Quarterly.* **25**(1):129-141.

Pelikan, P., 2003, Bringing institutions into evolutionary economics: Another view with links to changes in physical and social technologies, *Journal of Evolutionary Economics.* **13**(3):237-258.

Picot, A., Dietl, H., and Franck, E., 2005, *Organisation: Eine ökonomische Perspektive,* Schäffer-Poeschel: Stuttgart, 2005.

Reimers, K., 1996, The non-market preconditions of electronic markets: Implications for their evolution and applicability, *European Journal of Information Systems.* **5**(2):75-83.

Reimers, K., 2000, Automating Coordination Mechanisms - Markets, Hierarchies, and Associations, in: *Proceedings of 23rd Information Systems Research Seminar in Scandinavia (IRIS 23),* Vol. 2, pp. 1417-1439

Roberts, P. W., and Greenwood, R., 1997, Integrating transaction cost and institutional theories: Toward a constrained-efficiency framework for understanding organizational design adoption, *Academy of Management Review.* **22**(2):346-373.

Scharpf, F. W., 1993, Games in Hierarchies and Networks – Introduction, in: *Games in Hierarchies and Networks,* F. W. Scharpf, ed., Campus Verlag, Frankfurt/M., pp. 7-23.

Thorelli, H. B., 1986, Networks: Between Markets and Hierarchies, *Strategic Management Journal.* **7**(1):37-51.

Williamson, O. E., 1985, *The economic institutions of capitalism,* The Free Press: New York, NY.

Williamson, O. E., 1991, Comparative economic organization: The analysis of discrete structural alternatives, *Administrative Science Quarterly.* **36**(2):269-296.

Williamson, O. E., 1994, Transaction Cost Economics and Organization Theory, in: *The Handbook of Economic Sociology,* N. J. Smelser, and R. Swedberg, eds., Princeton University Press, Chichester, pp. 77-107.

Williamson, O. E., 2000, The New Institutional Economics: Taking Stock, Looking Ahead, *Journal of Economic Literature.* **38**(3):595-613.

Wise, R., and Morrison, D., 2000, Beyond the Exchange: The Future of B2B, *Harvard Business Review.* **76**(6):86-96.

Chapter 5

Portfolio Management of R&D Collaborations in Mobile Commerce

Volker Mahnke, Mikkel Lucas Overby, and Lars Engels Nielsen*
Copenhagen Business School

Abstract: Many companies in the cross section of telecommunication and mobile technology engage in R&D collaborations to manage uncertainty, create synergies and learn. While the challenges of managing individual collaborations are well documented, little is known on how to systematically manage several R&D collaborations simultaneously. We use modern portfolio theory as an analogy to show how companies active in mobile telecommunication manage risks and create synergies by simultaneously engaging in several inter-firm collaborations.

Key words: Portfolio theory, risk, synergy, R&D collaboration, mobile commerce

1. Introduction

The forces of technological change create new demands and increase competition in high-tech business fields such as wireless commerce. Global competitive battles require firms to adapt to rapidly changing environment. Under high degrees of uncertainty, R&D collaborations often outperform go-it-alone and acquisition-based strategies (Teece, 1992; Hagedoorn, 1993; Doz and Hamel, 1996). However, finding and maintaining the optimal mix of collaborations is not a straightforward matter to managers concerned with mastering new technology, developing capabilities, and marketing innovative high tech products. A recent McKinsey study (2002) concludes from a

---

* We gratefully acknowledge research funding of the Mobiconomy project at Copenhagen Business School.

survey of 500 firms that too often collaborative portfolios grow into a random mix of ventures assembled over the years by various business units; that overall performance measurement and coordination of the collaborative portfolio is lacking; and that alignment between a company's overall competitive strategy and its various collaborative activities is often missing. While the literature on *individual* collaboration is large (e.g., Ireland et al, 2002 for a review), studying the challenges of simultaneous management of multiple collaborations is a neglected issue in both research and managerial practice (e.g., Harbison and Pekar, 1998; de Man and Duysters, 2002).

The key question of this chapter is *how to manage portfolios of R&D collaborations?* To date very limited academic guidance is available to inform decision-making in the management of portfolios of R&D collaboration. In particular guidance is needed on how to manage risk and create synergies among several individual R&D collaborations that compose a particular firm's portfolio. In the following, the paper briefly outlines what is meant by portfolio management of collaborative R&D and explores how insights from portfolio analysis can help manage key risks and contribute to the creation of synergies when a set of relationships is managed as a portfolio rather than a set of discrete contracts. A managerial framework is offered introducing risk diversification and portfolio synergies as two key variables portfolio managers of R&D collaborations need to consider. The framework is illustrated through examples from mobile commerce.

2. Managing portfolios of R&D collaborations

Just as financial portfolio management helps hedge against market uncertainties, collaborative portfolios help understanding the risks and opportunities of several inter-firm collaborations pursued simultaneously. Numerous terms and concepts from the financial portfolio analysis literature have parallel applications in the context of managing collaborative portfolios. Modern Portfolio Theory (MPT) founder Harry M. Markowitz (1952) formulated the portfolio problem as a choice of the mean and the variance of a portfolio of assets that exploits the effects of asset return correlation to diversify portfolio risks (Elton and Gruber, 1997). Markowitz's student William F. Sharpe (1963, 1970) encouraged application of MPT outside the original domain of financial asset management, suggesting that portfolio theory is concerned with decisions involving outcomes that cannot be predicted with complete certainty, that uncertainty needs to be acknowledged, and that the interrelationship among outcomes is dealt with explicitly. We use analogue reasoning to show how MPT can inform the systematic management of a portfolio of R&D collaborations.

Analogue reasoning demands careful consideration of whether MPT insights meaningfully translate into the context of collaborative portfolios. For example, R&D collaborations differ from shares and bonds as an asset type. A financial investor is rarely in the position to impact the performance of individual bonds and shares, but seeks to optimise portfolio performance by combining financial assets, as well as through timing of their purchase and sales (Lubatkin and Chatterjee, 1994). Likewise, managers of R&D collaborations may optimise the return/risk relation of their relational portfolio through combining several alliance contracts, as well as clever timing of new collaboration or the termination of unproductive ones. In addition, however, companies can actively influence performance by searching for synergies between individual collaborations (Kale, Dyer and Singh, 2001; Anand and Khanna, 2000). Finally, whereas monetary returns on financial investments are easily appropriated (because rights to financial assets and their cash flows are well defined), capturing returns on inter-firm collaboration is more difficult, for example because defining property rights to jointly developed capabilities as return to collaborative efforts is inherently complicated (Hamel, 1991; Inkpen and Beamish, 1997).

Despite these differences, there are strong similarities making analogy reasoning suitable. A financial portfolio is defined as a set of assets; a portfolio of collaboration is a collection of inter-firm relationships. A financial portfolio is diversified in the risk of individual securities; a collaborative R&D portfolio seeks to diversify risks inherent in relationships. In line with MPT's risk diversification logic, the "reduction, minimizing and sharing of uncertainty in R&D" has been identified as a leading motive for high-tech firms to engage in R&D collaborations (Hagedoorn, 1993; Mowery et al., 1996). Finally, in both types of portfolios, managers seek to utilize interdependencies between outcomes. Outcome correlations in financial portfolios help for example reduce return variability, while outcome correlations between R&D relations lead to risk reduction and synergy creation.

The managerial objective pursued by our framework suggested below is to show how to improve the risk/return profile of a firm's collaborative R&D portfolio. The next section introduces our framework by discussing and illustrating its key dimensions.

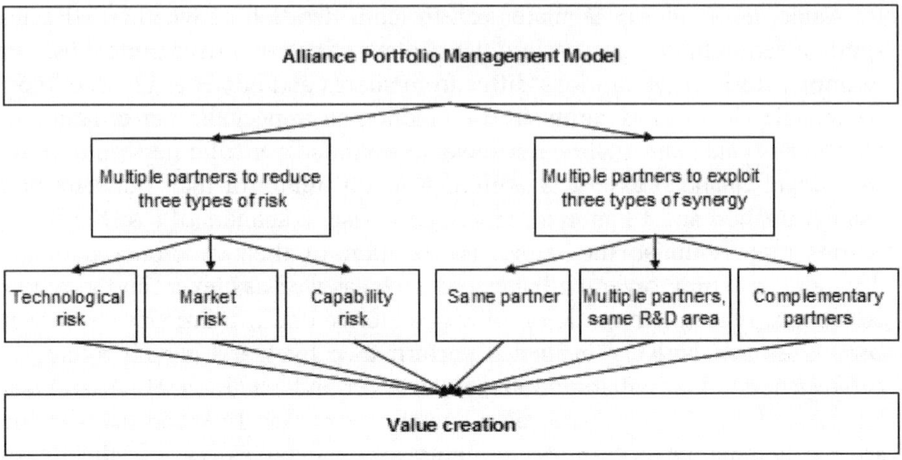

Figure 1: Alliance Portfolio Management Framework

2.1 Identify and diversify collaborative R&D risks

If a company confined itself to a single R&D collaboration it would suffer the full drawback if this relation fails to meet expectations. Portfolios of R&D collaboration diversify away part of the R&D risks that stem from 'putting all eggs in one basket.' Of particular relevance are two types of risks that typically characterize R&D collaboration: (1) technology risks, and (2) market risks. These are defined in the following and illustrated through examples from the world of mobile commerce. Subsequently we show how companies deal with such risk by engaging in multiple R&D collaborations.

Technology and capability risks. In high-tech industries, technology standard races among competing technologies imply technology risks at the firm level (Anderson and Tushman, 2001). Discontinuous technological change initiates an era of ferment during which the new technology competes against both old technologies and multiple emerging versions of the new technology. A company might not be sure about the value creating potential of a partner's technology as compared to own and others parallel technology developments. Thus two central questions are: What technology will win? Will we have access to capabilities required to master the winning technology? Consequently, positioning in relevant technological trajectories becomes critical for firms to reduce their exposure to technology obsolescence risks. Engaging in multiple R&D collaborations is a means to diversity technology risks by supporting access to required capabilities. An illustrative example is found in the market for operating systems for mobile handsets. In 1998 Motorola joined forces with Nokia, Ericsson (today Sony-Ericsson), and Psion in a joint venture named Symbian to develop and support an open operating system for current and next-generation mobile information and communication services (Samsung and Siemens later joined). The operating system (OS) is a central component of mobile devices, and being the leading producer in this market allows companies to be influential in standard interface development between computing and telephony. As Ancarani and Shankar (2003) suggest, the Symbian OS may drive standards for the interoperation of data-enabled mobile phones with mobile networks, content applications, and services. Hence, allying to develop and support a specific OS can decrease technology risks. Symbian, however, is currently fighting a technology standard war against Microsoft. Microsoft has launched its own mobile operating system and also sought and has achieved strategic support from leading industry players such as network operator Orange and, notably, handset manufacturer Motorola. In this way Motorola is placing its bets on two horses. While Motorola sold its shares in Symbian in 2003, the company did not abandon Symbian's technology or the partnerships to companies advocating the standard. Rather it hedges its bets and has several Symbian and Microsoft-based products in the pipeline. Hereby, Motorola reduces its technology risk, for instance in terms of lock-in, by betting on both competing technologies and their promoting companies.

Market risks. In highly turbulent market environments, uncertainties prevail on how to commercially exploit technology even if its superior performance can be ascertained. Such uncertainties concern what customers will ultimately demand and pay for. In mobile commerce, market risks for new data services are substantial. High uncertainty prevails about which future killer applications will drive revenue generation, which content types will attract customers, and customers' willingness to pay. NTT DoCoMo CEO Tachikawa recently noted that the lessons learned from the launch of the infamous i-mode wireless Internet service in 1999 renders up-front predictions of future killer applications illusive (Economist, 18.07.2002). In response, NTT DoCoMo emphasizes resources and time for experimentation "because our customers will decide [the commercial success of new applications]" and hence, "experimentation is key" (Boston Consulting Group, 2002). NTT DoCoMo's experimentation strategy is enacted through its attempts at cooperative service development with several leading software vendors: In April 2001 NTT DoCoMo teamed up with German software leader SAP to develop systems and corporate services, as well as explore possibilities to jointly market such services in the firms' existing markets. In November 2001, a similar alliance was forged with IBM's Lotus Software unit to jointly develop and globally market wireless multimedia business solutions. Simultaneously, to further diversity market risk, NTT DoCoMo was seeking additional system integrator partners to "help harness the full capabilities of its high-speed 3G services" (Reuters, 08.02.2002), and consequently, an additional R&D cooperation with the software maker Oracle was forged.

The above examples suggest that by engaging in multiple R&D collaborations portfolio risks can be reduced through diversification in two major ways. Firstly, if a company makes a split in its R&D budget between two collaborations it reduces risk exposure by creating a portfolio of collaboration. If one relationship fails, the other might still work. Secondly, and less trivially, risk is reduced where negative movements in some relationships are partially compensated by positive ones in others. A good example are mobile operating systems: In prior years Symbian did very well, but the opposite may be true for MS mobile operation services in the next few years. Despite its merits, managing risks in collaborative portfolios is only a first step. By considering synergies as a crucial return dimension, collaborative portfolios can be constructed that exhibit superior risk and returns to any single R&D collaboration.

2.2 Managing returns: identify and exploit portfolio synergies

In addition to evaluating benefits of individual R&D partnerships, managers of collaborative R&D portfolios need to identify and exploit synergies among their R&D collaboration, the sources of which include (1) partner-specific capabilities - synergies stemming from engaging in multiple alliances with the same partner; and (2) combinative capabilities - synergies obtained through engaging in several collaborations within the same area of R&D.

Partner-specific synergies rest on repeated interaction. Synergies in R&D collaborations may stem from repeated interactions between two partnering firms. Often synergies result in the form of new collaborative business ideas and opportunities generated by success in previous collaboration. Examples of sources of partner-specific synergies include repeated ties with the same partner and leveraging inter-firm routines (Dyer and Singh, 1998). Over time, partnering experience leads to successful conflict management supporting continued collaboration despite high uncertainties signifying R&D activities, and the accumulation of inter-firm trust and partner-specific absorptive capacity (Ring and Van de Ven, 1994; Doz, 1996; Mowery et al., 1996). HP is well-recognized for its alliance capability. The firm has a dedicated alliance function that manages the firm's portfolio of external relations to alliance partners. In 2003 HP and Disney entered a 10 year strategic alliance to co-develop new technologies with a focus on content delivery (including mobile content). HP had previously worked extensively with Disney and had among other things, overseen Disney's e-mail consolidation project, merging 190 locations in 40 countries with 17 systems into one central system. It has also provided the company with more than 70.000 desktops, 10.000 servers and – in Disney's Orlando resorts alone – 13.000 LaserJet printers. Likewise, before becoming part of HP, Compaq was heavily involved with Disney. Compaq was the technology provider and sponsor of a Disneyland exhibit in 1998 called Innoventions. In 2000, Compaq and Walt Disney Internet Group announced a three-year agreement naming Compaq as the preferred provider for the Mouse's online presence. As Bob Iger of Disney explains, valuable pre-existing relationships with both Compaq and HP helped clear the way for the deal (Computer Dealer News, 24.10.2003). One of the reasons is that learning in and about inter-firm routines (Hamel, 1991; Makhija and Ganesh, 1997; Dyer and Singh, 1998) presents a source of synergies, as established patterns of interaction may be leveraged across multiple R&D projects. Members of partnering firms have long-established work groups that collaborate on product roadmaps, technology standards and industry trends. "The advantage gained by leveraging all of those established working relationships is huge..." explains an alliance manager of HP, "...we knew we could deliver our systems, and it would work together with all the other parts. Our people have worked with the partner before, which means it all comes together so much more quickly." As the case illustrates, existing inter-firm product development routines can form the basis for the synergetic advantages multiple R&D collaboration with the same partner.

Combinative synergies rest on multiple partnerships. Combinative synergies are reaped across R&D alliances with different partners performing similar and/or complementary activities. Nokia has taken a first mover position in merging the handheld game console and mobile telephone markets with the development of its N-gage gaming phone. While Nokia linked up with several game developers, the lack of market knowledge within gaming resulted in an unattractive first model of the phone that has so far been a commercial failure. Among the reasons is a lack of market penetration in Korea and Japan, both markets account for over 50% of the total gaming market and require the mastery of mobile computing standards that N-gage does not support. Are there reasons to expect that Nokia should have engaged in multiple partnerships with, for example, telecom providers in these markets to increase the likelihood of success while competing against gaming giants such as Sony, Nintendo, and Sega? NTT DoCoMo and Sony Computer Entertainment Inc. have recently pooled complementary R&D resources to jointly develop and market services for a new i-mode/Playstation entertainment network. The companies formed a joint venture in 2003 to develop new services based on mobile phones equipped with Sony's IC Card technology. Other R&D collaborations preceded this alliance. NTT DoCoMo formed wireless application R&D collaborations with the two global leaders simultaneously, namely Sony Playstation and SEGA, to develop mobile gaming applications for the consumer segment. Gaming was seen as a key revenue driver so that in August 2000 NTT DoCoMo and Sony announced plans to link their blockbuster products: (1) NTT DoCoMo's i-mode Internet service enabled with Java for rich graphics and (2) Sony's PlayStation game console to enable users to play the same game at home and outside (Reuters, 29.01.2001). Almost simultaneously, NTT DoCoMo announced another R&D collaboration with Japanese SEGA, a key competitor of Sony, which aims to fuse i-mode with SEGA's NAOMI video arcade machines installed in arcade centres nationwide in Japan.

By engaging in several R&D collaborations simultaneously, combinative capabilities develop allowing a company to leverage learning from one alliance to another. The sharing and combination of strategic knowledge and technologies across R&D collaborations leads to synergies that are hard to obtain in a single R&D relationship. In a study of the Toyota knowledge sharing network, Dyer and Nobeoka (2000) found ample evidence of valuable sharing of product and process technologies across similar suppliers. A parallel can be found in mobile telecommunication where the Dutch network operator KPN Mobile has launched i-mode mobile multimedia services in the Netherlands, Germany, and Belgium through a strategic partnership with Japanese NTT DoCoMo. Through the partnerships NTT DoCoMo has transferred the core constructs of its business model to KPN. Also the partnerships established by NTT DoCoMo with leading content providers such as Disney, CNN and Reuters has been transferred to Europe. Whereas the i-mode services in Europe initially experienced a slow take-off period, the adoption has now accelerated and in early 2004 KPN registered its first million i-mode subscribers. Simultaneously, NTT DoCoMo has engaged in a similar alliance with AT&T Wireless in the US to facilitate the rapid establishment and development of i-mode technology and know-how to boost mobile multimedia services in the U.S. market as well.

The above examples of partner-specific and combinative synergies suggest that through engaging in multiple R&D collaborations, portfolio synergies may be obtained. Firstly, a company can gain synergies through repeated collaborations with the same partner. By doing so, inter-firm routines and prior learning can be leveraged. Secondly, by engaging in several similar or complementary relations (Richardson, 1972), the firm develops crucial absorptive capacity (Cohen and Levinthal, 1990) bringing the focal company into a learning advantage in a particular R&D area. We have exemplified portfolio synergies with reference to a focal firm's relationships only, but partner firms will have portfolios of relationships on their own. While this may lead to potentially conflicting interests, it may well increase the value of a particular partner in the focal firm's portfolio. In any case, the value of a particular relationship must be assessed by the focal firm through analyzing its stand alone value and, importantly, through the synergies it contributes to the portfolio of existing relationships.

3. Conclusion and managerial implications

We have provided several examples of firms utilizing the portfolio rationale for mitigating specific risks and exploiting specific synergies. A managerial framework is proposed to this end based on analogue reasoning from portfolio theory and empirical evidence from the mobile telecommunication sector. A portfolio of R&D collaborations is often more than the sum of its parts. Because not all relationships perform the same way, a portfolio of many relationships usually offers a superior overall balance between risk and return relative to any single collaboration.

In particular, it is argued that two managerial levers are useful to complement the parallel individual management of the focal firm's R&D collaborations. Multiple collaborations are a means to diversify and thereby reduce collaborative risks of a portfolio in terms of three critical risk classes associated with R&D: market risks, technology risks, and capability risks. Up to a certain point, allocations of small percentages of R&D funds to additional riskier relationships (as compared to current relations), for example to explore emerging technology, can actually reduce the risk of the overall portfolio if they do not operate on the same technology trajectory. Small investments in such additional R&D collaborations can have a great impact on the risk profile of an existing collaborative portfolio. Moreover, the total returns of a collaborative portfolio can be increased by identifying and exploiting synergies among collaboration. Synergies will be larger, the less diverse and the more similar R&D collaborations are. At the same time R&D collaborations with greater technology differences yield more learning possibilities. Thus, crucially by simultaneously considering synergy and risk of additional collaboration, the focal firm exploits interdependencies (both positive and negative) among collaborations. To ensure proper allocation of resources to R&D collaborations, not only the value and costs of a particular relationship must be assessed. Just as is the case of financial portfolios, performance and risk must be regarded for the portfolio as a whole.

References

Anand, B., and Khanna, T., 2000, Do firms learn to create value? The case of alliances, *Strategic Management Journal.* **21**(3):295-315.

Ancarani, F., and Shankar, V., 2003, Symbian: Customer interaction through collaboration and competition in a convergent industry, *Journal of Interactive Marketing.* **17**(1):56-76.

Anderson, P., and Tushman, M., 1990, Technological Discontinuities and Dominant Designs: A Cyclical Model of Technology Change, *Administrative Science Quarterly.* **35**(4):604-633.

Anderson, P., and Tushman, M., 2001, Organizational Environments and Industry Exit: the Effects of Uncertainty, Munificence and Complexity, *Industrial and Corporate Change.* **10**(3):675-711

Booz, Allen and Hamilton, 2000, *The allianced enterprise: breakout strategy for the new millennium,* Fifth in a series of viewpoints on alliances, Online publication.

Boston Consulting Group, 2002, *The Promise of Mobile Telecom: An Interview with Keiji Tachikawa, CEO of NTT DoCoMo,* Technology and Communications.

Chandler, A., 1990, *Scale and scope - the dynamics of industrial capitalism,* Belknap Press, Cambridge, MA.

Computer Dealer News (24.10.2003); *HP and Disney forge an IT development deal.*

Davies, A., and Brady, T., 1998, Policies for a complex product system, *Futures.* **30**(4):293-304.

de Man, A., and Duysters, G., 2002, *Navigating the network economy: positions, roles & tactics,* presentation by the centre for global corporate positioning (cgcpmaps.com) at the ASAP Summit Chicago, March 11-13, 2002.

Doz, Y., 1996, The evolution of cooperation in strategic alliances: initial conditions or learning processes?, *Strategic Management Journal.* **17**(Summer Special Issue):55-84.

Doz, Y., and Hamel, G., 1996, *The use of strategic alliances in implementing technology strategies*, INSEAD Working paper 95/22/SM, pp. 1-41.

Dyer, J., and Nobeoka, K., 2000, Creating and managing a high-performance knowledge-sharing network: the Toyota case, *Strategic Management Journal.* **21**(3):345-367.

Dyer, J., and Singh, H., 1998, The relational view: cooperative strategy and sources of interorganizational competitive advantage, *Academy of Management Review.* **23**(4):660-679.

Economist (18.07.2002); *The telecom crisis: Too many debts; too few calls.*

Elton, E., and Gruber, M., 1997, Modern Portfolio Theory, 1950 to date, *Journal of Banking and Finance.* **21**:1743-1759.

Funk, J., and Methe, D., 2001, Market- and committee-based mechanisms in the creation and diffusion of global industry standards: The case of mobile communication, *Research Policy.* **30**(4):589-610.

Hagedoorn, J., 1993, Understanding the rationale of strategic technology partnering: interorganizational modes of cooperation and sectoral differences, *Strategic Management Journal.* **14**(5):371-385.

Hamel, G., 1991, Competition for competence and interpartner learning within international strategic alliances, *Strategic Management Journal.* **12**(Summer Special Issue):83-103.

Harbison, J., and Pekar, P., 1998, *Smart Alliances – A Strategy & Business Book, Booz-Allen & Hamilton,* Jossey-Bass Publishers.

Inkpen, A., and Beamish, P., 1997, Knowledge, bargaining power and international joint venture instability, *Academy of Management Review.* **22**(1):177–202.

Ireland, D., Hitt, M., and Vaidyanath, 2002, Alliance Management as a Source of Competitive Advantage, *Journal of Management.* **28**(3):413-446.

Kale, P., Dyer, J., and Singh, H., 2001, Value creation and success in strategic alliances: Alliancing skills and the role of alliance structure and systems, *European Management Journal.* **19**(5):463-471.

Katz, M., and Shapiro, C., 1985, Network externalities, competition and compatibility, *American Economic Review:* **75**(3):424-440.

Lubatkin, M., and Chatterjee, S., 1994, Extending modern portfolio theory into the domain of corporate diversification: Does it apply?, *Academy of Management Journal.* **37**(1):109-137.

Makhija, M., and Ganesh, U., 1997, The relationship between control and partner learning in learning-related joint ventures, *Organization Science.* **8**(5):508-527.

Markowitz, H., 1952, Portfolio selection, *Journal of Finance.* **7**(3):77-91.

McKinsey, 2002, Managing an alliance portfolio, *The McKinsey Quarterly.* **2002**(3):28-39.

Mowery, D., Oxley, J., and Silverman, B., 1996, Strategic alliances and interfirm knowledge transfer, *Strategic Management Journal.* **17**(Winter Special Issue):77-92.

Oxley, J., 1997, Appropriability hazards and governance in strategic alliances: A transaction cost approach, *Journal of Law, Economics and Organization.* **13**(2):387-409.

Poppo, L., and Zenger, T., 2002, Do formal contracts and relational governance function as substitutes or complements?, *Strategic Management Journal.* **23**(8):707-725.

Porter, M., 1980, *Competitive Strategy,* Free Press, New York.

Porter, M., 1985, *Competitive Advantage: Creating and Sustaining Superior Performance,* Free Press, New York.

Reuters (08.02.2002); *NTT DoCoMo says seeking systems integration partner,* time posted: 10:01.

Reuters (29.01.2001); *Japan's DoCoMo, Sony to extend alliance overseas,* time posted: 08:53.

Richardson, B., 1972, The organization of industry, *Economic Journal.* **82**(327):883-896.

Ring, P., and Van de Ven, A., 1992, Structuring cooperative relationships between organizations, *Strategic Management Journal.* **13**(7):483-498.

Ring, P., and Van de Ven, A., 1994, Developmental processes of cooperative interorganizational relationships, *Academy of Management Review.* **19**(1):90-118.

Sharpe, W., 1963, A simplified model of portfolio analysis, *Management Science.* **9**(2):277-293.

Sharpe, W., 1970, *Portfolio Theory and Capital Markets,* McGraw-Hill, New York.

Sigurdson, J., 2004, *The Sony Ercisson Endeavour Part 1*, Working Paper, April 7 2004, Stockholm School of Economics.

Teece, D., 1992, Competition, cooperation, and innovation: organizational arrangements for regimes of rapid technological progress, *Journal of Economic Behavior and Organization.* **18**:1-25.

Teece, D., 1996, Firm organization, industrial structure, and technological innovation, *Journal of Economic Behavior and Organization.* **31**(2):193-224.

Tushman, M., and Anderson, P., 1986, Technological Discontinuities and Organizational Environments, *Administrative Science Quarterly.* **31**(3):439-465.

Chapter 6

The Role of Social Capital in Managing Relationships with IT Suppliers

A Case Study in Electronic Commerce

Kai Riemer
University of Münster

Abstract: Contemporary E-Commerce solutions are often developed and delivered in inter-firm setups with various business partners involved. Furthermore, E-Commerce projects are often characterised by innovative, ill-structured tasks that depend on new technologies to develop new business concepts. Management of E-Commerce projects and the subsequently resulting relationships with business partners thus is challenging and demanding. Surprisingly, project and partner management issues in E-Commerce have been largely unaddressed so far. Based on case study research, this paper takes an inter-firm perspective of E-Commerce and addresses characteristic features of multi partner E-Commerce projects. We argue that management in complex inter-firm relationships must to a significant extent rely on informal and social mechanisms of coordination due to the non-contractible nature of ill-structured tasks. Social capital theory referring to the value of social relationships and networks is used to guide this research. Based on our case study analysis, we are able to distinguish different types and life-cycle phases of E-Commerce relationships and subsequently to identify different roles of social capital. By applying social capital theory we are not only able to point out management implications, but also to enrich the general discussion of social aspects in inter-firm relationships which to date is largely dominated by concepts like trust and culture.

Key words: Relationship Management; Supplier Relationships; Social Capital; Electronic Commerce; IT Outsourcing.

1. Introduction

Information is increasingly important in today's society and likewise information-based services play a vital role in the portfolios of contemporary companies. Web-based services and electronic commerce become more and more important and the sophistication and complexity of E-Commerce offerings is increasing with the maturing of the sector. In this paper we argue that the success of Business-to-Consumer E-Commerce ventures is not only dependent on a marketable value proposition or a well-designed and viable business model, but that the management of E-Commerce projects and of the network of partners who are involved in creating and delivering the solution is equally important.

1.1 Inter-firm nature of electronic commerce

Contemporary E-Commerce solutions are often developed and delivered in multi party setups creating network business models that lead to new roles for the participating partners and that involve the design of novel electronic and organisational networks (Riemer et al., 2002). A number of recent developments fuel this trend. Firstly, there is a general trend towards inter-firm partnering with suppliers and other business partners increasingly contributing to the value creation of contemporary companies (Arthur D. Little, 2001). As Sheth and Sharma put it: "Organizational buying is dramatically shifting from the transaction oriented to the relational oriented philosophy" (Sheth and Sharma, 1997). Secondly, there is a growing need and willingness to outsource even complex IT services and to jointly develop and manage information systems with external partners (Lee et al., 2003). Finally, this trend is increased by the nature of information services, particularly those in E-Commerce where web-based services can be syndicated, distributed and integrated into third party web solutions via electronic networks (Wehrbach, 2000).

Consequently, E-Commerce relies on a twofold networking perspective: not only is it based on electronic networks for the delivery of web-based products and services, but also on organisational networks of partnering firms to develop solutions and deliver services. Management in this context needs to adopt an inter-firm network or relationship perspective. This is especially important since these IS-intensive relationships pose challenges of complexity and uncertainty stemming from the ambiguity of IS development projects in general and their inter-firm nature in particular.

1.2 A relationship management perspective

The usefulness of adopting a relationship view of inter-firm activity rather than one that merely focuses on discrete transactions has long been accepted (e.g. Dywer et al., 1987). A relationship view recognizes the long-term value of collaboration (creating new value together) in contrast to short-term exchange (getting something back for what one puts in immediately) (Kanter, 1994). As for other areas, the relationship is the appropriate unit of analysis in understanding inter-firm management issues in the IT arena, in particular in E-Commerce. Drawing from recent work on IT outsourcing, Kern and Willcocks state that the "concern for management has been how to handle the venture and manage the relationship to achieve the outsourcing objectives." (Kern and Willcocks, 2002)

Relationships with IT suppliers and other partners to jointly develop EC applications and services need dedicated management attention and require the adoption of a partnership perspective (also Lee et al., 2003). Not only is the joint development of E-Commerce solutions complex and challenging, the resulting multi-partner networks for the subsequent delivery of the services also has to be managed. A partner relationship management perspective is thus necessary to fully understand challenges and management practices of contemporary E-Commerce ventures.

1.3 Multi-dimensional view of inter-firm relationships

Inter-organisational relationships are complex multi-level setups comprising various organisational levels with strategic as well as technological implications (Hutt et al., 2000). Consequently, scholars have distinguished different dimensions for the analysis of inter-firm relationships and their value for the participating companies. Wilson and Jantrania distinguish economic, strategic, and behavioural dimensions of relationship value (Wilson and Jantrania, 1997). Similar, in reasoning on contemporary outsourcing research, Lee et al. distinguish economic, strategic and social relationship dimensions that have to be integrated to fully understand IT outsourcing (see Lee et al., 2003):

- The economic dimension is concerned with the economic benefits of inter-firm relationships comprising cost efficiencies, transaction costs or other benefits like quality improvements achieved through collaboration.
- The strategic dimension comprises the goals, resources, competencies, technologies and ultimately all factors that contribute to achieving collaborative advantage by partnering in inter-firm relationships.
- The social dimension finally takes into account the importance of people working in the inter-firm relationship. It covers issues like trust, culture, social bonding and inter-firm team building.

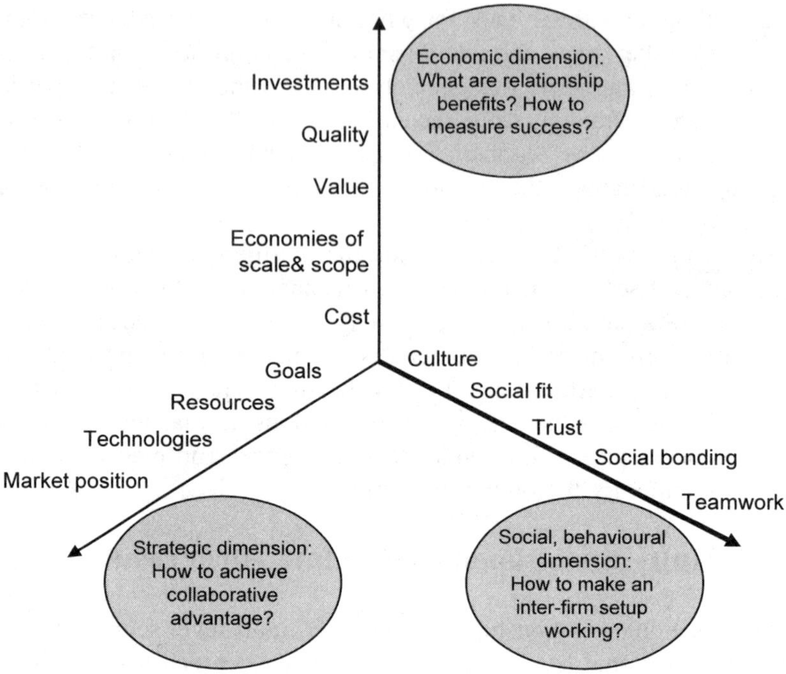

Figure 1. Dimensions of inter-firm relationships (adapted from Lee et al., 2003)

2. Social dimensions of inter-firm relationships

This paper focuses on the social or behavioural dimension of inter-firm relationships. From a behavioural point of view, EC ventures that involve contributions from business partners can become complex and challenging to manage. The more firms are partnering and the more complex the joint development tasks are, the more people are likely to be involved, which leads to a high organisational complexity. Sobrero and Toulan state that managing product development relationships with suppliers becomes "complicated even more by the fact that these relationships are comprised not simply of one person on each side but rather of many." (Sobrero and Toulan, 2000) In these projects the relevant knowledge and expertise is typically dispersed among several individuals from different departments in the collaborating firms. This makes these inter-firm projects generally complex social arrangements. Management thus has to deal with a network of people from different organisational backgrounds who have to collaborate in inter-firm teams.

2.1 Need for a better understanding of the social dimension

Surprisingly, the social dimension is the least researched dimension of inter-firm relationships. However, scholars have stated the need to further focus on the social and inter-personal aspects within inter-firm relationships (e.g. Kanter, 1994, Olk and Earley, 2000, Hutt et al., 2002). Oak and Earley claim that in researching relationships the social perspective has been largely ignored so far and Kanter moans about the lack of management focus on social issues in managing strategic alliances: "Yet, too often, top executives devote more time to screening potential partners in financial terms than to managing the partnership in human terms."(Kanter, 1994). Similarly, Hutt et al. conclude that "many alliances fail to meet expectations because little attention is given to nurturing the close working relationships and interpersonal connections that unite the partnering organizations" (Hutt et al., 2002). An understanding of informal inter-personal contacts is thus fundamental to achieve success of inter-firm relationships (see also Zeffane, 1995). The study reported in this paper took the position that social relationships matter. It thus focussed on the role of social relationships and their features in different types of relationships with E-Commerce suppliers. Further justification for this approach comes from the already mentioned field work of Kern and Willcocks: „Indeed, interview participants noted that it is essential to know the person and/or people you are dealing with in the other firm. It seemed that the better client managers got to know their partnering vendor managers the better the overall relationship worked." (Kern and Willcocks, 2002). Before the empirical study is introduced, the understanding of the social dimension of inter-firm relationships has to be expanded.

2.2 Non-contractible issues and the need for social stabilization

Inter-organisational relationships cannot be fully governed by contracts due to a high proportion of non-contractible issues. Håkansson and Gadde argue that inter-firm complexity creates uncertainty, so that it is often too costly to try to cater for all possible situations in contracts. Rather, the relationship itself has to provide the security for the partners (Gadde and Håkansson, 1997). As Hutt et al. put it: "Legal documents that establish an alliance and specify the boundaries in elaborate detail are never complete and exhaustive. (…) To resolve issues and move the alliance forward, personal relationships must develop and supplement formal role relationships." (Hutt et al., 2000)

Thus, inter-organisational relationships have to be lived and matched by relationships between individuals in the partnering companies. Rather than relying on contracts, the partnering firms and their managers are dependent on a "web of inter-personal connections" (Kanter, 1994). This is especially the case in the fast moving E-Commerce arena with its ever-changing technologies and the dynamics of business models and services that require ongoing adaptations in the relationships which cannot be laid down in contracts. The inter-personal, often informal relationships play a significant role in stabilizing these rather fragile arrangements on the basis of trust and bonding: "It is impossible to cover all conceivable issues in agreements and contracts. There must be space in which informal, personal one-to-one contact takes over." (Gadde and Håkansson, 1997). Consequently, Sheth and Sharma argue that for effective supplier relationship management, organizations will have to learn about and invest in bonding processes. (Sheth and Sharma, 1997). Wilson and Jantrania find that "it is clear that the individuals who must interact with each other within the context of the relationship need to have some positive level of social bonding for the relationship to reach its full potential." (Wilson and Jantrania, 1997). Consequently, it is argued that inter-personal relationships are supposed to have a positive influence on relationship success in that they stabilize the relationship and informally ensure the willingness of individuals to collaborate with other people in the setup.

2.3 Importance of inter-firm social capital

While the importance of the social aspects in inter-firm relationships has been stated by other scholars, research so far is largely limited to the issue of trust. However, it can be argued that this perspective is limited and that trust can only partly explain behavioural issues and does not take into account the above mentioned cognitive issues. Furthermore, the concept is rather abstract and difficult to grasp for management purposes. Therefore, social capital as a more holistic concept has been chosen to inform this research. The concept comprises trust but also covers the cognitive dimension of collaborative group work. Furthermore, the capital metaphor suggests that an organisation can invest in inter-firm relationships, in particular in the social relationships among individuals with the prospect of deriving collaborative benefits. As Håkansson and Gadde argue, organisations should see the inter-firm relationship as "an investment which, in terms of resources, makes it comparable to machinery or equipment used over a long period of time." (Gadde and Håkansson, 1997). On an individual or a group level, these investments can be interpreted as social capital. Another reason for choosing social capital is that the participating managers in the empirical research connected well with the idea of interpreting relationships as capital and that it is worthwhile investing in those relationships, be it the own personal ones or those between employees in the joint teams. The capital metaphor also takes into account that social bonding, trust, commitment and shared understanding have to develop over time, hence the notion of investing into social relationships that provide benefits in the long run.

3. Social capital theory

Social capital theory comprises an emerging body of concepts that acknowledges the inherent value of social structures, such as social relationships, networks and groups. Social capital refers to the value of membership in a social group and the benefits that individual actors derive from their social relationships. From an organisational point of view, social networks and relationships in this respect function as valuable resources that enable individuals to act as groups and to undertake complex actions like joint knowledge work (Nahapiet and Goshal, 1998). In this respect social capital can be seen as a necessary complement to human capital (Coleman, 1988). Whereas human capital refers to the knowledge and capabilities of individuals, social capital takes into account the social fabric among these individuals that is necessary for effective collaboration to take place. It thus refers to the capabilities of a team to act collaboratively.

Social capital is an umbrella concept, which integrates concepts from the sociological, organisational and social-psychology realm (Adler and Kwon, 2002). As it has been interpreted and used in many different ways, its definition is rather confusing and weak. Instead of adopting one particular viewpoint, social capital provides a comprehensive structuring and characterisation of the relationships (e.g. Nahapiet and Goshal, 1998). In doing so, the unit of analysis of social capital application, different dimensions of social capital, as well as social capital outcomes have to be distinguished and clarified.

3.1 Unit of analysis: Individuals, groups and organisations

Social capital has been applied at different levels of analysis. Blyler and Coff generally distinguish between organisational and individual social capital, but mention the existence of intermediate levels like social capital in groups or teams (Blyler and Coff, 2003). Individual-level social capital refers to the benefits that an individual derives from a network of relationships or the position within a social network. Organisational or group-level social capital on the other hand refers to the benefits derived from the social relationships among the individuals within the social collective in facilitating social action (Adler and Kwon 2002).

Although it is important to clarify the unit of analysis, the distinction comes down to two main perspectives: an internal and an external perspective of social capital (Adler and Kwon, 2002). From the external perspective, social capital can be defined as the benefits that actors (individuals, groups, organisations) derive from relationships with other actors. Internal social capital refers to the benefits that social collectives (groups, organisations) derive from their internal relationships among individual actors as members of the collective. In this sense, the same relationships can provide individuals with social capital (external) as well as the group of which the individuals are part of. Table 1 provides an exemplary collection of definitions that correspond with the two perspectives.

Table 1. Definitions of social capital (taken from Adler and Kwon, 2002)

Perspective	Definition	Authors
External (Individual-level)	"the aggregate of the actual or potential resources which are linked to possession of a durable network of more or less institutionalized relationships of mutual acquaintance or recognition"	Bourdieu (1985)
	"the ability of actors to secure benefits by virtue of membership in social networks or other social structures."	Portes (1998)
	"the process by which social actors create and mobilize their network connections within and between organisations to gain access to other social actors' resources."	Knoke (1999)
Internal (Group-level)	"the ability of people to work together for common purpose in groups and organisations."	Fukuyama (1995)
	"features of social organisation such as networks, norms, and social trust that facilitate coordination and cooperation for mutual benefit."	Putnam (1995)
Both internal and external	"the sum of the actual and potential resources embedded within, available through, and derived from the network of relationships possessed by an individual or social unit. Social capital thus comprises both the network and the assets that may be mobilized through that network."	Nahapiet, Goshal (1998)

The unit of analysis in this study is the inter-firm relationship, in particular the individuals and teams engaged in joint action at the boundaries of two organisations. The study compares different type of inter-firm relationships in order to find the requisite type of social capital that is required to govern those relationships. Whereas some relationships might only require single relationships between certain boundary spanning individuals, others might need group-level social capital to enable collaboration in inter-firm teams.

3.2 Dimensions of social capital

Different aspects of social relationships contribute to social capital. According to Nahapiet and Goshal, three general dimensions of social capital can be distinguished (Nahapiet and Goshal, 1998). Firstly, the structural dimension comprises the actual relationships that provide the opportunity for accessing resources or acting together; secondly, the relational dimension refers to the motivation of individuals to act collaboratively with others; and thirdly, the cognitive dimension describes the ability of these individuals to collaborate on the basis of a shared understanding and collective goals.

The structural dimension of social capital comprises the connections a social actor holds with other actors or the connections among individuals in a social group (depending on the perspective). Social relationships in this sense create the opportunity for collaboration (Adler and Kwon, 2002). One proposition of social capital is that through social relationships people get access to resources (e.g. information) that are held by others. Social relationships in and between groups thus constitute information channels allowing people to exchange information, which is a basic prerequisite for knowledge creation and thus any complex innovative work to take place (Nahapiet and Goshal, 1998). Besides this, network structure in terms of group closure refers to the level of interconnection between the members of a social group and is defined as "the average strength of the relationship between team members." (Reagans and Zuckerman, 2001). Network density allows for the observance of social norms in groups (Coleman, 1988) and facilitates trust and thus strengthens the so called "absorptive capacity" of a group, the ability to accumulate and create new knowledge (Cohen and Levinthal, 1990).

The relational dimension of social capital refers to the willingness of people to act collaboratively. On a group level this means subordinating their individual desires to group objectives (Leana and van Buren, 1999). The dimension comprises trust, norms and obligations. Individuals need to trust to be willing to collaborate with others. Trust is defined as the willingness to take a risk or to accept the vulnerability towards others in an interaction (e.g. Meyerson et al., 1996). Norms refer to a form of immanent control enforced by a social group on its individual members. Norms like openness, teamwork and an emphasis on collaborative rather then competitive behaviour are likely to enforce cooperative individual behaviour (Nahapiet and Goshal, 1998). Finally, obligations are created by acting collaboratively towards others. Obligations can function as social credits and ensure collaborative behaviour by others in the future. This is referred to as the generalized reciprocity of social capital based on mutual obligations (Putnam, 1995): "I'll do something for you, because I assume that at some later stage you'll do something for me".

The cognitive dimension refers to the ability of people to act together; it comprises shared understanding (Nahapiet and Goshal, 1998) and collective goal orientation to ensure the effectiveness of collaboration (Leana and van Buren, 1999). The idea is that people have to align their mental models and to establish a shared language and codes to be able to collaborate effectively (be it in a group or a single relationship). This dimension of social capital connects to a stream of research in social psychology called "socially shared cognition" (e.g. Levine and Moreland, 1991). It acknowledges that mental functioning is socially situated in its environment and that for effective social action in (work) groups the individuals' mental models have to be aligned, e.g. that people have to find a common ground for interpreting the environment through communication (Clark and Brennan, 1991). Social capital in this sense derives from the level of socially shared cognitions in a work group, which is an important determinant of its effectiveness (Levine and Moreland, 1991).

In this study, it is explored whether different inter-firm relationships show differences in the nature of social capital, what type of social capital is needed in different relationships, and what the contingencies are that distinguish those relationships.

3.3 Social capital outcomes

Drawing from the internal and external perspective of social capital, the benefits of social capital are basically twofold. External (e.g. individual-level) social capital enables the social actor to access resources like information or knowledge that is held and provided by other actors. This can be called the "allocative efficiency" of social capital. On the other hand, internal (group-level) social capital facilitates social action among the group members in that it motivates and enables collaborative behaviour ("adaptive efficiency"). As shown in table 2, the three dimensions of social capital all contribute to these outcomes by providing opportunity, motivation and ability to act collaboratively or to access or provide resources.

The outcomes of social capital can be distinguished into has informational and collaborative benefits. Informational benefits are related to improved information flow and information exchange: Individuals are able to access information through their social, often informal relationships, and groups are able to process information effectively when they possess sufficient social capital, especially in terms of the cognitive aspects. Social capital thus facilitates information flows and enhances information processing capacity of groups. On the other hand, the collaborative benefits of social capital refer to the enhanced willingness and ability of group members to act together. The collaborative ability results from trust, norms and a shared group understanding as introduced above.

Table 2. Conceptualisation of social capital

	Structural	Relational	Cognitive	Outcome
Individual-level	Number of ties with other individuals Network position	Relational trust Reciprocal obligations	Socially shared cognition Common ground	Facilitates access to resources Allocative efficiency
Group-level	Network density (group closure) Network configuration	Norms Group trust Bounded solidarity	Socially shared cognition Common ground	Facilitates social action Adaptive efficiency
Outcome	Opportunity	Motivation	Ability	Benefits

4. Research approach and cases

The underlying assumption of this study is that social relationships matter as a means of coordination in inter-organisational supplier relationships and that for collaborating organisations and their managers it is worthwhile to invest in those relationships in order to achieve the above mentioned outcomes. The study explores the nature of social capital and its role dependent on the type and characteristics of different inter-organisational relationships.

Little comprehensive or detailed research is available dealing with the social aspects of inter-organisational relationships apart from research on trust and cultural fit. Scholars tend to mention and point to the relevance of social relationships (e.g. Kanter, 1994; Zeffane, 1995), but only few empirical studies have been conducted so far. Kern and Willcocks researched the relationship level of outsourcing partnerships, but the social aspects were only one of an array of issues they included. Their study is useful in that it shows the significance of the topic but does not embark on a dedicated enquiry of the specific area (Kern and Willcocks, 2002). Olk and Earley reason theoretically about different types of inter-personal relationships in strategic alliances but do not undertake an empirical study (Olk and Earley, 2000). One empirical study was conducted by Hutt et al., who have done in-depth research of a single alliance looking at the inter-personal issues within the arrangement. Their findings show the management importance and tackle various issues like asymmetry in alliance perception among the involved parties etc. (Hutt et al., 2000). However, the study presented here is different in that it focuses more narrowly on the role of inter-personal relationships, but researches across different relationships to reason on the differing role of social capital in different relationships and situations. The general research question is: *What is the role of social capital in different E-Commerce supplier relationships and what are contingencies?*

4.1 Research method

Since there was only little prior understanding regarding the social dimension of inter-firm relationships, a qualitative case study approach was chosen to explore the role and nature of social relationships within inter-firm relationships. The author began with carrying out long and rich semi-structured interviews (Flick, 1996) with two managers who were responsible for large E-Commerce solutions at the time and thus in charge of the corresponding networks of relationships with IT suppliers. After conducting these interviews, a set of relationships was sampled to be followed up using the same type of interviews with the counter part managers on the supplier side. Although explorative in nature, the interviews were based on a pre-designed interview guide that specified the areas of interest and led the interviewer through the interview. In a first part, this interview roadmap incorporated rich context covering the background and reasons for the collaboration, the history of the relationship and a rich description of each focused relationship. In the second and more specific part of the interviews, it covered the role of social relationships and group issues comprising the dimensions and perspectives of social capital. The interviews aimed at exploring the usefulness and role of social relationships within the inter-firm setups and how managers deal with those relationships[7]. In so doing, the case context, social capital evidence in the case, social capital benefits (and some risks), as well as management implications where covered.

Interviews were tape recorded and transcribed. The areas and detailed concepts of the interview roadmap were coded. The respective relationships were characterised in several dimensions such as task nature, product criticality, partner symmetry, strategic relevance etc. In a similar way, evidence for social capital in the relationships was extracted and distinguished into the detailed level categories that were derived from the conceptualisation of the theory as presented in the theory chapter. The further analysis was then undertaken using cross-case analysis techniques for exploring relations within the data (cp. Miles and Huberman, 1994). Essentially, tables were used as cross-case displays to explore relations between relationship characteristics

---

[7] In talking about those relationships, interviewees often also referred to these as “informal contacts”, “connections” or “informal networks of people”.

(and other possible contingencies) and social capital attributes. The findings of this analysis are presented in the next chapters, as well as aggregated high level versions of the cross-case analysis tables.

4.2 Cases

The study was conducted in two European companies (FINANCE and TELCO[8]) focusing on their network of inter-firm relationships with IT suppliers that are contributing to their E-Commerce solutions. At the time, FINANCE was a start-up in the European E-Commerce arena providing an integrated online banking, brokerage and finance portal for end consumers[9]. As such, FINANCE concentrated on managing the customer service processes and decided to source a significant amount of services from different types of suppliers. Not only were the banking and brokerage functions outsourced, but also the development of the EC solution was undertaken in cooperation with a range of partners. Many financial services as well as web services were sourced from suppliers. The resulting partner network was indeed very complex, especially in the early start-up and development stages.

TELCO is a large telecommunications and Internet service provider. It is the second largest player in its national market challenging the formerly governmental owned incumbent. TELCO provides ADSL and ISDN dial-in services, as well as typical E-Commerce services, e.g. a content portal and an online shop. In doing so, it manages a network of suppliers that contribute to the telecommunications infrastructure, to various web services, as well as through providing consultancy and software development services.

Both FINANCE and TELCO source various services through a network of relationships with suppliers. It was important for our study to segment these networks and to select partner relationships that represent typical segments for follow-up interviews. We essentially followed the segmentations that were provided by the managers of the case companies, but integrated them in one framework that classifies E-Commerce services and the related

---

[8] Research was conducted in German language and all quotes had to be translated. Names of all companies have been anonymised using fictitious names that represent the respective business area of the companies.

[9] Being a typical start-up venture during the boom time of Internet business and E-Commerce, FINANCE was founded in 1999 and started operations in 2000. Due to the venture capital market drying up and the decision of the investors not to follow up with new investments, FINANCE had to sell its operations in 2002. Our research covers the period of solution development and early stages of operations and was not directly affected by the disinvestment decision.

supplier relationships regarding their relevance and critical importance for the overall solution and business model.

4.3 Relationship segmentation and sampling

Although not working with an explicit supplier segmentation, the FINANCE manager quoted to manage around 15 - 20% strategic relationships with high priority and deep integration, a middle range of around 30% that are characterised by alternating periods of joint collaboration and periods of low activity and finally a group of 50% non-strategic relationships. Strategic suppliers typically were responsible for core services like the banking and brokerage procedures or the core web infrastructure. One of the most important partners was BANK, a private bank that provided core banking services for FINANCE. WEBCONSULT, an Internet consultancy was seen to be part of the middle range suppliers showing certain periods of high interaction. WEBCONSULT provided various consultancy services, but was also responsible for the development of the user front end of the web solution. A typical non-strategic partner was CONTENT, a web content provider that provided customised online news letters for FINANCE customers. This non-strategic relationship was characterised by low relation specific investments from both sides and thus low barriers to switching.

The TELCO manager also segmented its E-Commerce suppliers in three groups: Firstly, high priority partners provide core services that have to have 24 hour availability with just 15 minutes of recovery time in case of breakdowns. Such services are for example the network infrastructure services. Typical partners are WEBCONSULT who are responsible for web server hosting and INFRA-NET, who provide various dial-up infrastructure services. A second group of partners delivers services that are also quite important but do not require the same 24 hour availability and thus are different in terms of joint process setups. Services in this category are also not core to the primary service delivery. A typical partner is DEVELOPER, who developed and maintains the online self administration service for TELCO customers. Finally, all non-core services are characterised by low criticality. As such, E-NEWS as a content provider provides online news content and also maintains the online news and discussion group functionality on the TELCO web site.

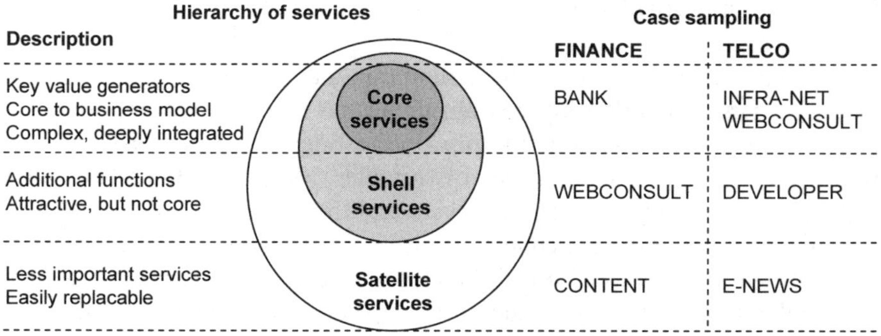

Figure 2. E-Commerce services and case sampling

Based on these segmentations, a hierarchy of E-Commerce services and accordingly a segmentation of the corresponding partners that provide these services can be identified. This hierarchy corresponds with what Belz et al. describe as the service performance system, which is based on a core product (or service) with additional layers of services around it (Belz et al., 1991, for another application also see Riemer and Totz, 2003). Following the service segmentations, three layers can be distinguished: a core layer with essential services, a shell layer with additional non-core but still important services and a ring of satellite services for which suppliers can be replaced quite easily. Core services comprise the core network and infrastructure services; shell services provide additional web site functionality and typical satellite services comprise the provision of low impact content, like online weather maps, that can be substituted with services from other suppliers. Relationships with suppliers in the three segments are distinctly different in terms of strategic relevance, frequency of interaction and the joint tasks undertaken within the relationships. Since the responsible managers were seeing differences between those partners and were dealing with these relationships in different ways, one company in each group was selected for closer examination in the study. Selections were made on the basis of typicality and accessibility. Relationships with the partners in the core category were dealt with in the primary interviews with the case company managers, while follow up interviews were conducted with partners of the shell and satellite categories. Figure 2 gives an overview of the services and the corresponding case examples.

5. Case analysis

The data analysis started from the assumption that the type of service and the resulting partner relationship has an impact on the role and importance of social capital within the relationship. Interestingly, the cross-case analysis revealed a more complex interplay of variables. Not only is the role of social capital dependent on the type of service and the corresponding partner relationship, but it is also dependent on different episodes in the relationship life-cycle. In fact, a three variable interplay was found to impact on the role of social capital. Firstly, the relationship episode was identified as the main dividing variable with further distinctions being made within the episodes. Two relationship episodes were prevalent in both case examples and all of the corresponding relationships, with a clear distinction being made between a project phase and a subsequent routine/operations phase. Within the project phase, the role of social capital was then found to be dependent on the complexity of the joint projects. And finally, within the routine phase, the role of social capital is contingent on the strategic dependency between customer and supplier. The variables and their representation in the cases will be explained in this chapter (see also figure 3 below), with the detailed findings regarding the role of social capital following in the next chapters.

5.1 Relationship episodes

The project phase typically is the initial stage of a supplier relationship characterised by the development of a new business model or new E-Commerce services and their integration to an existing E-Commerce solution. The subsequent routine phase refers to the actual service provision that may extent over a longer period of time. In fact, this transition from project to routine phase was quoted to be the point in time where a formal relationship between the two companies is established, where a service level agreement (SLA) is being formulated, which usually leads to the perception of "having a relationship". In the two cases, this transition was also seen as marking a vital change in the role and responsibilities of the supplier and thus in the interaction between the customer and the supplier. The TELCO manager quotes:

> *"It isn't quite the case that we happen to get into a new relationship. There will always be a project; when a new product is envisioned. (...) Well, I think to develop an application is one side. But [for a supplier] to be able to provide the service and support afterwards really is the other side!" [Manager TELCO]*

The FINANCE manager reported that during the project phase the work was perceived as being more of a joint effort, whereas its completion and the launch of the final solution marked the transition from partnership to outsourcing relationship. It was also stated, that within this relationship further follow-up projects may occur:

> *"I think it is quite cyclic. (...) I think at the beginning it was a joint thing, because it was new to the market and we built it together. The BANK colleagues had quite a good visibility and an image gain [from it] as well. Then came a point where the mere outsourcing, the merely operational issues were focused. Just recently we started a wave where some bigger releases and changes – product changes – are planned. That's more of a strategic collaboration again." [Manager FINANCE]*

Therefore, it can be stated that, whereas the project phase needs management attention regarding the service development with joint teams, the transition from project to operations usually means that detailed contracts and service level agreements are formulated to govern the subsequent service delivery. The role of the supplier changes from being a development partner to being an outsourcing provider with the establishment of a more formalized interaction process between the two parties.

5.2 Project complexity

Within the project phase, the role of social capital was found to be dependent on the project complexity. High project complexity typically results from the complexity of the partner network and the nature of tasks to be jointly undertaken. High complexity in this sense means a high degree of ill-structured tasks that are characterised by significant interdependency between the partnering companies, which requires intensive inter-firm interactions and joint team work. On the other hand, tasks with low complexity can be prespecified, which leads to less interdependency so that either party is able to work largely independently. Services that are specifically (and jointly) designed and developed to match the customer's needs require complex and often innovative project work during the project phase. The tasks thus might be ill-structured with the schedule of the project and its exact outcome not known in advance. These tasks require more than the customisation of built-to-order standard software solutions, which results in high task interdependency between the customer and the supplier organisation. In such a project employees from the partnering companies have to work closely together, which was found to require rich group-level social capital in terms of the relational and cognitive dimension, e.g. the motivation, commitment and shared understanding necessary for effective collaborative processes.

High complexity was present in the FINANCE case with the development of a new E-Commerce business model. Not only did this work involve a high degree of innovative, complex, and challenging tasks, the project was found to be even more complex due to the complexity of the partner network. This resulted in a high level of interdependency across partnering companies:

> *"The complexity resulted, to stay with the example, from the fact that there are not only the relationships to be managed between the FINANCE people and the suppliers, but also between supplier people and sub-supplier people. (...) We've called that the fifth party syndrom. (...) And there is another issue which increases the complexity and makes it more difficult. It isn't just that you hold relationships with multiple partners, that is one thing, and that tasks have to be coordinated, but there was also the time pressure and concurrency of tasks. That made it almost impossible to coordinate." [Manager FINANCE]*

People in this setup had to cope with a high uncertainty and ambiguity due to the inter-firm nature of the setup, the size of the partner network, and a lack of formal organisational structures. Social capital in the form of group structures and informal contacts in the inter-firm network was found to play a vital role as a prerequisite of collaboration and coordination.

A similar picture was drawn in the other case. The TELCO development projects with the core partner WEBCONSULT and the INFRA-NET partners were also characterised by high task complexity and consequently high interdependency between the partners. Significant task complexity was also found in the project with DEVELOPER characterised by joint design work between technicians and software developers of the two companies. Social relationships were found to be generally highly important, to provide the work group with collaborative abilities and what the TELCO manager called "the ability to carry out tasks blindly."

5.3 Strategic dependency

Within the supplier portfolio of the two case companies, different degrees of strategic dependency were found. Usually, the customer company was found to be highly dependent on a supplier when the supplier was deeply integrated into the service production process and the company's operations. As the TELCO manager notes:

> *"For a company like ours, we have to be honest here; we have a 100% dependency on partners that are clearly integrated into our production. We have a 100% dependency on WEBCONSULT; because, if the infrastructure that they built for us doesn't work, we really have a problem." [Manager TELCO]*

It can be argued, that relationships of high strategic dependency require greater management attention and thus social stabilization than relationships with little operational integration.

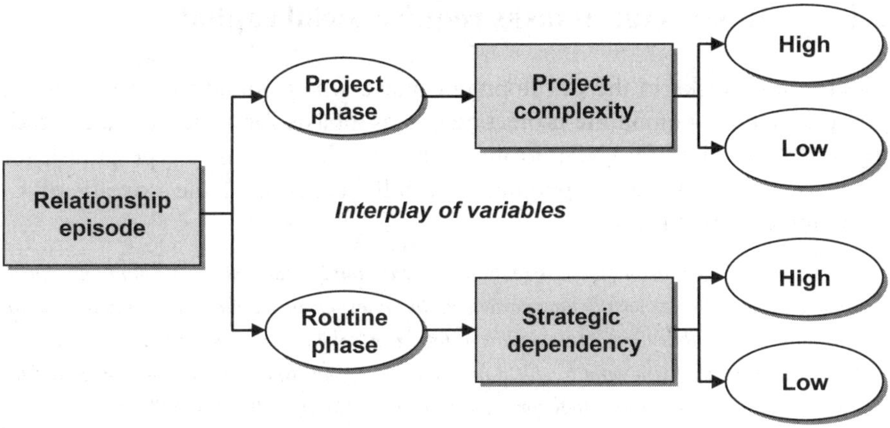

Figure 3. Two level structure and interplay between variables

The following chapters present the findings and are organised along the two stage distinction of the variables (see figure 3). Firstly, the role of social capital in different types of joint projects is explained, followed by the routine phase with the role of social capital discriminated by the strategic dependency between the partners. The analysis will be completed by integrating these findings into one single framework and by presenting some management implications.

6. Social capital in the design and development phase

The role of social capital in the design and development phase was found to be contingent on the project complexity. Drawing from the service segmentation (see figure 3 above) two types of partner projects can be distinguished. Projects that aimed to develop core and shell-level services were found to be characterised by significant task complexity, whereas projects to establish satellite services are rather well-structured. Examples for the first group are the FINANCE banking services (sourced from BANK) and the web platform (developed with various partners including WEBCONSULT). In the TELCO case, the projects with WEBCONSULT and the INFRA-NET partners (core), as well as the shell-level partnership with DEVELOPER belong to this category. In contrast, for the setup of satellite-level services (CONTENT and E-NEWS) the process was well specifiable; a standard solution had to be customised to be integrated into the customer systems and, consequently, social capital played a less important role in the governance of the project.

6.1 Ill-structured tasks require social capital

Ill-structured tasks in the development phase where found to require strong group structures among the project people as a basis for a shared understanding to derive. The FINANCE project for example was a new type of task for many of the participating people, especially because of the novelty of E-Commerce at the time.

> *"One important reason [for this ambiguity] was simply that there were many unexperienced people. Not generally unexperienced, but unexperienced with the particular type of project. I'd say that for ninety percent of the people who were involved, it was their first Internet project, if you want to call it an Internet project. But let's say the online part [of the project] was absolutely new for most of them." [Manager WEBCONSULT]*

The novelty of the project led to a high level of ambiguity and uncertainty in the initial project phase that required ongoing discussions. Even more importantly, tasks were ill-structured with the project venturing into an innovative area. This contributed to the ambiguity and made ongoing alignments necessary in order to define and agree upon the project tasks, as well as to make continuous adaptations throughout the project. To be able to engage in these discussions, people had to establish a shared understanding and shared references for the interpretation of project matters in order to understand each other. Personal relationships between employees were found to be crucial and had to be established and encouraged by the management very early in the project:

> *"Over time, more and more of our operational people established direct connections into the organisation. That is unavoidable. (...) It is not possible to do such a project without these connections. You cannot separate these issues. We did of course try to establish these connections early. Myself for example, at a time when I was involved in parts of the IT architecture, I took our developers over, at a time where - from a strictly rational point of view - it was not absolutely necessary; just for them to get to know these people. In the end, you have to facilitate these informal contacts." [Manager WEBCONSULT]*

In doing so, it was found to be important to give employees the time and opportunities to meet and actually build these social relationships as well as to achieve the required joint understanding as a group.

> *"I think that are important issues [the relationship building]. To somehow understand your counterpart. And you have to give your employees the opportunity to actually establish these relationships." [Manager FINANCE]*

A similar picture was drawn in the other case by the TELCO and the DEVELOPER manager. Learning to collaborate in the beginning of a new project was seen as a necessary prerequisite for effective collaboration. People had to get to know each other, establish relationships and learn how to deal with each other:

"Typically, in new relationships that we establish, the [supplier] people first have to come and work at our site, so that we can learn to work together." [Manager TELCO]

According to the TELCO manager, the quality of social relationships in complex inter-firm projects crucially contributes to the overall performance and success of the development projects.

„With companies where we have poor relationships or where we are personally not that close, we have problems with the [project] duration and we also have much higher cost. And in these cases we also have much more [negative] discussions.“ [Manager TELCO]

As a result of the case analysis, it can be argued that people have to establish social relationships with other team members as a basis for learning how to collaborate and thus as a prerequisite for engaging in ill-structured and novel project tasks. As Clark and Brennan put it, two people or a group cannot begin to coordinate the task at hand "without assuming a vast amount of shared information or common ground – that is mutual knowledge, mutual beliefs, and mutual assumptions." (Clark and Brennan, 1991) In the same way Levine and Moreland state that "groups function best when their members view the world from a common perspective." (Levine and Moreland, 1991) This is especially important when the tasks are rather complex in that they can be fulfilled by various members of the group and in many ways, or when the right way of execution for a task is yet to be found. In this case, it is important for the group members to agree on what those tasks are and who will perform them (Levine and Moreland, 1991). And to be able to do so, the team members need to share a common understanding about the group itself, its members and the tasks at hand. Even more so when the task is of innovative nature and involves extensive creation of new knowledge like it is the case in E-Commerce software and service development.

According to Nonaka and Takeuchi (1995), knowledge creation is a social process that generally begins with a process of sharing tacit knowledge among individuals with the aim of deriving a group-level understanding of the tasks to create a basis for successful collaboration (Nonaka and Takeuchi, 1995). Consequently, people in inter-firm setups, who have different backgrounds and different views of the world, have to find a shared cognitive basis for their collaborative work. They have to "learn to communicate more effectively by developing a better understanding of how each uses language, the categories that are important to them, the heuristics they employ, and the forms of verbal and nonverbal shorthand and codes they use." (Nohria and Eccles, 1992). Ill-structured tasks as prevalent in the case examples require investments in rich (group-level) social capital to enable effective collaboration, especially in the cognitive social capital dimension.

6.2 Complex inter-firm setups require informal social networks

Especially during the start up and development phase, FINANCE maintained a large network of active relationships with partners contributing to the business model in various ways. Furthermore, some of the partners brought in sub-contractors, so that the resulting network was growing even bigger. At the peak time, around 80 companies were contributing to the solution, although the core of the network only consisted of a fraction of this total number. However, the resulting network turned out to be almost unmanageable. The network complexity combined with the task complexity led to a situation, where the formal project management methods were found to be limited in governing the inter-firm project. The network was too large to be coordinated centrally.

Here, with an inter-firm network too complex to be governed by formal central project coordination mechanisms, social capital in the network can be interpreted as a substitute for the lacking formal structures. This finding is well in line with findings by Hutt et al who researched the social dimension in a complex inter-firm alliance. They found that inter-personal relationships play a vital role for the information flow within large alliances in that "a web of interpersonal connections provides the information-flow circuits" (Hutt et al., 2000). In the same way, FINANCE was eager to bring together the relevant partners and bridge apparent holes in the network setup by encouraging the creation of social relationships between the various suppliers' representatives who had to work together due to the high interdependence of tasks across supplier companies.

> *"We repeatedly tried to bring together the respective people. (...) We took this so far that we said, there is the advertising agency, there is the web consultancy, and there are the Java developers, so that they all can get to know each other and roughly know, well, because at some stage the Java developer who works at the content management system has an impact on the web consultancy and they again have to be aligned with the branding people, because those in the end create the ads and so forth and so forth." [Manager FINANCE]*

With the network size reportedly being large and the impact of formal coordination being limited, boundary spanners turned out to be very important to coordinate information flows within the network. The WEBCONSULT manager reflects on his own role in the network:

"I really spent days in the FINANCE office quite frequently to do nothing else than to look into the office and to chat to these guys. And then to walk to another office and to tell this guy what the other just said, because the one who worked 15 meters down the corridor hadn't talked to the other one for four months, although they were working on related systems parts. Really, to do this deliberately is an important point, I think." [Manager WEBCONSULT]

Boundary spanners or relationship promoters are actors who develop a dense network of social relationships; they are thus well connected within the social network and can multiply information and bridge gaps. According to Walter, "relationship promoters are persons who intensively shape and advance interorganisational exchange processes; they do this on the basis of their network of good personal relationships with significant actors of the partner organisations (…) as well as their ability to develop and use new network relationships." (Walter, 1999) Boundary spanners thus hold a high level of (individual-level) social capital that the organisation might capitalize in governing the entire network. Hutt et al. further argue that boundary spanners also contribute to producing a shared interpretation of goals and common agreement on norms and work roles within the inter-firm network (Hutt et al., 2000).

Although it was found that informal coordination mechanisms based on social relationships played a vital role in the FINANCE network, it turned out that the informal day-to-day work had to be complemented by formal mechanisms to document project decisions and outcomes. Whenever this was not sufficiently done, problems arose due to unclear specifications or decisions that had been made between some people in the network without notifying others. Consequently, it can be concluded that social capital in a complex network is a necessary means of enabling effective information flows and collaborative work, but that it has to be complemented with formal documentation procedures:

"...hard to say, but I would say that is a part of it. I would say that without these informal channels you can't get this [the project] to be working. Important is to also establish as many channels as possible for the rather formalised communication." [Manager WEBCONSULT]

Moreover, people who built social relationships and were part of the social networks within the inter-firm network had a better identification with the project and were quoted to be more motivated to contribute to the project:

"These people who are really part of the informal networks and thus also better understand what their contribution is, these people have a significantly better identification with the whole [project] and thus also a better motivation. The motivation was worst with those people who really were only brought in for a particular task and who never had any

personal contact with someone else, except with their own manager." [Manager WEB-CONSULT]

It can be argued that people, who are not able to establish relationships with people from partner organisations in complex projects, are likely to become dissociated and lack motivation, because they are not part of the information flows within these informal social networks. As Putnam notes, people who are working in a virtual setup are in danger of becoming "socially as well as physically remote" (Putnam, 2001). This aspect connects with the relational dimension of social capital. Without being part of the work group by virtue of having relationships with other employees, people lack trust in contributions of others and are not bound by social norms and obligations of the group and thus are less likely to show collaborative behaviour.

Motivation to act collaboratively in the inter-firm project was further found to be challenged by the diversity within joint teams, with people coming from different organisational backgrounds and having different views of how tasks should be approached. Regarding this, other scholars found that members of teams with diverse knowledge and different professional backgrounds face the challenge of integrating their knowledge and are likely to have higher levels of social uncertainty than in homogeneous teams (Anand et al., 2003). Diverse teams in an inter-organisational context are even more challenging: "The major challenge with these teams is enhancing the likelihood that integration and (knowledge) creation actually occurs (Anand et al., 2003)." Major problems here are the cultural barriers (see Hall, 1995). People from different organisations do things differently, they say things differently, and they behave differently. This can lead to competitive behaviour, especially when people insist on solving the joint problem in their usual way. This was reported in the TELCO case with IT people often engaging in competitive behaviour when insisting on a particular way of solving a software issues. Establishing social relationships as a basis for the joint work beforehand reportedly reduced this egoistic and opportunistic behaviour. People are then more likely to understand other people and to engage in collaborative instead of competitive behaviour:

"The egoistic, the small minded, the dogmatic [behaviour] is clearly diminished with the personal relationships. That is absolutely clear." [Manager TELCO]

If groups and their managers are not able to overcome the social barriers that result from intra-team differences and diversity, they might enter a "downward spiral of misunderstandings, mistrust of intention, conflict and a broken relationship." (Hall, 1995). We conclude that when people have to work in complex setups with other people from partner organisations, social relationships are a means of providing the necessary information flows, connectedness, identification with the project and motivation to contribute. It also reduces opportunistic and competitive behaviour. From a managerial perspective, it is thus worth investing in these social relationships. Consequently, they can be interpreted as a form of social capital due to the above mentioned benefits for the organisation.

6.3 Role of social capital in complex inter-firm projects

Social capital plays a vital enabler role in complex inter-firm projects. Social relationships and sufficient group structures are important for people to engage in complex and ill-structured tasks. Work groups have to develop a shared understanding and shared views of the world to be able to carry out ill-structured tasks. Furthermore, social networks are important to complement or even substitute formal coordination mechanisms in complex inter-firm setups with many suppliers and high task inter-dependencies across organisational boundaries. Social networks allow for effective information flows. Being part of these social networks is positively related to individuals' identification with the project and the motivation to contribute to the joint work. Furthermore, social relationships are seen to have a significant impact on project outcomes and directly related to performance. As the TELCO manager puts it:

> *"The better the personal relationships are, the more successful are the projects. This can be the distinction between success and failure. We did observe that projects failed because the personal relationship, the connection between the companies actually wasn't right." [Manager TELCO]*

It is concluded that complex inter-firm projects require rich social capital on both the group level and the individual level. Teams need sufficient group-level social capital and individuals within large inter-firm setups have to be well connected through informal social networks. Consequently, people have to invest in social capital to become part of the project work. All three dimensions of social capital – structural, relational and cognitive - were found to be important in the cases (see table 3). In terms of its outcome, social capital was found to provide both informational and collaborative benefits. It enables collaboration in teams as well as information flows within the social network.

Table 3. Role of social capital in complex inter-firm projects

Perspective	
Individual level	Individuals in the inter-firm setups need social capital to be part of information flows and to be able to collaborate. Some individuals act as boundary spanners/relationship promoters. Individuals connect via social ties with others and access information and impact decisions.
Group level	Groups need to derive a shared understanding and norms to be able to collaborate on ill-structured tasks.
Dimension	
Structural	Densely woven social networks enable effective information flows. Boundary spanners play a vital role by bridging structural holes in the social network.
Relational	Social relations ensure identification with the project and the motivation to contribute to collaborative work. High levels of trust are based on social relationships with others.
Cognitive	Ill-structured tasks require alignment of mental models and shared understanding to evolve; enables effective collaboration.
Outcome	
Informational	Informal structures (social networks) play paramount role in distributing information quickly and effectively, especially in large networks.
Collaborative	Social relationships provide collaborative ability.

6.4 Role of social capital in well-structured projccts

Both the CONTENT relationship with FINANCE and the E-NEWS relationship with TELCO are content delivery partnerships. Both suppliers customise and syndicate standard content and content services to various clients (e.g. newsletters and discussion forums). They are thus typical E-Commerce players in the marketplace (Wehrbach, 2000). Both suppliers also produce customer specific content and services.

The role of CONTENT was to produce an online newsletter that was delivered to FINANCE's end customers. The initial project involved planning and designing the news content and the production of a pilot version. In addition, the online delivery solution had to be technically implemented. In order to achieve this, CONTENT had to customise its online delivery system to create an interface with the FINANCE systems. Both tasks did not require joint team work apart from initial meetings to discuss and agree upon project details. Consequently, roles were perceived as being a clear customer-supplier relationship with CONTENT working to meet FINANCE expectations. The work was undertaken independently by CONTENT's employees with occasional inter-firm interactions to clarify details. Communication then was mainly based on email.

A similar picture was drawn in the other case with E-NEWS syndicating its real-time news content and its discussion fora to TELCO's web platform. Apart from these standard services, a customised discussion forum was created in which TELCO's customers are now able to discuss TELCO-specific technical issues. The forum is moderated by TELCO people, although the system is hosted on the E-NEWS system. The initial project was mainly concerned with selecting the right news services from the E-NEWS portfolio and the customisation of the technical systems to allow real-time online integration between the E-NEWS content management system and the TELCO web system. Again, the work could be well specified in initial meetings and the customer and supplier roles were clearly separated. Communication between the two parties mainly relied on email and telephone.

Consequently, the well structured tasks required a much more limited role of social capital. There was no need for intensive investments in group structures, since tasks were not ill-structured but rather straight forward. Nevertheless, social capital was found to have positive effects on an individual level. Bilateral social relationships between the responsible software developers as well as between the project managers improved the communication and information flows. Good personal relationships were also quoted by the suppliers to have a positive impact on the motivation to work together:

> *"Well, I regard this [to know the counterpart at FINANCE] very important. The motivation is different then. You can much better adapt to the partner. And it makes things easier when you have contact later, when you try to clarify something, and also to reduce barriers. It also works better via email then." [Manager CONTENT]*

Social relationships thus provided the people with a better understanding for each other and were important for the supplier to know the customer's needs and to adapt to their requirements; this of course had a positive effect for the customer, too. Another positive aspect was that the communication became richer and more pleasant as a good relationship improved the motivation to work together.

> *"[The advantage of having a good relationship is] that you get to know each other better, that you better know the other's needs and that you do not only talk about the dry stuff, but that you talk about general interests in conversations." [Manager E-NEWS]*

In conclusion, good social relationships provide richer communication and the motivation to spend time on the project and allow for a better predictability of the customers' needs. It was thus found to be beneficial by the suppliers' managers. In sum, social capital plays a supporting role in well-structured projects with a positive direct effect but ultimately not paramount for the success. Group-level social capital is not required and benefits of social capital in the relationship are largely informational with better access to information across organisational boundaries and also better understanding of the other party's needs. Table 4 summarizes the findings.

Table 4. Role of social capital in well-structured inter-firm projects

Perspective	
Individual level	Social relationships between people in the inter-firm relationship support effective project work. Group-level social capital is not necessary.
Dimension	
Structural	Merely bilateral social relationships.
Relational	Having a good personal relationship is motivating for working together and spending time on the project.
Cognitive	Good relationships allow people to better judge each others' behaviour and needs (predictability).
Outcome	
Informational	Accessing information provided by people in the partner organisation easier with good relationship.
Collaborative	Better bilateral understanding and predictability.

7. Social capital in the routine and operations phase

The role of social capital in the routine and operations phase was found to be contingent on the strategic dependency between customer and supplier. Suppliers offering core services were found to be deeply integrated into the customers operations, with the customer being strategically dependent on the performance and service quality of these suppliers. Examples are the FINANCE partnership with BANK and the TELCO relationships with WEBCONSULT and the INFRA-NET partners.

Shell-level and satellite-level services were found to be less strategic since the customer was not strategically dependent on the supplier. Here, the supplier typically provides services like content delivery or takes care of the maintenance of a software solution. FINANCE for example did not regard itself strategically dependent on WEBCONSULT after finishing the web site development project; the same applies to the TELCO project with DEVELOPER. Finally, the content delivery relationships with CONTENT and E-NEWS were also not strategically important. Consequently, abandoning such a relationship was seen as being possible at any time.

7.1 Role of social capital in strategic relationships with high dependency

Companies are highly dependent on those suppliers who provide core services that are deeply integrated into their service portfolio. These relationships were found to be socially stabilized via investments in relationships with key employees from supplier companies. Although service delivery in E-Commerce is mainly based on electronic network linkages and usually highly automated, the underlying personal linkages were found to match those electronic linkages for the sake of social stabilization:

"There are the operational linkages for once, what is being exchanged. In our business, this is all electronic of course, with only little human intervention. ...but this is accomplished by communication processes which try to safeguard that." [Manager FINANCE]

A key issue here was the management of the transition from the project to the operations phase. In the FINANCE case, relationship management was found to be professionalised during that transition with specific relationship managers being applied as primary responsible contacts for the supplier people. In so doing, the organisation was able to capitalize on existing social capital that was build during the project phase. These personal relationships allowed for effective decentralized coordination of operations-related issues on the basis of electronic communication.

But at the same time new inter-personal relationships had to be built between technical and operations people who are responsible for the day-to-day business and who were not (directly) involved in the project. The key here was to get these people involved early enough. It was found that it was not sufficient that the primary relationship managers had a good relationship with each other; operational people also had to be well connected.

Especially important were emergency and service recovery processes in case of systems' break downs. The supplier's employees were found to be a very important component in this process. To ensure quick and pragmatic service recovery, good personal relationships between customer and supplier employees were seen as very important. TELCO operates a so-called on-call-process where supplier's employees have to be available 24 hours a day for notification via email, SMS and mobile phone. Inter-personal relationships with these operations people turned out to be very important in this process: not only do the supplier's people know the customer's problems better; they are also more motivated to help and solve problems. This was acknowledged by TELCO's manager. Nurturing of those relationships was found to be beneficial:

"In case of an emergency the [supplier's] people are the most important component. (...) They are of course treated differently [by us]. I mean, look at Jack[10], when he visits us, he is always warmly greeted. And we also thank him one or two times more often and we talk to him. When he wants to talk to us, we always take the time, that's pretty clear. We know

---

[10] Name was changed.

how important he is. He is actually much better integrated into our organisation than other people. He also knows our headaches, he also knows our problems, and we appreciate that we can expose our problems to him, because we know that he will not abuse our trust and knowledge." [Manager TELCO]

These social relationships can certainly be interpreted as a form of social capital for the organisation as they provide a better motivation of the suppliers' people and in the end a better overall service quality. It was noted that suppliers showed higher commitment whenever the personal relationship was good. It can be argued that suppliers' people are more likely to spend more time on a customer contract if they are engage in positive personal relationships with people in the customer organisation. These relationships are thus very valuable for both customers and suppliers. As the TELCO manager argues:

"It pretty much depends on the particular person. Jack from WEBCONSULT for example. He is incredibly valuable for TELCO. And for WEBCONSULT he is also quite valuable. If Jack was to move, we'd have to ask ourselves: what comes next?" [Manager TELCO]

These findings confirm the literature on supplier management; for effective supplier relationship management, organisations have to invest in bonding (Sheth and Sharma, 1997) and social stabilization to accomplish the formal relationship that is fixed in contracts (Gadde and Håkansson, 1997). It is concluded that social relationships between key boundary spanning people on both the management and the operational level benefit the customer organisation in terms of relationship stabilization and better service delivery respectively. On the other hand, these relationships also benefit the supplier organisation, because the customer is satisfied and the contract is safeguarded.

Whereas the inter-firm operations might also work without good interpersonal relationships, social capital was clearly found to be positively related to the relationship outcome. Social capital as such supports operations and service delivery and ensures the motivation of supplier personnel to act collaboratively and pragmatically or to make an extra effort to support the customer operations. Social capital is individual level and mainly relational in nature with trusting relationships contributing to motivation and commitment. Social capital also has a structural component with people being able to access necessary information across the organisational boundary more easily based on their relationships. Social capital thus also contributes to better information flows between the organisations. Table 5 summarizes the findings.

Table 5. Role of social capital in strategic supplier relationships

Perspective	
Individual level	Social relationships between people in the inter-firm relationship support operational processes. Group-level social capital is not necessary.
Dimension	
Structural	Merely bilateral social relationships.
Relational	Good personal relationships contribute to supplier personnel being motivated to solve problems pragmatically and quickly and to spend time on the project.
Cognitive	Supplier personnel know customer problems and needs (predictability).
Outcome	
Informational	Accessing information from people in the partner organisation is easier with a good relationship.
Collaborative	Better motivation and thus better collaborative behaviour and commitment.

7.2 The role of social capital in non-strategic supplier relationships

As expected, interactions in the relationships with shell-level and satellite-level service providers turned out to be not very complex. Services are delivered automatically and electronically via Internet platforms with minimal inter-personal interaction (e.g. content delivery). Not surprisingly, social capital was found to play only a minor role in this type of relationships. Although there still has to be a personal contact between the two companies, this usually only existed between a few people. The initiative to maintain the relationship came clearly from the supplier side.

DEVELOPER for example established a formal delivery relationship with TELCO based on a service level agreement that subsequently only required minimal direct interaction in the day-to-day business. But motivated by the prospect of further joint activities, the DEVELOPER manager was still interested in holding the personal relationship with his TELCO counterpart. A similar picture was drawn by the E-NEWS manager, who interpreted the personal relationship mainly from a sales perspective:

"...when you ask, where these social contacts pay off, that is to keep the customer. We want to keep collaborating with TELCO and we have to be competitive and we want to keep this rapport. That's why I think these relationships play a role; to maintain them." [Manager E-NEWS]

Such relationships can be interpreted as being part of a deliberate key account management from the supplier side based on the intention to increase the contract and to participate in future activities. The social relationship is thus mainly to stay in contact and to get access to information regarding the latest customer developments. As CONTENT's manager notes:

"I would also intensify the contacts in the operations phase, to be closer to the customer; reflecting that self-critical, to be able to predict the customers movements a little bit better." [Manager CONTENT]

Maintaining these relationships may also be beneficial from the customer's point of view, because it can significantly reduce search cost, when new project activities are planned. And it might also lower the time and cost it takes to get started working together on a new project, as was explicitly mentioned by FINANCE's manager. Social capital thus is mainly seen as playing what can be called a "lubricant" role. Social relationships provide easy access to new business opportunities or likewise access to experienced suppliers. While not significantly contributing to the current operations, social capital functions as a potential with prospective benefits in the future. Social capital is based on rather weak social ties (Granovetter, 1992) with mainly informational benefits for the two parties (see table 6 for a summary).

Table 6. Role of social capital in non-strategic supplier relationships

Perspective	
Individual level	Weak social ties to stay in contact. Social capital as future potential; may be part of key account management approach on the supplier side.
Dimension	
Structural	Bilateral social relationships between individuals of the two companies as future potential, often maintained out of people's individual interest.
Outcome	
Informational	Supplier accesses information about future activities at the customer end. Customer able to reduce cost in searching for competent suppliers and starting new projects due to existing social capital.

8. Framework and management implications

Several roles of social capital in managing inter-firm relationships with IT supplier in E-Commerce have been discussed. The case study findings suggest that social capital is a useful concept to research the social dimension of inter-firm relationships and that a two level distinction of variables explains the role of social capital in these relationships. Firstly, a distinction in project and operations phase is necessary since the roles of the partnering companies, their interactions, as well as the tasks to be undertaken change significantly with the transition from project to operations phase. This has an effect on the role of social capital. Whereas the project phase needs intensive investments in social capital, managers of the partner companies can capitalize on and maintain existing social capital throughout the operations phase. Secondly, we have to make further distinctions within the two phases. In the project phase, the role of social capital is dependent on the complexity of the joint project regarding task and network complexity. In the subsequent operations phase, it is the strategic dependency between the partner firms that discriminates the role of social capital. Figure 4 illustrates the distinction between the two relationship episodes.

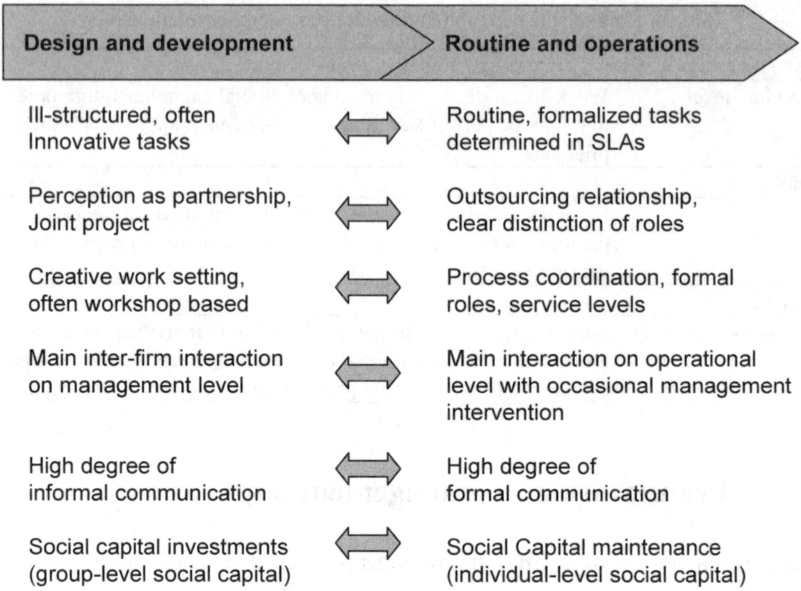

Figure 4. Transition between project and operations phase

8.1 Integration of findings into one comprehensive framework

Drawing on the case study findings, social capital can play three different roles in E-Commerce supplier relationships. Firstly, in complex projects it plays an enabler role. Social capital on a group-level enables collaboration in projects with ill-structured tasks and complex network setups. Without sufficient group structures to ensure trust, motivation, and a shared group understanding, effective collaboration in joint teams is unlikely to happen. Secondly, in non-complex projects with well-structured tasks as well as in the operations phase of strategic supplier relationships, social capital plays a supporter role. Whereas the inter-firm relationship might function without this social capital, it was nevertheless found to have a positive effect on project outcomes and service quality. Finally, in non-strategic supplier operations, social capital is rather unimportant, but was found to play the role of a lubricant providing certain potential value for further activities between the two organisations. Supporter and lubricant type social capital is largely of an individual-level type associated with bilateral relationships between individuals across the organisational boundaries. Table 7 integrates the findings in one comprehensive framework and connects them with the initial segmentation of different types of E-Commerce services. Moreover, the empirical study also provides management implications.

Table 7. Contingency model explaining the role of social capital in E-Commerce relationships

<table>
<tr><th rowspan="2">Services delivered by supplier</th><th colspan="2">Project phase</th><th colspan="2">Operations phase</th></tr>
<tr><th>Tasks</th><th>Role of social capital (SC)</th><th>Tasks</th><th>Role of social capital (SC)</th></tr>
<tr><td>Core:
Core solution and critical applications</td><td>Joint design and implementation of often novel and innovative EC solutions.</td><td rowspan="2">ENABLER:
Group-level social capital enables collaboration through trust, motivation, and a shared understanding as well as effective information flows.</td><td>Supplier integrated in day-to-day service delivery/operations. Exception handling processes are crucial.</td><td>SUPPORTER:
Individual-level SC ensures information flows and motivation, stabilizes supplier relationship.</td></tr>
<tr><td>Shell:
Additional services with 2nd rate criticality</td><td>Joint design & specification, but independent implementation by the supplier.</td><td>Maintenance of solution, small changes and improvements.</td><td rowspan="2">LUBRICANT:
Individual-level social capital as potential for future activities and for reducing search cost.</td></tr>
<tr><td>Satellite:
Non strategic services, e.g. content syndication</td><td>Well-structured product/service customisation according to customer specifications.</td><td>SUPPORTER:
Individual-level SC allows for effective communication, motivation and predictability.</td><td>Standardised service delivery, usually entirely automated using electronic linkages (e.g. web content delivery).</td></tr>
</table>

8.2 Management implications

In inter-firm relationships, formal governance structures often do not match the requirements of ill-structured and innovative tasks. To ensure that effective collaboration actually occurs, managers have to take into account the importance of the social aspects of inter-firm collaboration. This study has shown that inter-personal relationships play a significant role in inter-firm collaboration in IT supplier relationships. However, not all relationships can be treated equally. Rather, a segmentation approach provides the necessary distinction to determine the relevance of the social aspects in managing these relationships. Managers have to take care of social capital according to the requirements of the particular relationship. This includes the manager's own individual social capital with people at the partner site as well as the social capital among the employees of the joint work group in an inter-firm project.

Managers thus should invest in social capital with the prospective benefits of better collaboration and information flows (according to the segmentation provided in table 7). The underlying rationale is to facilitate the emergence of social networks as a social infrastructure for the day-to-day interactions. In other words, social capital investments are directed to create and maintain a social network that spans firm boundaries to facilitate collaborative action and information flows. However, when trying to do this, managers face a dilemma: Social capital is most urgently needed at the beginning of a complex joint project, where people need to collaborate in complex design tasks. However, with companies just joining forces to collaborate, social capital is not readily available at that point in time.

Consequently, managers have to pay attention to social capital investments at the very beginning of an inter-firm venture. In doing so, they face a second dilemma in that it is hardly possible to invest in social capital directly. A person trying to deliberately engage in social interactions for the sake of social capital benefits is likely to be perceived as exploiting someone's favour. Individual social capital arises as a by-product of social interactions with others. By acting collaboratively in the day-to-day actions one gains social credits serving as social capital afterwards. Thus, social capital stems from authentic behaviour and cannot be forced, but has to evolve over time (Tymon and Stumpf, 2003). The same applies to group-level social capital. Neither can social relationships among people be established by order, nor can social norms or shared understanding be designed and implemented. Relationships and norms emerge as a by-product of social interaction between people over time. Nevertheless, managers can indirectly invest in social capital by creating the right environment in which social capital grows and by influencing the opportunities for fruitful social interactions to take place.

In doing so, it is important to bring the relevant people together early enough. Employees from both parties need opportunities to meet and build social relationships. Start-up workshops and other joint events help to facilitate social contacts. These can be either project related workshops or professional team-building events being held by a third-party consultant. Dedicated events and early collocation create the necessary rich environment to engage in face-to-face interactions that are necessary to build this social capital in the beginning of new projects. Such rich social capital cannot derive by computer-mediated communication only; the TELCO manager states:

> *"...of course we see, that they get to know each other personally. It is always important in the beginning, that the relationship is not only established via phone or electronically, but that the people come together, for example in the implementation or test phase [in the project]." (Manager TELCO)*

Electronic communication lacks the richness to deliver all the needed tacit, non-verbal but "visual cues that are easily observable in face-to-face setting" (Andres, 2002). Collocation is thus seen as a means of establishing social relationships with the employees of the supplier firm. People have to learn to collaborate through engaging in a process of grounding to align their mental models and to derive a shared understanding.

While electronic communication is quite limited in creating rich social capital, social capital in turn can be seen as a basis for effective electronic communication to take place, especially in the later stages of the collaboration after it has successfully been built. In the examined cases, social relationships among the collaborating employees were found to be important in reducing misunderstandings and misinterpretations when communicating using electronic media. Remote collaboration is prevalent in most inter-firm relationships as the collaborating companies are on rarely co-located. Sufficient social capital then has to emerge as a basis for people to use ICT to complement their face-to-face interactions. As Nohria and Eccles put it: "This is because an extensive, deep, robust social infrastructure of relationships must exist so that those using the electronic media will truly understand what others are communicating to them." (Nohria/Eccles, 1992). By establishing these social relationships, employees learn to communicate with each other, to interpret the partners' messages and to identify themselves with the other side which can be seen as a necessary prerequisite for remote collaboration via electronic media. As one manager noted:

> *"Generally, I think that once you've met and you remember a face, you can see that face when you take the phone and that makes a difference. You can identify better with the other side when you have such a clue." [Manager DEVELOPER]*

Besides creating the right environment for social interactions to take place, there is more that managers can do to facilitate the emergence and deployment of social capital. When selecting people for joint teams, managers should also pay attention to the collaborative skills of employees rather than just focusing on task-related knowledge. And in case people with prior involvement with the partner firm exist, managers can further capitalise on their existing social capital in creating joint teams. Managers should also positively award collaborative behaviour and encourage employees to build and foster social relationships. Here, another dilemma becomes obvious: Generally, humans tend to invest in relationships with others whom they like and who are similar to them. However, the rather difficult relationships with people whom one does not like need often more attention in order to find a way to get along with these people. Here, managers should encourage employees to deliberately sit down with those people and work on the relationships. Otherwise clubs and islands of collaboration might fragment the inter-firm social network with people not spanning cultural gaps.

Furthermore, it is also useful to find people who establish strong social networks over time and who act as relationship promoters (see above). By empowering these actors, managers can make better use of their social capital in that information flows are improved and social integration is further fostered. These actors are also vital in spanning the social gaps in large networks. Last but not least, the managers' own behaviour is important to create a positive climate for social capital emergence. Managers should lead by example by showing social behaviour that is collaborative, consistent and authentic. Table 8 summarizes management implications and social capital dilemmas.

Table 8. Management implications of social capital in inter-firm relationships

Dilemmas of managing social capital	
Dilemma 1	Social capital is most urgently needed at the beginning of a project, but the least likely available at that stage.
Dilemma 2	Investments in social capital are important, but direct investments are not possible. Social capital is a by-product of interactions that emerges over time.
Dilemma 3	People tend to invest in good relationships with people they like and who are similar, although difficult relationships might need investments more urgently.
Management propositions	
Segment relationships	Make distinctions between different types of inter-firm relationships and align management behaviour regarding the social aspects accordingly.
Create opportunities for social interactions	Workshops, events and collocation are important for rich social capital to emerge, especially group-level social capital in terms of joint understanding. Social capital is important as basis for effective remote collaboration using electronic communication
Select people	Take into account social and collaborative skills and existing social relationships of people. Pay attention to relationship promoters.
Encourage people	Reward collaborative behaviour and encourage people to invest in social relationships, also in the difficult ones.
Lead by example	Managers should display consistent behaviour that is authentically collaborative.

9. Conclusion

This paper presents an empirical study on the social dimension of inter-firm relationships. It was argued that an understanding of the social aspects of inter-firm collaboration is important for an effective management of relationships with IT suppliers; reason being a lack of formal structures in general and the complex nature of IT projects in particular. It has been shown that social capital theory is useful in informing this type of research. Social capital theory as an umbrella framework integrates various perspectives and constructs dealing with collaboration; it starts from the social relationship as its main entity, which allows for better operationalisation than more abstract concepts like trust. In fact, it turned out, that the managers in the empirical inquiry connected well with the capital metaphor and the idea of regarding social relationships as a form of investment.

The author opted to undertake an explorative study due to the fact that little prior research was available on the social aspects of inter-firm relationships. Thus, a theory building approach was chosen to gain understanding on what role social capital might play in different types of inter-firm collaborations. Two cases in the E-Commerce sector with a number of different IT supplier relationships were research. In so doing, it turned out that, against the initial assumptions, it was not sufficient to distinguish between different kinds of E-Commerce services and the corresponding supplier relationships to explain the relevance of the social dimension. Rather, the case data revealed a more complex contingency model that is based on three variables: the relationship episode, the project complexity and the resulting strategic dependency. Based on a two level interplay of these variables social capital plays three distinct roles that were identified as being an "enabler", a "supporter", and a "lubricant" role (see table 8). The main contribution of this study is a framework that distinguishes different roles of social capital in inter-firm relationships with IT suppliers. Besides, some suggestions for managers on how to deal with social capital investments could be provided.

However, the study has certain limitations. First of all, only two, albeit quite typical and interesting cases have been researched that gave access to a variety of relationships. Thus, a follow-up study aimed at replicating this research approach to other cases could add further insights; especially since a subsequent study could start from these findings and try to prove the provided framework. A second limitation is the narrow focus on E-Commerce relationships. Although the author is confident that the findings are generalisable and will be e.g. be applicable to other IT-related relationships, a second study could venture into other areas of IT outsourcing and IT-enabled collaboration. And since this study aimed at gaining a general understanding of the role of social capital in inter-firm relationships it was limited in the depth of researching certain aspects of social capital. Further studies could focus on single dimensions of social capital and thus gain deeper understanding on issues like the cognitive processes of grounding in an inter-firm context in the presence of social diversity. Nevertheless, the author believes that this study makes a contribution to the research of inter-firm relationships in general and those of complex IT supplier relationships in particular.

References

Adler, P. S., Kwon, S. W., 2002, Social Capital: Prospects for a new concept, *Academy of Management Review.* **27**(1):17-40.

Anand, V., Clark, M. A., Zellmer-Bruhn, M., 2003, Team Knowledge Structures: Matching Task to Information Environment, *Journal of Managerial Issues.* **15**(1):15-31.

Andres, H. P., 2002, A comparison of face-to-face and virtual software development teams, *Team Performance Management.* **8**(1/2):39-48.

Arthur D. Little, 2001, Partnering. Challenges for the old and new economy. Facts - Assessments - Recommendations based on a global Arthur D. Little survey (September 2001), http://www.adlittle.de/asp/orderpublications.asp?ID=28.

Belz, C., et al., 1991, *Erfolgreiche Leistungssysteme,* Schäffer, Stuttgart.

Blyler, M., Coff, R. W., 2003, Dynamic Capabilities, Social Capital and Rent Appropriation: Ties that split Pies, *Strategic Management Journal.* **24**(7):677-686.

Bourdieu, P., 1985, The forms of capital, in: *Handbook of theory and research for the sociology of education,* J. G. Richardson, ed., Greenwood, New York, pp. 241-258.

Clark, H. H., Brennan, S. E., 1991, Grounding in Communication, in: *Perspectives on Socially Shared Cognition,* L. B. Resnick, J. M. Levine, and S. D. Teasley, eds., American Psychological Association, Washington DC, pp. 127-149.

Cohen, W. M., Levinthal, D. A., 1990, Absorptive Capacity: A New Perspective on Learning and Innovation, *Administrative Science Quarterly.* **35**(1):128-152.

Coleman, J. S., 1988, Social capital in the creation of human capital, *American Journal of Sociology.* **94**:95-120.

Dywer, F. R., Schurr, P. H., Sejo, O., 1987, Developing Buyer-Seller Relationships, *Journal of Marketing.* **51**(2):11-27.

Flick, U., 1998, *An Introduction to Qualitative Research,* SAGE Publications, London et al.

Fukuyama, F., 1995, *Trust: The social virtues and the creation of prosperity,* Free Press, New York.

Gadde, L. E., Håkansson, H., 1997, The Changing Role of Purchasing: Reconsidering Three Strategic Issues, in: *Understanding Business Markets,* D. Ford, ed., The Dryden Press, London, pp. 430-444.

Granovetter, M., 1992, Problems of Explanation in Economic Sociology, in: *Networks and organizations: structure, form, and action,* N. Nohria, and R. Eccles, eds., HBS Press, Boston, pp. 25-56.

Hall, W., 1995, *Managing Cultures - Making Strategic Relationships Work,* John Wiley & Sons, Chichester.

Hutt, M. D., Stafford, E. R., Walker, B. A., Reingen, P. H., 2000, Case study: Defining the social network of a strategic alliance, *Sloan Management Review.* **41**(2):51-62.

Kanter, R. M., 1994, Collaborative Advantage: The Art of Alliances, *Harvard Business Review.* **72**(4):96-108.

Kern, T., Willcocks, L. P., 2002, Exploring relationships in information technology outsourcing: the interaction approach, *European Journal of Information Systems.* **11**(1):3-19.

Knoke, D., 1999, Organizational networks and corporate social capital, in: *Corporate social capital and liability,* R. T. Leenders, and S. M. Gabbay, eds., Kluwer, Boston, pp. 17-42.

Leana, C. R., van Buren III, H. J., 1999, Organizational Social Capital and Employment Practices, *Academy of Management Journal.* **24**(3):538-555.

Lee, J. N., Huynh, M. Q., Kwok, R. C., Pi, S. M., 2003, IT outsourcing evolution - Past, present, and future, *Communications of the ACM.* **46**(5):84-89.

Levine, J. M., Moreland, R. L., 1991, Culture and Socialization in Work Groups. in: *Perspectives on Socially Shared Cognition,* L. B. Resnick, J. M. Levine, and S. D. Teasley, eds., American Psychological Association, Washington DC, pp. 257-279.

Meyerson, D., Weick, K. E., Kramer, R. M., 1996, Swift Trust and Temporary Groups, in: *Trust in Organizations,* R. M. Kramer, and T. R. Tyler, eds., SAGE Publications, London, pp. 166-195.

Miles, M. B., Huberman, A. M., 1994, *Qualitative Data Analysis: an expanded sourcebook,* 2nd ed., SAGE Publications, London.

Mintzberg, H., Raisinghani, D., Théoret, A., 1976, The Structure of unstructured Decision Processes, *Administrative Science Quarterly.* **21**(2):246-275.

Nahapiet, J., Ghoshal, S., 1998, Social capital, intellectual capital, and the organizational advantage, *Academy of Management Review.* **23**(2):242-266.

Nohria, N., Eccles, R., 1992, Face-to-Face: Making Network Organizations Work. in: *Networks and organizations: structure, form, and action.* N. Nohria, R. Eccles, eds., Boston, Harvard Business School Press.

Nonaka, I., Takeuchi, H., 1995, *The knowledge-creating company: How Japanese companies create the dynamics of innovation* New York, Oxford University Press.

Olk, P., Earley, C. P., 2000, Interpersonal Relationships in International Strategic Alliances - Cross-Cultural Exchanges and Contextual Factors, in: *Cooperative Strategy,* D. Faulkner, M. de Rond, eds., Oxford University Press, New York, pp. 307-323.

Portes, A., 1998, Social capital: Its origins and applications in modern sociology, *Annual Review of Sociology.* **24**(1):1-24.

Putnam, R. D., 1995, Bowling Alone: America's declining social capital, *Journal of Democracy.* **6**(1):65-78.

Putnam, L., 2001, Distance Teamwork - The Realities of Collaborating with Virtual Colleagues, *Online.* **25**(2):54-58.

Reagans, R., Zuckerman, E. W., 2001, Networks, Diversity, and Productivity: The Social Capital of Corporate R&D Teams, *Organization Science.* **12**(4):502-217.

Riemer, K., Klein, S., Gogolin, M., 2002, Network Business Model Configuration - New Roles for Dynamic Network Arrangements, in: *Challenges and Achievements in E-business and E-work - Proceedings of e2002 Conference,* B. Stanford-Smith, E. Chiozza, and M. Edin, eds., IOS Press, Amsterdam et al., pp. 892-899.

Riemer, K., Klein, S., 2003, Challenges of ICT-enabled Virtual Organisations: a Social Capital Perspective. in: *Proceedings of the 14th Australasian Conference of Information Systems (ACIS),* Perth, Nov 26-28.

Riemer, K., Totz, C., 2003, The many faces of personalization - an integrative overview of mass customization and personalization, in: *The Customer Centric Enterprise: Advances in Mass Customization and Personalization,* M. M. Tseng, F. T. Piller, eds., Springer Verlag, New York/Berlin, pp. 35-50.

Sheth, J. N., Sharma, A., 1997, Supplier Relationships - Emerging Issues and Challenges, *Industrial Marketing Management.* **26**(2):91-100.

Sobrero, M., Toulan, O., 2000, Task Partitioning, Communication Activities, and the Performance of Supplier Relations in Product Development, in: *The flexible Firm. Capability Management in Network Organizations,* J. Birkinshaw, and P. Hagström, eds., Oxford University Press, Oxford, pp. 21-42.

Tymon, W. G., Stumpf, S. A., 2003, Social capital in the success of knowledge workers, *Career Development International.* **8**(1):12-20.

Walter, A., 1999, Relationship Promoters: Driving Forces for Successful Customer Relationships, *Industrial Marketing Management.* **28**(5):537-551.

Werbach, K., 2000, Syndication: The Emerging Model for Business in the Internet Era, *Harvard Business Review.* **78**(3):84-93.

Wilson, D. T., Jantrania, S., 1997, Understanding the Value of a Relationship, in: *Understanding Business Markets,* D. Ford, ed., The Dryden Press, London, pp. 288-304.

Zeffane, R., 1995, The widening scope of inter-organizational networking: economic, sectoral and social dimensions, *Leadership & Organization Development Journal.* **16**(4):26-33.

Chapter 7

The Influence of Power Relations on Interorganisational Identification in Buyer-Supplier Relationships of the Automotive Industry

Daniel Corsten[*], Gunther Kucza[°] and Marion Peyinghaus[#]
[*]London Business School; [°]Holcim AG, Zurich; [#]POM AG, Zurich

Abstract: This paper focuses on gaining sustainable competitive advantage in supply chain collaboration. It is based on an empirical study of more than 200 buyer-supplier relationships in the Automotive industry. Our analysis is dedicated to answering the question why and under what conditions some supplier-buyer relationships are more successful than others. Latest research in the automotive industry has revealed that suppliers engaged in committed and obliged relationships with their buyers perform better compared to the average. Drawing on Social Identity Theory, we assume that successful relationships result from interorganisational identification among supply chain members. Moreover, we hypothesise that interorganisational identification is predominantly influenced by interorganisational power strategies. Therefore, based on our research model, we examine the interdependence between power and identity and subsequently, effects of organisational identity on collaborative success.

Key words: Social Identity Theory, Power Relations, Supplier-Buyer Relationships, Automotive Industry

1. Introduction

Research in automotive supplier relations has shown that Japanese suppliers perform better than suppliers in the U.S. (Cusumano and Takeishi, 1991; Dyer and Nobeoka, 2000). Several researchers have emphasised the necessity of trust, interorganisational interaction, knowledge sharing mechanisms, mutual assistance, social relations, and cooperative behaviour in supplier-buyer relationships (Nishiguchi and Baudet, 1999; Mac Duffie and Helper, 1997; Larson 1992). Nevertheless, other factors beyond relational contracting may affect supplier's loyalty and obligation. Gulati and Lawrence (1997) have found in their study of supplier relationships in the automotive industry that relationships with embedded ties perform better than alternative sourcing arrangements. Kogut (2000, 414) assumes that dense networks foster a "sense of collective identity", whereas Dyer and Nobeoka (2000) even recognise identity creation processes in Japanese supplier networks. According to Wood and Gray (1991), collective identity might be one of the reasons for increasing collaboration effectiveness. Considering the Japanese supplier network, Toyota effectively motivated suppliers to participate in their network and created conditions that helped suppliers to strongly identify with this network (Dyer and Nobeoka, 2000, 351). While the German automotive industry differs in organisation and conditions from the Japanese model, we would like to investigate if supplier identification will emerge even without Japanese management practices and their particular institutions. If supplier identification is an effect that appears also in the German automotive industry, the preconditions and consequences may deviate from the initial presumptions made within the Japanese automotive research. In our project we empirically investigate the extent to which organisational identity exists in the context of supplier-buyer relationships and analyse important antecedents and consequences.

Although the concept of organisational identity is often discussed in the literature (Bhattacharya et al., 2002; Dutton et al., 1994; Ashforth and Mael, 1989), the study of organisational identity in business-to-business relationships is mostly neglected. A study which uses Social Identity Theory to frame hypotheses about market orientation and interorganisational relationships has been conducted by Steinman et al. (2000). Likewise, Scott and Lane (2000) focus on a stakeholder approach to organisational identity. Other conceptual developments and empirical studies discuss interpersonal cooperations within organisations (McAllister, 1995), the cognitive identification of art museum members (Bhattacharya et al., 1995), alumni (Mael and Ashforth, 1992), MBA students (Elsbach and Kramer, 1996), employees (Elsbach and Glynn, 1996) or citizens (Bhattacharya and Elsbach, 2002). A general lack of studies in the organisational literature on "individual's identification with organisations of which they are not members" has been recognised by Elsbach (1998, 232).

Social identification is the perception of belonging to a group with the result that the person itself identifies with that group. In addition, organisational identification is a specific form of social identification in which people define themselves in terms of their memberships in a particular organisation

(Ashforth and Mael, 1989; Dutton et al., 1994; Mael and Ashforth, 1995). Tajfel (1978) have explicitly defined that social identification has both cognitive and affective components. In detail, the concept describes the "individual's knowledge that he belongs to a certain group, together with some emotional and value significance to him of that membership" (Tajfel, 1978; 31). Subsequently, organisational identification engages with the individual's feelings, actions and believes (Harquail, 1998). Although the concept is derived from an individual level, we assume that it might be applicable to an interorganisational level. Kahn (1993) reports that consistently recurring acts suggest the likelihood of underlying organisational patters. Likewise, Huy (1999) argues that organisational norms and routines related to feelings mirror organisational behaviour and either expressing or evoking certain emotional states. Although several antecedents accounting for individual's identification have been proposed in the literature (Mael and Ashforth, 1992; Bhattacharya et al., 1995; Bergami and Bagozzi, 2000; Bhattacharya and Elsbach, 2002) we expect that identification on an interorganisational basis depends on related but slightly different factors.

2. Practical relevance of organisational identity

In the last decade, many large firms have been undergoing a transformation, typically moving away from vertical integration towards more external contracting of key activities, thereby building complex networks of suppliers (Nohria and Eccles, 1992). In addition, the nature of buyer-supplier relationships in industrial markets has shifted in recent years from confrontation towards a more cooperative situation. In particular, many buyers have changed their relationships with component suppliers from traditional arm's length relations driven by competitive structures towards new arrangements based on cooperative structures. These take the form of "cooperative relationships" (Bensaou, 1997), "extended enterprises" (Dyer, 2000), "alliances" (Spekman, 1988; Heide and John, 1990) or "partnerships" (Anderson and Narus, 1990).

In contrast to these changes in the character of buyer-supplier relationships, conflicts and opportunism remain a reality in industrial markets (Scheer and Stern, 1992; Kumar et al., 1995a, 1995b). The intensity of competition and consolidation processes on the industry level seeds mistrust and fosters disingenuous behaviour. However, Kumar, Scheer and Steenkamp (1998) have found that as dealer-supplier interactions increase, dealers' punitive actions directed toward suppliers are restrained. In this context, cooperation or the mutual comprehension of the need to satisfy end customers results in improved performance for both participants in the relationship. As

Carlisle and Parker (1989, 5) mentioned, "if customer and supplier firms can recognise their common ground in a shared interest in capturing the consumer sales which actually nourishes them both, it should be possible for them to work creatively and effectively together to capture that sale for their product".

Overall, there is a growing interest in relational contracting and other hybrid forms of governance based on long-term cooperative arrangements. In particular, the automotive industry is a prime example for cooperation. Automobiles are developed and manufactured by Original Equipment Manufacturers (OEM) and their supplier networks, which produce as much as 70 percent of the value of the vehicle. Consequently, the cost and quality of an automobile are a function of the productivity of a network of firms working in cooperation (Dyer and Nobeoka, 2000). In addition, the automotive industry is mainly affected by consolidation processes. Supply base rationalisation forces car manufacturers to form closer relations with their key suppliers. Likewise, first-tier suppliers have begun to rationalise their own supplier base and to invest in long-term partnerships. Due to these developments, suppliers are not only impelled to deliver products of higher quality at lower costs in shorter time than in the past but also to manage other parts of the supply chain strategically (Scannell et al., 2000). In contrast to strategic management improvements at all levels of the supply chain, car manufacturers are loosing control over their supplier base. Equally, they face the problem that knowledge and in-house capabilities are moved to their first- or second-tier suppliers. Long-term cooperative arrangements may compensate these effects.

Researchers have found that Japanese automotive networks have been superior at labour productivity, inventory reductions and knowledge diffusion (Dyer and Nobeoka, 2000; Liebermann and Asaba, 1997). Dyer and Nobeoka argue that the reason has to do with the fact that Japanese car manufacturers have developed a "strong identity for the network" (2000, 351). Equally, collaboration literature suggests that the effectiveness of collaboration increases when stakeholders have a shared purpose (Wood and Gray, 1991; Gray 1989). In this sense, Kogut (2000) argues that those dense networks also foster a sense of collective identity which supports coordinated exchange. Following his former research work, a shared identity does not only lower the cost of communication, but establishes explicit and tacit rules of coordination (Kogut and Zander, 1996). Further automotive research (Mac Duffie and Helper, 1997) explains what is meant by a shared identity: Creating an identity for a collective means that the individual members feel a shared sense of purpose with the collective. Specifically, the identity of a firm is defined by the organisational boundaries which dedicate who is and who is not a member of the organisation. The border is established by shared goals and values, and by patterns of interaction among individuals that give rise to a common language and common frameworks for action. With regard to the underlying research setting, Dyer and Nobeoka (2000) argue that the Japanese model provides evidence that the concept of a shared identity is not only applicable to firms but also to networks or network dyads.

Following the assumption of Turner (1982, 1984) that social identification affects the outcomes conventionally associated with group formation, including intra-group cohesion, cooperation, altruism, and positive evaluation of the group, we estimate that a mutual social identity has a positive effect on the quality of buyer-supplier relationships. Likewise, Pratt (1998, 171) argues that "identification is a fundamental task of organisations: Organisations must engender identification to facilitate their functioning." Furthermore, according to Cheney (1983) organisational identity helps organisations to retain control over their members. This might be an answer for loosing supply chain control by car manufacturers. All equal and according to latest research attempts, the concept of organisational identification offers a positive evaluation on a firm, inter-firm and network level and it is not restricted to the automotive industry.

3. Theoretical foundation and literature review

This research project is mainly influenced by sociological theories about social identification, which have been recently discussed in organisational behaviour research (Mael and Ashforth, 1992; Dutton et al., 1994, Bhattacharya and Elsbach, 2002). Organisational identification, the key element of this study, is a specific form of social identification in which individuals define themselves in terms of their membership in a particular organisation (Ashforth and Mael, 1989; Dutton et al., 1994; Mael and Ashforth, 1992; Mael and Tetrick, 1992).

The concept of identification was first developed in a systematic way by Freud (1922) who addressed the process whereby a person assimilates itself to other persons or objects. Later on, this rather psychological perspective was applied to group behaviour where identification came to signify individual's attachment to the group (e.g.; Rothman, 1965) or people's adoption of the group attitudes (Kelman, 1958).

Simon (1947) was one of the first organisation science scholars to introduce the concept of organisational identification, highlighting thus its importance for organisational decisions. Simon described that "identification is the process whereby the individual substitutes organisational objectives ... for his own aims as the value-indices which determine his organisational decisions" (1947, 218). Afterwards March and Simon (1958) developed the ideas of organisational identification further, proposing a theory that was mainly based on a psychological point of view. Recently, organisation theorists have concentrated on a more explicitly social view of identification, namely on Social Identity Theory (SIT).

Social Identity Theory, a theory of inter-group relations, first developed by Tajfel and Turner (1979) and further elaborated by Ashforth and Mael (1989), focuses on connective links between individuals and social entities. SIT rests on people making social comparisons between in-group and out-group, or between self as in-grouper or others as out-groupers, in order to construct a sense of who they are and how they are evaluated (Hogg, 2000; Hogg et al., 1995). Tajfel (1981, 255) explains that SIT is concerned about how social categories serve as "a system of orientation which helps to create and to define the individuals place in society". Thus, in the perspective of SIT, the defining characteristics of the social categories with which an individual feels membership (e.g., nationality, religious affiliation, profession) comprise an individual's social identity (Tajfel, 1981; Tajfel and Turner, 1979).

In case of organisational identification, employees become attached to their organisations when they incorporate the characteristics they attribute to their organisation into their self-concepts. To the extent that an organisation possesses attributes that are perceived by the employees as being positive and valuable, the employees have a basis for reinforcing self-esteem and defining self-worth (Pratt, 1998; Bergami and Bagozzi, 2002). Once identified, individuals sense a feeling of oneness with the organisation, which involves the perceived experience of its success and failures (Mael and Tetrick, 1992). Furthermore as employees identify with their firm, employees' individual self-perceptions are likely to become depersonalised so that employees see themselves as interchangeable representatives of the organisation (Bergami and Bagozzi, 2000).

However, identification does more than afford a definition of membership; it also effects the attribution of self-interested behaviour (Kogut and Zander, 1996). Turner (1982) explains that "social identity is the cognitive mechanism which makes group behaviour possible" (1982, 21) and emphasised in a later study (1985) the powerful impact of identification on both members' affect and behaviour. Indeed, several scholars recognised the impact of organisational identification on the well-being of the organisational members and the organisation itself (Cheney, 1983; O'Reilly and Chatman, 1986; Ashforth and Mael, 1989; Mael and Ashforth, 1992; Pratt, 1998; Elsbach and Bhattacharya, 2001). For instance, Ashforth and Mael (1989, 29) explain that identification with the organisation's offer on the one hand is a mechanism whereby the individual can reify the organisation and feel loyal and committed to it per se. Otherwise, the authors argue that identification provides an indirect path through which socialisation may enhance the incorporation of organisational values and beliefs. Similarly, Turner (1982, 1984) asserts that organisational identification leads to group formation, including intra-group cohesion, cooperation, and altruism.

However, identification research has to date focused primarily on clarifying employees' relationships with their organisation (e.g., Pratt, 2000, Dutton et al., 1994), members' relationships with non-profit organisations (e.g., Arnett et al., 2003; Bhattacharya et al., 1995; Mael and Ashforth, 1992; Dukerich et al., 2002) or consumers' relationships with companies (Bhattacharya and Sen, 2003; Ahearne et. al., in press). Elsbach (1998, 232) acknowledges that there is a lack of research in the organisational literature on "individuals' identification with organisations of which they are not members". Except of several conceptual studies, empirical evidence regarding identification processes in the context of business-to-business relationships is not existent. For example, recently Rowley and Moldoveanu (2003) and formerly Scott and Lane (2000) have used social identity theories to explain stakeholder group actions. Further, Steinman et al. (2000) discuss social identification in the context of differences in customers' and suppliers' market orientation. Peteraf and Shanley (1997) propose effects of strong strategic group identities. Ring and Van de Ven (1994, 99) assume that identification is a fundamental force to establish and maintain interorganisational relationships. This assumption is equally supported by Johnsen et al. (2002) in the context of international joint ventures. In the same line, Ashforth and Mael (1989, 28) have hypothesised earlier that a positive organisational identity attracts the recognition, support and loyalty of not only organisational members but also of other stakeholders. Finally, MacDuffie and Helper (1997) firstly introduced the concept of organisational identification in the automotive business, which was recently further elaborated in Dyer and Nobeoka's case study about the Toyota network (2000). But despite this amount of research, a lack of empirical validation of the concept in business-to-business relations exists.

Thus, a fundamental problem in SIT is that research is principally conducted at the group level of analysis rather than at the organisational level. Pratt outlines that the question, "under what conditions do organizations come to identify with one another" (1998, 192), is not answered yet. As a result, research in Social Identity Theory demands to broaden the concept on an organisational level and express that "one of the biggest challenges to research on organisational identification is to go beyond the group level of analysis" (Pratt, 1998, 192). Consequentially, scholars claim for an interorganisational orientation of the concept to enable the development of cooperative relations among departments within a large organisation or among firms in a larger business context (Hogg and Terry, 2000). Thus this research would like to give an answer and explain the conditions that facilitate or impede identification on an interorganisational level.

4. Research model

Relational contracting has figured prominently in the marketing channel literature (Dwyer et al., 1987; Heide and John, 1990). Referred to as a relational exchange, suppliers and customers remain autonomous entities, but develop long-term, cooperative exchange relationships. These relationships go well beyond the short-term contracts that govern traditional market transactions. To employ this strategy means both for suppliers and for car manufacturers to accept an extra effort in relationship care. These efforts are linked to relationship issues of trust and commitments or pledges to the channel partner (Anderson and Weitz, 1992), and relative power and dependence (Anderson and Narus, 1990) of the partners. Equally, relationship management is concerned with psychological bonds of memberships, such as identification (Bhattacharya et al., 1995). This research project attempts to combine these approaches and tries to point out how the different constructs are related with each other. We will mainly focus on power relations and underlying organisational identification processes and will further investigate the role of commitment. Thus, we will evaluate antecedents, outcomes, and interaction effects of these psychological bonds.

4.1 Power relations as antecedents of organisational identity

Social identification occurs even in the absence of strong leadership or membership interdependence (Ashforth and Mael, 1989). Nevertheless, SIT proposes several organisational factors, which cause or enhance individual's identification: distinctiveness of the group values and practices, prestige of the group, salience of the out-groups, and factors traditionally associated with group formation. These factors are related with group formation and cover for example themes of interpersonal interaction, similarity, linking, proximity and shared goals (Ashforth ans Mael, 1989, 25). Although these factors are not mandatory according to SIT they are used by individuals as fundamentals for categorising (Turner, 1984). Categorisation is proposed by SIT as a basic element of the identification process and sufficient for identification to occur. Otherwise the diffusion of formal and informal groups in organisations indicates that categorisation is unlikely to be the only factor in identification.

Recently conducted conceptualisations of organisational identification see it as a form of social identification whereby a person comes to view him- or herself as a member of a particular social entity, the organisation. We extend this perspective from person-organisational level to an interorganisational level.

Identification on an individual's level happens through cognitive processes of categorisation, where the individual forms self-categories of organisational membership and individual's similarities with others in the organisation (Scott and Lane, 2000). Tajfel (1978) explains social identity as "the individuals knowledge that he belongs to certain social groups, together with some emotional and value significance to him of that membership" (1978, 31). However, as an individual identifies increasingly with an organisation, the self-perception tends to become depersonalised. In detail, identification is similar to the degree to which an individual defines him- or herself by the same attributes that he or she believes define the organisation (Dutton et al., 1994).

However, identification is not static. Individuals and organisations mutually "shape one another over time" (Ashforth, 1998:214). Respectively, the extent of individual's identification is varying according to the social context. Research in organisational behaviour has found that treatment by authorities influences individual's degree of identification. This will be demonstrated by changes in their view about the organisation, or by deviations in the individual's behaviour and attitudes (Tyler, 1998). Therefore, particular treatments shape feelings of obligation toward the organisation as well as rule-following behaviour. Drawing these findings on our empirical setting and on an interorganisational level, we assume that the customer's use of power will have a main impact on the supplier's level of identification.

According to the power typology by French and Raven (1959) we focus on the following two types of power: Non-coercive power and coercive power. Non-coercive power is based on the supplier's perception that the customer can mediate the reward for it. This type of power is also frequently discussed as reward power. Typical rewards that customers may be able to give suppliers are favourable treatment and shared expertise and information. Otherwise, coercive power, or punishment power, is based on the supplier's perception that the customer has the ability to mediate punishments. Examples would be unexpected sanctions or if the customer withholds advice, information, or services. We expect that the behavioural patterns chosen by the customer significantly count for the level of supplier's identification.

In order to respond to the question "under what conditions do organizations come to identify with one another" (Pratt, 1998, 192), we focus on conditions, which may foster or impede identification processes and refers

therefore to the use of coercive and non-coercive power. Studies analyzing identification on an organisational level propose that constructive and extensive interaction between stakeholders and the focused organisational entity enhance stakeholders' strength of organisational identification (Johnson et al., 2002; Peteraf and Shanley, 1997; Scott and Lane, 2000). In particular, theorists analyzing inter-firm identification are convinced that close and embedded interactions in contrast to arm-length ties are responsible for identification processes on an organisational level. Thus, we postulate that non-coercive power is the preferable power strategy for customer firms in actively managing their working relationships to foster organisational identification with their supplier. In turn, previous research has shown that coercive use of power in inter-firm relationships seriously weakens their collaborative nature and confirms the widely accepted proposition regarding the negative consequences of using coercive power in order to create close bonds among the parties.
Thus, we hypothesise:

> ***H1a:*** *The higher the level of buyer's use of non-coercive power, the higher the degree of the supplier's organisational identification with the buying firm.*

> ***H1b:*** *The higher the level of buyer's use of coercive power, the lower the degree of the supplier's organisational identification with the buying firm.*

4.2 The influence of organisational identity on collaboration quality

Ashforth and Mael (1989) were the first who clearly determined the role of organisations in individual's social identities. They describe the process of identification as the individual's perception of feeling a "oneness with or belongingness to an organisation" (Mael and Ashforth, 1992, 104). While most prior research has investigated identification in formal membership context, both theory and recent examinations (Elsbach, 1998; Scott and Lane, 2000) propose that identification with organisations can occur even in the absence of formal membership. To summarise this discussion and to apply it to the underlying empirical setting, we assume that members from the supplier organisation will think of themselves as belonging to customer organisations. Although formal membership is absent, we expect that the supplier's employees will feel a kind of oneness with the customer organisation.

Although not only positive types of identification are feasible (e.g., Ashforth, 1998; Dukerich et al., 1998; Elsbach, 1999), we estimate some worthwhile effects of organisational identification. Related research on organisational behaviour outlines the strong relation between commitment, socialisation, lower in-group conflict and increase in behaviour congruent with the organisation's objectives with identification processes (e.g., Van Maanen and Schein, 1979; Dutton et al., 1994; Mael and Ashforth, 1995). Even Cheney (1983) provides a long list of organisational benefits that are deducted from member identification. Here, however, we look at terms of organisational identification that will affect both the supplier and the customer organisation in a positive manner. Given that "social identification enables the individual to conceive of, and feel loyal to, an organisation or corporate culture" (Ashforth and Mael, 1989, 26), the concept of organisational identification describes one of the most beneficial situation in which people can interact.

Bergami and Bagozzi (2000) have found that social identification processes boost and encourage behaviours for the benefit of co-members. Several researchers point out that organisational identification has implication for citizenship behaviour (Bergami and Bagozzi, 2000; Dutton et al., 1994). We assume that these evaluated positive outcomes count also on an interorganisational level. Scott and Lane (2000) argue in their conceptual approach on stakeholder's organisational identity that if identification with a group increases, the motivation to reach group goals is rising likewise. While positive attachments of individual's identification are concerned with helpful and supportive behaviours, the internalisation of values and norms or higher levels of interaction (Bhattacharya et al., 1995; Dutton et al., 1994; Mael and Ashforth, 1989), the related effects on an interorganisational level might be different. We assume that the concept of organisational identification may bridge the gap between the buyer and the supplier organisation. Furthermore we expect that while the buying organisation is becoming part of the supplier's in-group, the degree of agreement between the two organisations will increase. Likewise as Steinman et al. (2000) proposed in their study, we argue that organisational identity will transform an "us versus them" thinking between the buyer and supplier organisation into a consensus among them.

The ultimate purpose of any company is to maximise profits (Conner, 1991). Therefore organisational performance has become an important dimension of empirical research (Dess and Robinson, 1984). Researchers frequently take the performance of organisations into account when investigating such organisational phenomena as efficiency and effectiveness in the context of interorganisational relationships. However, organisational performance is a complex and multidimensional phenomenon, even more so in an interorganisational context. Anyway, we assume that organisational identity has an impact on collaborative quality, which we define as relational success, financial performance as well as satisfaction.

Thus, we hypothesise:

H2a: *The higher the level of supplier's identification with the buying firm, the higher the relational success within the buyer-supplier relationship.*

H2b: *The higher the level of supplier's identification with the buying firm, the higher the financial performance of the supplier organisation.*

H2c: *The higher the level of supplier's identification with the buying firm, the higher the supplier's satisfaction with the buyer-supplier relationship.*

4.3 Moderating effects on supplier's identification and relational outcomes

Commitment is generally viewed as the strength of the relational ties among channel members and has long been central to the social exchange literature (Blau, 1964; Morgen and Hunt, 1994; Gruen et al., 2000). We expect that commitments have interaction effects on the relation between supplier's organisational identity and relationship outcomes.

Morgan and Hunt (1994, 23) define relationship commitment "as an exchange partner believing that an ongoing relationship with another is so important as to warrant maximum efforts at maintaining it." Similar to organisational identification, the focus of organisational commitment is the relationship between an individual member and the particular organisation. The two concepts are often merged or subsumed in the existing literature (Dutton et al., 1994; Buchanan, 1974; Meyer and Allen, 1991). However, Mael and Ashforth (1989) differentiate both from each other despite their similarities. Finally, Mael and Tetrick (1992) show that organisational commitment and organisational identification are conceptually distinct. They argue that organisational identification must be organisation-specific because it is a particular organisation that is seen by individuals as being self-defining (Pratt, 1998; Mael and Ashforth, 1995; Bhattacharya and Rao, 1995). Otherwise, organisational commitment needs not to be organisation-specific because the concept simply comprises a strong belief in the value and norms of the organisation and not in the organisation per se. In addition, Pratt (1998) argues that "the most salient distinction is that identification explains the individuals-organisations relationship in terms of an individuals self-concept; organisational commitment does not." Likewise Meyer and Allen (1991) believe that commitment is equated with the acceptance of organisational values, whereas identification is equated with sharing organisational values and beliefs.

Research on organisational identity has widely examined the strong relation between commitment and organisational identity (Ashforth and Mael, 1989; Dutton et al., 1994; Bergami and Bagozzi, 2000). We broaden up this perspective and presume that commitment also plays a significant role in the context of interorganisational identification. Thus, we hypothesise:

> ***H3:****The higher the degree of supplier's commitment to the buying firm, the higher the effects of supplier's organisational identification on supplier's perception of* ***(H3a)*** *relational success,* ***(H3b)*** *financial performance and* ***(H3c)*** *the level of satisfaction with the buyer-supplier relationship.*

One meaning of identifying is "to recognise". This meaning is made salient when individuals identify with an organisation that they believe has values and beliefs that are similar to their own. In these terms, individuals use organisations that they perceive as similar to their own image in order to define themselves. Researchers in SIT describe this process as identification through affinity (Pratt, 1998, 174). Specifically, identification is related to the consistency between people's self-concepts and their perceptions of the organisation. This means that individuals seek similar organisations. Likewise Mael and Ashforth (1995) argue that individuals who perceive themselves to be similar to an organisation are more likely to identify with that organisation. In general, individuals who identify with an organisation want to be known as being assimilated with it.

Indeed, Dutton et al. (1994) have found that the higher the degree of fit between the person and the organisation, the higher the similarity between the perceived organisational identity and a person's self-concept. Consequently, the higher the person-organisation fit, the stronger a member's organisational identification. Effectively, organisational identification is described by the congruence between organisational and individual values (Hall and Schneider, 1972). Similarly, we assume that a mutual fit on an interorganisational level will influence the identification process. Thus, we hypothesise

> ***H3:*** *The higher the level of partner fit between the buyer and the supplier organization, the higher the effects of supplier's organisational identification on supplier's perception of* ***(H3d)*** *relational success,* ***(H3e)*** *financial performance and* ***(H3f)*** *the level of satisfaction with the buyer-supplier relationship.*

4.4 Research model

Based on the related literature and the practitioner interviews, we have developed an underlying research model (see figure 1), subsequently for the concepts of antecedents and consequences of organisational identity within buyer-supplier relationships. This model summarises the described research hypothesises. The research hypothesises are implemented in the figure and visualised through arrows.

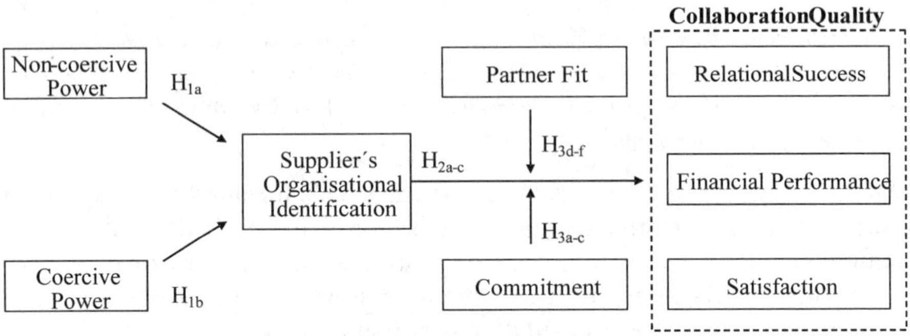

Figure 1. Research Model

5. Research methodology

The level of analysis is the relationship between the supplier and the buyer organisation. Drawing on SIT, we investigate these relationships regarding underlying psychological bonds in terms of power and identity. In order to understand the dynamics in buyer-supplier relationships, we have not only studied extant literature in the areas of supply chain management and relational marketing but also supplemented this knowledge with in-depth interviews with several key informants from the German speaking automotive industry.

The exploratory interviews served as a basis for the quantitative research step. Derived from the first findings the research model is established and the underlying hypotheses are developed. Although the in-depth interviews provided us with substantial information, it was beyond the scope of our research project to collect data through interviews from a large sample. We decided to collect the data through survey questionnaires administered to relevant managers across a large sample of automotive supplier firms. The quantitative research allows us to measure perceptions and make generalisations about the collective behaviour of organisations within the automotive industry. Thus, the objective and the context of this research project have driven the employed research methodology.

5.1 In-depth interviews

To determine the concept of organisational identity and interorganisational power, we first gathered preliminary information from a series of personal interviews. We conducted in-depth interviews with German or Swiss car manufacturers as well as their suppliers. The interviewees were mainly General Managers and Directors of Purchasing, Sales or Logistics. The questions were broad and open-ended to enable informants to define the situation themselves. Most of the interviews were conducted personally, the others by phone. A typical interview lasted about an hour. The interviews were audio-taped and transcribed. Participants and the research team reviewed the transcriptions, identifying gaps in the narrative and suggesting additional data collection. The reviews often led interviewees to provide more detailed background information. By allowing all the participants to review their transcriptions we could offset some of the bias normally associated with retrospective interviews.

The first findings from theses interviews, along with an extensive research of social identity literature, convinced us that the concept of organisational identity was likely to exist even between organisations within the German speaking automotive industry. Although the interviewees had often not explicitly defined their self-perceptions as "identification", a list of other affiliated statements indicated that the concept of organisational identity is present in the minds of many people. The preliminary findings also suggested that the organisational identification is important enough to affect suppliers' or customers' behaviour or the outcome of the dyadic relationship. The following quote illustrates the identified practical relevance:

> *"In relationships it is important to keep your own identity, yet in some cases a mutual identity is helpful and sometimes already even existing."*

5.2 Data collection and sample

The scope of the study has been defined as the German speaking automotive industry. The survey was supported by the European Commission in the context of the DOMINO project (Dynamic Organisational Management for Interfirm Network Orchestrations, IST-2000-29545). We used a mailing list company that provided us with names, addresses, and limited organisational information.

As contact persons we identified either the general manager, the sales manager or in other cases the marketing manager or the logistic manager. We expect no significant difference between the different types of informants. We see our respondents as representatives of their respective firms, not of a specific subgroup within the firm. Questionnaires were sent per mail. Most of the respondents returned the paper version, others used the online version. After four weeks e-mail reminders were sent out. Participants without e-mail addresses were contacted by phone. 267 questionnaires have been returned. After subtracting 43 questionnaires that were not sufficiently filled out, the sample size consisted of 224 suppliers.

5.3 Measurement

Based on the 12 expert interviews and the literature review, items and questions were generated to test the theory of the underlying research project. Whenever possible, we used construct definitions and measures available from the literature to improve content validity. Where a new scale had to be developed, we were guided primary by construct definition and the scales utilised in organisational research. We consulted practitioners and academics in order to ensure the right understanding and interpretation of the questions. This led us to several further adjustments to our questionnaire. The resulted items are listed in Appendix A.

5.3.1 Interorganisational identity

The dependent variable in our research project is the degree of supplier's identification with the customer's organisation. Suppliers identification is measured by adapting Mael and Ashforth`s (1992) scale (see the items used for the construct interorganisational identity in Appendix A). The strength of the supplier's organisational identification reflects the degree to which the content of the individual's self-concept is tied to his or her organisational affiliation. When organisational identification is strong, the organisation-based content is salient and central (Stryker and Serpe, 1982) and organisational affiliation is a prevalently used concept for self-definition (Kramer, 1991).

5.3.2 Power

For our empirical study we focus on customer's enacted power from the subjective supplier's perception. Use of power (also referred to as influence strategies) can be conceptualised as an exercise of a coercive versus non-coercive power. The constructs are based on Geyskens and Steenkamp (2000). The customer's use of a non-coercive power base involves reward and assistance, the customer's use of a coercive power base involves punishment (see the items used for the construct power in Appendix A)

5.3.3 Relational success

The development of the construct relational success is mainly influenced by findings based on our in-depth interviews. The items cover a wide range describing successful interactions between firms on an operational level. The operationalisation includes questions about the delivery rate of defective parts, the delivery reliability and the generated profits in the specific relationship. Similarly, we asked these questions compared to other relationships of the firm.

5.3.4 Financial performance

Financial performance is a complex and multidimensional phenomenon. Operationalising such a complex concept is inherently difficult. In our study, we focused on popular measures related to financial performance, such as return on assets[11], return on investments[12], and return on sales. In this context we have to emphasise that we asked in our study only for the subjective perception of the aforementioned dimensions of financial performance. This means respondents had to assess how their company performs compared to their competitor according these measures[13]. Dess and Robinson revealed in their study of organisational performance measures that there is a strong correlation between subjective measures and objective measures of organisational performance (Dess and Robinson, 1984).

5.3.5 Satisfaction

In order to measure satisfaction, we used Jap's (2001) operationalisation and her 3-item scale. The author utilised the construct to describe the relationship quality. We adopted this method by assessing supplier-buyer relationships. O`Reilly and Chatmann (1986), Ashforth and Mael (1989) or Mael and Tetrick (1992) predicted formerly the influence of organisational identity on satisfaction.

---

[11] 'Return on total assets' is commonly viewed as one operational measure of the efficiency of a firm with regard to the profitable use of its total asset base (Ansoff, 1965; Bourgeois, 1980; Gale, 1972).

[12] Ansoff asserts that 'return on investment' is a commonly and widely accepted yardstick for measuring business success (Ansoff, 1965).

[13] In order to avoid that an exceptional good or bad year leads to distortion in the results the average over the last three years was used for all aforementioned economic performance measures.

5.3.6 Partner fit

Kale et al. (2000) emphasised the importance of the organisational fit between alliance partners with respect to the complementary and compatibility of the partners. We adopted this approach but altered the items. While Dutton et al. (1994) argued that the degree of fit between the person and the organisation, or the degree of similarity, is determining for organisational identity we selected items to highlight the compatibility factor. Applied to the interorganisational context, these items cover congruence between different firms. The congruence is described by the similarity of the particular organisational objectives, cultures, management styles, and employee characteristics.

5.3.7 Customer's commitment

We adopted the construct customer commitment on the bases of the paper by MacDuffie and Helper (1997) about Honda's approach to create lean suppliers. The items of the construct are aligned with this case study. We expect that if the customer's firm is offering and executing support the supplier tends to perceive a much stronger affiliation to this customer, which will moderate the result of supplier's organisational identity on the performance outcomes in a significant way.

6. Applied statistical methods

For the full sample we conducted exploratory factor analyses to purify the scales. Adapting Anderson and Gerbing's (1988) two step approach, acceptable measurement models were developed prior to conducting tests of the hypothesized relationships between constructs. In the beginning we validated the measurement model through confirmatory factor analysis and tests for unidimensionality, reliability and validity of the constructs. Afterwards, we employed regression analysis to test our moderator/mediator model (Backhaus et al., 2000). Regression analysis is recommended as a method for testing moderating effects if at least one of the variables, predictor or moderator, is continuous. Linear moderating effects are tested by adding the product of the moderator and the predictor variable to the regression equation. Moderator effects are indicated by significant effects of the product of both moderator and predictor variable while controlling for the direct effect of both (Baron and Kenny, 1986).[14]

Employing a moderator/mediator model contributes to the understanding and complex functioning of a phenomenon. Mediation takes place, if one predictor causes another predictor, which then causes the dependent variable. Moderation means that the effect of one predictor on the dependent variable depends on or varies across levels of another predictor (Heath, 2001, 94). For moderating effects, we tested mediation using the three-step mediated regression approach suggested by Baron and Kenny (1986). To test moderation effects or interaction effects we used Sharma et al. (1981) proposed approach.

For the statistical analysis we used the AMOS 4.0 Statistical Software as well as SPSS Version 10.0. The software enables a stringent test of unidimensionality, reliability and validity for measure validation. When the measurement validation is terminated, the regression analysis follows. Estimating adequate measurements of constructs using confirmatory factor analysis before conducting test of hypothesis is a recognised methodology in related research (e. g., Heide and John, 1990).

7. Measurement models for interorganisational identity

On the basis of Anderson and Gerbing's (1988) recommendation, we developed measurement models before testing the hypothesised relationships between the constructs. A measurement model describes how well the observed indicators serve as a measurement instrument for the latent variables (Jöreskog and Sörbom, 1993). It is specified by assigning indicators to a specific latent variable or construct based on theory and prior to employing confirmatory factor analysis (Bollen, 1989).

Since including all constructs in one measurement model would have resulted in a highly complex model, which cannot be estimated using structural equation modelling techniques (Anderson and Narus, 1990; Bentler and Chou, 1987), we separated three measurement models respectively for the antecedents, the focal construct with the moderators, and the outcome constructs.

---

[14] An important property of the moderator variable is that unlike the predictor-mediator relation where the predictor is causally antecedent to the mediator, moderators and predictors are at the same level with regards to their role as causal variables antecedent or exogenous to certain criterion effects. Moderator variables always function as independent variables, whereas mediating events shift roles from effects to causes, depending on the focus of the analysis (Baron and Kenny, 1986).

7.1 Measurement models

The first measurement model comprises interorganisational power as enabler of interorganisational identity. The second measurement model contains the focal construct identity and two moderating constructs, commitment and partner fit. The third measurement model estimates three outcome constructs, relational success, financial performance and satisfaction.

7.2 Evaluating measurement model fit

Since a number of fit indices are available in the output of AMOS 4.0 we were guided by three criteria for selecting fit indices, namely, relative independence of sample size, accuracy and consistency to assess different models, and ease of interpretation aided by a well defined continuum or pre-set range (Marsh et al., 1988).

Based on the stated criteria, we report the chi-square (χ^2) and three other fit indices that are generally used and recommended in related research: the Tucker-Lewis-Index (TLI), the Comparative-Fit-Index (CFI) and the Root Mean Squared Error of Approximation (RMSEA). These indices are all scaled on a pre-set, continuum (0 - 1) for easy interpretation and are all relatively independent of sample size effects.

Chi-square (χ^2): Although the chi-square is the most common method of evaluating fit, this fit index is highly sensitive to sample size and the significance test can be misleading (Marsh et al., 1988; Medsker et al., 1994; Hulland et al., 1996; Baumgartner and Homburg, 1996). The chi-square compares the actual observed matrix with the estimated matrix. A 'non-significant' low chi-square value indicates a good fit, i.e. that both matrices do not differ significantly. However, when the sample size exceeds 200 observations, significant differences are bound to be found. Unfortunately, a minimum sample size of 200 observations is recommended to obtain stable parameter estimates. Thus, we interpreted the chi-square test statistic with caution when evaluating our measurement models (Medsker et al., 1994; Hulland et al., 1996; Baumgartner and Homburg, 1996).

Tucker-Lewis index (TLI): The Tucker-Lewis index (TLI), also known as the non-normed fit index (NNFI), compares a proposed model's fit to a nested baseline or null model. Additionally, the TLI measures parsimony by assessing the degrees of freedom from the proposed model to the degrees of freedom of the null model (Marsh et al., 1988). The TLI also seems resilient against variations in sample size and, thus, is highly recommended. An acceptable threshold for this index is .80, although .90 or greater is recommended (Hulland et al., 1996; Baumgartner and Homburg, 1996).

Comparative fit index (CFI): Bentler developed the comparative fit index (CFI) as a non-centrality parameter-based index to overcome the limitation of sample size effects (Bentler, 1990). This index ranges from 0 - 1, with .80 representing an acceptable fit and .90 or greater a preferred fit (Hulland et al., 1996; Baumgartner and Homburg, 1996).

Root mean squared error of approximation (RMSEA): The root mean squared error of approximation (RMSEA) index, a parsimony measure, measures the discrepancy between the observed and estimated covariance matrices per degree of freedom. The RMSEA measures the discrepancy in terms of the population and not the sample. Thus, the value of this fit index is expected to better approximate or estimate the population and not be affected by sample size. Furthermore, the RMSEA accounts for potential artificial inflation due to the estimation of too many parameters. Again, values run on a continuum from 0 to 1, with values falling between .05 to .08 deemed acceptable (Medsker et al., 1994; Hulland et al., 1996; Baumgartner and Homburg, 1996).

7.3 Measurement model for antecedents of interorganisational identity

We conceptualised the measurement model antecedents for interorganisational identity as two first-order models.

Assessment of Unidimensionality: Measurement model 1 showed unidimesionality as the CFI (.997) and TLI (.950) were far above the benchmark of .90 and the RMSEA (.061) below the recommended level of .08. Also, the chi-square (χ^2=23.973; 13 degrees of freedom) for measurement model 1 (interorganisational power as antecedents of interorganisational identity) was not significant (p=.031).

Table 1. Measurement results for interorganisational power as antecedents of interorganisational identity

Measurement Model Organisational Enablers	Items	Cronb. Alpha	Compo. Relia.	Varian. Extr.	Fit Measures
Non-Coercive Power	3	.76	.76	.52	$\chi^2_{(13)} = 23.973$
Coercive Power	4	.86	.86	.61	CFI = .997
					TLI = .994
	9				RMSEA = .061

Assessment of Reliability: All measures showed adequate reliability. Both Cronbach's Alphas and composite reliabilities were estimated as .76, .86, for non-coercive power and coercive power, thus exceeding the preferred level of .70. Average variance extracted for the two constructs was higher than the suggested .50 (i.e. .52, .61).

Assessment of Convergent Validity: The model showed convergent validity. The factor regression coefficients between the latent variable and the indicators of measurement model 1 are statistically significant, i.e. minimum t-value. AMOS critical ratio was 8.057, $p<.001$ and mostly far above .70. The parameter estimates were 5 to 10 times as large as the standard errors.

Assessment of Discriminant Validity: An exploratory factor analysis of the 7 items of measurement model 1 demonstrated a clear separation, with each item loading highest on the factor it was hypothesised to measure. Moreover, the correlation between the two constructs were low (phi-matrix values .26) they were significantly below unity ($p<.001$) and the latent correlation between the two constructs plus/minus twice the standard error (i.e., .72) did not include 1.0.

7.4 Measurement model of interorganisational identity and for moderators of interorganisational identity

Measurement model 2 contains the two moderators of interorganisational identity. Partner fit and commitment. An exploratory factor analysis of the 10 items of measurement model 2 demonstrated a clear separation, with each item loading highest on the factor it was hypothesised to measure. The measure validation procedures produced the following results (see table 2).

Assessment of Unidimensionality: Although the chi-square (χ^2=50.805, 32 degrees of freedom) for measurement model 2 was significant ($p<.001$), the overall fit was more than acceptable, because the CFI (.997) and TLI (.995), were clearly above the usually recommended level of .90 and the RMSEA (.051) below the recommended level of .08.

Table 2. Measurement results for focal construct and moderators of interorganisational identity

Measurement Model Moderators	Items	Cronb. Alpha	Compo. Relia.	Varian. Extr.	Fit Measures
Identity	3	.90	.91	.76	$\chi^2_{(32)} = 50.805$
Commitment	3	.92	.93	.81	CFI = .997
Partner Fit	4	.88	.91	.77	TLI = .995
	10				RMSEA = .051

Assessment of Reliability: The preferred level of .70 for Cronbach's Alpha (Composite reliability in brackets) was exceeded by all three constructs:

Identity .90 (.91), commitment .92 (.93) and partner fit .88 (.91). Variance extracted was .76 for identity, .81 for commitment, and .77 for partner fit thus always clearly higher than the benchmark of .50.

Assessment of Convergent Validity: The model showed convergent validity. Factor regression coefficients are above .70 and significant (smallest critical ratio was 10.33, p<.001) and parameter estimates were 20 to 50 times as large as the standard errors.

Assessment of Discriminant Validity: We expected identity, commitment and partner fit to be correlated. However, since correlation between commitment and partner fit (.55) plus/minus twice the measurement error (.93) does not include one, we concluded that discriminant validity does no pose a problem.

7.5 Measurement model for outcomes of interorganisational identity

Measurement model 3 contains three outcome measures of interorganisational identity: relational success, satisfaction and financial performance. The measure validation procedures for economic performance and capability development produced the following results (see table 3):

Table 3. Measurement results for outcome measures of interorganisational Identity

Measurement Model Outcome	Items	Cronb. Alpha	Compo. Relia.	Varian. Extr.	Fit Measures
Relational Success	3	.78	.80	.57	$\chi^2_{(24)} = 31.211$
Satisfaction	3	.86	.88	.70	CFI = .999
Financial Performance	3	.94	95	.86	TLI = .998
					RMSEA = .036

Assessment of Unidimensionality: Measurement model 3 showed unidimesionality as the CFI (.999) and TLI (.998) were far above the benchmark of .90 and the RMSEA (.036) far below the recommended level of .08. Also, the chi-square (χ^2=23.973; 13 degrees of freedom) for measurement model 3 was not significant (p=.148).

Assessment of Reliability: Cronbach's Alpha (composite reliability) for relational success is .78 (.80), for satisfaction .86 (.88) and for economic performance .94 (.95) thus exceeding the preferred level of .70. Variance extracted was .57 for relational success, .70 for satisfaction, and .86 for economic performance respectively and thus higher than the benchmark of .50.

Assessment of Convergent Validity: The model showed convergent validity. The parameter estimates were mostly greater than .80, statistically significant (minimum t-value, i.e. AMOS critical ratio was 8.053, p<.0001) and the parameter estimates were 30 to 50 times as large as the standard errors.

Assessment of Discriminant Validity: Discriminant Validity is evidenced as the correlation confidence interval between the three constructs were low (phi-matrix values .26, .26, .36) and the latent correlation between any two of the three constructs plus/minus twice the standard error (.48, .43, .65) did not include 1.0.

8. Analysis and results

In the theory section we proposed 11 core hypotheses for organisational identification, antecedents, moderators and outcome measures. Following Anderson and Gerbing's (1988) two step approach, and after having established validity and reliability of the conceptualised constructs, we proceeded with a test of the hypotheses that were developed in our model. Tests of hypotheses are conducted through the use of hierarchical moderator regression (Jap, 2001). For each outcome measure the model includes the main effect and interaction terms of both moderator variables. We used factor scores instead of averages because compared to averages they represent the sample specifics better. By averaging details of the sample characteristics can be diluted. We considered this a stronger argument than the disadvantage of factor scores that replication of the analysis by other researchers is impeded as the factor scores can only be computed based on the whole data set (Lastovicka and Thamodaran, 1991). We obtained the factor scores by performing a stepwise hierarchical exploratory factor analysis. The following construct-level correlation matrix formed the basis for the hypothesis testing (see table 4).

Table 4. Factor correlation table

	1	2	3	4	5	6	7	8
1 NONCOE_P	.760							
2 COE_P	.216 **	.860						
3 IDENT	.298 **	-.180 **	.900					
4 COM	.201 **	-.077	.475 **	.920				
5 P_FIT	.330 **	-.088	.518 **	.362 **	.880			
6 REL_SUC	.141 **	-.049	.311 **	.132	.171 **	.780		
7 SATISF	.277 **	-.172 **	.345 **	.422 **	.384 **	.188 **	.860	
8 FIN_PERF	.186 **	-.182 **	.265 **	.067	.221 **	.246 **	.284 **	.940

** Correlation is significant at the 0.01 level (2-tailed)

* Correlation is significant at the 0.05 level (2-tailed)

8.1 Effects of antecedents on organisational identification

Hypothesis 1a predicts that buyer's use of non-coercive power has a positive effect on supplier's organisational identification. A regression analysis found that the use of non-coercive power by the customer's organisation has a significant effect on the level of supplier's identification (standardised $\beta = .353$, $p < .001$, $R^2 = .151$). Likewise, hypothesis 1b is tested and approved by the same regression analysis (standardised $\beta = -.256$, $p < .001$, $R^2 = .151$). Therefore the analysis confirmed that customer's use of coercive power accounts for a reduced level of identification by the supplier firm. Additionally, we tested mediation effects according the approach of Baron and Kenny (1986)[15].

Table 5 presents mediated regression results for both coercive and non-coercive power in relation to the three outcome measures satisfaction, financial performance and relational success. The regression shows in each case a significant coefficient for the mediating variable identity and a decrease in the magnitude of the coefficients for the independent variables non-coercive and coercive power.

---

[15] A given variable may be said to function as a mediator to the extent that it accounts for the relation between the predictor and the criterion. Mediators explain how external physical events take on internal psychological significance. A variable functions as a mediator, when the mediator is regressed on the independent variable; secondly, the dependent variable is regressed on the independent variable; and thirdly, the dependent variable is regressed simultaneously on both the independent variable and the mediator (Baron and Kenny, 1986). According to Baron and Kenny, mediation is indicated for a independent variable – mediator-dependent variable relationship if the following conditions are met: The independent variable must affect the mediator in the first equation; the independent variable must affect the dependent variable in the third equation; and finally, the effect of the independent variable on the dependent variable must be less in the third equation than in the second equation (Baron and Kenny, 1986).

Table 5. Mediated regression results

	Focal Construct IDENT		Dep. Variable SATIF	Dep. Variable FIN_PERF	Dependent REL_SUC		Dep. Variable SATIF	Dep. Variable FIN_PERF	Dependent REL_SUC
Independent Variables		Independent Variables				Independent Variables			
(Constant)	.000	(Constant)	-.002	-.001	-.001	(Constant)	-.004	-.004	-.004
	(.062)		(.063)	(.116)	(.066)		(.061)	(.115)	(.064)
NONCOE_P	.353 [a]	NONCOE_P	.326 a	.418 [a]	.159 [c]	NONCOE_P	.245 [a]	.309 [c]	.061
	(.063)		(.065)	(.121)	(.069)		(.067)	(.126)	(.070)
COE_P	-.256 [a]	COE_P	-.235 a	-.409 [a]	-.079	COE_P	-.167 [c]	-.318 [c]	.004
	(.063)		(.065)	(.120)	(.069)		(.066)	(.124)	(.069)
						IDENT	.246 [a]	.331 [b]	.299 [a]
							(.067)	(.126)	(.070)
R^2	.151	R^2	.128	.083	.026	R^2	.179	.111	.100
F	19.700 [a]	F	16.179 [a]	9.919 [a]	2.910 [d]	F	15.902 [a]	9.096 [a]	8.129 [a]

* Standard Error in Parantheses

[a] $p<.001$, [b] $p<.01$, [c] $p<.05$, [d] $p<.1$

All variables are factor scores.

9. Influence of organisational identity on collaboration quality

Hypothesis 2a proposes that the level of supplier's identification account for the relational success within the buyer-supplier relationship. The results of the conducted regression analysis provide strong support for this hypothesis and show a positive relation between supplier's level of identification and the supplier's perception of relational success. Likewise, we tested hypothesis 2b by regression analysis. The analysis outlines that organisational identification relates positively to the financial performance of the supplier firm. Thus, hypothesis 2b is confirmed. Further regression analysis examined the relation of organisational identification and supplier's satisfaction. As expected, the analysis supports hypothesis 2c and approved a positive effect. All results are shown in table 6 and are significant on a $p<0.001$ level.

Table 6. Effects of Organisational Identification on Outcome Measures

	Dep. Variable SATIF	Dep. Variable FIN_PERF	Dependent REL_SUC
Independent Variables			
(Constant)	-.004	-.005	-.003
	(.063)	(.117)	(.064)
IDENT	.349 [a]	.483 [a]	.314 [a]
	(.064)	(.118)	(.065)
R^2	.119	.070	.097
F	29.874 [a]	16.690 [a]	23.684 [a]

* Standard Error in Parantheses

[a] p<.001, [b] p<.01, [c] p<.05, [d] p<.1

All variables are factor scores.

9.1 Moderating effects on supplier's identification and outcome measures

Before describing the hypothesis testing procedure in detail we will briefly describe what moderator variables are and how they can be tested.

„A moderator is a qualitative (e.g., sex, race, class) or quantitative (e.g., level of reward) variable that affects the direction and/or strength of the relation between an independent or predictor variable and a dependent or criterion variable" (Baron and Kenny, 1986, 1174). The underlying approach to test for moderation effects uses the procedure suggested by Cohen and

Cohen (1983) and follows the recommendation of Baron and Kenny (1986) and Aiken and West (1991). Therefore, a basic moderator effect is represented as a (significant) interaction between the moderator and the independent variable and can be linear or quadratic. Thus, a moderator hypothesis is supported, if the coefficient for the corresponding interaction term is statistically significant and possesses the predicted sign. In other words, if a positive relationship between a predictor and a moderator variable exists, a significantly positive interaction term suggests that the relationship between the predictor and criterion variables is strengthened, whereas a negative interaction term would weaken it. Further, Sharma et al. (1981) argued that to prove a moderating influence of C on A's relation with B, you have to model:

1. $B= b_1 + b_2 A$, to show a main effect for A,
2. $B= b_3 + b_4 A + b_5 C$, and show no main effect for C because if there is a main effect it would be a 'quasi moderator',[16]
3. $B= b_6 + b_7 A + b_8 C + b_9 A{*}C$, and show an effect for the A*C interaction term, and a lower beta coefficient for A in this equation (b_7) than (b_2) in the first equation.

Therefore, the authors' demand for inclusion of the main effect is consistent with several researchers' work. To avoid confusion with the main effect test of interorganisational power we tested main and moderating effects separately.[17]

In addition, several researchers suggested slightly different testing criteria, not distinguishing between moderators and quasi-moderators. For instance, Lehman et al. (1998) argued that two conditions have to be met so that interaction effects are proven. The test is successful when the beta coefficient of the interaction term is significantly different from zero, and equivalently, if adding the variable increases the variance explained (R^2). Irwin (2001, 98) argues that "the partial regression coefficient on the interaction term is the only indication whether there is a moderation effect" or not. Similarly, Aiken and West (1991) argue for interaction effects even in the presence of main effects and evade discussions of pure and quasi-moderators.

Furthermore, our approach starts with the simplest model of organisational identity and subsequently adds further effects, always requiring that

---

[16] Quasi moderation relaxes the requirement that the moderator is neither related to the dependent variable nor to the independent variable (Sharma et al., 1981).

[17] This is conforming to Irwin's (2001) caution that the beta coefficient of the main effect in a single regression is not equivalent to the beta coefficient of the variable in the regression including the interaction term. Researchers name the effect of the focal variable in the moderated regression analysis 'simple effect' instead of 'main effect' to avoid misinterpretations (Aiken and West, 1991).

the more complex model explains more of the variance coefficient (R^2) of the investigated dependent variable (Cote, 2001). Secondly, we check for the significance of the interaction term. Each of the added effects must be based on theory (Cote, 2001). We have carefully investigated possible interaction effects for the constructs of our model, yet only those for which hypotheses were developed had sufficient basis in theory. Hence, our model is the most complex we could build based on theory.

According to these explanations our analysis found that supplier's commitment significantly moderated the effect of supplier's organisational identification on relational success. The regression analysis displays interaction effects of commitment and supports therefore hypothesis 3a ($p < .05$). According to hypothesis 3b supplier's commitment moderates the effect of identification on financial performance as well. Against the assumptions, the regression analysis does not support this hypothesis. The interaction effect is not significant. Otherwise, a moderated regression analysis displays interaction effects for commitment and satisfaction ($p< .01$). Moreover, commitment has in addition a significant main effect on satisfaction. According to Sharma et al. (1981) the moderator has to show no main effect on the outcome variable because if there is a main effect it would be a "quasi moderator" (Lehmann, 2001). Whereas, referring on conditional effects, Aiken and West (1991) argue for interaction effects even in the presence of main effects. Following the argumentation of the authors, hypothesis 3c is supported. Thus, commitment moderates the effect of supplier's identification on relational effects and satisfaction. All results are presented in table 7.

Further moderating effects are found by regression analysis for partner fit. Regression results display in some extent interaction effects for partner fit and supplier's identification on the various outcome measures. In hypothesis 3d we predicted that partner fit moderates the relation of supplier's identification on relational success. The hypothesis is supported and shows significant interaction effects ($p< .05$). Similarly, hypothesis 3e is confirmed and supports moderating effects of partner fit on supplier's identification and financial performance. Interaction effects are predicted on a significance level of $p< .1$. Against prior assumption, hypothesis 3e is not supported. The regression analysis doesn't indicate significant interaction effects for partner fit and supplier's identification on satisfaction. All results are presented in table 7.

Table 7: Moderated regression analysis for commitment and partner fit

	Dep. Variable REL_SUC	Dep. Variable FIN_PERF	Dep. Variable SATIF		Dep. Variable REL_SUC	Dep. Variable FIN_PERF	Dep. Variable SATIF
Independent Variables				Independent Variables			
(Constant)	-.003	-.003	-.011	(Constant)	-.152 [c]	-.160	-.113 [d]
	(.064)	(.116)	(.058)		(.074)	(.138)	(.068)
IDENT	.310 [a]	.434 [b]	.086	IDENT	.272 [a]	.408 [b]	.037
	(.080)	(.146)	(.073)		(.080)	(.148)	(.073)
COM	-.015	-.161	.323 [a]	COM	.127	-.065	.511 [a]
	(.077)	(.140)	(.070)		(.098)	(.181)	(.090)
P_FIT	.021	.235 [d]	.244 [a]	P_FIT	-.031	.186	.197 [b]
	(.076)	(.138)	(.069)		(.076)	(.140)	(.069)
				IDXPFIT	.160 [c]	.222 [d]	.020
					(.070)	(.129)	(.064)
				IDXCOM	.161 [c]	.110	.211 [b]
					(.070)	(.130)	(.064)
R^2	.097	.086	.250	R^2	.151	.105	.289
F	7.862 [a]	6.869 [a]	24.310 [a]	F	7.690 [a]	5.086 [a]	17.651 [a]

* Standard Error in Parantheses

[a] p<.001, [b] p<.01, [c] p<.05, [d] p<.1

All variables are factor scores.

10. Discussion

Overall our results provide important insights into the dynamics and implications of buyer-supplier relationships. Although most extant literature emphasises structural factors to explain relationship success, the results of our study highlight the need to pay greater attention to social concerns and behavioural patterns in relationship management. These aspects of relationship management play a greater role in explaining and determining key relationship objectives such as relationship success, financial performance and satisfaction. All relationship performance measures are best achieved through high levels of supplier's identification. Supplier's identification bases on a feeling of affiliation that is going beyond expressions of trust and loyalty. Subsequently, the supplier's perception of oneness or unity with the customer's organisation builds the bases for beneficial effects within the business to business relationship. These beneficial effects are reflected here by the before mentioned outcome measures of relationship success, financial performance and satisfaction. Although positive evaluations of social identification in individual-organisation relationships have been shown in earlier research, this study for the first time presents desirable effects of social identification procedures in an interorganisational context. The study shifted the level of analysis from an individual to an organisational perspective, examining social bonds not only between individuals but also between organisations. Following the assumptions of several researchers in organisational behaviour that social identification counts on an individual level (Cheney, 1983; Dutton et al., 1994; Mael and Ashforth, 1989, 1995), our study broadens their application and supports these theories in the context of organisations. Methodologically, this study is the first to explore the effect of social identification in an interorganisational context on a quantitative basis.

Social Identity Theory (Ashforth and Mael, 1989) proposes several organisational factors that cause or enhance individual's identification. Individuals and organisations mutually shape one another over time (Ashforth, 1998). Thus, the extent of the individual's identification is varying according to the social context. We predicted the same procedure in the context of organisations. Adopted from social identity research on an individual level, we examined the influence of coercive and non-coercive power used by the customer on the level of supplier's identification. Comparable to individual identification processes, organisations respond to treatments such as punishment or reward by other organisations. The results of this study show that the levels of identification deviate according to the different kinds of power practices. Coercive power, referring to the supplier's perception that the customer has the ability to mediate punishments, is negatively related to the supplier's level of identification. These results support Tylers (1998) research on authority relations and treatment effects on social identification. On the other hand, the use of non-coercive power by the customer is positively related to the supplier's level of identification. The results endorse former research that helpful and supportive behaviour is going along with identification processes (Scott and Lane, 2000; Bhattacharya et al., 1995; Dutton et al., 1994). Nevertheless, Ashforth and Mael (1992) presented a study in which they found that strong organisational identification was associated with tyrannical behaviour of managers toward their subordinates. SIT explains that once an authority is confirmed and established, individuals accept punishments without dis-identification. Our study provides insight that reasons for identification differ in an organisational context from an individual setting. However, SIT research indicates a significant need for further research in power-identity relations and demands for integrating power aspects into the framework of social identification (Bouchikhi et al., 1998, 41). The results of this study support these claims and try to contribute to further discussions about power and identity relations.

The results of this study support the findings of previous social identification studies within an individual's context. But more importantly, this study extends the general understanding of when and how suppliers identify in this research context by investigating moderating constructs of the main effect. The analysis shows moderating effects for commitment and partner fit. The difference or congruence of organisational identification and organisational commitment has long been discussed in the literature. The results of this study provide insights that the two constructs are conceptually distinct and unique. However, literature (Mael and Tetrick, 1992) and results are suggesting a strong relation between them; some scholars even viewed identification as being integral to commitment processes (Dutton et al., 1994). But the conceptualisation of commitment tends to focus on the economic reasons for staying with or leaving an organisation. Specifically, it focuses on supplier's investments and calculations of losses and benefits as explanatory mechanisms for commitment. In turn, identification is conceptualised by emotional participation in failures and successes. Identification is therefore described by the psychological attachment that occurs when members adopt the defining characteristics of the organisation as defining characteristics for themselves. Referring to the economic aspects of commitment, the level of commitment displays a stable and relatively constant situation. According to identification research (Scott and Lane, 2000) a self-definition process becomes scripted and schematised to the extent that the social reality is consistent. The direct influence of importance of commitment in relationship management is widely examined by Morgan and Hunt (1994). While commitment itself is regarded as a key factor for achieving valuable relational outcomes, more than ever identification plus commitment contribute to relational success and supplier's satisfaction.

Additionally, the analysis showed that the level of partner fit is moderating the relation between identification and relational success as well as financial performance. Hereby, partner fit is dealing with shared objectives and goals rather than with complementary resources and capabilities. Further research in SIT (Ashforth and Mael, 1989) supports this moderating effect whereas similarity, proximity, shared goals are seen as basic factors for identification processes. Furthermore, a lack of congruence between the goals or expectations of related groups may impede joint identification (Ashforth and Mael, 1989:30). However, researchers even defined organisational identification as congruence between organisational and individual values (Hall and Schneider, 1972). This study provides insights that this even counts on an organisational level. While Dutton et al. (1994) hypothesised a strong relation of the degree of similarity and identification processes, this study shows interaction effects of identification and partner fit on relational success and financial performance. The positive impact of partner fit in alliances is assessed by Kale et al. (2000). Otherwise the interaction effect is explained in theory by people's motivation to maintain consistency between their self-perceptions and behaviour (Festinger, 1957; Dutton et al., 1994). Therefore, favourable relational outcomes are expected if suppliers identify, even more, if a congruence between the supplier's and a buyer's firms exist.

Before coming to the conclusion we would like to outline several limitations of this study. As is the case in most large-sample studies of relationships, we have responses from just one of the relationship partners. Although estimating dyadic properties by surveying one side of the dyad is relatively common in interorganisational exchange theory (Mohr and Spekman, 1994; Zaheer and Venkatraman, 1995; Artz, 1999; Kale et al., 2000) and not necessarily problematic (John and Reve, 1982), it is possible that the supplier's perception of the relationship specific constructs may be different from the customer's. It would be advantageous to get an assessment from both suppliers and customers. Therefore, taking a true dyadic perspective in the data collection by not sampling only one side of the channel dyad would improve our measurements and increase confidence in the study's results. However, we argue similar to Provan and Skinner (1989) and Arzt (1999) that this limitation may not have been so important as to invalidate our results. Moreover, our study must be viewed in the context of the particular distribution channel of the German automotive industry in which the study was conducted. Therefore, its limitations can be seen in the restricted research field and its specific focus on the automotive industry. The automotive industry is influenced by a wide range of specific key factors, such as environment, policies, members and stakeholders, competition and production complexity. Large differences are known to exist between industries; that would certainly influence results. Therefore, our results must be seen in the specific background of the automotive industry and can not be transferred directly into common findings or into other industrial settings. Thus, we cannot claim generalisability of our research model across countries and industry boundaries. Also, it would be helpful to complement our perceptual data with archival data. Although the use of perceptual data is accepted in related research, supplementing our data with archival data would allow cross-examination of data sources and help validate our findings, particularly with regards to the measuring of financial performance. However, given the fact that most of the companies in our sample are privately owned, it may be difficult to obtain real performance data. Nevertheless, a link to real performance outcomes would be desirable to increase the validity of our results. Likewise, we recognize that the constructs included in our study are only a portion of the potentially relevant variables that might have been included. Although the variance explained in our sub models is significant, it is still relatively small. This suggests that additional moderators are needed to explain fully the effects of supplier's organisational identification on outcome measures. Apparently, outcome measures are affected by organisational identification, partner fit and commitment; however, other constructs may also play an important role. At least, identification processes develop over time. Further research might be going beyond this cross-sectional data and emphasises the dynamic perspective of the concept. Further research should be taken that into account.

11. Conclusions

This research project is one of first empirical studies that investigates identification processes on an interorganisational level and provides some empirical evidence to emphasise the significance of power practices and identification processes in relationship management. Indeed, this study showed that the kind of power use impedes or fosters the level organisational identification. In turn, organisational identification accounts significantly for relationship success. Thus, the right use of power practices helps customers to achieve relationship objectives and to bind the suppliers to themselves. To the extent that identification processes are responsible for relationship success, customers can benefit from managing carefully their reward and punishment system.

Additionally, this study showed that relationship success is quite higher if congruence between the buying and the supplying firm exists. While deep identification requires investments of time, people, or capital, firms have to choose carefully their relationship partners. Similarly, identification processes are more effective in enduring and long-living partnerships, where the supplier is committed to the customer. Customer firms have to take into account, that relationship success due to identification aspects might be lesser in emerging relationships. In summary, long-lasting relationships with partners of high similarity and conformity are best suited for reaping identification gains. By examining organisational identity in the context of supplier-buyer relations, we hope to contribute to a more comprehensive understanding of the social identity phenomenon in vertical relationship management.

References

Ahearne, M., Bhattacharya, C. B., Gruen, T., in press, Antecedents and Consequences of Customer-Company Identification: Expanding the Role of Relationship Marketing, *Journal of Marketing.*

Aiken, L. S., West, S. G., 1991, Multiple Regression: Interpreting Interactions, Sage, Thousand Oaks, CA.

Anderson, E., Weitz, B., 1992, The Use of Pledges to Build and Sustain Commitment in Distribution Channels, *Journal of Marketing Research.* **29**(1):18-34.

Anderson, J. A., Gerbing, D. W., 1992, Assumptions and Comparative Strengths of the two Step Approach, *Sociological Methods & Research.* **20**(1):321-333.

Anderson, J. C., Gerbing, D. W., 1988, Structural Equation Modeling in Practice: A Review and Recommended Two-Step Approach, *Psychological Bulletin.* **103**:411-423.

Anderson, J. C., Narus, J. A., 1990, A Model of Distributor Firm and Manufacturer Firm Working Partnerships, *Journal of Marketing.* **54**(1):42-58.

Ansoff, H. I., 1965, *Corporate Strategy*, McGraw-Hill, New York.

Artz, K. W., 1999, Buyer-Supplier Performance: The Role of Asset Specificity, Reciprocal Investments and Relational Exchange, *British Journal of Management.* **10**:113-126.

Arnett, D. B., German, S. D., Hunt, S. D., 2003, The Identity Salience Model of Relationship Marketing Success: the Case of Nonprofit Marketing, *Journal of Marketing.* **67**(2):89-105.

Ashforth, B. E., 1998, Becoming: How Does the Process of Identification Unfold?, in: *Identity in Organisations: Building Theory through Conversations,* D. A. Whetten and P. C. Godfrey, eds., Sage, Thousand Oaks, CA, pp. 232-237.

Ashforth, B. E., Mael, F., 1989, Social Identity Theory and the Organization, *Academy of Management Review.* **14**(1):20-39.

Ashforth, B. E., Mael, F., 1992, *The Dark Side of Organisational Identification,* Paper presented at the Academy of Management Meeting, Las Vegas.

Backhaus, K., Erichson, B., Plinke, W., Weiber, R., 2000, *Multivariate Analysemethoden - Eine anwendungsorientierte Einführung,* 9th Edition, Springer, Berlin, Heidelberg.

Baron, R. M., Kenny, D. A., 1986, The Moderator-Mediator Variable Distinction in Social Pschychological Research: Conceptual, Strategic, and Statistical Considerations, *Journal of Personality and Social Psychology.* **51**:1173-1182.

Baumgartner, H., Homburg, C., 1996, Applications Structural Equation Modeling in Marketing and Consumer Research: A Review, *International Journal of Research in Marketing.* **13**:139-161.

Bentler, P. M., 1990, Comparative Fit Indexes in Structural Models, *Psychological Bulletin.* **107**:238-246.

Bhattacharya, C. B., Rao, H., Glynn, M. A., 1995, Understanding the Bond of Identification: An Investigation of its Correlates among Art Museum Members, *Journal of Marketing.* **59**(4):46-57.

Blau, P. M., 1964, *Exchange and Power in Social Life,* John Wiley & Sons, New York.

Bensaou, M., 1997, Interorganisational Cooperation: The Role of Information Technology - An Empirical Comparision of U:S: and Japanese Supplier Relations, *Information System Research.* **8**(2):107-124.

Bentler, P. M., Chou, C. P., 1987, Practical Issues in Structural Equation Modelling, *Sociological Methods and Research.* **16**:78-117.

Bergami, M., Bagozzi, R. P., 2000, Self-Categorization, Affective Commitment, and Group Self-esteem as Distinct Aspects of Social Identity in the Organisations, *British Journal of Social Psychology.* **39**:555-577.

Bergami, M., Bagozzi, R. P., 2002, *Antecedents and Consequences of Organisational Identification and the Nomological Validity of the Bergami-Bagozzi Scale,* Working Paper, Marketing Department, Jones Graduate School of Management, Rice University.

Bhattacharya, C. B., Elsbach, K. E., 2002, Us versus Them: The Roles of Organisational Identification and Disidentification in Social Marketing Initiatives, *Journal of Public Policy & Marketing.* **21**(1):26-36.

Bhattacharya, C. B., Rao, H., Glynn, M. A., 1995, Understanding the Bond of Identification: An Investigation of its Correlates among Art Museum Members, *Journal of Marketing.* **59**(4):46-57.

Bhattacharya, C. B., Sen, S., 2003, Consumer-Company Identification: A Framework for Understanding Consumers' Relationships with Companies, *Journal of Marketing.* **67**(2):76-88.

Bollen, K. A., 1989, *Structural Equations with Latent Variables,* John Wiley and Sons, New York.

Bouchikhi, H., Fiol, C. M., Gioia, D. A., Golden-Biddle, K., Hatch, M. J., Rao, H., Rindova, V., Schulz, M., 1998, The Identity of Organizations, in: *Identity in Organisations: Building Theory through Conversations,* D. A. Whetten, P. C. Godfrey, eds., Sage, Thousand Oaks, CA, pp. 33-80.

Bourgeois, L., 1980, Performance and Consensus, *Strategic Management Journal.* **1**(3):227-248.

Buchanan, B., 1974, Building Organisational Commitment: The Socialisation of Managers in Work Organisations, *Administrative Science Quarterly.* **19**:533-546.

Carlisle, J. A., Parker, R. C., 1989, *Beyond Negotiation: Redeeming Customer-Supplier Relationships,* John Wiley, New York.

Cheney, G., 1983, On the Various and Changing Meanings of Organizational Membership: A Field Study of Organizational Identification, *Communication Monographs.* **50**:342-362.

Cohen, J.; Cohen, P. (1983); Applied Multiple Regression/Correlation Analysis for the Behavioural Science, Erlbaum Press. Hillsdale, N.J.

Conner, K. R. (1991); "A Historical Comparison of Resource-Based Theory and Five Schools of Thought within Industrial Organization Economics: Do We Have a New Theory of the firm?

Cote, J., 2001, "VI.E Mediators and Moderators," in Structural Equation Modelling, *Journal of Consumer Psychology.* **10**(1/2):83-100.

Cusumano, M. A., Takeishi, A., 1991, Supplier Relations and Management: A Survey of Japanese, Japanese-Transplant, and U.S. Auto Plants, *Strategic Management Journal.* **12**:563-588.

Dess, G. G., Robinson, R. B., 1984, Measuring Organizational Performance in the Absence of Objective Measures: The Case of the Privately-held Firm and Conglomerate Business Unit, *Strategic Management Journal.* **5**:265-273.

Dukerich, J., Kramer, R. M., Parks, J. M., 1998, The Dark Side of Organizational Identification, in: *Identity in Organizations: Developing Theory Through Conversations,* D. Whetten and R Godfrey, eds., Sage, Thousand Oaks, CA, pp. 245-256.

Dukerich, J. M., Golden, B. R., Shortell, S. M., 2002, Beauty Is in the Eye of the Beholder: The Impact of Organisational Identification, Identity, and Image on the Cooperative Behaviour of Physicians, *Administrative Science Quarterly.* **47**(3):507-533.

Dutton, J. E., Dukerich, J. M., Harquail, C. V., 1994, Organizational Images and Member Identifications, *Administrative Science Quarterly.* **39**:239-263.

Dwyer, F. R., Schurr, R. H., Oh, S., 1987, Developing Buyer-Seller Relationships, *Journal of Marketing.* **51**(2):11-27.

Dyer, J. H., 2000, *Collaborative Advantage - Winning Through Extended Enterprise Supplier Networks,* Oxford University Press, Oxford.

Dyer, J. H., Nobeoka, K., 2000, Creating and Managing a High-Performance Knowledge Sharing Network: The Toyota Case, *Strategic Management Journal.* **21**:345-367.

Elsbach, K. D., 1998, The Process of Social Identification: With what Do we Identify?, in: *Identity in Organisations: Building Theory through Conversations,* D. A. Whetten, P. C. Godfrey, eds., Sage, Thousand Oaks, CA, pp. 232-237.

Elsbach, K. D., Bhattacharya, C. B., 2001, Defining Who You Are by What You're Not: A Study of Organizational Disidentification and the NRA, *Organization Science.* **12**(4):393-413.

Elsbach, K. D., Glynn, M. A., 1996, Believing your own "PR": Embedding Identification in Strategic Reputation, in: *Advances in Strategic Management,* J. A. C. Baun, J. E. Dutton, eds., JAI Press, Greenwich, CT, pp. 63-88.

Elsbach, K. D., Kramer, R. M., 1996, Members Responses to Organisational Identity Threats: Encoutering and Countering the Business Weeks Rankings, *Administrative Science Quaterly.* **41**:442-476.

Festinger, L., 1957, A Theory of Cognitive Dissonance, Harper and Row., New York.

Fornell, C., Larcker, D. F., 1995, Evaluating Structural Equation Models with Unobserved Variables and Measurement Error, *Journal of Marketing Research.* **18**(1):39-50.

French, J. R., Raven B., 1959, The Bases of Social Power, in: *Studies in Social Power,* D. Cartwright, ed., University of Michigan, Institute for Social Research, Ann Arbor, pp. 150-167; reprinted in: Studies in Managerial Process and Organizational Behavior, J. H. Turner, A. C. Filley, and R. J. House, eds., Scott, Foresman and Co., Glenview, Ill., pp. 72-81.

Freud, S., 1922, *Group Psychology and the Analysis of the Ego,* Boni and Liveright, New York.

Gale, B., 1972, Market Share and Rate of Return, *The Review of Economics and Statistics.* November 1972:412-423.

Geyskens, I., Steenkamp, J.-B., 2000, Economic and Social Satisfaction: Measurement and Relevance to Marketing Channel Relationships, *Journal of Retailing.* **76**(1):11-32.

Gray, B., 1989, *Collaborating: Finding Common Ground for Multiparty Problems,* Jossey-Bass, San Francisco, CA.

Gruen, T. W., Summers, J. O., Acito, F., 2000, Relationship Marketing Activities, Commitment, and Membership Behaviours in Professional Associations, *Journal of Marketing.* **64**(3):34-49.

Gulati, R., Lawrence, P., 1997, *Organizing Vertical Networks: A Design Perspective,* Working paper, J. L. Kellogg Graduate School of Management, Northwestern University.

Hall, D. T., Schneider, B., 1972, Correlates of Organisational Identification as a Function of Career Pattern and Organisational Type, *Administrative Science Quarterly.* **17**(3):340-350.

Harquail, C. V., 1998, Organizational Identification and the "Whole Person": Integrating Affect, Behavior, and Cognition, in: *Identity in Organisations: Building theory through conversations,* D. A. Whetten, P. C. Godfrey, eds., Sage, Thousand Oaks, CA, pp. 223-231.

Heath, T., 2001, Structural Equations Modeling, *Journal of Consumer Psychology.* **10**(1/2):83-100.

Heide, J. B., John, G., 1990, Alliances in Industrial Purchasing: The Determinants of Joint Action in Buyer-Supplier Relationships, *Journal of Marketing Research.* **27**(1):24-36.

Heide, J. B., John, G., 1992, Do Norms Matter in Marketing Relationships?, *Journal of Marketing.* **56**(2):32-44.

Hogg, M. A., 2000, Social Identity and Social Comparison: Theory and Research, in: *Handbook of Social Comparison,* J. Suls and L. Wheeler, eds., Kluwer Academic, Plenum Publishers, New York.

Hogg, M. A., Terry, D. J., 2000, Social Identity and Self-Categorization Processes in Organisational Contexts, *Academy of Management Review.* **25**(1):121-140.

Hogg, M. A., Terry, D. J., White, K. M., 1995, A Tale of Two Theories: A Critical Comparison of Identity Theory with Social Identity Theory, *Social Psychology Quarterly.* **58**(4):255-269.

Hulland, J., Chow, Y., Lam, S., 1996,Use of Causal Models in Marketing Research: A Review, *International Journal of Research in Marketing.* **13**:181-197.

Huy, N. Q., 1999, Emotional Capability, Emotional Intelligence and Radical Change, *Academy of Management Review.* **24**:325-345.

Irwin, J., 2001, "VI.E Mediators and Moderators" in Structural Equation Modelling, *Journal of Consumer Psychology.* **10**(1/2):83-100.

Jap, S. D., 2001, "Pie Sharing" in Complex Collaboration Contexts, *Journal of Marketing Research.* **38**(1):86-99.

Jöreskog, K., Sörbom, D., 1993, *Structural Equation Modeling with the SIMPLIS Command Language,* Scientific Software International, Chicago.

John, G., Reve, T., 1982, The Reliability and Validity of Key Informants Data from Dyadic Relationships in Marketing Channels, *Journal of Marketing Research.* **19**(4):517-524.

Johnson, J. P., Korsgaard, M. A., Sapienza, H. J., 2002, Perceived Fairness, Decision Control, and Commitment in International Joint Venture Management Teams, *Strategic Management Journal.* **23**:1141-1160.

Kahn, W. A., 1993, Caring for Caregivers. Patters of Organisational Caregiving, *Administrative Science Quaterterly.* **38**:539-563.

Kale, P., Singh, H., Perlmutter, H., 2000, Learning and Protection of Proprietary Assets in Strategic Alliances: Building Relational Capital, *Strategic Management Journal.* **21**:217-237.

Kelman, K. C., 1958, Compliance, Identification, and Internalization: Three Processes of Attitude Change, *Journal of Conflict Resolution.* **2**(1):51-60.

Kramer, R. M., 1991, Intergroup Relations and Organizational Dilemmas: The Role of Categorization Processes, in: *Research in Organisational Behaviour,* L. L. Cummings, B. M. Staw, eds., **13**:191-226.

Kogut, B., 2000, The Network as Knowledge: Generative Rules and the Emergence of Structure, *Strategic Management Journal.* **21**:405-425.

Kogut, B., Zander, U., 1996, What Firms Do? Coordination, Identity, and Learning, *Organization Science.* **7**:502-518.

Kumar, N., Scheer, L. K., Steenkamp, J.-B., 1995a, The Effects of Supplier Fairness on Vulnerable Resellers, *Journal of Marketing Research.* **32**(1):54-65.

Kumar, N., Scheer, L. K., Steenkamp, J.-B., 1995b, The Effects of Perceived Interdependence on Dealer Attitudes, *Journal of Marketing Research.* **32**(3):348-356.

Kumar, N., Scheer, L. K., Steenkamp, J.-B., 1998, Interpendence, Punitive Capability, and the Reciprocation of Punitive Actions in Channel Relationships, *Journal of Marketing Research.* **35**(2):225-235.

Larson, A., 1992, Network Dyads in Entrepreneurial Settings: A Study of the Governance of Exchange Relationships, *Administrative Science Quarterly.* **37**:76-104.

Lastovicka, J. L., Thamodaran, K., 1991, Common Factor Score Estimates in Multiple Regression Problems, *Journal of Marketing Research.* **28**(1):105-112.

Lehmann, D., 2001, Structural Equations Modeling: VI.E. Mediators and Moderators, *Journal of Consumer Psychology.* **10**(1/2):83-100.

Lehman, D., Gupta, S., Steckel, J., 1998, *Marketing Research,* Addison-Wesley-Longman, Reading, MA.

Liebermann, M., Asaba, S., 1997, Inventory Reduction and Productivity Growth: A Comparison of Japanese and U.S. Automotive Sectors, *Managerial and Decision Science.* **18**:73-85.

MacDuffie, J. P., Helper, S., 1997, Creating Lean Suppliers: Diffusing Lean Production throughout the Supply Chain, *California Management Review.* **39**(4):118-134.

Mael, F. A., Tetrick, L. E., 1992, Identifying Organisational Identification, *Educational & Psychological Measurement.* **52**(4):813-824.

Mael, F. A., Ashforth, B. E., 1992, Alumni and their Alma Mater: A Partial Test of the Reformulated Model of Organizational Identification, *Journal of Organizational Behavior.* **13**(2):103-123.

Mael, F. A., Ashforth, B. E., 1995, Loyal from Day One: Biodata, Organisational Identification, and Turnover among Newcomers, *Personnel Psychology.* **48**(2):309-333.

March, J. G., Simon, H. A., 1958, *Organizations,* John Wiley & Son, New York.

Marsh, H. W., Balla, J. R., McDonald, R. P., 1988, Goodness-of-Fit in Confirmatory Factor Analysis: The Effect of Sample Size, *Psychological Bulletin.* **103**(3):391-410.

McAllister, D. J., 1995, Affect- and Cognition based Trust as Foundations for Interpersonal Cooperation in Organizations, *Academy of Management Journal.* **38**(1):24-59.

Medsker, G. J., Williams, L. J., Holahan, P. J., 1994, A Review of Current Practices for Evaluating Causal Models in Organizational Behaviour and Human Resources Management Research, *Journal of Management.* **20**(2):439-464.

Meyer, J. P., Allen, N. J., 1991, A Three-Component Conceptualization of Organisational Commitment, *Human Resource Management Review.* **1**(1):61-89.

Mohr, J., Spekmann R., 1994, Characteristics of Partnership Success: Partnership Attributes, Communication Behaviour and Conflict Resolution, *Strategic Management Journal.* **15**:135-152.

Morgan, R., Hunt, S., 1994, The Commitment-Trust Theory of Relationship Marketing, *Journal of Marketing.* **58**:20-38.

Nishiguchi, T., Beaudet, A., 1999, Fractal Design: Self-Organizing Links in Supply Chain Management, *Logistics in the Information Age, 4th ISL,* Florence, Italy.

Nohria, N., Eccles, R., 1992, *Network and Organizations: Structure, Form and Action,* Harvard Business School Press, Boston, MA.

Peteraf, M., Shanley, M., 1997, Getting to Know You: A Theory of Strategic Group Identity, *Strategic Management Journal.* **18**(Summer Special Issue):165-186.

Pratt, M., 1998, To Be or Not to Be: Central Questions in Organisational Identification, in: *Identity in Organisations: Building Theory through Conversations,* D. A. Whetten, P. C. Godfrey, eds., Sage, Thousand Oaks, CA, pp. 171-208.

Pratt, M., 2000, The Good, the Bad, and the Ambivalent: Managing Identification among Amway Distributors, *Administrative Science Quarterly.* **45**(3):456-493.

Provan, K. G., Skinner, S. J., 1989, Interorganizational Dependence and Control Predictors of Opportunism in Dealer-Supplier Relations, *Academy of Management Journal.* **32**:202-212.

O'Reilly, C., Chatman, J., 1986, Organizational Commitment and Psychological Attachment: The Effects of Compliance, Identification, and Internalization on Prosocial Behavior, *Journal of Applied Psychology.* **71**(3):492-499.

Ring, P. S., Van De Ven, A. H., 1994, Developmental Processes of Cooperative Interorganizational Relationships, *Academy of Management Review.* **19**(1):90-118.

Rothman, J., 1965, *Minority Group Identification and Intergroup Relations: An Examination of Kurt Lewin's Theory of Jewish Group Identity,* New York.

Rowley, T. J., Moldoveanu, M., 2003, When Will Stakeholder Groups Act? An Interest- and Indentity-Based Model of Stakeholder Group Mobilization, *Academy of Management Review.* **28**(2):204-219.

Scannel, T. V., Vickery, S. K., Dröge, C. L., 2000, Upstream Supply Chain Management and Competitive Performance in the Automotive Supply Industry, *Journal of Business Logistics.* **21**(1).

Scott, S. G., Lane, V. R., 2000, A Stakeholder Approach to Organisational Identity, *Academy of Management Review.* **25**(1):43-62.

Scheer, L. K., Stern, L. W., 1992, The Effect of Influence Type and Performance Outcomes on Attitude toward the Influencer, *Journal of Marketing Research.* **29**:128-142.

Schlenker, B. R., 1986, Self-Identification: Toward an Integration of the Private and the Public Self, in: *Public Self and Private Self,* R. F. Baumeister, ed., New York: Springer-Verlag, New York, pp. 21-62.

Schlenker, B. R., 1985, Identity and Self Identification, in: *The Self and the Social Life,* B. R. Schlenker, ed., McGraw-Hill, New York, pp. 65-99.

Sharma, S., Durand, R. M., Gur-Arie, O., 1981, Identification and Analysis of Moderator Variables. *Journal of Marketing Research.* **28**:291-300.

Simon, H. A., 1947, *Administrative Behaviour,* Free Press, New York.

Spekman, R. E., 1988, Strategic Supplier Selection: Understanding Long-Term Buyer Relationships, *Business Horizons.* (July-August):75-81.

Steinman, C., Deshpandee, R., Farley, J. U., 2000, Beyond Market Orientation: When Customers and Suppliers Disagree, *Journal of the Academy of Marketing science.* **28**(1).

Stryker, S., Serpe, R. T., 1982, Commitment, Identity Salience and Role Behaviour: Theory and Research Example, in: *Personality, Roles and Social Behaviour,* W. Ickers, E. Knowles, eds., Springer-Verlag, New York.

Tajfel, H., 1978, *Differentiation between Social Groups*, Academic Press, London.

Tajfel, H., 1981, *Human Groups and Social Categories: Studies in Social Psychology,* Cambridge University Press, New York.

Tajfel, H., Turner, J. C., 1979,An Integrative Theory of Intergroup Conflict, in: *The Social Psychology of Intergroup Relations,* W. G. Austin, S. Worchel, eds., Brooks/Cole, Monterey, CA.

Turner, J. C., 1982, Towards a Cognitive Redefinition of the Social Group, in: *Social Identity and Inter-group Relations,* H. Tajfel, eds.,Cambridge University Press, Cambridge, pp.15-40.

Turner, J. C., 1984, Social Identification and Psychological Group Formation, in: H. Tajfel, eds., *The Social Dimension: European Developments in Social Psychology,* Vol. 2, Cambridge University Press, Cambridge, pp. 518-538.

Turner, J. C., 1985, Social Categorization and the Self-Concept: A Social Cognitive Theory of Group Behaviour, in: *Advance in Group Processes,* E. J. Lawler, ed., JAI Press, Greenwich, CT, pp. 77-122.

Tyler, T. R., 1998, The Psychology of Authority Relations, in: *Power and Influence in Organizations,* R. M. Kramer, M. A. Neale, eds., Sage Publications, Thousand Oaks, CA.

Van Maanen, J., Schein, E. H., 1979, Towards a Theory of Organizational Socialization, in: B. M. Staw, eds., *Research in Organizational Behavior,* JAI Press, Greenwich, CT, pp. 209-264.

Wood, D. J., Gray, B., 1991, Towards a Comprehensive Theory of Collaboration, *Journal of Applied Behavioural Science.* **27**(2):139-162.

Zaheer, A., Venkatraman, N., 1995, Relational Governance as an Interorganizational Strategy: An Empirical Test of the Role of Trust in Economic Exchange, *Strategic Management Journal.* **16**:373-392.

Appendix A

Organisational Identity (based on Mael and Ashforth 1992)

1. If someone criticises our customer, it feels like a personal insult.
2. If someone praises our customer, it feels like a personal compliment.
3. When we talk about our customer, we usually say we rather than they.

Customer's use of non-coercive power (based on Geyskens and Steenkamp 2000)

1. When our firm complies with this customer's suggestions, we get more favourable treatment from this customer.
2. We receive benefits or services from this customer when we follow their recommendations, but not when we disregard their recommendations.
3. If we do what this customer wants, they reward us.

Customer's use of coercive power (based on Geyskens and Steenkamp 2000)

1. This customer undermines or punishes our firm when we do not follow their guidelines and recommendations.
2. If we don't do what this customer wants, this customer provides poorer service and becomes difficult to work with.
3. If your firm rejects this customer's suggestions, we will receive harsher treatment from this customer.
4. If we don't do what this customer wants us to do, they withhold resources and/or services that are important to our firm.

Relational Success

Comparing other customer relationships we have with this customer...
1. ... a better failure rate.
2. ... a better delivery reliability.
3. ... a higher level of profits.

Financial Performance

Based on the last three years and comparing other firms...
1. ... is our sales revenue clearly greater.
2. ... is our return on total assets (ROA) clearly higher.
3. ... is our return on investment (ROI) clearly better.

Satisfaction with the collaboration (based on Jap 2001)

1. Our collaboration with the customer has been a successful one.
2. Our collaboration with the customer has more than fulfilled our expectations.
3. We are satisfied with the outcomes from this collaboration.

Commitment (based on Kumar, Scheer and Steenkamp 1995a)

1. Even if we could, we would not drop this customer because we like being associated with it.
2. We want to remain a member of the customer's network because we genuinely enjoy our relationship with it.
3. Our positive feelings towards this customer are a major reason for continuing the relationship with it.

Partner Fit (inspired by Kale, Singh and Perlmutter 2000)

There is a high similarity between us and our customer because,...

1. ... the employees are comparable.
2. ... the objectives agree with each other.
3. ... the organisational cultures fit together.
4. ... the management styles are related.

Note: All items were measured on seven-point scales, with "strongly disagree" and "strongly agree" as the anchors.

Chapter 8

Performance Measurement in Supply Chain Networks

The case of fast moving consumer goods

Dimitris Papakiriakopoulos
Athens University of Economics and Business

Abstract: In the area of Management Control Systems research efforts focus primarily on the development of performance measurement systems for a single organization. However, collaboration practices create common areas of interest among organizations. To this end, integrated performance measures are required. In a collaborative context facilitated by an IT infrastructure, organizations have the opportunity to develop a common performance measurement system. This chapter briefly presents some widely discussed theoretical issues in the area of performance measurement as well as some practical considerations. Based on case study research in the area of Fast Moving Consumer Goods, I present a concise method to realize which performance measures are available on the top of the IT infrastructure. At the same time, the chapter addresses the challenges and problems of a single performance measure, showing that the measurement method is important although sometimes complex.

Key words: Performance measurement; collaboration; store replenishment process.

1. Introduction

The design and development of performance measurement systems is part of the management control function (Simons, 1995). The field attracts the interest of various researchers and includes few concepts, methods and tools, which are increasing due to lack of an accepted and consolidated theory (Otley, 1999). Management control has the constant need to capture the efficiency and the effectiveness of a company, and performance measurement is the actual and concrete instrument to cover this need (Churchman, 1959;

Eccles, 1991). In this chapter I examine the employment of performance measurement in the context of a complex system.

Within the last years organizations tend to collaborate more and more, by establishing strong relationships with each other. In such complex settings performance is still an open issue. In the performance measurement literature most of the studies refer to a single organizational setting. Although the organizations are able to identify the need for collaboration and form a network structure, the answer of how well they collaborate is an ambiguous issue, due to the multidisciplinary set of participants, different objectives and different understandings. To this end the motive of research is coming from the fact that performance measurement systems are studied in majority within the context of a single organization, which is considered as limitation because networks are constituted by various partners who have individual needs and specific management practices for control.

This paper focuses on the development process of a performance measurement system in a collaborative context in the fast moving consumer goods industry (FMCG), utilizing advanced IT infrastructure. The fast moving consumer goods industry is characterized by the involvement of various suppliers and retailers, with hundred geographically dispread retail outlets. Each training partner maintains its own performance measurement system in isolation (Lambert, 2001; Dekker, 2004). The objective of the research is to illustrate why it is important for a network formation to develop a common performance measurement system. To this end, I also present issues related to the accuracy and reliability of the common performance measures.

In the first section I briefly present background literature of the performance measurement field, addressing the research streams, the types of performance measures and the role of the IT. The last is certainly important for my research due to the fact that most of the network formations are utilizing the supportive role of the IT. Moreover the information infrastructure is the main source for the development of performance measures. The problems of developing common performance measurement systems are addressed in the third section, where I present a detailed account of performance measurement initiatives in the FMCG industry and a case study, in order to highlight the opportunities and barriers during the development of a common performance measurement system for all the trading partners.

2. Performance measurement

Performance measurement encompasses management questions regarding what to measure, how to measure it and how these measures can help managers to design corrective actions. According to Simons (2000), systems of performance measurement involve a number of performance measures used to systematically measure the performance of the firm. In the next sections I provide a brief discussion of performance measurement systems and the basic types of performance measures as described in the wide literature on the topic.

2.1 Perspectives on performance measurement

Originally the purpose of performance measurement systems had been the auditing of the financial results of the organization, thus the majority of systems were incorporating accounting methods (Argyris, 1990; Collins, 1982). However, various researchers have argued that only the financial perspective of performance could not accurately draw the exact situation of the organization (Kaplan and Norton, 1992). Over the last decade various performance measurement frameworks have been proposed, seeking to handle the multi-disciplinary nature of the field and overcome the limited scope provided by the accounting methods (e.g. Activity Based Costing) (Anderson and Young, 1999; Krumwiede, 1998). The balanced scorecard (Kaplan and Norton, 1992), the results and determinants (Fitzgerald, 1991), the performance pyramid (McNair, 1990), EP^2M (Adams and Roberts, 1993), and the performance prism (Neely, 2002) are some examples of performance measurement frameworks including both financial and non-financial measures. Nowadays performance measurement discussion has shifted closer to the concept of performance management systems, which are the formal, information-based routines and procedures, managers use to maintain or alter patterns in organizational activities (Simons, 2000). These systems focus on conveying financial and non-financial information that influences decision making and managerial action. Taking into account how researchers are considering the issues of measuring performance, it is possible to identify three major research perspectives in the area of performance measurement.

- **Strategic-Operational:** The control function examines the alignment between operational excellence and strategic objectives (Govindarajan & Fisher, 1990; Langfield, 1997). Simons (2000), for example, argues that systems of performance measurement should assist managers in tracking the implementation of business strategy by comparing actual results against strategic goals and objectives. Although the strategic importance of performance measurement systems has been emphasized in the normative literature during the past decade (e.g. Anthony et al., 2001; Dixon et al., 1990; Kaplan and Norton, 1996; White, 1996), the performance measurement instruments can also be of operative nature. Within this perspective a number of operative uses of performance measurement have been proposed, in order to signal deviations from operational plans, to manage change, to motivate employees, as a means for communication, to allocate resources, to facilitate comparisons (benchmarking), and to determine the bonuses to be awarded (Euske, 1984; Sieger, 1992; Olian and Rynes, 1991; Daniels et al., 1994; Thor, 1991; White and Flores, 1987).

- **Organizational:** Performance measurement systems are examined as a medium to study the governance/coordination mechanism of the organization (Ouchi, 1978; Jermier, 1998). Typical issues concern the management mechanisms of the organization as well as the design/development process of such mechanisms. This powerful approach thoroughly examines the importance of human factor in the organization. Thus structural and governance artifacts are the main hooks of research. The organizational approach usually examines issues like employee satisfaction, organizational flexibility etc.
- **Accounting:** Although it is the most obvious and sometimes the most critical, it had received both great attention and criticism during the last decade (Otley, 1999). The objective of the accounting perspective is to allocate cost to certain functional areas of the organization (Kaplan, 1994). The task might seem manageable, however specific issues like cost hierarchy and cost allocation, and the desired level of cost detail, are issues that every organization needs to tackle (Cooper, 1990). A typical performance measurement system which derives from this perspective is the budgetary control (Otley, 1978).

The existence of various and sometimes contradictory perspectives can be attributed to the multidisciplinary nature of the field. This plurality reinforces the importance of the factors that affect the success of the control function. However we argue that the selection of a solid research perspective at the early stage of designing a performance measurement system is mandatory and affects the design and development method. For instance, if someone would like to build a management reward system following a strategic-operational approach, then he would probably need to rank the employees based on some specific criteria (sales or productivity measures). In the case of the organizational research approach, it is more likely to study issues related to the social ties and the power of one employee to other groups. Finally, if the research approach takes an accounting angle, then the rewards will be provided to the employees that better manage cost related issues. When there is a single control objective, different performance measurement system can be developed by changing the approach.

The development of a single performance measurement system cannot entirely fulfill the management needs of the organization. The organization needs to maintain a number of systems to track performance, depending on the purpose of the development approach (Tarr, 1995; Dixon et al., 1990). Nevertheless, measurement systems are dynamic, and the managers have to frequently revisit the objectives, methods and results in order to fit the measurement procedure in the shifting organizational planning needs (Neely et al., 1995).

2.2 Types of performance measures

Performance indicators are the main ingredients of performance management systems. Many typologies of performance indicators have been proposed, but the following two types are the most important and widely used:

- **Financial vs. non-financial indicators:** On the one hand, financial indicators are expressed in monetary terms, and act as the basis for the production of various important ratios (e.g. cost per unit). Non-financial indicators on the other hand are expressed in non currency terms. Some articles published in the area of TQM stressed the fact that financial indicators are less proactive than non-financial, and emphasized the complementarity between these types of indicators (Kueng, 2000; Jeans & Morrow, 1990). A study by Fitzgerald et al. (1992) shows that performance measurement in the UK has broadened its focus to include also non-financial measures. Other studies show that USA companies had also included non-financial indicators, while Japanese companies at the same time, had already employed non-financial measures, due to Just In Time production (Germain and Droge, 1997; Choi and Liker, 1995; Daniel and Reitsperger, 1991). A representative measurement system of this category is the Balanced Scorecard. According to the creators of Balanced Scorecard, a balanced view provides a more illustrative picture of the organization's performance (Kaplan and Norton, 1992).
- **Lagging vs. leading indicators:** Anthony et al. (2001) and Kaplan and Norton (1995) make a distinction between 'outcome' and 'driver' measures. Thus, outcome (lagging) measures indicate the result of a decision making/strategy (e.g. increased market share) and inform management what has happened. By contrast, leading indicators (e.g. order cycle time) show the progress of key areas of business. Outcome measures could indicate only the final result, whereas driver measures might be used at a lower level and indicate the cumulative evolution that will ultimately affect the outcome. Representative accounting methods of this category are the Economic Value Adding and Activity-Based-Costing.

In general the distinction between financial and non-financial indicators is well established, but this is not the case of the leading and lagging indicators. According to Dutta (1999), a performance indicator might be leading in some cases, and lagging in other cases, concluding that this notion is relative and case dependent. To this end, these types of performance indicators are useful in order to better organize the design of the performance measurement system through the incorporation of different types of measures in a single performance measurement system.

Apart from the categories of indicators, and the selection of the appropriate performance measurement framework, the importance of the development method must be noted. Normally the development of a performance measurement system requires the identification of the critical activities, establishment of performance indicators and performance targets, data (measures) collection, analysis of the actual performance and comparison with the target measures, communication of the results etc (Zairi, 1994; Kennerley and Neely, 2000; Bourne et al., 2000). The completion of each task might require specific techniques (e.g. utilization of heuristic methods, observation, market research etc), which necessitates the involvement of several people with different skills and competences. However the result of a performance measurement system might not always be the desired one. For example if the inventory levels of a supplier are increasing unexpectedly then managers in all probability will think that the marketing function of the firm has a problem because sales have decreased. This is translated in performance measurement terms as the re-examination of the partners' satisfaction, the competitive forces and forecasting model (performance measures). This straightforward approach is based on the weak assumption that there is a causal relationship between the sales (results) and the procedure (marketing actions), which in turn might disorient the whole effort of measuring performance in the firm. Issues like the quality of the materials, behavioural issues of the employees and others might be the cause of decreased sales volume.

This example raises two important questions which will be further discussed in the next sections. The first question is what to measure, and the second is how to measure it. Both of these questions are applicable when developing a measurement system, whether it is for a single organization or a collaborative working context. Although there isn't a totally acceptable recipe for these questions, we can utilize a few practical considerations. We argue that these considerations are primarily important during the design and development phases of a performance measurement system.

2.3 The role of information technology in performance measurement

The wide body of literature has long recognized the essential role of information as the corner stone of performance measurement systems (Willcocks and Lester, 1999). Information technologies could turn in operational mode a performance measurement system. Currently, information technologies help to model business processes and identify critical activities, collect data and process the result. The technological support could be expressed in a manifold manner utilizing different tools. In more detail the existing technologies are:

- **Data repositories and networks:** Information systems store transactional data (sales, invoices, orders etc), that can be further exploited for performance measurement purposes. From data repositories is easy to extract the required information and produce a user-friendly form (e.g. using OLAP technologies). In addition, data repositories could store customer's feedbacks and through appropriate procedures provide the measurement results (e.g. collect complains from a call-center or web). A good example of turning transactional data into performance measures and thus to valuable management information is coming from the field of the ERP implementation projects, where all the available data are stored in a central repository and by adding a performance measurement module, the organization is able to monitor various performance indicators in real time (e.g. inventory levels, product sales etc). In general data repositories and data communication networks are important enablers for the development of performance measurement systems.
- **Process development software/Simulation:** Business process models are the communication basis for all the persons involved in most of the phases of performance measurement. The quality of modeling is subject to the next guidelines of modeling: correctness, clarity, relevance, comparability, economic efficiency and systematic design (Becker et al., 1995). Software tools (e.g. ARIS) enable the process modeling in accordance to the guidelines. Apart from modeling business processes, some software tools provide simulation functionality. Simulation can serve as an adequate descriptive and experimental instrument for the design of complex measurement systems.

Although briefly presented, information technology has a significant role in the development of performance measurement systems. Moreover, information and communication technologies (e.g. Web, XML etc) support the collaborative relationships between trading partners. Collaboration implies a durable relationship and a strong commitment to a common goal (Ring and Van de Ven, 1992; Chiu, 2002). From a managerial perspective collaboration is the set of activities and the predetermined communication method used in order to archive a common goal[18]. Various scholars have been extensively examining collaboration implications (Cravens and Piercy, 1994; Jarillo, 1988; Powell, 1990). Although the focal point of these studies is different, most of them tend to agree on the origin of the factors forming the collaboration (market related factors, technological developments etc.) (Almassy and Baatz, 1992; Vyas et al., 1995; Nohria et al., 1991; Gulati, 1999). Lately Austin (2000) has moved beyond the traditional thinking of collaboration, and addressed the collaboration success between nonprofit organizations and businesses, stressing the importance of collaboration without translating the collaboration in monetary terms. To this end, considerable attention has been devoted to determine the advantages and limitations of strategic partnerships (e.g. selection of a suitable partner, and the development of collaboration plans), and it is surprising that far less attention has been placed on studying the performance of a collaboration (Dekker, 2004). A major reason for the high failure rate of alliances is that few have developed a formal performance measurement system, while the reliability of the selected performance indicators do not safeguard their existence in the long run, due to the incorporation of financial indicators only (Cravens et al., 2000).

3. The case of collaborative replenishment process in the grocery retail sector

The selection of a case study is recommended in this research in order to illustrate the problems emerging during the development of performance measurement systems. In more detail, the selected case includes many major product suppliers (currently offering more than 4.000 different products) and a retail chain which has four central warehouses and 200 geographically disperse retail stores. The product suppliers and the retail stores are collaborating through an IT infrastructure in a daily base in order to effectively accomplish the product replenishment business process. We argue that the supply chain examined in this case constitutes a network, due to the involvement of different actors, executing various activities and the existence of a high degree of interdependence (Holmberg, 2000).

---

[18] From a marketing and strategic perspective collaboration is used synonymously with the term strategic alliance (Biemans and Brand, 1995).

A strategic - operational perspective was followed for the design of a new performance measurement system. This approach allows focusing at the level of the collaborative replenishment business process, which is rather new in the working practice of the trading partners.

Before the mediation of the collaborative platform both suppliers and retail chain were managing their individual isolated performance measurement systems. Depending on several factors, each Performance Measurement System was serving different needs. For instance some suppliers were using a performance measurement system in order to provide rewards to the salesmen, while other suppliers were using their own PMS as a negotiation base with the suppliers. Moreover the retail chain was using various individual islands of performance measurement systems. The retail chain had a measurement system for every central warehouse in order to track the inventory levels, and at the same time other performance measurement systems were developed in order to evaluate the effectiveness and efficiency of the retail stores.

The essential characteristic of the business model of the case is the existence of a collaboration platform. This platform is used to facilitate the store ordering replenishment process, by concentrating the suppliers, the central warehouses and the retail stores. Suppliers and retailers were utilizing their individual Performance Measurement Systems (marked in the next picture as PMS). Our work was to develop a totally new PMS utilizing the information sources exchanged though the collaboration platform in order to gather more reliable and accurate performance measure than the existent. The collaboration platform has the capabilities to host the new performance measurement system because it aggregates detailed information, regarding the transactions between suppliers and the retail chain. To this end, the New PMS will not replace the existing systems but it will extend the control capabilities of the collaborating organizations delivering almost real time valuable information.

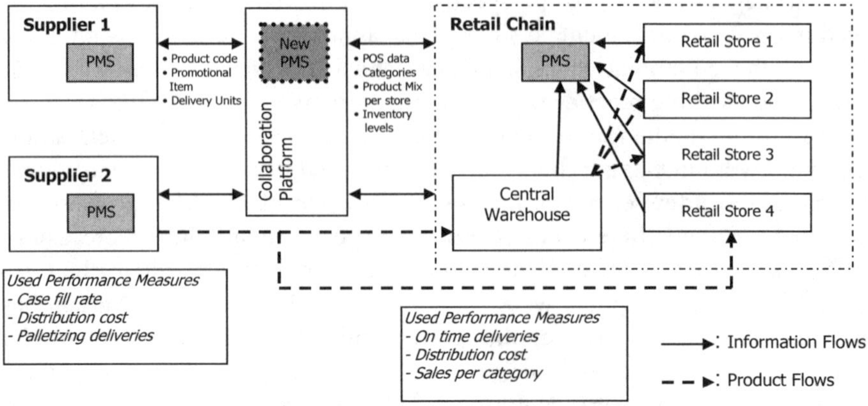

Figure 1. The structural arrangement of the case

Figure 1 depicts that the existing Performance Measurement Systems of the organizations are currently isolated. Moreover, some indicative examples of existing performance measures used by the suppliers and the retail-chain are listed. A supplier organization is monitoring the case fill rate, which addresses issues regarding the effectiveness of the ordering business process. Although the retail chain is heavily involved in the ordering process, managers do not address the issue of inbound logistics, because it is rather complicated, since a supplier can deliver products either to the central warehouse or directly to the retail store. In the case that a performance measure is maintained only from one organization within a bilateral relationship, then the only concern is whether the collaboration platform has the required information to support it. However there are cases, where a performance measure is maintained by all the organization in the supply chain network. The distribution cost is a performance measure that exists in all the PMS of the organizations of the supply chain network. Each organization calculates the distribution cost following a different approach (measurement method), which is a barrier to the new PMS, because the results are not comparable. Thus it is necessary that all the players agree regarding the measurement method of the distribution cost. Finally the new PMS is able to develop totally new performance measures that have not been used extensively used. For example the development of a measure for addressing the Out-Of-Shelf situations for all retail stores at a daily base is innovative and the players of the supply chain network have different motives for having this information. The supplier organization would like to know the Out-Of-Shelf situations for its own products because it could perceive more clearly the presence it has in the retail stores. The retail chain would exploit this information in order to support consumer loyalty, because the existence of the right product, at the right place, the right time is vital for retail operations.

To this end, the development of the new PMS is shaped by the investigation of two different questions. The first is the identification of the appropriate performance measures that investigate the efficiency and the effectiveness of the collaborative replenishment process. This question initiates the discussion regarding what is important to measure and how the performance measures could help the managers of the supply chain network to make the right decisions and design corrective actions. Assuming that the managers decided to identify what is important to measure, the next question is how to measure it. The measurement method is a crucial part of every management control system and several criteria had been proposed (e.g. flexibility, reliability, utilization, ease to understand, accuracy etc.). For the purpose of our study we concentrated our attention mainly on the reliability and the accuracy attributes of the measures. All the measures are assumed to be understandable due to the fact that the managers of the supply chain network proposed them. Moreover all the performance measures would be offered at a daily base to all the trading partners. Having an accurate, reliable and easy to use measure, we assumed that the managers would utilize it, thus the adoption of the new collaborative PMS would be subject to other issues (e.g. ethical, commitment of the managers, trust between the partners).

3.1 Industry characteristics and performance measurement initiatives

Lean supply chain programmes, like Efficient Consumer Response (ECR), which has revolutionized the grocery business, are built on collaboration among companies, replacing the traditional competitive relationships (Joint industry ECR project, 1994). The influence of these innovative practices combined with technical advancements underlines the urgency to reconsider which management approaches would be the most effective in this new reality. The key roles that constitute a supply chain are suppliers, manufacturers, distributors, wholesalers, retailers and consumers. Depending on the level of analysis, it is possible that one company assumes multiple roles.

Apart from the roles of the industry, various practices like Vendor Management Inventory (VMI), Continuous Replenishment Product (CRP), Just-In-Time (JIT) etc. have already increased the effectiveness of distribution channel, inventory control, and production scheduling. Furthermore, technological artifacts have made supply chain management within the grocery industry even more successful. Technical systems like Electronic Data Interchange (EDI), Computer-Assisted Ordering (CAO), and Automatic Replenishment Program (ARP) illustrate a technological mature industry, utilizing innovative information infrastructures. Speakman et al. (1998) argue that over the twenty last years relationships between the players of supply chains has shifted from fierce competition to collaboration. Since the key enablers of collaboration are trust and commitment it is obvious that information sharing and joint planning activities are critical for the successful operation of the supply chain. For example, Seven-Eleven-Japan shares information (e.g. detailed product sales, product market share etc) with various suppliers in order to determine store inventory levels and optimal shelf space and allow collaborating partners to develop more accurate production plans, design more efficient promotional plans etc.

Typical examples of performance measurement efforts in the grocery retail sectors are the Global ECR Scorecard and the SCOR model. The Global ECR Scorecard aims to assess how well the trading partners are collaborating in the total supply chain. It focuses on the supplier-retailer relationships and provides all the required tools to the trading partners in order to realize the problems of their relationships. A more complicated model is SCOR, which helps companies to address supply chain issues, measure performance and identify performance improvement objectives. SCOR includes all the supply-chain metrics, the formula associated with the metrics and a reference to best practices and their associated technology (Stewart, 1997). Both of these efforts have not been adopted by the trading partners in our case. Most of the organizations involved within the industry have developed their individual performance measurement systems, which eventually formed many performance measurement islands, each one carrying an isolated organizational model. Thus, we argue that in order to establish a sound basis for measuring the performance, a common performance measurement framework is required. Since it is not possible to develop a one-fits-all framework, we exploited an alternative option, which was to enroll the trading partners (suppliers and retailers) to a common collaboration territory. In the next section a brief description of a fast moving collaboration case is provided, which was the common reference point for our research.

3.2 R-L case setting

R-L acts as an intermediary between supermarkets and their suppliers, supporting their business transactions and exchange of information via its B2B electronic collaboration infrastructure. The company focuses on the improvement of the different stages in the supply chain from suppliers to end-consumers through the use of advanced web-technology and new logistics models. R-L innovations include a collaborative store-ordering model supported by the daily exchange of point-of-sale data between retailer and manufacturer.

According to ECR, numerous inefficiencies exist in the collaboration with trading partners. The suppliers have reported inefficiencies regarding the high inventory levels, high out of stock situations, lack of visibility along the supply chain, while retailers identified problems regarding the forecast accuracy, the shelf availability, rush orders etc. (Joint Industry ECR Project, 1994). From the presented inefficiencies in the supplier's side, it is worth mentioning the problem of high out-of-stock situations; the high returns rate and of course the general long lead times. Accordingly, in the retailers side we should stress the low forecast accuracy, the low on-shelf availability and generally the fact that the replenishment it is not consumer based.

Utilizing principles of Collaborative Planning Forecasting and Replenishment (CPFR), a retailer and consumer goods firm (manufacturer) can work together to jointly create a single, combined promotion calendar in advance of the selling period which could subsequently be up-dated on a real-time basis over the Web (Holmstrom et al., 2002). The retailer can also provide point-of-sale (POS) data, longer-term promotional plans, prescribed inventory levels, etc. for the consumer goods trading partner. Both firms can create sales and order forecasts. The retailer can then electronically transmit the retail forecast to the manufacturer. A collaborative system can be used to compare that forecast to the manufacturer's own forecast. Discrepancies or exceptions can be identified and appropriate managers advised. Working together, the "team" can decide on one, i.e. collaborative, forecast extending across the supply chain.

Both suppliers and retailers are interested in having a common and accurate view of the performance in order to minimize the negotiation efforts. The daily interaction between suppliers and the retailers is based on the individual impression that every trading partner holds regarding the efficiency and the effectiveness of the replenishment process. In the daily agenda of collaboration, suppliers and retailers need to come up with agreements regarding what to order, how much to order, from where to order, where to store, which products should be included in the product mix of the stores, which products to promote at which store etc.

The new business process is about trading partners sharing information and collaborating on a daily basis in order to support the store replenishment process. This model brings together over the Web the expert opinion of the product suppliers and the unique knowledge of the store managers with the ultimate objective to eliminate out-of-shelf situations, while maintaining optimum levels of stock throughout the supply chain. It is a new collaborative practice that supports the daily store-replenishment process, based on the online-sharing of critical information such as: sales data (POS), store assortments, stock-level in the store, promotion activities, out-of-shelf alerts, etc. This process is supported an IT collaborative platform dedicated in the enablement of daily online sharing of all the required information, the sales forecasting and order generation, the online collaboration of the trading partners, and finally the order exchange and status tracking.

From a performance measurement perspective, the existence of a collaboration platform is a crucial precondition for designing and developing a new common performance measurement system. Since suppliers and retailers have already implemented isolated performance measurement systems for various purposes (e.g. a budgetary control system), it is preferable to develop a totally new measurement system, rather than combine performance measures from every single organization. To this end the new performance measurement system will address only the collaborative replenishment process and will coexist with the rest of performance systems. However there is the possibility that the new performance measures will introduce some complexity issues. Cases where a new performance measure is already monitored by few suppliers (so it is not new for all the trading partners), or a new performance measure is important for some (but not all), force us to rethink that a new performance measurement is a concept highly dependent on contextual factor. Thus, it should be carefully treated. The resolution of such problems was based on the joint design and development of the "new" performance measurement system, focusing only at the area of product replenishment business processes.

3.3 Deciding for proposed measures

The R-L collaborative network early realized the opportunity to exploit transactional data and build a comprehensive performance measurement system, utilizing the capabilities of IT. This requirement was partially covered from a custom reporting application (based on OLAP technology). Although the provided reports met the expectations of the suppliers and of the retail chain, further improvements and innovation were required in the performance measurement, because the incorporated measures met in an isolated way the management needs of the suppliers or the retailer and could not evaluate the efficiency and effectiveness of the collaborative business process.

In order to decide what could be measured, we started from reviewing the relative literature and practitioners handbooks and made a long list of candidate performance indicators (Schneiderman, 1996; Gunasekaran, 2004; Lambert and Cooper, 2000; Gunasekaran et al., 2001; Van Hoek, 1998; Beamon and Ware, 1998; Accenture, 2002) Additionally, attention has been paid to other CPFR cases within the retail industry, because the specific case follows the principals of this initiative (Seifert, 2002). The reduction of the list has been done on the basis of the applicability of the measures to the case and the requirement that each measure is important both to supplier and retailer.

Having available information like Points Of Sales (POS) data, store assortment and promotional activities, estimations of the inventory level, suggestive order from supplier etc., we concluded that few of the performance indicators could be implemented at the top of the collaboration platform. The existing data was also a constraint in the design of the new measurement system, since they implicitly determined what it could be measured.

The importance of each measure has been determined through expert opinion, where various managers from suppliers and the retail company had been interviewed. It is worth mentioning that the suppliers and retailers suggested evaluating the whole performance system during a pilot testing, rather than asking for the importance of each measure, because the answers would be biased to the specific needs of each manager. As a result, we built a set of specific performance indicators which were acceptable by suppliers and retailers. The nature of all performance indicators was non-financial while we had lagging and leading indicators. The next table illustrates some of the proposed performance measures that the trading partners wanted to be developed.

Table 1. Indicative performance measures for the R-L collaborative network

Performance measure	**Description**
Sales Forecast Accuracy	It is a non-financial, leading indicator. It describes the ratio between the forecasted numbers of sales divided by the actual sales for a specific product. If the measure is close to 1, then the forecast ability is considered as high. This measure is considered to be important for promotional and seasonal items
Perfect orders	It is a non-financial, lagging indicator and expresses the operational effectiveness of logistics function. It is the ratio between the number of perfect orders delivered (a perfect order meets the requested product, quantity and time having the necessary invoices) divided by the number of delivered orders. In the case only the products delivered by the central warehouse of the retail chain are included
Inventory Level at the store	It is a non-financial, leading (for retailer) indicator. It shows the availability of the product in the store
Out-Of-Shelf	It is a non-financial, both leading (for retailer) and lagging (for supplier) indicator. It expresses the situation where a product is not at the shelf, although it has to be. It is calculated per store

The Sales Forecast Accuracy expresses the differences between the actual sales of a product and what has been estimated to sale. Usually it is expressed in terms of the index

$$SFA = \frac{actual\ sales}{forecasted\ sales}.$$

Currently the SFA measure is calculated both by suppliers and the retailer. Since the issue of forecasting is rather complex, the measures gained differ between the trading partners, which is a cause for negotiations. In the context of the R-L case such fluctuations are expected to be minimized because of the employment of the CPFR practice.

The second measure concerns the logistics operations. The Perfect Orders Measure expresses the ability of the supply chain to deliver to the retail store an order that is complete, accurate, on time, and in perfect condition. The measure is calculated using the following formula:

$$PO = \frac{\#\ of\ perfect\ orders}{\#\ of\ total\ orders}$$

As the supplier and retail chain have to their disposal trucks delivering products to the store, then it is interesting to investigate how well these logistic networks operate. The recent adoption of Cross Docking increases the importance of the PO performance measure and the logistic and inventory managers of the collaborative networks stressed the significance.

Related to the Perfect Order Measure is the *Inventory Level at the Store* (ILS). The later depicts the inventory level for each product. Generally speaking the store manager's objective is to maintain low inventory levels, without losing sales from stock out situations (zero inventory). Having a precise picture of the inventory, store managers would be able to place orders timely, and avoid stock out situations. The inventory levels are generally calculated using the following formula

$$ILS = 1 - \frac{\#\ of\ sold\ items}{\#\ of\ received\ items},$$

which describes the percentage of the remaining unsold products. Although the ILS formula does not provide an accurate view of the inventories, it is used in order to illustrate that the determination of the inventory level is a tradeoff between the number of ordered products and the demand.

The last selected measure is the Out-Of-Shelf (OOS), which describes the shelf availability at the store level. Within the retail industry the existence of the product at the shelf is crucial and refers to the last 50 yards problem, where the product might exists in the store, but not at the right place (e.g. the shelf is empty, but few units of the products exist in the backroom of the store). The Out of Shelf rate is calculated based on the

$$OOS = \frac{\#\ products\ not\ on\ the\ shelf}{\#\ products\ in\ store\ mix}.$$

The product availability is an issue for investigation by both for suppliers and the retailer. The suppliers need to know reliably which stores distributes their products, while on the retailer side the measure of OOS would allow the investigation of the effectiveness of the shelf replenishment process.

For the purpose of this study, we will provide details regarding the measurement methods for the Inventory Level at the store (ILS) and of the Out-of-shelf (OOS). The Inventory Level at the Store was selected to show differences between making a performance measurement system at a single firm level and at a network level. The Out-Of-Shelf measure demonstrates the complexity of developing a performance measurement.

3.4 Developing the inventory level at the store measure

The identification of the Inventory Levels at the store is related with Shelf Availability. Usually the inventory levels are examined at the central warehouse, but for this study the interest shifted at the store level. If a retail store has enough quantity stored in the backroom in order to face the future consumer demand, at least within the lead time of replenishment cycle, then the shop is unlike to come to the predicament of stock out. Since it is unrealistic to count the inventory level at the end of the day for all the products, a more "sophisticated" approach is required. Some researches suggest the management of inventory levels could be supported through the information acquired by calculating the stock levels through the difference between the number of ordered products and the number of items sold within a period, which in most of the cases is not a reliable measure. According to Kang and Gershwin (2003) it is very difficult to maintain perfect inventory records at the store level, which is further translated as an obstacle to achieve higher performance. The causes of the inventory inaccuracy discussed by Kang and Gershwin (2003) are the stock loss, transaction error, inaccessible inventory, and incorrect product identification.

The inventory inaccuracy problem does not allow the development of an accurate inventory management system into a full extent, where all the products would be monitored for each store. However it is interesting to examine at which number of products (coverage) such system would work, in the context of the retailer (single firm level). Principally the inventory levels are determined by comparing the total sales (S) from the total ordered quantity (Q) for a specific product. Nevertheless the ordered quantity conditionally approximates the sales volumes.

1. Some products are delivered directly from the supplier to the store (Direct Store Delivery Products – DSD) (e.g. fresh food, milk) and consequently the retailer cannot have an accurate view of the inventory for these SKUs (Store Keeping Units), due to the fact that the orders are placed directly from the retail stores to the supplier. Thus the required information is placed on the supplier information infrastructure and not in the internal replenishment system of the retailer.
2. The salesman (supplier side) in order to convince the store manager to include a new product in the product assortment offers a small quantity of a product. This quantity is considered as sample order and it is not recorded at the retailer side. In case the store manager agrees to include this product into the store's assortment, the total sales would be somewhat higher than the total ordered quantity. Consequently for the particular product it would not be easy to determine the exact level of inventory
3. The stores are not isolated and the transfer of small volumes of products between neighboring stores is acceptable by the retail chain. This practice obviously amplifies the inventory inaccuracy problem.
4. Finally damages of the products, returns, thefts or invoicing discrepancies are factors that affect the accuracy and reliability of the estimated inventory levels.

For the purpose of out study, we examined the number of products that a retail chain could accurately estimate their inventory levels. In doing so, we selected nine representative stores and thoroughly examined the consistency between sales and orders for all the products for a five-month period. Through the analysis we classify all the products under three major categories

- The first category is called CWH (Central Warehouse) indicating that this product is delivered in majority through the central warehouse. In the CWH case the total sales (S) of the product are less than the ordered quantity (Q).
- The second category is labeled as DSD (Direct Store Delivery), which prompts that the product is delivered directly from the supplier to the store. In this case, the product appears to be sold for a long time but there are no orders stored in the information infrastructure (Q=0).

- Last but not least are the products that are not meeting one of the above classes. The UNK (Unknown) category includes all the products that are sold within a five-month period but the order levels for the specific products could not support the observed sales velocity. This class demonstrates the fluctuations and inconsistencies of store replenishment process and mainly addresses the reasons 2-4 as mentioned above as well as the causes of inventory inaccuracies proposed by Kang & Gershwin (2003).

The next figure illustrates the distribution between the CWH, DSD and UNK classes of products in the selected stores. The green bar expresses the number of products delivered by the central warehouse, and with the red bar we show how many products are delivered by the supplier. Finally with the yellow colour, we indicate the number of products that belong to the UNK class. All the aforementioned classes are calculated for the sample stores. On the one hand Store1 is the largest store, offering over 4.000 different products, while on the other hand the smallest store (Store9) merchandises approximately 1300 different products. As figure 2 presents, most of the products (approximately 48%) are coming from the central warehouse, regardless the store size. This is an expected result, because the ordering cost from the central warehouse is lower compared with the ordering cost from the direct delivery, reflecting the fact that store managers prefer to order from the central warehouse, in order to minimize cost elements.

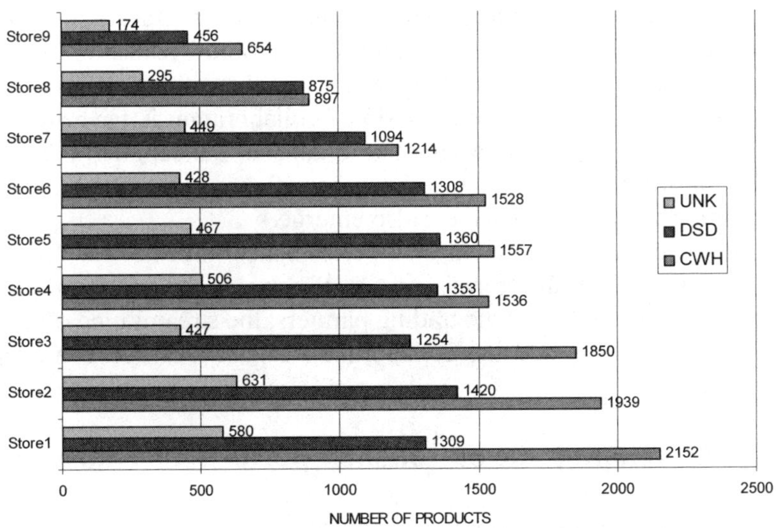

Figure 2. Distribution of products across the three classes

The number of products delivered directly to the store varies between 35%-40%, depending on the store size. Smaller and medium size stores, tend to replenish more frequently products directly from the supplier due to limited store space, while the large stores which have considerable larger backroom facilities have the capability to maintain safety stocks, thus reduce direct interaction with the supplier directly. In addition 10% (mainly fresh foods, milk) of the DSD products are delivered only by the supplier to the store, thus this is the lowest threshold of the DSD products. The rest of the products (that are neither CWH nor DSD) were classified under the UNK label. In average, this class represents the 14% of products. Recall for this class of products that there is not a specific method to accurately estimate the inventory levels, because it reflects the inconsistencies both of the information infrastructure and the replenishment process.

At this point we draw two alternative scenarios. According to the first scenario, the retail chain individually exploits its information infrastructure in order to develop the performance indicator for monitoring the inventory levels at the store. As presented above, the measure would be applicable only for half of the products. The existence of high levels of UNK products would decrease the reliability (45% estimated) of the indicator, due to noisy data. The low reliability number is considered by experts as the main barrier for the development of such a measure.

According to the second scenario, the retail chain collaborates with multiple suppliers, following the CPFR practice. In this scenario the inventory levels are calculated based on the various information sources shared by the retailer and its suppliers. In this scenario it is possible to track almost 90% of the products (while the rest 10% cannot be captured because of exceptions due to promotional and seasonal products) and the estimated reliability approximates 80%. Although the scenario of collaboration is far better, issues like trust between suppliers and retailer, quality of the supplier's data, compatibility of different infrastructures, number of suppliers that are interesting at developing such an approach etc also emerge.

To this end the development of a performance indicator for monitoring the inventory levels at the store is a tradeoff between the quality of the sales and orders data provided by the trading partners, the streamlining of the store replenishment process and the collaboration capabilities between suppliers and retailer.

3.5 Developing the out-of-shelf performance measure

Out-of-shelf (OOS) refers to the problem that a product is not on the shelf for customers to pick-up. According to Gruen et al. (2002) the OOS rate is close to 8.3 percent worldwide, which is considered as high, while an accepted level (determined by suppliers and retailers) is close to 2 percent. Similar results, regarding the severity of the problem are reported by Roland Burger (2002). Moreover it has been found that the OOS rates of promoted items are much higher, which consequently affects the promotional effectiveness measure (Gruen et al., 2002). In general, retailers and suppliers are looking for a measurement method to determine the OOS rates and undertake corrective actions. Suppliers are looking for this information because it is an index regarding the presence of their products in the stores, while the retailer wants to provide the right product at the right place for consumers.

The current practice for measuring the OOS is based on surveys/physical auditing. This means that employees need to frequently visit the store's shelf and count the OOS situations. However the high cost of measuring the shelf availability and the dynamically changing states of the shelves are the major drawbacks for approximating the problem. The OOS problem is examined through two major perspectives. The first is a consumer oriented perspective, coming from the marketing literature, which mainly addresses the reaction of consumer when he/she cannot find a product on the shelf. This approach takes into consideration consumer loyalty and underlines the importance of the problem, since supply chains tend to be consumer driven. The second approach focuses on the management of the business operations. Activities like category management, inventory management and supply chain management are combined to settle effectively the problem of OOS situations. Within the management approach various models exist, dealing with the stock-out problem, but do not fully address the OOS. In principal, the term stock-out is used in the literature to describe the situations where the product does not exist in the store, and consequently does not exist in the shelf either.

Several researchers have developed models addressing mainly the issue of stock-out under certain circumstances, but the out-of-shelf problem has not been examined in detail. An approximation measurement method for the OOS situations is referred as the European OOS Index (EOI), so there is the option either to employ the EOI or to develop a new measurement method for the collaborative platform. The EOI is utilized only for products having sales velocity over 10 items per day and sales volatility ($\mu_{i,s}/\sigma_{i,s}$, for the i-product at s-store) lower that 1. a product is characterized as OOS if it satisfies the precondition of sales velocity and sales volatility and additionally the day into consideration sold zero items.

The quantification method of the EOI functions as a precondition for the OOS situations. In order to examine the measure characteristics of the EOI, we conducted an experiment. In more detail, we selected 9 representative retail stores and using a stratified clustering technique, we developed clusters having as stratification variables the sales velocity and the sales volatility. In addition, we added one isolated cluster including only the promotional items.

From each cluster we randomly selected 11 products that had been monitored for one week by inspecting the product shelf availability at each store. The collection of such dataset permitted us to perform several tests regarding the "behavior" of the EOI. We developed a software component for calculating all the required statistical measures and validated the EOI against the results of the physical survey. Few basic findings follow:

- The precondition of the EOI is supported only by 5% of products, which are the fast-moving goods. These items belong to important categories which cover almost 22%-36% of total sales per store.
- The EOI captures only the total OOS situations. The partial OOS (means that during the day the self was empty) cannot be identified.
- The EOI captured all the total OOS cases for the whole reporting period, which means it is 100 percent accurate. However the results of the EOI contained also products that were characterized as OOS, but according to the physical survey they had been on the shelf. The noise level that EOI introduces in the result set is up to 25 percent, which means that from the results of the algorithm only 75 percent is definitely an OOS situation.
- The EOI is sensitive to seasonality. In more detail products introduced in the store to cover the high seasonal demand would probably support the precondition of the EOI after the seasonal period as well. The utilization of exponential smoothing or other techniques that removes the seasonal component did not produce satisfactory results.

The calculation of sales volatility and sales velocity for each day of the week (e.g. calculating six different $\mu_{i,s}/\sigma_{i,s}$, one for each day) decreases the noise of the index. This happens because the sales, the daily average and the daily standard deviation are considerable different between the days (e.g. the sales on Saturdays are significantly different than on Tuesdays for a wide variety of products).

To this end, we consider that the employment of the EOI is satisfactory for the fast moving items, but there are important limitations. The EOI does not address about 95% of the store products, so it is of limited usage. This fact motivated us to develop of a new measurement method. The objective of the new method is to extend the EOI to slow moving products, working independently from the sales volatility and sales volume. Including parameters like past orders, the time interval between non-zero sales, the estimation of the inventory levels etc., we move towards the deployment of a new index to identify the OOS situations which do not request a physical audit.

4. Conclusions

The development of a performance measurement system in a collaborative context has been discussed in this paper. Although organizations in supply chain networks have the permanent need to measure performance, performance measurement systems are usually isolated. Related studies are fragmented by the fact that they examine the needs of a single organization, which is too restricting for the development of a common performance measurement system within a network context. The raise of collaborative supply chain networks triggered a set on strategic, organization or market related issues. However the improvement efforts require the existence of a common performance measurement system that minimizes negotiations between the trading partners and can act as an arbitrary instrument of control. Every organization participating in a network formation has a view of efficiency and effectiveness for the narrow boundaries of the single firm, but the efficiency and effectiveness of the whole supply chain network cannot be derived through the existing isolated performance measurement systems.

The supply chain networks represent a mature network formation with open issues regarding measuring performance. Suppliers and retailers can determine what to measure, but the available information infrastructure cannot support this management need. As presented with the ILS measure, it is preferable to develop ILS measure at a network context and avoid the discrepancies of the single firm level. Nevertheless this option requires additional efforts from all the trading partners. The study of the OOS measure raised issues regarding the method of measuring. The proposed measure of EOI is not satisfactory within a real business environment and the adoption of such a measure requires resources from all trading partners. In conclusion the development of a common performance measurement system is not magically derived from the existing measurement systems of the trading partners, because the management control functions in network formations is rather complicated and the needs of the whole network differ from the individual needs of the single firms.

References

Antony, R., Govindarajan, V., 2001, *Management Control Systems,* 10th Edition, McGraw-Hill Irwin, New York.

Accenture, 2002, *European CPFR Insights.* ECR Europe Publications. http://www.ecrnet.org.

Almassy, E., and Baatz, B., 1992, Strategic Alliances: 455 electronic executives say rugged individualism is fading, *Electronic Business.* March:38-42.

Anderson, S., and Young, M., 1999, The impact of contextual and process factors on the evaluation of activity-based costing systems, *Accounting Organizations and Society.* **24**(7):525-559.

Argyris, C., 1990, The dilemma of implementing controls: The case of managerial accounting, *Accounting, Organizations and Society.* **15**(6):503-511.

Austin, J., 2000, *The collaboration challenge,* Jossey-Bass Publishers, San Francisco.

Beamon, B., and Ware, T., 1998, A process quality model for the analysis, improvement and control of supply chain systems, *Logistics Information Management.* **11**(2):105-113.

Becker, J., Rosemann, M., and Schuette, R., 1995, Guidelines of good modeling, *Wirtschaftsinformatik.* **37**(4):435–445.

Biemans, W., and Brand, M., 1995, Reverse Marketing: a synergy of purchasing and relationship marketing, *International Journal of Purchasing and Materials Management.* 31(3):29-37

Bititci, U., Turner, T, and Begemann, C., 2000, Dynamics of performance measurement systems, *International Journal of Operations and Productions Management.* **20**(6):692-704.

Bourne, M., Mills, J., Wilcox, M., Neely, A., and Platts, K., 2000, Designing, implementing and updating performance measurement systems, *International Journal of Operations & Production Management.* **20**(7):754 –771.

Burke, M., Rupinski, M., Dunlap, W., and Davison, H., 1996, Do situational variables act as substantive causes of relationships between individual differences variables? Two large-scale tests of 'common cause' models, *Personnel Psychology.* **49**(3):573-598.

Chiu, M.-L., 2002, An organizational view of design communication in design collaboration, *Design Studies.* **23**(2):187-210.

Choi, T., and Liker, J., 1995, Bring Japanese continuous improvement approaches to U.S. manufacturing: The roles of process orientation and communications, *Decision Sciences.* **26**(5):589-620.

Churchman, W., 1959, Why measure, in: W. Churchman, and P. Ratoosh, eds., *Measurement: Definition and Theories,* John Wiley & Sons, New York.

Collins, F., 1982, Managerial accounting systems and organizational control: A role perspective. *Accounting, Organizations and Society.* **7**(2):107-122.

Cooper, R., 1990, Implementing an activity-based cost system, *Journal of Cost Management.* **4**(1):69-78.

Cravens, D., and Piercy, N., 1994, Relationship marketing and collaborative networks in service organizations, *International Journal of Service Industry Management.* **5**(3):39-53.

Cravens, K., Piercy, N., and Cravens, D., 2000, Assessing the performance of strategic alliances: Matching metrics to strategies, *European Management Journal.* **18**(5).529-541.

Daniel, S., and Reitsperger,W., 1991, Linking quality strategy with management control systems: empirical evidence from Japanese industry, *Accounting, Organizations and Society.* **16**(7):601-618.

Daniels, C., and Rosen, A., 1994, *Performance Management: Improving Quality and Productivity through Positive Reinforcement,* 4th ed., Performance Management Publications, Tucker, GA.

Dekker, H., 2004, Control of inter-organizational relationships: evidence on appropriation concerns and coordination requirements, *Accounting, Organizations and Society.* **29**(1).27-49.

Dixon, J., Nanni, A., and Vollman, T., 1990, *The New Performance Challenge - Measuring Operations for World-Class Competition,* Irwin, Homewood, IL.

Dutta, S., and Manzoni, J., 1999, *Process Re-engineering, organizational change and performance improvement,* McGraw-Hill.

Eccles, J., 1991, The performance management manifesto, *Harvard Business Review.* **69**(1):131-137.

Euske, J., 1984, *Management Control: Planning, Control, Measurement, and Evaluation,* Addison-Wesley, Reading, MA.

Germain, R., and Dröge, C., 1997, Effect of Just-In-Time Purchasing Relationships on Organizational Design, Purchasing Department Configuration, and Firm Performance, *Industrial Marketing Management.* **26**(2):115-125.

Govindarajan, V., and Fisher, J., 1990, Strategy, control systems and resource sharing: effects on business-unit performance, *Academy of Management Journal.* **33**(2):259–285.

Gruen, T., Corsten, D., and Bharadwaj, S., 2002, *Retail Out-Of-Stocks: A worldwide examination of extent causes and consumer response,* The Food Institute Forum (CIES, FMI, GMA).

Gulati, R., 1999, Network location and learning: the influence of network resources and firm capabilities on alliance formation. *Strategic Management Journal.* **20**(5):397–420.

Gunasekaran, A., Patel, C., and Tirtiroglu, E., 2001, Performance measurement and metrics in a supply chain environment, *International Journal of Operation & Production Management.* **21**(1):71-87.

Gunasekaran, A., Patel, C., McGaughey, R., 2004, A framework for supply chain performance improvement, *International Journal of Production Economics.* **87**(3):333-347.

Holmberg, S., 2000, A system perspective on supply chain measurement, *International Journal of Physical Distribution and Logistics Management.* **30**(10):847-868.

Holmstrom, J., Framling, K., Kaipia, R., and Saranen, J., 2002, Collaborative planning forecasting and replenishment: new solutions needed for mass collaboration, *Supply Chain Management.* **7**(3):136-145.

Jarillo, C., 1988, On strategic networks, *Strategic Management Journal.* **9**(1):31-41.

Jeans, M., and Morrow, M., 1990, Performance measurement in the UK industry, *Journal of Cost Management for the Manufacturing Industry.* **3**:51-64.

Jermier, J., 1998, Critical perspective on organizational control, *Administrative Science Quarterly.* **43**(2):235-256.

Joint Industry ECR Project, 1994, *Performance Measurement: Applying Value Chain Analysis to the Grocery Industry,* Report published by ECR.

Kang,Y., and Gershwin, S., 2003, Information Inaccuracy in Inventory systems, Auto-ID Center, University of Washington, [available at http://cell1.mit.edu/papers/kang-gershwin-autoid04.pdf , Last Accessed 18 November 2004

Kaplan, R., and Norton, D., 1992, The balanced scorecard - measures that drive performance, *Harvard Business Review.* **70**(1):71-79.

Kaplan, R., and Norton, D., 1995, *Translating Strategy into Action: The Balanced Scorecard,* Boston, MA, Harvard Business School Press.

Kaplan, R., 1994, Management Accounting (1984-1994): Development of new practice and theory, *Management Accounting Research.* **5**:247-260.

Kennerley, M., and Neely, A., 2000, Performance measurement frameworks: a review, in: *Proceedings of Performance Measurement 2000: Past Present and Future Conference*, Robinson College, Cambridge, 19-21 July, pp. 291-298.

Krumwiede, K., 1998, The implementation stages of activity-based costing and the impact of contextual and organizational factors. *Journal of Management Accounting Research.* **10**:240 –277.

Kueng, P., 2000, Process performance measurement system: a tool to support process-based organizations, *Total Quality Management.* **11**(1):67-85.

Lambert, D., and Cooper, M., 2000, Issues in supply chain management, *Industrial Marketing Management.* **29**:65-83.

Lambert, D., and Pohlen, T., 2001, Supply chain metrics, *The International Journal of Logistics Management.* **12**(1).

Langfield, K., 1997, Management control systems and strategy: a critical review. *Accounting, Organizations and Society.* **22**:207-232.

Neely, A., Gregory, M., and Platts, K., 1995, Performance measurement system design – a literature review and research agenda, *International Journal of Operations & Production Management.* **15**(4):80-116.

Nohria, N., and Garcia-Pont,C., 1991, Global strategic linkages and industry structure, *Strategic Management Journal.* **12**:105-124.

Olian, D., and Rynes, L., 1991, Making total quality work: aligning organizational processes, performance measures, and stakeholders, *Human Resource Management.* **30**(3):303-333.

Otley, D., 1978, Budget use and managerial performance, *Journal of Accounting Research.* **16**(1):122-149.

Otley, D., 1999, Performance management: a framework for management control system research, *Management Accounting Research.* **10**:363-382.

Ouchi, W., and Johnson, J., 1978, Types of organizational control and their relationship to emotional well-being, *Administrative Science Quarterly.* **23**:293-317.

Ouchi,W., 1978, A conceptual framework for the design of organizational control mechanisms, *Management Science.* 25(9):833-848.

Powell, W., 1990, Neither Market nor Hierarchy: Network forms of organization, *Research in Organization Behavior.* **12**:295-336.

Reichlestein, S., 2000, Providing managerial incentives: Cash flows versus accrual accounting, *Journal of Accounting Research.* **38**(2):243-269.

Ring, S., Van de Ven, H., 1992, Structuring cooperative relationships between organizations, *Strategic Management Journal.* **13**:483-498.

Roland Berger, 2002, Full shelf satisfaction. Reducing the out-of-stocks in the grocery channel. Grocery Manufacturers of America (GMA).

Schneiderman, A. M., 1996, Metrics for the order fulfillment process (part 1)', *Journal of Cost Management.* 10(2):30-42.

Seifert, D., 2002, *Collaborative Planning Forecasting and Replenishment,* Galileo Press, Bonn.

Sieger, M., 1992, Manage your numbers to match your strategy, *Management Review.* 8(2):46-48.

Simons, R., 1995, *Levers of Control: How Managers Use Innovative Control Systems to Drive Strategic Renewal,* Harvard Business School Press.

Simons, R., 2000, *Performance measurement and control systems for implementing strategy: text & cases,* Prentice Hall, Upper Saddle River, NJ.

Speakman, R., Kammouff, J., and Myhr, N., 1998, An empirical investigation into supply chain management: a perspective on partnerships, *Supply Chain Management.* 3(2):53-67.

Stewart, G., 1997, Supply-chain operations reference model (SCOR): the fisrt cross-industry framework for integrated supply-chain management, of their supply chain, and to support, *Logistics Information Management.* 10(2):62–67.

Tarr, J., 1995, Developing performance measurement systems that support continuous improvement, *Hospital Material Management Quarterly.* **17**(3):59-67.

Thor, G., 1991, Performance measurement in a research organization, *National Productivity Review*, pp. 499-507.

Van Hoek, R., 1998, Measuring the unmeasurable – measuring and improving performance in the supply chain, *Supply Chain Management.* **3**(4):187-192.

Vyas, N., Shelburn, W., and Rogers, D., 1995, An analysis of strategic alliances: forms, functions and framework, *Journal of Business and Industrial Marketing.* **10**(3):47-60.

White, G. P., 1996, A survey and taxonomy of strategy-related performance measures for manufacturing, *International Journal of Operations & Production Management.* **16**(3):42-61.

White, M., and Flores, B., 1987, Goal setting in the management of operations, *International Journal of Operations & Production Management.* 7(6):5-16.

Willcocks, L., and Lester, S., 1999, *Beyond the IT Productivity Paradox,* John Wiley & Sons, Chichester.

Zairi, M., (1994), *Measuring Performance for Business Results*, Chapman & Hall, London.

Chapter 9

Examining the Emerging Dynamics of an Information Infrastructure

The case of introducing a web-based collaboration platform in the construction industry

Nasos Nikas and Angeliki Poulymenakou
Athens University of Economics and Business

Abstract: The focus of this chapter is on the implementation of collaboration technologies in the context of the construction industry. Our empirical setting involves the introduction of a web-based collaboration platform for progress monitoring, co-ordination of project activities, project record keeping, information sharing and exchange in a construction consortium, constituted of geographical dispersed business units and organizations. This research seeks to identify and understand impacts in management and work arrangements in the emerging network information infrastructure.

Key words: Information infrastructure; collaborative technologies; work practices; project management.

1. Introduction

The construction industry in general is highly fragmented compared to other manufacturing industries. Danwood et al. (2002) mention that this fragmentation is due to the uniqueness of its production processes and the products themselves. Each construction project is unique by its nature and must be delivered in certain time and budget. The complexity of the construction processes is such that accomplishing this objective is proving to be difficult under the existing delivery processes.

Generally, the construction industry is considered to be divisive and fragmented, where construction parties pay attention to conforming to contractual requirements while the organizations participating in the construction are characterized by heterogonous structures and processes. The execution of a construction project requires a variety of organizations that are temporarily combined to create a 'temporary multiorganization' (TMO) (Cherns and Bryant, 1984) to exchange information. When construction problems arise, relevant organizations have to work together to determine appropriate concessions and compromises before solutions can be obtained (Alty, 1993). The construction industry is centered on projects in which organizations work together within the duration of these projects. Each project is unique in the sense that there are 'properties' of construction problems that are inseparable from the project itself.

It is worth noticing that the fragmented nature of the industry limits the scope of co-operation among the various participants in construction consortia. IT is premised to increase co-operation and collaboration in construction projects by facilitating new ways of communication. This then would result in the establishment of a web of communication networks, which in turn seek to facilitate the operations of the construction parties. In this case one of the most important goals of IT is to play a supporting and enabling role within the pre-existing network in terms of managing the communication, the collaboration, the workflow and the flow of documentation among the networked organizations.

The case study in this chapter uncovers the many challenges with regards to the implementation of web-based collaboration technologies, and the continuing work of developing effective work practices related to this particular type of technology. Changing the work habits towards more collaborative behaviour has been proved difficult. Furthermore, other IT tools supporting individuals' work practices are far more popular and widespread in use than collaboration tools in the specific industry. This chapter is based on the experiences and observations of the authors, by extensively interviewing the IT consultant involved in the implementation process, by reviewing internal project documentation, and by observing usage of a web based collaborative platform by a project consortium. This approach falls within widely accepted practices for qualitative data collection (Myers, 1997).

2. The need for adopting collaboration technologies in the context of the construction industry

In the information era, a responsive IT infrastructure is crucial to the flexibility and constantly changing needs of a business organization (Broadbent et al., 1998). The highly competitive business environment is forcing organizations to re-evaluate totally their processes and structures, indicating an increasing need for networking and cooperative arrangements. Although Information Technology (IT) is often emphasized as an important enabler for this organisational transformation, there is a propensity to overplay the role of IT in this restructuring, by offering the potential for collaboration across geographical and organisational boundaries (Baskerville and Smithson, 1995). Internet based systems provide the capabilities of sharing, diffusing and managing information across time and space. Such systems are mentioned in the literature as web-based collaboration platforms (Munkvold, 1999; 2003).

However, little research has been conducted so far regarding web-based collaboration in distributed organisational environments (Munkvold, 1999). Construction is a multi-organisation process with heavy dependence on exchange of large complex data and information. The successful completion of a project depends on the accuracy and timing of information exchange within the construction consortium. Thus, an information lattice is created where actors diffuse and exchange various categories of information. Rojas and Songer (1999) note that two-thirds of the construction problems were caused by inadequate coordination and inefficient means of communication of project information and data. To this end, web-based platforms for the construction necessitate efficient management of information in terms of its structure and use.

Interorganizational systems exist to support and implement cooperation and strategic alliances, between two or more organisations (Heide and John, 1990). Economies of scale, specialisation, rationalisation, and global competition are also cited as possible reasons for these partnerships. Information technology is referred to as the enabling means that will not only support, but also enable interorganizational coordination activities (Bensaou, 1996). By using sophisticated IT applications (e.g. web-based technologies), coordination, collaboration and the accomplishment of the work itself may become independent of time and space and can be carried out by distributed groups (Wigand et al., 1997) and organisational settings. The notions of coordination and collaboration may imply increased complexity of tasks and processes. In this respect, organisations strive for solutions or mechanisms that will be able and capable for organising the work by its nature, and such a mechanism is project management. The basic purpose for initiating a project is to accomplish some goals. The reason for organising the tasks as a project is to focus on the responsibility and authority for the attainment of the goals on an individual or small group. Project management is expected to coordinate and integrate all activities needed to reach project's goals (Meredith and Mantel, 1995). A great deal of project management involves avoiding problems, tackling new ground, managing a group of people and trying to achieve very clear objectives quickly and efficiently (Greiss, 1995). Specifically, the purpose of introducing the new collaborative platform in the construction consortium is because it was considered as an enabling mechanism for improving project management and control as well as a tool for improving collaboration practices among the involved actors. However, the introduction of such a system consequently implies alterations on the notion of managerial control (i.e. the control of the project manager over the project), its scope and rationale (Ciborra, 2000).

The Royal Institute of British Architects (2000) provides well-defined roles for different project participants such as architects, engineers, surveyors, planners, project managers, contractors and sub contractors in a construction project. These roles are focused on managing and co-ordinating the project information and the flow among the various participants with the aim of satisfying the objectives of each stage in a construction project. The overall role of project management, in this scenario, is to harmonize the functions of planning, communicating, monitoring and control in order to meet the project's overall objectives as defined by the scope, time, cost, quality, and client satisfaction. However, each individual process requires close collaboration between actors (Coyne and Lee, 2000).

This research seeks to identify and understand impacts in management and work arrangements in a network organizational setting created specifically by the introduction of a new information system supporting collaboration and information resource sharing to improve project management practices. In general, groupware or collaborative technologies are expected to support team's activities, such as planning, coordination, decision making and so on (Ngwenyama and Lyytinen, 1997). Concomitantly other authors claim that there is a great lack of understanding of the complex social activity that is constitutive of groupwork (Kling, 1991; Grudin, 1991). Loosemore and Lee (2001) note that construction consortia are formed from a respective number of participant organizations which, viewed as social organizations, adds more to their divisive nature. Social groups within social organizations develop "norms" to influence values and priorities of their members causing them to interpret incoming messages from ''out-groups'' in a certain way. These norms also vary among the different professional backgrounds of the actors who participate in construction projects meaning that what is considered reasonable, rational, logical and self-evident for one person may be unreasonable, illogical and obscure to another.

In this chapter we present an illustrative case study which highlights the social intricacies and afflictions in the process of articulating the complexity of implementing a specific groupwork technology. Grudin (1991; 1994) suggests that the failure to address the social dimension of groupware implementation leads to user rejection of otherwise well-designed applications. In this respect we assert that the aforementioned issues should be addressed in the implementation process of such systems and more specifically there is a great need for a systemic analysis of the implementation of groupwork technologies in view of the particulars of groupwork situations. Failing that, even if rapid technological applications provide appropriate tools for developing communication and data exchange systems, our research study reveals how a problematic implementation process may lead to their abandonment. Successful implementation of a new Information and Communication Technology (ICT) application is critical for achieving its effective use. Munkvold (1999) notes that despite the enormous interest in how IT can be used for supporting new organisational forms, there are only a few empirical studies on the process of implementation for supporting collaboration in distributed organisational arrangements. Hence, the introduction of a new collaborative technology affects pre-existing organisational structures, but more importantly the people that are going to use this technology, and there is a great discrepancy between how people perceive this kind of change and how they manage it (Orlikowsi and Hofman, 1997).

The exploratory case study presented in this chapter, indicates that implementing and deploying a new infrastructure does not only concern organizational and technological matters. Important dynamics are also emerging from a rising tension between the network and single organizational aspects of the information infrastructure in use. We have chosen to focus our analysis beyond traditional IT implementation approaches in distributed organizational environments (Cooper and Zmud, 1990; Munkvold, 1999), onto the evolving tension between organizational arrangements and technological flexibility. Furthermore, the research findings extracted from the study illustrate how an emerging information infrastructure implementation context, may denote additional complexity compared to inter-organizational IT implementation, arising from a greater level of autonomy among geographical dispersed business units, geographical barriers and technological constraints. Thus, our understanding on the concept of information infrastructures deployment may be broadened by capturing and better understanding the intricacies and afflictions that are rising from the internal dynamics underlying this process (Ciborra, 2000).

2.1 The reality of managing projects in construction

Multiple co-ordination and communication activities have to take place between project participants in a construction project. However, the Internet alone cannot create an environment of interoperability among the various participants in construction projects (Alshawi et al., 2000). This is mainly attributed to the type and format of the exchanged data/documents as well as to the different hardware and software systems in organizations. Data exchange can be generally defined as the process of transferring relevant/ common information between different construction parties with the aim of minimizing data re-entry and duplication. Data exchange can take place across several organizations, construction applications, professionals, etc. Such an exchange involves different types and amounts of information depending on the nature of the organization, experience, project, etc. Poor communication and coordination often results in misunderstandings, misinterpretations and ignorance of information that seriously affects the performance of a construction project in terms of quality, time, cost and value, which may result in serious delays regarding project completion. Peters (1981) argues that in a construction project its status is constantly changing from that of an idea or a concept through to feasibility studies, execution and finally completion. But nowadays construction projects are far more complicated than ever before. They involve huge capital investments, embrace several disciplines, widely dispersed project participants, quality standards etc. Alshawi et al. (2003) notes that these factors coupled with high-speed technological advances in Information and Communication Technology have influenced project management practices, towards taking advantage of newly developed management tools and the latest technology. He also states that current project management practices are often isolated and concerned with managing problems related to individual stages of the projects. Specifically he locates project management problems to the following causes:

- **Lack of adequate communication:** Communication deals with producing, issuing and circulating of reports/documents and having meetings from time to time among the project participants so that the proposed timing, method and strategy are made available and understood. To this end, communication is also important to monitor and control the project's activities according to the project plan. Hence, problems in communication result often to additional expenditure due to reworking. Reworking often occurs due to conflicting information and information not received in time to the parties concerned. The Built Environment and Transport Panel (1998) states that 30% of construction rework is attributable to process-related problems.
- **Lack of automating the processes of a whole project:** During the last decade significant developments in technology have resulted in the production of very powerful software packages for the construction. However, such applications resulted improvements in specific construction phases such as planning, estimating, design etc. but contributing at a minimum with regards the processes that are taking place at the project level. To this end, IT system solutions that are widely available today are rather isolated applications resulting in a broad spread of stand-alone applications packages with no communication facilities. The incompatibility between hardware and software mentioned earlier has seriously pre-

vented project managers to access information when needed. To this respect an integrated system that facilitates smooth flow of information between the various stages of a project seems more than necessary.

3. Case description

The construction consortium examined in the Greek construction industry is a temporary, project driven organizational network. Dimer S.A., a Greek construction company, is the prime contractor of the construction consortium. Dimer has adopted a web-based collaboration platform in order to improve co-ordination of project work (in this case the network's mission concerns the construction of a new hospital wing), monitoring and reporting the progress of the construction project. The temporary organisational network, i.e. the consortium, consists of five geographically dispersed partners bound by contractual agreements (Technical and Financial Annexes). This case concerns collaborative technology mediation of complex coordination processes (e.g. task allocation, time scheduling, coordination of the building process) among multiple organizations (prime contractor, contractors and their various sub-contractors) participating in the consortium. Hence, the collaboration platform is contribution to the creation of an emergent network information infrastructure.

Formally, a contract has been signed from the prime contractor (Dimer S.A) and the construction site manager, an independent company, which lists several goals and tasks to be achieved. The prime contractor decided to implement the new information system in the construction phase of the project for improving project's performance, monitoring and control. The case setting concerns the monitoring practices of a construction site remotely by the prime contractor. Several parties joined together to construct a new side-wing of a hospital. The project lasted eight months and its construction budget reached almost 6 million Euros. The construction site was located in an agricultural area 300 km away from the head offices of the prime contractor and its project manager.

The introduction of the collaborative platform was embedded in the set-up of a network of collaborating organizations, bringing together complementary (or cumulative) skills, competencies, technology know-how regarding the various aspects of the project under way. Network participants were collaborating with each other in accordance to the project work flow. We note that a construction project is constituted of two distinct phases, - the planning/design and the construction phase. This study concerns the study of the construction phase, which is often the most tightly controlled, but often ends up being the most problematic and time-consuming stage. This is due, in part, to its potential high complexity and to difficulties in coordination. Information captured in shop drawings, approvals, change orders, inspections, and reviews all add to the "actual construction."

The construction phase typically is planned in more detail than any other construction project stages (design stage, bidding, etc.), but it often ends up being the most troublesome, particularly for the prime contractor. This is due, in part, to the high complexity and coordination difficulties that the prime contractor confronts with both contractors and sub-contractors. It is very difficult from the prime contractor's side, to monitor all the processes and the coordination activities that evolve during the construction process. Decision-making and conflict resolution demand a highly structured information environment, where the prime contractor can easily retrieve the information needed in order critical and objective decisions to be made. Otherwise, an unstructured information environment might lead to false decisions due to an incomplete representation of the situation.

The complex nature of the construction phase requires extensive communication and collaboration among the various subcontractors. The construction phase is comprised of a group of multiple sub-processes, or various phases: feasibility study, architectural programming, conceptual design, design development, bidding, construction, and facilities management. Each individual process requires collaboration of multiple consulting groups that comprise each process. In particular, the collaboration of many consultants is necessary in the design development phase. For instance, the civil engineer, mechanical engineer, electrical engineer, and experts of other specialized faculties need to cooperate for the successful development of a design. The construction site manager communicates on a daily basis with the construction workflow supervisor and on a regular basis with the raw material supplier. Specific pieces of information such as shop drawings, approvals, change orders, inspection reports, and reviews all augment the actual construction work. Management, in this case project management in a network setting, is required to meet tangible goals related directly to project performance (such as monitoring costs, assuring quality, meeting time schedules) as well as intangible goals such as establishing mutual trust and sharing a common vision. During the construction phase, efficient and effective collaboration among the network participants is critical.

3.1 The collaboration technology

The collaboration technology introduced from the prime contractor tailored to support the following services:

- project progress monitoring,
- co-ordination of project activities,
- project record keeping,
- information sharing and exchange within the construction consortium.

The system comprises a management platform available through the Internet, addressing the specific needs of the construction industry. It offers users instant information access via the Internet. It is an integrated management information system while it also supports daily project operations and administration by providing a construction site diary and communication logs (create/update project plan, timesheets), collaboration and communication (online meetings, video conferencing, chatting, redlining), document workflow, real time requests for information (RFIs) and task assignments to project members (permissions, authoring, logs, redlining). The introduction of the new Information System posits new management challenges to be addressed concerning the handling and diffusion of information resources among the network nodes. A prerequisite for efficient and effective collaboration is supposed to accurate and timely handling and monitoring of the exchanged information among the construction consortium and the management of the emerging information lattice. Internet based systems provide the capabilities of sharing, diffusing and managing information across time and space.

The type of information that can be exchanged using the functionalities of the platform can be categorised into two groups according to Alshawi et al. (2003); the element/objects and the document groups. Information exchanged at the document group level could be characterised as quite detailed (e.g. details of an invoice), while at the element/object level it normally refers to simply viewing or sharing images such as drawings by users. Transferring information at the element/object level requires common standards that enable information to be transferred freely between applications. On the other hand transferring document level information can be performed through the internet as attachments to messages handled by the web-based application.

The table below illustrates the information entities exchanged during project's lifespan allocated in the two groups of information mentioned above.

Table 1. Types of information exchange

Element/objects	Document groups
Notices to proceed	Field orders: Forms Used to facilitate minor changes to the requirements that do not require a change order.
Meeting minutes	Construction site photos and drawings
Change order: the formal document that defines what changes in the project scope is required and identifies the associated changes to the time frame	Punch List: A document that summarizes corrections and schedules of activities
Change orders requests: Can be submitted by the Prime Contractor or the Project Manager in response to a field order	Project progress reports
Invoices, Orders and cost sheets	Contracts, manuals and certificates of insurance
	Request for Information (RFI): Used to obtain formal responses

3.2 Roles and responsibilities

The following actors have been appointed by the prime contractor organisation as users of the system:

1. CEO of the prime contractor
2. Project Manager
3. Procurement manager
4. Construction work flow supervisor
5. Construction site manager

The CEO of the prime contractor is the person holding overall responsibility and accountability by the project's client (in this case a Health authority) for the completion of the project (i.e. the construction of the new hospital wing). To this end, the CEO brought about the collaboration system for monitoring the overall construction process of the project. The project manager was located both at the construction site and at the head offices of the prime contractor. He was responsible for managing and controlling this particular project and also responsible for reporting to the prime contractor all the relevant information about project's progress and completed tasks according to time schedule. The procurement manager was located at the head offices of the prime contractor and was responsible for supplying the construction site manager with materials and equipment. He was assigned to reviewing the requests sent from the construction site manager and authorized from the project manager to proceed in the delivery of the requested materials and equipment. The project manager and the prime contractor had the responsibility to monitor the whole process. The construction workflow supervisor was responsible for informing and consulting the construction site manager about revisions on the technical details of project activities by submitting field orders. He was responsible for monitoring particular tasks related to the feasibility study, and, architectural and conceptual design. The construction site manager was responsible for constructing the side wing of the hospital according to the drawings and studies produced in the design phase and he was obligated to follow the instructions given from the project management and the workflow supervisor as well. He was also obliged to carry out tasks as scheduled and to report back to the project management on project's progress. The following figure illustrates the interactions and the information flow that took place in the hospital project between the involved actors.

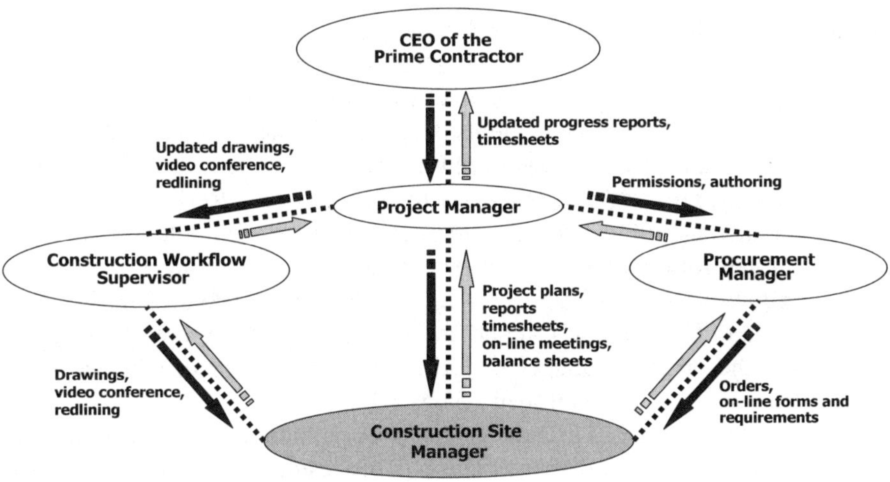

Figure 1. Information flow and interactions within the consortium

4. Research findings

As mentioned earlier the purpose for implementing this collaborative web-based platform in the construction consortium was for improving project management and control of the construction processes. The design of the system was based on supporting 'typical' business processes that usually take place in the construction phase. The system was implemented as an "as is" IT application with minimum customization on its main functions. Each organization participating in the project had its own established internal processes and sub-processes supporting them. Adoption of the system meant that organizations ought to re-organize their internal processes of storing and diffusing information in order to avoid reworking. Formal processes for this were not established and a high degree of adhocracy on the way work evolved occurred. The specific processes that the system called to facilitate were:

- Procurement of raw materials and equipment
- Revising of the implementation study/plan (architectural study, feasibility study and, electric and mechanical studies)
- Compilation of periodic and ad hoc reports
- Project monitoring

Prior to the introduction of the system, information exchange was conducted through saving drawings in CDs and then sending them to the interested parties. The introduction of the system shifted the consortium's expectations regarding the efficacy of document exchange since it featured electronic storage and diffusion of documents through the web. A second goal to achieve by using the system was to reduce the need for face to face meetings to negotiate progress of and revisions to project work. Reductions in time spent over such activities was expected because the system allowed the storage and organization of project information such as meeting minutes, actions, comments requests, approvals and notifications generated during project's lifespan. This function aimed to improve also the project manager's work since the project manager would be instantly aware of who has published what, when it had been seen and by whom.

However, we observed that the type of information exchanged in the consortium had a high degree of abstraction. This resulted in the lack of appropriate information trails, which in turn made the users unable to enact particular tasks and processes within the system. Activities such as "requests for information" (RFIs) did not have a standardized form required to enable the user to cross-reference them to certain tasks or specific processes involved. On the contrary they contained just a simple file description and offered the opportunity to choose a single or a group of recipients. A request for information (RFI) was initially hailed as a powerful functionality of workflow support designed to structure communication between the Construction Site Manager and the Project Manager regarding the design of the project or other issues affecting the project. However, an RFI is only effective if the question is formulated clearly, the question is answered properly, and the answer is provided in time as to not affect the construction schedule. An RFI typically originates from a vendor, supplier or subcontractor, who submits the question to the Project manager. Once the question is answered, the process reverses itself as the response makes its way back to the originator.

During the process of making necessary revisions to the implementation study/plans, the construction workflow supervisor was responsible for maintaining the adherence of revised work elements to the basic premises of the original feasibility, architectural, electric and mechanical studies as specified in the project's contract. This type of information is referred to the element/object level, such as plans and drawings. The project manager illustrates bellow the complexity of the amendment process in the construction project:

> *"Our purpose for introducing the system to the consortium was to reduce paperwork and bureaucracy. Previously, the usual procedure to exchange high capacity files was to save them in CDs and courier them to the interested parties. This meant that we needed at least one day to deliver a drawing to a recipient. We estimated that we were going to exchange at least 10 CDs full of drawings, plans and other types of documents during the construction phase, which could be translated to the loss of 10 very valuable work days. We had great expectations from the system because it would facilitate a web-based document inventory, accessible at any time. However, established procedures in the construction are very difficult to change. For example, when a drawing had to be amended, the revised version of the drawing as well as the instructions following it, needed to be in hard copy form in order to be confirmed by the architect's signature. The receipt of the drawing had also to be acknowledged to both the project manager and the prime contractor in writing. Therefore, sending these documents electronically failed to complete these endorsement procedures. The mixing of hard and electronic copies in the participant organizations made it extremely difficult to process the right information whenever it was necessary."*

This resulted in mistakes and misinterpretation of information because the documents exchanged were not up-to-date and instantly available. Team members confronted daily the risk of working on information that was out-of date, or incomplete. This increased site visits and time spent in meetings to resolve misunderstandings. However, if we consider what Scanlin (1998) points out, that communication comprises about 75-90% of a project manager's time and hence that information needs to be up-to-date and available on demand, we may conclude that communicating information by electronic means hampered seriously the effectiveness of the project control by the project manager. Alshawi et al. (2003) note that despite the fact that many construction organizations are using IT to improve specific processes/applications, the construction industry still traditionally insists on issuing hard copy documentation as against electronic forms for auditing and record purposes.

The introduction of the system necessitated changes in the nature of both specialists' and managers' work, towards more collaborative work practices. The system imposed the electronic documentation of project work. For example, besides the actual construction of the hospital wing the construction site manager had to submit forms, send orders and keep the project's diary electronically, and distribute RFIs instead of using former means of communication, such as the telephone or fax. The focus of his work was divided now between construction supervision and solving problems in the construction site and documenting work in progress in a previously unknown level of detail. The lack of standardized information trails, tasks and procedures in conjunction with the low level of understanding that a person might have when introduced to a new means of communication, resulted in growing hesitation and uncertainty to the construction site manager on system's use and capabilities. We also found that a real problem with the training courses provided for the construction site manager which proved to be inefficient and resulted most of the difficulties met regarding the use of the system. The IT consultant states:

> *"...the construction site manager participated to the training courses offered to all users simultaneously and not individually due to time restrictions. There was a great hurry for starting the construction work and the training courses were being based on an earlier version of the platform than the one which was finally released. However, we noted to the prime contractor that the construction site manager had a low IT literacy level, and that he would need some extra courses to attend in order to be ready with the release of the system. But the prime contractor claimed that time was not enough and that the construction site manager has been doing this job for almost two decades and he knows his work better than everybody else..."*

The introduction of the system in the work environment resulted in an increasing aggravation of some actors against the system. For example, the compilation of periodic progress reports on time and with a certain level of accuracy, proved a complex and time consuming process for the construction site manager. This resulted in serious delays in sending the reports to the project manager, which in turn made him merely incapable of finding the information he was seeking in a timely fashion, often ever at all.

Furthermore, delays in the ordering, purchasing and invoicing practices resulted in delays in supplies being received and led to less collaboration between the construction site manager and the procurement department. For example, many delays occurred from the integration of the existing material procurement system with the new platform, which did not integrate well procurement information with project plans and schedules. This limited the stock control of the materials and consequently accurate predictions of the resource requirements for the project were not created. Finally, poor communication and collaboration among between the procurement department and the construction site manager was the outcome of the overall lack of the system's integration to cater this need.

5. Discussion

5.1 Implications for project management

Project management and control include progress monitoring, co-ordination of project activities, project records keeping and information exchange. Monitoring is about collecting, recording and reporting information concerning any and all aspects of project performance that the project manager or others in the organization wish to know. It is important to note that monitoring, as an activity, should be kept distinct from controlling (which used the data supplied by monitoring to bring actual performance into approximate congruence with planned performance. What is important for project managers in general is to know the ease of finding the information they need, when it is needed. A primary concern is to ensure that all parties interested in the project have available, on a timely basis, the information needed to exercise effective control over the project. From our study we extract the critical role of introducing and adopting a common information classification scheme. Problems indicated when the project manager could not find the information needed when needed (RFIs, progress reports, invoices, etc.). This problem occurred because as mentioned earlier the set of action plans that describe what is being done in the construction site, in accordance to the planned level of resource usage for each task, work package and work unit in the projects, was not explicitly supported as information elements by the system's functions.

5.2 Implications to information diffusion

The collected information consisted of periodic progress reports, specification changes and alike. However, the project members were unable to determine precisely which of the available data should be collected and allocated to specific actors. Due to the ineffective organization of project documents, users tended to receive irrelevant information. Furthermore, the degree of the detail that the exchanged reports entailed, both in the reports themselves and in the input being solicited from the actors, was inappropriate: abstraction was very high and information was poorly structured. This resulted in a negative propensity on system's use and performance regarding some of the participant actors (e.g. construction site manager, procurement manager). Moreover, this situation made almost impossible for the project manager to instantly assess the information needed to monitor specific tasks. Each of the participant organizations kept to their own information standards of forms and documents that were being exchanged. Basically, there was also a high inadequacy of the de facto standards, related to the construction project processes. The inadequacy of formal standards of construction processes caused further inconsistencies and ambiguity in the information that was produced and exchanged. Thus, this resulted in diverse interpretations of information and users mis-perceptions regarding the system and its use.

5.3 Implications for collaborative work

Alshawi (2003) notes that the industry, the government and clients are all seeking to bring about change in the construction industry to improve quality, competitiveness and profitability and to increase value to clients. Our study revealed that actors' familiarity with the use of such technologies was very low. Furthermore, there was not customized training corresponding to specific roles and particular business processes. Hence, even the actors that were going to handle very specific tasks and processes were rather confused with the subject and the scope of their action. The construction site manager at the end considered using the system as "hosting a stranger" with regards to his every day work and claimed that it added only extra bureaucracy and time consumption. The system's capability of instant information diffusion also resulted in fears of exposure among the users. The prime contractor claimed that the technology destabilized current strategy and created imbalances, by failing to meet their current needs. The introduction of the system also created new ambiguity to the existing processes. The various problems with interoperability, instability and performance of the technology resulted in users developing mistrust in the new technology and thus, preferring to use substitute media, e.g. fax instead of e-mail.

In summary the introduction of this new IT application to support the construction phase collaborative practices had multiple implications in terms of management and work as a result of the emerging socio-technical dynamics of network information infrastructures. Specifically, new information entities emerged, and activities were enabled. The system had the potential to create a pool of documentation material on project practices, delineating and decomposing the corresponding construction phase tasks.

Nevertheless, an interesting issue is rising from the usage and the value of the stored information. In information infrastructures, stored information must be shared and common to its users (Ciborra, 2000). However, information management and sharing presuppose that this repository of information needs proper management and common definitions to be handled effectively. Specification of roles, tasks and processes is also a crucial aspect that needs further investigation. Finally, we note that in our case there was a limited installed base that could create more complex problems such as incompatibilities of integrating different technologies in use.

6. Conclusions

At the moment plenty discussions about how to proceed in the process of implementing and deploying an information infrastructure remain open and opinions diverge. Several research studies are now focusing on integrating the construction and collaboration processes through standardization of data by taking advantage of evolving technologies. Nevertheless, managing information as depicted above, and integrating construction and collaboration processes, do not lead necessarily to an efficient use of the web-based platform. Whether a new technology is introduced to one or many organizations, significant changes are implied not only to the organization using it, but also to its structure and core processes. This imposes major implications on the work conditions as far the introduction of a new IT application influences roles, tasks, co-ordination activities and so on. In this respect, these systems (platforms) necessitate the formulation of new formal and informal work procedures (i.e. roles, tasks, co-ordination activities) that need to be embedded into existing 'compulsory' processes as well as in informal norms. However, the definition of appropriate work tasks during the construction phase can be a laborious and tedious process. This is due to the unique nature of construction projects in general, which involves too many individual and different work tasks and makes their definition an expensive and time consuming process. At the same time, the design for many tasks in construction may be reused as templates in new projects. This, however, probably can take place within the same organization since the industry lacks standard processes and procedures adopted from the whole industry. For example, the tasks involved in the construction of a building floor may be reused with only minor alterations for each of the floors in the building, or other buildings as standard definitions for most tasks already exist from previous projects. Nevertheless, each organization in construction preserves its own internal processes and procedures described by different information standards. Construction organizations are keen to use systems to store and retrieve the activities associated with past projects in order to create an information repository for internal use. Finally, from an industry perspective the establishment of information and procedural standards is essential in order to contribute to the design and the adoption of such systems in an industrial level.

Traditional IS and other experts at the time being have not concluded in a specific design of such standards in construction like in other industries e.g. EDI, or XML based systems. Executives are getting worried because of existing solutions' lack of flexibility or because its implementation is too risky and expensive. The need for continuously organizational change requires similar change of the proposed solutions as well. Hanseth (2000) notes that flexible solutions are needed. But flexibility, contradicts with the concept of efficient information sharing and the apparent standardization that is needed to make it efficient. To this end, there is a need for new approaches on the concept of deploying information infrastructures. We propose a closed look at the significance of organizing practices in organizational change (Orlikowski, 1996). In this respect, we invoke Orlikowski to question the beliefs that organizational change must be planned, that technology is the primary cause of technology-based organizational transformation, and that radical changes always occur rapidly and discontinuously. Organizational transformation, implied by the implementation of a challenging information system should be seen as *"an ongoing improvisation enacted by organizational actors trying to make sense of and act coherently in the world."*

This study not only reveals already known implementation issues, but beyond that, the problem of interaction between technology and organization comes in light. Moreover, when analyzing information infrastructure redesign processes, it is crucial to understand the dynamics evolution within single-firms participating in the network, and the network as a whole. End-user participation may reduce the risk of true integration of the system with the business processes and will certainly reduce the risk of resource wastage and rewarding investment. Hence, this is a very time consuming process and requires from the organizations in the construction to reach a minimum of IT maturity met in other industries, like the manufacturing. People must acquire the necessary skills to benefit from the implementation of web-based collaborative technologies. Further investigation is needed to shift the focus of adoption efforts from ensuring system utilization to rethinking about work processes and negotiating a viable network strategy for accepting the new form of collaborative processes.

Acknowledgement

This research has been supported by the Hellenic Ministry of Education (25%) and the European Commission (75%) under the Operational Programme "Education and Primary Vocational Training" (EPEAEK II - http://www.epeaek.gr/).

References

Alshawi, M., and Ingirige, B., 2000, Web-enabled project management: An emerging paradigm in construction, *Automation in Construction.* **12**:349– 364

Alshawi, M., and Bingunath, I., 2003, Web-enabled project management: an emerging paradigm in construction, *Automation in Construction.* **12**:349-364.

Alty, J., 1993, 'Information Technology and the Construction Industry: Another Tower of Babel?, in: *Selected Papers from the Conference on Information Technology for Construction*, K. S. Mathur, M. P. Betts, and K. W. Tham, eds., World Scientific Publications, pp 3-15.

Bensaou, M., 1997, Interorganizational Cooperation: The Role of IT, *Information Systems Research.* **8**(2):107-124.

Baskerville, R., and Smithson, S., 1995, Information technology and new organisational forms: Choosing chaos over panaceas, *European Journal of Information Systems.* **4**(2):66-73.

Built Environment and Transport Panel, 2000, Foresight: Making the future work for you, Construction Associate Program, in: DETR, *Rethinking construction (The Egan Report).*

Broadbent, M., Weill, P., and Neo, B. S., 1999, Strategic Context and Patterns of IT infrastructure capability, *Journal of Strategic Information Systems.* **8**(2):157-187.

Ciborra, C. U., 2000, *From Control to Drift*, Oxford University Press, Oxford et al.

Cherns, A. B., and Bryant, D. T., 1984, Studying the client's role in construction management, *Construction Management and Economics.* **2**:177-184.

Cooper, R. B., and Zmud R.W., 1990, Information technology implementation research: a technological diffusion approach, *Management Science.* **36**(2):123–139.

Cordella, A., and Simon K. A., 2000, Global and Local dynamics in Infrastructure Deployment: The Astra Hassle Experience, in: *From Control to Drift*, C. U. Ciborra, ed., Oxford University Press, Oxford et al., pp. 172-192.

Coyne, S. O., and Lee, J., 2000, Managing building product information on the web, in: *Proceedings of the Conference on Implementing IT to Obtain a Competitive Advantage in the 21st Century*, H. Li, Q. Shen, D. Scott, and P. E. D. Love, eds., Hong Kong Polytechnic University Press, Hong Kong, pp. 856-868.

Danwood, N., Akinsola, A., and Hobbs, B., 2002, Development of automated communication of system for managing site information using internet technology, *Automation in Construction.* **11**.

Greiss, G., 1995, *Project Managent Demistyfied: today's Tools and Techniques*, 2nd ed., E & FN Spon, UK.

Grudin, J., 1991, CSCW Introduction, *Communications of the ACM.* **34**(12):31-34.

Grudin, J., 1994, Computer-supported cooperative work: History and focus, *IEEE Computer.* **27**(5):19-26.

Hanseth, O., 2000, The Economics of Standards, in: *From Control to Drift,* C. U. Ciborra, ed., Oxford University Press, Oxford et al., pp. 56-70.

Heide, J.B., John, G., 1990, Alliances in Industrial Purchasing: The Determinants of Joint Action in Buyer-Supplier Relationship, *Journal of Marketing Research.* **27**(1):24-35.

Kling, R., 1991, Cooperation, Coordination and Control in Computer Supported Work, *Communications of the ACM.* **34**(12):83-88.

Meredith, J.R., and Mantel, S. J., 1995, *Project management: A managerial approach*, John Willey & Sons, New York.

Munkvold, B.E., 1999, Challenges of IT implementation for supporting collaboration in distributed organizations, *European Journal of Information Systems.* **8**(4):260–272.

Munkvold, B.E, 2003, *Implementing Collaboration Technologies in Industry: Case examples and Lessons learned*, Springer, London et al.

Myers, M.D., 1997, *Qualitative Research in Information Systems*, (http://www.misq.org/misqd961/isworld)

Ngwenyama, O. and K. Lyytinen, 1997, Groupware As Action Constitutive Rule-Resource Sets: A Social Action Analysis of Groupware Environments, *Computer Supported Cooperative Work.* **6**(1):71-93.

Peters, G., 1981, *Project Management and Construction Control*, Construction Press, London.

RIBA, 2000, *Architect's Plan of Work*, RIBA Publications, UK.

Rojas, E. and Songer, A., 1999, Web-centric Systems: A New Paradigm for Collaborative Engineering, *Journal of Management in Engineering, ASCE.* **15**(1):39-45.

Orlikowski, W. L, 1996, Improvising Organisational Transformation Over Time: A situated change perspective, *Information Systems Research.* **7**(1):63-92.

Orlikowski, W.J., and Hofman, D., 1997, An Improvisational Model of Change Management: The Case of Groupware Technologies, *Sloan Management Review.* **42**(2):11-22.

Scanlin, J., 1998, The Internet as an enabler of the Bell Atlantic project office, *Project Management Journal.* **29**(2):6-7.

Wigand, R.T., Picot, A., Reichwald, R., 1997, *Information Organisation and Management,* Wiley & Sons, New York.

Chapter 10

Unraveling the Virtual University

The case of eMaster Postgraduate programme

Elpida Prasopoulou, Angeliki Poulymenakou and Nancy Pouloudi
Athens University of Economics and Business

Abstract: This chapter critically explores the vision of a university "without walls" that has dominated these last years the discussions in academia and industry alike. In examining the efforts of a distributed virtual university to foster collaboration among the various participating actors through the establishment of a common technological infrastructure, we found that technological coupling is not enough in itself. In particular, the analysis showed that there are a number of defining factors namely, (1) task characteristics, (2) communication interface, and (3) frames that must be aligned for any effort to create a distributed virtual university to be successful. To this end, we examine in depth each of these defining factors and discuss the assumptions that lead universities to rely on technology to foster collaboration. We conclude by discussing the implications of the vision for a "virtual" university for both academic research and practice.

Key words: Virtual university; technological coupling; tasks; technological frames; communication interface.

1. Introduction

The advent of advanced information and communication technologies that enhance interconnectivity among geographically distributed organizations and permit communication beyond space and time boundaries triggered a vivid discussion, in academia and industry alike, on the forthcoming knowledge revolution that is going to overthrow many traditional institutions and especially universities (e.g. Brown and Duguid, 2002; Cornford, 2000). The image of a university without walls connecting faculty, students, alumni, potential learners and companies in an expansive, organic network form embracing change and adaptability suddenly dominated discussions on the future of academic institutions. Even more, this vision of a flexible institution embracing new technologies did not remain at a strictly conceptual level. Many existing institutions started to incorporate the advanced technologies available to them in order to offer a new learning experience to their students and a new way of work to their faculty.

However, the rush of the virtual university focused both the debate and the attempts to materialize it on the technological infrastructure and not on the people actually using it. The majority of institutions trying to virtualize part or the totality of their operations opted for the ad hoc implementation of technological solutions like internet-based courses, collaboration platforms or e-mailing lists hoping that users are going to embrace it in their everyday activities. This top-down approach of technology introduction to an academic setting, although quite widespread in practice, has been largely ignored by the researchers examining the virtualization of the university. Yet this issue is of great importance, since technological appropriation is crucial for any attempt towards virtualization to succeed. How do the users, be they faculty or students, of the new learning and collaborating technologies feel about the new reality introduced to them? Do they find it easy to accept the new teaching and learning environments? How do they incorporate the new technologies in their existing practices, if they do it at all?

In this paper we investigate how the partners of eMaster (a pseudonym) postgraduate programme, a consortium of ten universities, negotiated the virtual organizing required for the collaboration of their members in various joint activities. More specifically, the paper analyses how users in an academic setting deal with *technological coupling*, the ad hoc introduction of a common technological infrastructure between universities collaborating in a virtual environment. In the following section, the theoretical underpinnings of the virtual university are reviewed. Our research design and data collection methods are presented in section 3, followed by a description of eMaster. The main body of the paper focuses on the analysis of the ways eMaster members negotiated virtual collaboration in two specific instances and the major organizing principles that stem out of this experience. Section 6 discusses the effects of technological coupling in virtual environments. Finally, the last section presents the conclusions of the paper.

2. Virtualizing the university

The potential of new types of interaction among geographically distributed, functionally and/or culturally diverse entities enabled by advanced forms of information and communication technologies (DeSanctis and Monge, 1999) triggered a great, academic and business, interest in virtual forms of organizing. This vision for new, lean and flexible organizations influenced greatly the discussion on the future of universities and especially business schools. Higher education has been at the epicenter of vivid debates on economic development and growth ever since knowledge and learning became of paramount importance for the advancement of society (Van Baalen and Moratis, 2001). This increased interest in the future of universities in combination with the advances in ICT led many proponents of virtualization to predict that digital media and information networks will undermine the position of universities as the locus of knowledge production and dissemination (Cornford, 2000).

The virtual university became the hallmark of many info-enthusiasts who saw "books and libraries as little more than containers, education as little more than infodelivery, learning as infoconsumption" (Brown and Duguid, 2002). With such an understanding of the educational process and with a focus on providing maximum value in terms of time and money many scenarios describing potential forms of virtual universities emerged (see Table 1 for a summary). Cunningham et al. (1997) describe the virtual university as a situation where "students never meet a lecturer face to face in a classroom, never physically visit the on-campus library; in fact, never set foot on the campus or into an institutional lecture-room or learning centre". In a similar vein, Chellappa et al. (1997) propose a scenario in which the Virtual University takes educational material from many content providers and from educators on demand, customizing it to student demands and distributing through an open technological infrastructure. Harris (2000) in his work presents a range of virtual arrangements with varying purposes. In the one extreme he places the "learning utility" where the purpose of virtual learning is the maximization of student numbers and in the other the "interstitial model" where advanced learning technologies are combined with more conventional ones. Van der Perre and his associates (2000), finally, have coined the concept of the distributed virtual university which combines the characteristics of a consortium of universities to the idea of virtuality.

Table 1. Visions of the virtual university

Cunningham et al. (1997)	… a situation where students never meet a lecturer face to face in a classroom, never physically visit the on-campus library; in fact, never set foot on the campus or into an institutional lecture-room or learning centre
Morrissey (2002)	Universities that provide an "anytime, anywhere" virtual classroom model using ICT platforms to deliver courses and degree programs for both resident and non-resident students.
Antonucci and Cronin (2001)	A synthesis of traditional academic principles with an exciting, dynamic non-traditional learning model involving the delivery of college level courses and university-style services via the Internet.
Moratis and van Baalen (2002)	The networked business school deploys a hybrid form of virtualization, in order to be able to deliver low-cost, mass-customized courses for large numbers of students, while at the same time it commits to principles of personalization, differentiation, and blended learning in its offerings, enabling low-scale and high-cost provision of education for particular markets, too.
Dumort (2000)	The university of tomorrow is more likely to offer a mix of on-campus and internet-based off-campus courses in order to respond to increasing need for accessibility, diversity, flexibility and affordability of education services
Chellappa et al. (1997)	A VU does not have a traditional campus, professors' offices, or a library; instead, there are electronic workspaces and global libraries that provide richer functionality and features than their physical analogs. A VU focuses on developing skills and expertise by mass customizing content on demand rather than providing terminal degree programs with homogeneous and predetermined curricula.

What is common in all these scenarios is according to Cornford (2000: 509) "the decomposition of the university as a particular place and its recomposition as a set of wholly mediatized relationships, tied together by information and communications technologies (ICTs)". This focus on the technological backbone of the virtual university rather than the reactions of the faculty or the students is obvious also in accounts of real-life examples of universities that incorporate virtual types of interactions in some of their functions. Pease (2000) in her analysis of the Jones International University celebrates mainly the technological innovativeness of the institution which provides a flexible and convenient leaning environment. Schneider et al. (2000) in their account of the interactive web-based Master of Arts in Gerontology launched by the Leonard Davis School of Gerontology discuss briefly students concerns only to center their analysis on the design of the program. Finally, Dumort (2000) in his overview of the development of new media in the higher education systems of the European Union and USA insists mainly on the technological aspects of these advances highlighting innovative approaches in the introduction of ICT in the learning process.

It is therefore obvious that the discussion on the virtual university is rife from technological determinism. The new "intellectual/electronic infrastructure" (Ives and Jarvenpaa, 1996) is not only considered by the majority of researchers as the primary medium for providing education but also as the basic enabler of organizational change leading to the retooling of the university. Even criticism on the idea of the virtual university tends to focus primarily on technology stressing the disadvantages of virtualization. Newman and Johnson (1999), for example, criticize the oversimplified underlying assumptions of the virtual university that tend to ignore the role of apprenticeship and the situated nature of knowledge generation. Similarly, Brown and Duguid (2002) question the vision of a totally virtual university since they claim that there are many complex issues related to learning, knowledge, communities, organizations and institutions that must be incorporated in the debate.

The missing element in the current debate on the virtual university is the people that use the new technologies namely the faculty and the students. Centering the discussion on technological advances and its advantages and disadvantages the existing literature is failing to study how the faculty, the students and the other members of the academic community are actually coping with this radical shift in the nature of their activities.

Our intention in this chapter is to develop the problematic by examining issues pertaining to the *appropriation* of ICT-enabled learning practices in a virtual environment. We examine a real-life instance of a specific model of virtual university, that of the distributed virtual university (Van der Perre et al. 2001). In this model, Van Baalen and Moratis (2001) explain that "the use of ICT is of central importance to its functioning not only in the sense of providing education through ICT, but also to establish networking between participating universities that initiate activities together". However, is technology in itself enough to propel collaboration between different institutions in a virtual environment? How do faculty and students adapt their practices to the new technological realities? Recent studies (e.g. Edmondson et al. 2001) have shown that the implementation of a new technology disrupts the existing organizational routines. Zollo et al. (2002) established a clear link among the development of common inter-organizational routines in strategic alliances and the process of learning among partners. However, thus far, there is no clear evidence that the implementation of a technological solution in a distributed, inter-organizational environment is going to be appropriated by the users or that is going to lead to the establishment of joint practices.

3. Research design and method

The need of this particular research endeavour to be longitudinal in nature, yet real-time in terms of observation (Van de Ven, 1992), indicated the case study approach as the most appropriate research method. Case study incorporates the empirical context in the research design (Hartley, 1998) and this permitted a holistic, in depth investigation (Tellis, 1997) of the processes involved in the phenomenon under study.

For the collection of empirical data the eMaster Postgraduate programme has been selected. eMaster is a specific, unique, bounded system with patterned behaviour (Stake, 1994) that can reveal interesting insights in the way technology can harness inter-university collaboration in a virtual environment if its particularities are pondered upon as the case study method implies. The main drivers behind its selection were its polycentric character as well as the geographical dispersion of the participating institutions, which demanded intense communication and collaboration.

Research drew both on archival data, in-depth interviews and informal discussions with participants in the consortium as detailed below. The aim was to recreate and thus understand the contextual frames of reference (Van de Ven, 1992) of the partners in order to record the reaction of faculty and students to the introduction of novel technological solutions in teaching and assess their subsequent influence in the establishment of inter-organizational collaboration in a virtual environment. For this reason, the first round of interviews aimed at retracing the basic events of eMaster's formation and acquiring a solid picture of the consortium. The process of interviewee identification was quite simple in concept and was followed in a manner consistent with that used in other research efforts as well (e.g. Doz, 1996). First, the participants that enjoyed the most visibility in the eMaster program were interviewed, namely the director of the program and some faculty members actively involved. These interviews revealed other persons involved in the alliance, which were consecutively interviewed. This process came full circle when the persons suggested had already been interviewed. During this first interview stage, an intense research in archival data also took placc in order to trigger the memories of the interviewees and reduce the selective retrospective bias of the participants (Golden, 1992). This retrospective case history (Van de Ven, 1992) delivered an account of the major events during eMaster's process. The outcome was used as the basis of the second round of interviews where participants were asked to commentate on these events with emphasis on instances affecting tasks common to all alliance parties, which also involved use of ICT.

In addition to the interview material a variety of other complementary sources of information were deployed in order to gain richer insights to the phenomenon. These included archival data, which consisted mainly of e-mails and minutes of the Executive Board meetings, as well as data derived from informal discussions with eMaster members, participation in eMaster meetings, informal discussions with key eMaster players and various teaching activities, which fed research with an in-depth knowledge of eMaster routines and practices and acted as a supplementary source of empirical findings. The data gathered through this methodology was analyzed according to the qualitative methods of inductive analysis (e.g. Miles and Huberman, 1984) in order to ensure viability and rigor.

4. eMASTER postgraduate programme

The eMaster consortium evolved out of the need for a more up-to-date executive education regarding the changes ICT brought to managerial practices. This need has been formally expressed by the European Union, which, at the encouragement of G7, invited in 1997 a group of top-ranked business schools, business organizations and research centers to develop a new educational program for eCommerce. Although the initiative involved solely the creation of the curriculum, professors from ten universities decided to actually launch an international postgraduate program in eCommerce, which they called eMaster.

The founding core of the alliance included five large European Business Schools and one partner from the Unites States of America. In the beginning of the second academic year ("ring" in eMaster's terminology), the alliance, as a result of increasing demand, was also joined by four new members: two European universities and two from the North America.

The content of the postgraduate program offered by the consortium was arranged around three general streams, Business, Technology, and Policy and Law. Courses were classified in three main categories. The first included Internet-based courses, common for all eMaster partners, that were part of the technological stream. The second category included courses common in terms of topic but different or at least varying in terms of content. eMaster faculty was allowed to select their own material and teaching methods, however the core of the lessons was common as they involved a joint assignment called Virtual Team Exercises (VTE) that entailed the collaboration of students from all university members in multinational teams. Finally, eMaster included also school specific courses to capitalize on local expertise and comply with local policy and accreditation issues. As part of its innovative approach in teaching methods, eMaster offered also International Seminars three times per academic year as well as an in-company project at the end of the program.

The following sections describe and explain in detail the occasions where ICT was used as the backbone in eMaster's joint activities. To this end, the analysis focuses primarily on the preparation of two course categories, the Internet-based courses and the courses with common title that included Virtual Team Exercises. A major component of eMaster's curriculum, these two course categories represent a rich and interesting setting to examine in depth how consortium partners deployed the technological infrastructure at their service.

4.1 Internet-based courses

Internet based courses were part of the technology stream and aimed at providing an overview of the majority of technological issues regarding eCommerce. They included a variety of topics such as security, information systems, eCommerce. This plurality of content however did not satisfy the faculty or the students. Faculty members coming from different disciplines had difficulties in teaching all topics of the course. As one of the course designers stated:

> *"Faculty members could not easily teach that course. This was due to the fact that everybody originated from a different discipline. For example, the tutors with expertise in IT had no problem in teaching databases or somebody with IS expertise could easily teach the relevant topics. However, many had difficulties in analyzing some interdisciplinary issues or e-Commerce topics. They needed coaching themselves to cope with the demands of the course. This wasn't a single incident since many of the tutors involved in the course faced this kind of problem."*

Students on the other hand, expected something quite different than the content actually delivered. Students with a technology background were quite disappointed by the relevant lessons since they were quite easy for them while management-oriented students expected more emphasis on organizational issues.

The inability of the courses to satisfy the needs of both faculty and students does not originate solely in the different backgrounds of those two groups. Variety is always present in postgraduate courses without inhibiting educational practices. In eMaster, the core of the problem could be traced in the design phases of the Internet-based courses. eMaster directors, who set the requirements, could not provide specific guidelines to the persons who designed the courses while time was pressing and the resources were limited. As stated by one of the courses designers of the first Internet-based courses of the curriculum, T1:

> *"We did not have guidance regarding the content of the course. We had created a pilot that was presented during an Executive Board Meeting in Atlanta and as it was approved*

we continued to design the course trying to combine resources useful for technology apt students as well as beginners. However, at this point of time, dates were pressing and the Board did not have a clear idea on how the course should look like. So we designed T1 along the lines of the pilot already approved."

The interviews revealed that the task of designing the three Internet-based courses, although common to all eMaster members, was allocated by the Board of Directors to specific partners, which were solely responsible for the structure, the content and interface of the course with little, if any, interaction with instructors from the other institutions in the consortium. Responsible for the three technology courses were two European universities and a U.S. one. The first European University designed T1 ("eTechnology Infrastractures"), which was taught in the first academic year of eMaster. The task was undertaken by a team that tried to incorporate in the content the various suggestions of the partners but was especially guided by the eMaster Director of the university. Following its preparation and its distribution to the students, a brief period of familiarization of the faculty intervened. Every faculty member that was responsible for teaching T1 had the opportunity to comment on the course components and provide suggestions for amelioration. During that period, the European University team became subject to severe criticism, although unofficially, since the faculty and the directors themselves expected something quite different than the outcome. As time was not enough for radical changes, the final version taught to the students had few differences from the original. However, all the comments as well as material provided by faculty were incorporated in the second version of the course during Ring II.

4.2 Common courses and virtual team exercises

The second common task regarding course preparation involved eMaster courses that had a common topic for all partners. The actual content of the courses lied at the discretion of every professor. The courses were paired with projects (the Virtual Team Exercises), undertaken by groups of students from various university-members. This structure provided great freedom to the tutor, however, it demanded inter-faculty coordination and sometimes even collaboration for the benefit of the Virtual Team Exercises, which had to be grounded in common knowledge. This interaction never happened in practice since the consortium could not provide enough incentives to the tutors to challenge them into working in an inter-organizational environment. As one faculty member stated:

"At the beginning, I though collaboration with my eMaster colleagues was obligatory in order to create a common curriculum for the course. For that purpose, I contacted the

course manager. However, very soon I realized that collaboration was optional and furthermore not everybody was willing to participate. I had begun [working] with the will to discuss with other colleagues the topic itself since it was very innovative at the time. I saw an opportunity in discussing the content of a highly innovative course. In practice, this never happened because there wasn't enough motivation. Besides, there wasn't any specific task list. So, we didn't have to make time for this to happen. [...] Regarding this course eMaster provided me with a highly innovative title at the time. Nothing more. I was solely responsible for the teaching method and I had prepared the course according to my experience."

And yet the reluctance of faculty members to collaborate was not considered as something potentially harmful to the consortium. As one eMaster director acknowledged:

"Ultimately faculty will choose to collaborate or not, on their own volition. You can force them by terms of employment or whatever. In an executive program you try to find the best faculty who can teach in that type of a setting. It is a very special kind of setting and even good faculty in regular courses does not do very well in executive. Because they really have to relinquish a sheer amount of minute-by-minute control of the course to the students and a lot of faculty are only comfortable when they're totally in control of the course. And whether this also commensurates with their interest in collaborating internationally with other faculty you have to look at it as something of a bonus. If you say the most important think for me is that they collaborate internationally and secondarily that they do well in the classroom you would probably have a disaster in your hands from a delivery perspective. So you try to find people who seem to be able to deal with both ... But if you have to make a hard decision you come down on the side of good delivery in the classroom primarily."

The lack of collaboration among faculty members affected also the level of collaboration among students during Virtual Team Exercises. Since faculty members did not interact with each other they could not persuade students of the necessity of these exercises. As one student stated: "*Teachers weren't very committed to eMaster in order to sell it better to us*". Thus, students were motivated solely by their own pursuits in order to diligently accomplish these assignments. To this end, vexation was not something uncommon among students as this remark by one student indicates:

"Supervisors did not collaborate. The one did not know what the other had done. We had a marketing plan in VTE1 which took us a lot of time to achieve. Then in GTE2 we were forced to do a business plan. The brochure we received demanded questions already covered during VTE1. We were at a loss. We didn't know what we were supposed to do."

These differences made coordination of the Virtual Team Exercises rather impossible since Internet was the basic means of communication and therefore these exercises fell gradually into disuse as a practice.

5. Organizing principles for the virtual university

Pretty soon it became evident to both students and faculty that the available technological infrastructure was not enough in itself to foster collaboration. The problem was not solely technological since there were other elements missing as well. A closer look at the Internet-based courses and the Virtual Team Exercises allows us to move the discussion from what went wrong in the case of eMaster to a broader discussion on how universities can collaborate, in terms of teaching and learning, successfully in a virtual environment. In this section, we analyze three organizing parameters that must be taken into account early in the formation stage of a virtual inter-university collaboration: (1) fitting task characteristics to the inter-organizational context, (2) structuring a rich communication interface, and (3) fostering compatible frames.

5.1 Fitting task characteristics to the inter-organizational context

In eMaster both the Internet-based courses and the common courses with the Virtual Teams Exercises necessitated to design close collaboration between faculty members regarding the content. Because of the geographic dispersion of the consortium, the collaboration was based in e-mail lists, on-line chats and collaboration platforms like Blackboard™. Yet despite of the various electronic facilities available to the consortium, collaboration remained at minimum levels. As one faculty member stated during the interviews:

> *"I was assigned to coordinate the e-Law module at the consortium level. After a lot of effort I managed to get in contact with the other faculty members who were teaching e-Law in the participating universities. However, they were all reluctant to collaborate closer for the course."*

Even some of the eMaster directors admitted that collaboration between faculty members was quite problematic.

> *"The pinnacle of it was, some members of the faculty refused to share any of their course material with anybody else because of 'copyright' issues."*

Yet poor collaboration should not be attributed to particular faculty members who had problems with sharing and subsequently collaborating. In eMaster, as in many cases where inter-organizational networks try to foster collaboration in a virtual environment, a paradox arises. People are forced to collaborate and build interdependencies in tasks that in the physical environment are performed independently.

Education, as the literature suggests (Weick, 1976), is an idiosyncratic task. This means that the task is situated and cannot be formalized in the strict sense that tasks in industrial organizations are standardized and managed. This particularity of the educational process influences also the structure of universities as specific organizational forms. Universities are loosely coupled systems in the sense that "*coupled events are responsive, but that each event also preserves its own identity and some evidence of its physical or logical separateness*" (Weick, 1976). This type of organizational structure preserves independence for its participants in the fulfillment of their tasks. Moreover it reduces the necessity for coordination which is difficult to achieve in a highly autonomous environment and results in fewer conflicts that can arise when local needs are forced to fit in a unifying whole. So one may wonder "how can inter-organizational collaboration be fostered in such an environment when, in addition, this collaboration is virtualized"?

Although there is no easy answer to this question, the nature of the task and the interdependencies that can be introduced through it in the work practices of an inter-organizational network offer a starting point. The simple virtualization of an independent task as in the case of eMaster cannot trigger co-operation among people who are used to work independently. Moreover, the limitation of task commonality, at the consortium level, to trivial characteristics like common course titles is not going to harness collaboration since the rest of the task components can be performed locally. So a strategy to create a collaborative virtual environment is to design tasks that need to be performed in an interdependent way in the sense that each node of the network will be reliant on the others. However, such a rich and complex task structure posits more demands in other components of the inter-organizational arrangement and especially its communication interface.

5.2 Structuring a rich communication interface

In any type of inter-organizational arrangement the multiplicity of parties involved as well as the variety of organizational roles entail a highly complex communication interface within and across the organizations involved. However, the scope of this research endeavour demands communication interface to be described in terms of interaction across universities, among faculty members and among students regarding the aforementioned courses. The purpose is not to draw a detailed picture of the multiple communication paths across the alliance but to reveal the basic means of communication in eMaster in terms of persons involved and medium used.

In the case of Internet-based courses, interaction among students simply was not inscribed in their design. These courses were the only curriculum component identical for all eMaster partners. Moreover, technology courses involved intense use of information technology as part of the educational process. However, the interface design of each course included only the possibility for on-line tutoring, not interaction among students. Therefore, students could not interact during the sole scheduled common task while the exchange of ideas or experiences was left to their own initiatives. The use of the course interface as communication medium was never fully exploited for a more practical reason as well. Technology courses have been distributed to the students in the form of CD for convenience reasons so the on-line experience never actually unfolded to its true potential. As a faculty member stated:

> *"The technology course interface included mechanisms for on-line tutoring. However, in order to accommodate executive students we also distributed the course in CD's. This form was been more widely used with regards to the Internet."*

Irregularity, or rather absence of communication, characterized the interface among faculty members regarding common courses. The design of the Internet-based courses was not assigned to them and the actual designers never really communicated with faculty members during the creation of the T-courses. During the familiarization period before teaching, faculty members communicated mainly with the designer and seldom with each other. Additionally, the interface structure of the course was fostering interaction between tutors and students within the same institution and not across alliance partners. Since the Internet-based courses were taught from their CD version for practical reasons the possibility for communication across alliance partners was lost and interactions were limited within each institution, as in traditional programs.

In the case of Virtual Team Exercises, interface structure regarding students was frequent, however, the problem lied in the communication medium used for that purpose. Students were asked to coordinate their efforts though e-mails. However, this type of communication presented many problems in the context used, since the uncertainty and difficulty associated with the assignments demanded heavy coordination efforts that could not be achieved through electronic correspondence. Faculty on the other hand, had to communicate not only during the coordination of Virtual Team Exercises but also during the preparation of the courses related to them. For that purpose the alliance assigned a manager to each course who acted as intermediary among tutors. However, as stated in the interviews, this practice actually obstructed direct communication:

> *"... Since I communicated mainly with the course manager the actions of my colleagues teaching the same course in other universities were completely invisible to me. I did not*

even know who they were. Only if the course manager carbon-copied messages to other colleagues I could see their names in the e-mail."

Moreover, this course manager, as faculty members told us, did not have any specific task list therefore even communication with him faded after a while.

"... After a while it became obvious that the course manager didn't have any task list in reality. Even now I' m not sure what he actually did or even if he did anything for the course."

Thus, eMaster students and faculty never actually worked in a virtual inter-organizational environment. On the contrary, even during common tasks, interaction across universities was scarce to the detriment of the alliance. The structure of the communication interface deprived these two groups from the opportunity to collaborate closely and establish some sort of enduring and stable ties. Students could not interact properly because from inception the program never really anticipated the mechanisms that could support this kind of interaction. For faculty members, the basic barrier to a more intense and fruitful communication could be traced to the lack of motives to indulge into this kind of interaction. As a faculty member stated during interviews:

"Since there was not any specific task list, I could not see any value to interact with other faculty members. We were not obliged to deliver anything specific in the alliance so most of us opted not to get involved beyond teaching."

The poor communication among eMaster members and its consequences highlights the importance of a rich communication interface that can actually promote collaboration by linking together all the relevant communities. As Brown and Duguid (1995) argue, universities in their effort to codify knowledge in a way that can be studied and taught to others rely on a conversational paradigm which explains the importance of rich communication among members of the academic community. This is because conversations are:

"...complex and powerful social processes that involve silence as much as saying, knowing as much as information, and peripheral eavesdroppers as much as central interlocutors. Through first listening and slowly participating, people learn how to speak and when, what to say and to whom; they come to understand a community and practice from the inside, to recognize not only the accents, inflections, and jargon, but most of all the social significance of a practice. Conversation is the way understanding gets around" (Brown and Duguid, 1995)

So the absence of a mechanism that can support communication is a major omission in the structuring of a technological infrastructure that aspires to foster virtual collaboration at the inter-organizational level. First, because network members cannot really perform joined tasks under conditions of poor communication. Secondly, because with poor communication people do not build common frames regarding their work and remain with the mindsets of their respective organizations.

5.3 Fostering compatible frames

In the two previous sections we saw evidence of incompatible frames among eMaster stakeholders. Inconsistency initiated at the organizational level and subsequently influenced the perceptions of the consortium members for the common technology. More specifically, every eMaster director had different motives that triggered his involvement in the program. For example non-European partners wanted to cooperate with prominent business schools and found it hard to "sell the eMaster idea" in rings where these schools did not participate. Other directors wanted to participate in the consortium because of the eCommerce topic, while others just wanted to gain visibility by participating in an international consortium formed by renowned business schools. These different agendas influenced the alliance in a number of ways in terms of strategy and management, although, for the purpose of this research, we focus on the consequences of this discrepancy on the curriculum.

The variety of visions was primarily reflected in the recruitment of students where European and non-European universities had a different candidate profile as reference. European students were mainly corporate employees while US students were entrepreneurs that wanted to understand eBusiness in order to manage effectively their start-up companies. These discrepancies affected the content of the curriculum and especially the common courses. Internet-based courses had to be delivered in a satisfactory manner for all the students. However, the effort to combine in the Internet-based courses as many perspectives as possible in order to accommodate everybody did not satisfy students as it is evident in the following statement:

> *"The lessons were very peculiar also. There was a focus on issues that nobody cares about. Like in IT, there were lessons about encryption while people in the IT industry, like me, don't bother about them at all. It is a black box that somebody puts there. You don't have to sustain a lecture on this topic. Nobody cares."*

One of the course designers we interviewed attributed the failure of the Internet-based courses to the limited understanding and partial information students had about theses courses.

> *"We have tried to combine in T1 lessons for both technology and management oriented executives. For that choice we received severe criticism by the students, since many of them thought the content was childish. It was obviously childish since the purpose of the*

course was not to examine in dept technological issues. However, I think that students weren't really aware of what they ought to expect. I think they weren't properly informed."

The inability of the eMaster program to accommodate in the courses the variety of themes interesting the students led many participants to become abruptly aware of the gap between their initial aspirations in terms of curriculum and reality. Additionally, bonding mechanisms like Internet-based courses or Virtual Team Exercises gradually fell into misuse and were transformed into school specific routines. It is therefore evident that framing is an essential element of context. According to Orlikowski and Gash (1994) who first introduced the term, technology frames are:

"that subset of members' organizational frames that concern the assumptions, expectations, and knowledge they use to understand technology in organizations. This includes not only the nature and role of the technology itself, but the specific conditions, applications and consequences of that technology in particular contexts".

Especially, in an inter-organizational setting, framing can be proved crucial since it guides "sense making, for quickly coming to grips with a situation" (Doz and Hamel, 1998).

Technological solutions cannot harness the institution of common frames among partners in inter-organizational settings since they are the equivoque that must be jointly negotiated by the partners. So the implementation of a common technological solution will be treated by definition differently by the various partners of any inter-organizational arrangement. What can actually initiate interaction among partners for the different frames to be expressed and synthesis to start is an effective communication interface (Poulymenakou and Prasopoulou, 2004) and a careful task design that will induce partners to co-operate with each other and thus interact.

6. Technological coupling in virtual inter-organizational networks

Universities as a distinct organizational form can be viewed as loosely coupled systems tied together by a combination of join aspirations, conversational interaction and cross-fertilization between collaborating and occasionally competing communities of practice. This loose interaction between the various constituting components has been mainly induced by the idiosyncratic nature of education as a task and the autonomy that it brings to both faculty and students. The advent of new information and communication technologies that promise the digitization of the entire educational process and its recombination into cyberspace created new possibilities for the coupling of educational organizations.

In this chapter we discussed the possibility of technological coupling as a potential mechanism that can restructure universities to better fit in the new virtual environment. Technological coupling is the ad hoc introduction of a common technological infrastructure between universities collaborating in a virtual environment. Many universities inspired by the rhetoric of the new university "without walls" and the implicit technological determinism that characterizes it launched large scale projects to virtualize part of their operations. An even more advanced form of virtual university is the one that combines not only new technologies but also inter-university collaboration in various stages of the educational process. In this particular type of virtual university technological coupling has been proposed and in many cases, as the one examined here, implemented as the core around which the entire collaboration could be built.

From the analysis it became evident that in the case of eMaster there were a number of incompatible characteristics that affected the appropriation of the technological infrastructure. Tasks for every partner were defined, in their majority, so as to permit operation based on university specific routines. However, in order to ensure interaction, common tasks, namely the Internet based courses and the Virtual Team Exercises, were also assigned. The execution of these tasks involved heavy use of Internet-based mechanisms, which were embedded in these activities not only as a facilitating component but also primarily as a unifying mechanism among partners. Despite initial design these mechanisms never promoted collaboration and learning among partners because the common tasks were allocated to specific partners who performed them following their own, independent routines. Thus, task commonality never actually led to intense collaboration since poor execution prevented the establishment of joint inter-organizational practices.

A number of shortcomings existed in the structure of the communication interface among eMaster members making it circumstantial and eclectic regarding the communication paths followed. The main paradox could be traced to the absence of an interface mechanism in Internet-based courses. The consortium had not invested in fostering interaction in the sole common and technology intensive task of the program. This omission left a great opportunity to foster stable communication paths and facilitate the creation of social ties among participants (other than eMaster directors) totally unexploited. However this instance was not the only problem in eMaster's interface. Even the communication media used when interaction was anticipated were not the appropriate for the occasion. Students, for example, interacted through e-mail when the tasks entailed high uncertainty and thus more face-to-face communication was in order (Daft, Lengel, and Trevino, 1987). The poor design regarding interface caused profound disappointment to many eMaster participants leading to the gradual misuse of any communication attempts within an inter-organizational environment and the subsequent retreat in communication among school-specific actors.

In the analysis presented thus far it is evident that the interplay of task and communication interface structure with the Internet-based mechanisms embedded in joint activities affects mainly structural as well as operational characteristics of an inter-organizational virtual arrangement. Frames, on the other hand, affect technology at a more general level since they influence its very use within an inter-organizational context. Directors had very different visions regarding the role of eMaster, which led to the recruitment of students with very different educational needs and expectations regarding the program. This fact complicated curriculum. Especially in the common courses, where Internet-based mechanisms played a key role, context never satisfied both directors and students since the attempt to incorporate a wide variety of topics made the course imbalanced and unexciting. Problems in the use of technology led to it being used as a scapegoat for the lack of success of the Internet-based courses and thus its role as a unifying mechanism gradually fainted.

It is evident that technology in itself cannot trigger the formation of inter-organizational ties. Moreover, the implementation of a technological infrastructure as a coupling mechanism does not guarantee appropriation, as it is already known in the literature of information systems. The analysis showed that there are a number of defining factors namely; (1) task characteristics, (2) communication interface, and (3) frames that must be aligned for any effort to create a distributed virtual university to be successful. The existence of specific factors that actually foster or obstruct collaboration in inter-organizational environments has already been discussed in the strategic management literature with reference to strategic alliances. Doz (1996) in his work identified four initial conditions, *task definition* for all the parties, *organizational routines*, *interface structure* and *expectations,* that define to a large extent the outcome of any alliance. In this research we verified the importance of defining factors at the formation stage of any inter-organizational collaboration. Moreover, we identified the set of factors that affect inter-organizational collaboration in virtual environments and that fit to the particularities of the university as an organizational form.

Finally, through the discussion on the virtual university and the role of new advanced technologies in its operation, the need for a thorough restructuring of the university became explicit. To this respect Cornford's (2000: 520) work echoes the findings of our own research:

> *"These demands literally call into being a different, and more concrete, type of institution, one in which the heterogeneity of the institution is reduced in the sense that the various parts of the organization must be made to fit together and be aligned in the same direction. Indeed, what we have found is that attempts to build the virtual university from the bottom-up, course-by-course, without reconstructing the basic structures of the university appear to be very slow, labor intensive and highly prone to failure."*

The introduction of new technological solutions that foster advanced forms of interaction cannot be successful in a traditional environment. We must reconsider the way universities currently function, identify their core operations and assist them in their transition to an organizational form that will incorporate successfully the new technologies available.

7. Conclusions

The vision of an institution "without walls" is a powerful one, as the augmenting volume of business and academic literature shows. Such vision is based on the assumption that existing processes are going to be translated in information and thus into a form that is amenable to technologically mediated storage and distribution to enable mobility and re-combination in new ways and in new places. In this paper we critically examine the promise of the virtual university. More specifically we focus on a special case of virtual university which combines virtuality with inter-organizational collaboration. The purpose is to examine whether the ad hoc introduction of a common technological infrastructure can actually harness collaboration among different universities embodying the characteristics of loosely coupled systems.

Previous research examining real-life examples of virtual universities primarily focuses on the technological details of the underlying infrastructure (e.g. Pease, 2000; Schneider et al., 2000). Even critics of the virtual university tend to discuss the new arrangements introduced by technology at an abstract theoretical level without focusing on how or even if users are appropriating the available technological infrastructure. This paper makes a contribution in this area through the empirical investigation, in an inter-university consortium collaborating virtually in many instances, of the way technological coupling has been accepted by faculty and students. Moreover, the research delves into the basic parameters that influence technological coupling and provides a thorough analysis on the use of Internet-based mechanisms as teaching outlets and collaboration tools among students.

Specifically, empirical data provided enlightening insights on how particular instances during the formation of the inter-university consortium and the design of the common technology inhibit the adoption of innovative technological solutions for the execution of joint tasks at the consortium level. Research in eMaster has shown that incompatibility of three defining parameters, (1) task characteristics, (2) communication interface, and (3) frames or poor execution lead to internal tensions in the consortium and members tended to retreat to their own practices and abandon any common efforts that were associated with high degrees of uncertainty and potential discord. Therefore, technology could not act as the glue among consortium members because partners defined tasks and established communication procedures that did not foster cooperation in a virtual environment. The problem did not lie in purely technological issues but in the way cooperation was envisaged during formation.

Acknowledgements

The authors would like to thank Niki Panteli for her insightful comments in previous versions of this chapter.

References

Brown, J. S., and Duguid, P., 1995, Universities in the digital age. *Change: The Journal of the American Academy of Higher Education.* **28**(4): 10-19.

Brown, J. S., and Duguid, P., 2002, *The Social Life of Information*, 2nd ed., Harvard Business School Press, Boston.

Chellappa, R., Barua, A., and Whinston, A. B., 1997, An electronic infrastructure for a virtual university, *CACM.* **40**(9): 56-58.

Cornford, J., 2000, The virtual university is ... the university made concrete?, *Information, Communication & Society.* **3**(4): 508-525.

Cunningham, S., Tapsall, S., Ryan, Y., Stedman, L., Bagdon, K., and Flew, T., 1997, New media and borderless education: A review of the convergence between global media networks and higher education provision (No. 97/22), Department of Employment, Education, Training and Youth Affairs, Camberra.

Daft, R. L., Lengel, R. H., and Trevino, L. K., 1987, Message equivocality, media selection, and manager performance: Implications for information systems, *MIS Quarterly.* **11**(3): 355-366.

DeSanctis, G., and Monge, P., 1999, Introduction to the special issue: Communication processes for virtual organizations. *Org. Sc.*. **10**(6): 693-703.

Doz, Y. L., 1996, The evolution of cooperation in strategic alliances: Initial conditions or learning processes?, *Strategic Management Journal.* **17**(Special Issue: Evolutionary Perspectives on Strategy): 55-83.

Doz, Y. L., and Hamel, G., 1998, *Alliance Advantage: The Art of Creating Value Through Partnering*, Harvard Business School Press, Boston.

Dumort, A., 2000, New media and distance education: An EU-US perspective, *Information, Communication & Society.* **3**(4): 546-556.

Edmondson, A. C., Bohmer, R. M., and Pisano, G. P., 2001, Disrupted routines: Team learning and new technology implementation in hospitals, *Administrative Science Quarterly*. **46**: 685-716.

Golden, B. R., 1992, The past is the past - or is it? The use of retrospective accounts as indicators of past strategy, *Academy of Management Journal*. **35**(4): 848-860.

Harris, M., 2000, Virtual learning and the network society, *Information, Communication & Society*. **3**(4): 580-596.

Hartley, J. F., 1998, Case studies in organizational research, in *Qualitative methods in organizational research: A practical guide*, C. Cassell & G. Symon, eds., Sage Publications, London, pp. 208-229.

Ives, B., and Jarvenpaa, S. L., 1996, Will the Internet revolutionize business education and research?, *Sloan Management Review*. **37**(3): 33-41.

Miles, M., and Huberman, A., 1984, *Qualitative Data Analysis: A Sourcebook of New Methods*. Sage, Los Angeles.

Moratis, L. T., and van Baalen, P. J., 2002, The radicalization of the multiversity: The case of the networked business school, *The International Journal of Educational Management*. **16**(4): 160-168.

Morrissey, C. A., 2002, Rethinking the virtual university. *CACM*. **9**: 456-466.

Newman, R., and Johnson, F., 1999, Sites for power and knowledge? Towards a critique of the virtual university, *British Journal of Sociology of Education*. **20**(1): 79-88.

Orlikowski, W. J., and Gash, D. C., 1994, Technological frames: Making sense of information technology in organizations, *ACM Transactions on Information Systems*. **12**(2): 174 - 207.

Pease, P. S., 2000, The virtual university: Jones International University™, Ltd, *Information, Communication & Society*. **3**(4): 627-628.

Poulymenakou, A., and Prasopoulou, E., 2004, Adopting a life cycle perspective to explain the transition from technological innovation to alliance management, *Management Decision*. **42**(9): 1115-1130.

Schneider, E., Henke, M., and Renold, C., 2000, Targeting working professionals: A master's of arts in gerontology, *Information, Communication & Society*. **3**(4): 622 - 626.

Schultze, U., and Orlikowski, W. J., 2001, Metaphors of virtuality: Shaping an emergent reality, *Information and Organization*. **11**: 45-77.

Stake, R. S., 1994, Case studies, in *Handbook of Qualitative Research*, N. K. Denzin and Y. S. Linkoln, eds., Sage Publications, Thousand Oaks, CA, pp. 236-247.

Tellis, W., 1997, Introduction to case study, *The Qualitative Report*. **3**(2).

Van Baalen, P. J., and Moratis, L. T., 2001, *Management Education in the Network Economy*, Kluwer Academic Publishers, Boston.

Van de Ven, A. H., 1992, Suggestions for studying strategy process: A research note. *Strategic Management Journal*. **13**(Strategy process: Managing corporate self-renewal): 169-191.

Van der Perre, G., Roosendaal, H., and Van den Branden, J., 2001, The distributed virtual university, in *New Learning*, A. R. Trindade, ed., Universidade Aberta, Lisbon.

Weick, K. E., 1976, Educational organizations as loosely coupled systems, *Administrative Science Quarterly*. **21**(1): 1-19.

Zollo, M., Reuer, J. J., and Singh, H., 2002, Interorganizational routines and performance in strategic alliances. *Org. Sc.*. **13**(6): 701-713.

Part III
Conclusions

Chapter 11

Organizing Principles for Inter-firm Networks

Elpida Prasopoulou and Angeliki Poulymenakou
Athens University of Economics and Business

Abstract: Throughout this volume, we have reflected on the challenges that managers face in their everyday practice at the inter-firm level. Moreover, we have also examined a concise number of issues that must be addressed by them. Concluding this volume, it is only appropriate to present a comprehensive set of recommendations for network managers. Literature on network management includes an important number of recommendations on various issues troubling managers in such complex situations. However, a systematic, step-by-step grouping of such recommendations is still largely missing from the literature. In this chapter, we provide a set of managerial guidelines arranged according to a life cycle model of inter-firm cooperation. These guidelines are the outcome of in-depth research on specific instances of inter-firm networks as presented in the body of this volume. Specific actions are presented at each stage of the life cycle while a set of managerial implications is presented at the end of the chapter.

Key words: inter-firm networks; life cycle; dynamic view; organizing principles.

1. Introduction

Collaboration among organizations in the form of stable but flexible arrangements is a ubiquitous phenomenon driving organizational changes in the majority of industrial sectors (Doz and Hamel, 1998; Spekman et al. 1996). The turbulent environment created by technological advancements (Fulk, 2001) has prompted organizations into creating linkages among them in order to sustain competition and deal with vast changes in their markets (Miles and Snow, 1986). Technological change is not only driving inter-firm network formation, which is not new as an organizational phenomenon. It also enables new configurations which present novel characteristics if compared to inter-firm arrangements of previous decades (Fulk and DeSanctis, 1995). To this end, IT enabled inter-firm networks are a novel form of voluntary interorganizational cooperation which involve significant exchange, sharing, or co-development, and thus result in the formation of stable ties among partners that render commitments enduring and strong (Fulk and DeSanctis, 1999).

The IT-induced novelty of this organizational form in combination with its spread in the majority of industrial sectors introduced new realities in business practices and posited new challenges for managers involved in such arrangements (Ireland et al. 2002). A first striking difference in managerial practices is the necessity to add a new layer of analysis in the assessment of the external environment (Spekman et al. 1998). An inter-firm network, viewed from a single-firm's perspective, is a boundary between the firm and the industry. Each firm involved in such an arrangement must act as an integral part of a larger entity – the network – while at the same time is obliged to maintain its character as a unique and autonomous firm. This necessity of each firm to combine in its management practices two fundamentally different perspectives generates the demand for a novel design for inter-firm cooperation that will reconcile the need for autonomy and the urgency for coordinated action (Poulymenakou and Prasopoulou, 2004). This need is also transferred at the network level. Managing an inter-firm arrangement entails precisely the combination of the demands of various business entities in an outcome that can ensure viability and profitability of all the members (Poulymenakou and Prasopoulou, 2004). Nevertheless, inter-firm network management is not a simple aggregation of the needs and imperatives of the network members (Kale, Dyer, and Singh, 2001). On the contrary, it is more like a balancing act between different, frequently contradictory perspectives that must be accommodated into choices and actions that satisfy every partner in a way that minimizes conflict and leads to increasing trust (Ireland et al., 2002).

"The movement away from centrally coordinated, multi-level hierarchies" (Miles and Snow, 1992) and towards a new inter-firm organization of corporate life has preoccupied many authors who provided guidelines for the efficient management of inter-firm networks (e.g. Ireland et al., 2002; Ring, 2000; Spekman et al., 1996). However, a systematic, step-by-step analysis is still largely missing from the literature. In this chapter, we provide a set of managerial guidelines arranged according to a life cycle model of inter-firm cooperation. Life cycle models are a prominent way of describing the various stages of an inter-firm collaboration (De Rond and Bouchikhi, 2004). Nevertheless, most of the authors (e.g. D'Aunno and Zuckerman, 1987; George and Farris, 1999), with the notable exception of Kanter (1994) and

Spekman et al. (1996), concentrate on the characteristics of each stage or the relationships among the various stakeholders without providing specific guidelines for management to follow during those stages. It this chapter, each stage of the life cycle contains a concise list of managerial recommendations for a successful collaboration among the various partners. In the following section the existing life cycle models and their rationale are presented and analysed. The critical parameters that managers must take into account when joining an inter-firm network are overviewed in section 3. Section 4 presents the life cycle model and the managerial guidelines related to each stage. Finally, in section 5 we discuss the implications that stem out of such a view on network management.

2. A Dynamic view of inter-firm management

Investigation of the organizational processes involved in the formation and management of inter-firm networks is a persistent claim in organization and management literatures (Salk, 2005). Current research on inter-firm networks examines primarily the antecedent conditions of inter-firm formation and the structural properties of these arrangements (Ring and Van de Ven, 1994) presenting a static view of the phenomenon. There is however, a small number of researchers (e.g. De Rond and Bouchikhi, 2004; Doz, 1996; George and Farris, 1999) who focus on the very process of networking. The outcome of their endeavours is incorporated in a number of life cycle models identifying sequences of formative stages and the issues that need to be addressed by managers.

One of the first studies that adopted explicitly such a dynamic view is D'Aunno and Zuckerman's (1987) investigation of hospital federations. Acknowledging the multi-organizational nature of such collaborations the authors focus on the identification of specific stages during their life cycle. Their purpose was to identify which factors influence the transition from one stage to another, while at the same time they also presented a list of tasks to be performed by managers at each stage. Comparing to current life cycle models, the stages identified by D' Aunno and Zuckerman (1987) seem quite simple. However, this research effort signals a conceptual shift in network literature since it uses life cycle models as an explanatory device for network formation. Moreover, it sketches a management framework with specific tasks to be addressed by organizational members. In the same vein, Larson (1992) conducted a number of case studies on high-growth entrepreneurial firms where she identified three discrete phases on network formation. The first one groups the preconditions for the exchanges such as pre-existing relationships among the collaborating organizations. The second phase presents the conditions necessary for the establishment of inter-firm linkages such as mutual economic advantages while the third phase presents the factors which solidify the relationship among prospective partners.

Alluding to a linear sequence of evolution, inter-firm network formation has been also presented as a marriage where cooperation follows various stages from courtship to internal change (Kanter, 1994). The purpose of this metaphor was to stress the dynamic nature of inter-firm collaboration and prepare managers, at least at a mental level, to the realities of network management. Spekman et al. (1996) also propose a sequence of various stages ultimately leading to the establishment of inter-firm linkages. These are anticipation, engagement, valuation, coordination, investment, stabilization and decision. This life cycle model which is based on case studies in various business organizations engaged in inter-firm collaborations is more fine-grained than the previous ones presenting a longer set of stages which are further analysed into a set of issues that need to be tackled by managers.

Going further than the identification of successive stages and the listing of specific tasks or issues within each one of them, life cycle models present also interesting analyses on the governance mechanisms deployed by network partners. Lowndes and Skelcher (1998) used a four-stage life cycle model as framework in order to investigate governance mechanisms. They found that from the initial contacts among partners to the delivery of their programme and subsequent dissolution inter-firm arrangements adopt various governance mechanisms ranging from networking between individuals to formal hierarchical structures and even market mechanisms in order to accommodate the various stakeholders emerging at each stage and achieve the objectives set at the beginning of collaboration.

The evolution from early research efforts stressing on the formative stages themselves, to the later ones focusing more explicitly in the managerial issues of inter-firm networks (George and Farris, 1999) (see Table 1) instantiates the transition from the need to understand the phenomenon of network formation to an urgency to manage the inter-firm collaboration effectively (Ireland et al., 2002). The intuitive appeal of life cycle as a conceptual scaffold for the examination of inter-firm network management is closely linked to its easy association to the natural life cycle (George and Farris, 1999). However, according to Poulymenakou and Prasopoulou (2004) there are even more advantages to such a conceptual model:

Table 1. Life cycle models of inter-firm networks

Study	Focus	Life cycle stages
D'Aunno and Zuckerman, 1987	Application of life cycle model in hospital federations	Emergence of a coalition Transition to a federation Maturity of federation Critical crossroads
Larson, 1992	Examination of the role of social dimension in the control and coordination of inter-firm networks	Preconditions for exchange history Conditions to build mutual economic advantage, trial period Integration and control
Kanter, 1994	Managerial guidelines for the stages of a life cycle	Selection and courtship Getting engaged Setting up housekeeping Learning to collaborate Changing within
Spekman et al., 1996	Analysis of a life cycle model	Anticipation Engagement Valuation Coordination Investment Stabilization Decision
Lowndes and Skelcher, 1998	Mode of governance in various stages of the life cycle Relationships between stakeholders	Pre-partnership collaboration Partnership creation and consolidation Partnership programme delivery Partnership termination and succession

- **Continuity:** First of all, partners realize that their actions do not happen in vacuum. There is continuity in their decisions that must be acknowledged. To this end, partners need to carefully design the parameters that must be controlled and be very precise of their decisions and actions even from the initial stages of inter-firm network formation since they can significantly influence its entire course.
- **Step-by-step approach:** The definition of specific stages in the network life cycle permits partners to conceptualize the transitory phases that these inter-firm arrangements go through and adjust their practices in the special characteristics of each stage. Partners through a stage-by-stage approach can focus on the special needs of each stage while taking into account the more longitudinal needs of the inter-firm network.

The following sections built on the stages of the network life cycle management framework presented in Chapter 2. In accordance to the latest trends in inter-firm management research, we reflect on the challenges that managers face in their everyday practice at the inter-firm level. Moreover, in each stage we examine a concise number of issues that must be addressed by managers. The outcome, as presented in this chapter, is a set of recommendations which must be followed for a fruitful inter-firm collaboration. Before, however, delving into inter-firm network management we examine the critical parameters for the emergence of such cooperations.

3. Designing for cooperation: The critical parameters

The impressive variety characterizing networks (e.g. strategic alliances, supply chain hubs, dynamic focal networks) (Elmuti and Kathawala, 2001) stresses the importance of thorough planning before an organization initiates or enters a network arrangement (Ring, 2000). Managers have to assess a number of parameters that will permit them to gain a better appreciation of the dynamic environment in which they enter (Draulans, deMan, and Volberda, 2003). Among the various parameters proposed in the literature (e.g. Das and Teng, 2003; Saxton, 1997) we focus in two that we consider fundamental since they influence the needs and motives for inter-firm network formation as well as the issues that need to be tackled from a management perspective.

We first examine the general industry characteristics which shape the context in which inter-firm collaborations emerge (Vyas, Shelburn, and Rogers, 1995). Then we investigate the characteristics of the network itself, which influence greatly the issues that must be addressed by the management (Borys and Jemison, 1989). The examination of these two parameters as a management prerequisite in each inter-firm network serves a dual purpose. First of all, managers can focus on the issues that are of relevance in the particular characteristics of the industry and the inter-firm network in which they are. Additionally, they become aware of the complex character of a network arrangement and of the various tasks they need to perform in order to manage it successfully.

3.1 Industry characteristics

The flexible character of the network organization as well as its adaptability to various circumstances facilitated the spread of this organizational form in many industries (Doz and Hamel, 1998). However, the ecology of every industrial sector comprises different elements that influence greatly the characteristics of the emerging inter-firm arrangements (Madhavan, Koka, and Prescott, 1998). To cope with the idiosyncrasies of the industry in which the network operates, managers need first to assess a number of specific factors that describe the external environment of the inter-firm arrangement. These factors are the following:

Pace of change in the industry

The transition from one organizational archetype to another implies significant changes in any industry. Nevertheless, the pace of change is a parameter that varies across industrial sectors since innovation at the technological and institutional level does not influence uniformly the actors of every industry (Osborn and Hagedoorn, 1997). At the network level, managers need to distinguish primarily between *evolutionary* and *revolutionary* change in order to gain a realistic picture of the fermentations inside every sector.

In sectors where change is the outcome of longitudinal processes among the various actors of the industry, the evolving inter-firm networks have the character of strategic collaborations with a long-term perspective that bound together the participating entities (Osborn and Hagedoorn, 1997). This is precisely the case of the automotive industry as analyzed in the chapter of Corsten et al. The propensity of the players in the automotive industry to form inter-firm networks is mainly attributed to the degrading market conditions in the industry and the subsequent augmenting competition between the existing OEMs (Glaister and Buckley, 1996). OEMs, parts suppliers and other business entities in this industry need to collaborate in order to survive fierce competition within the European market and face the other OEMs from U.S. and Japan (Dyer, 1997). Nevertheless, this change in the market conditions has been gradual and does not threaten the existence of traditional roles in the industry. The very existence of OEMs is not questioned and the evolving inter-firm networks are coalitions of existing players that join their forces in order to compete other coalitions within the industry (Bensaou and Venkatraman, 1995).

The situation is quite different when change is the outcome of unexpected technological or institutional advances (Anderson and Tushman, 1990) that question the existence of traditional players, lower the entry barriers to innovative entities and lead to more flexible and precarious inter-firm combinations that can adapt to a volatile environment (Garud and Kumaraswamy, 1993). This is the case of the mobile service provides described by Mahnke et al. in this volume. The rapid technological advances in mobile and wireless applications cause great uncertainty on the roles each player is going to assume. Thus, inter-firm arrangements in this industry are too open-ended and transient focusing on the exploitation of specific applications and not to the formation of long-term relationships (Poulymenakou and Prasopoulou, 2004).

Degree of industry institutionalization

Another factor that influences the characteristics of the inter-firm networks that emerge in the various industrial sectors is the degree of institutionalization of the industry in which actors operate (Park, 1996). There are significant differences in the inter-firm networks that emerge out of *traditional, established industries* with the ones that emerge from *new, highly innovative* ones. This is due to the fact that in traditional industries, large companies dominate while in emerging industries the size of the players is considerably small following the young age of the sector itself. These differences in size can be translated in the degree of inertia inherent in each actor. In traditional industries the players are usually more conservative while in more innovative sectors, players are more positive to new arrangements.

In traditional industrial sectors where relationships among players are rather stable and there are large firms that dominate the market, the propensity towards inter-firm networking leads to stable arrangements that concentrate a significant number of players (Boddy, Macbeth, and Wagner, 2000). This is the case of the retail industry presented by Papakiriakopoulos in this volume. The network evolved in a traditional industry where players are mostly large retail companies and their suppliers. The collaboration among these major players, although technologically driven, does not lead to a solution that revolutionizes the existing structure of the industry. On the contrary, the inter-firm arrangement aimed at the consolidation of the traditional relationships and the creation of even stronger ties among traditional allies or old competitors. This proves that the degree of inertia in the system usually leads to inter-firm arrangements that sustain the traditional status quo in the industry.

In innovative industrial sectors however, the situation is quite different. The small size of the companies and the young age of the industry itself usually nurture more flexible and quite often provisional inter-firm networks (Hitt, Dacin, Levitas, Arregle, and Borza, 2000). The pharmaceutical companies described by Jørgsensen, and Vintergaard (this volume) create a network of partners around the in order to draw the necessary resources and expertise for their products. These networks are characterized by plug-and-play arrangements that mainly aim at the absorption of the knowledge of each partner (Vervest et al. 2004). Their example indicates that the small size of players in new industries and their inability to possess all the necessary resources is the primary reason for networking. However, the necessity for a variety of resources infuses these arrangements with a short-term character since the needs of each firm for various resources changes over time.

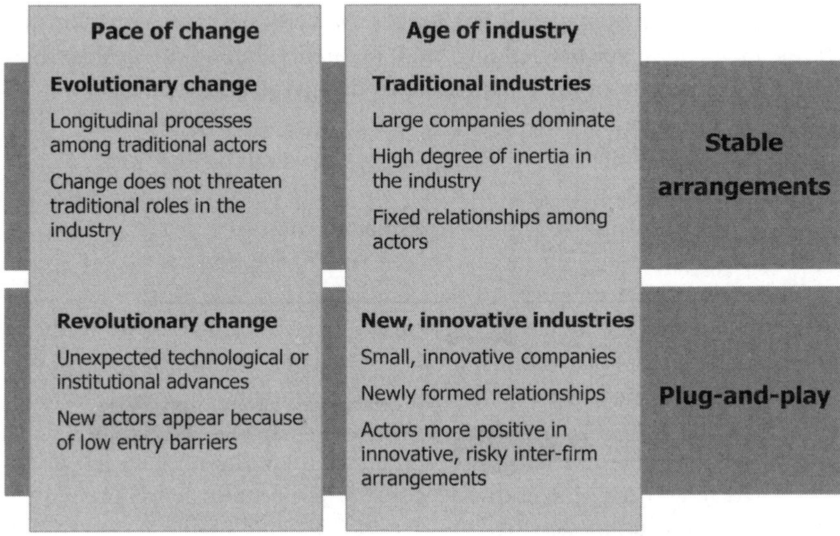

Figure 1. The influence of industry characteristics in the inter-firm network types

It follows that there are two prevailing forms of inter-firm networking, the stable arrangements and the plug-and-play arrangements. The stable arrangements like the OEM; the R-L network and the eMaster network emerge in traditional markets with established players where change occurs in an evolutionary way that does not disrupt existing relationships. The plug-and-play arrangements like Derma S/A on the contrary, are the products of new industries where revolutionary changes take place and small innovative companies join their forces in order to create a common pool of capabilities for their mutual benefit (Vervest et al., 2004).

3.2 Inter-firm network characteristics

The existence of multiple dominant variations around a generic cast is a unique characteristic of the network form of organizing that differentiates it from other organizational forms (Ebers and Jarillo, 1998). The possibility for various arrangements infuses this form with flexibility yet at the same time generates the need for some anchoring points against which managers can map the inter-firm networks in which they participate (Richardson, 1995). In this section we present an overview (Figure 2) of the most important themes in inter-firm network management. Thus we focus on issues of power among network partners, entry requirements and stability of these arrangements. We also discuss the role of IT in the formation and management of inter-firm networks. Within each issue we analyze only the extreme cases in order to vividly highlight the managerial challenges. Nevertheless, we consider these cases as ideal ones acknowledging that in reality inter-firm arrangements contain a combination of the characteristics discussed below.

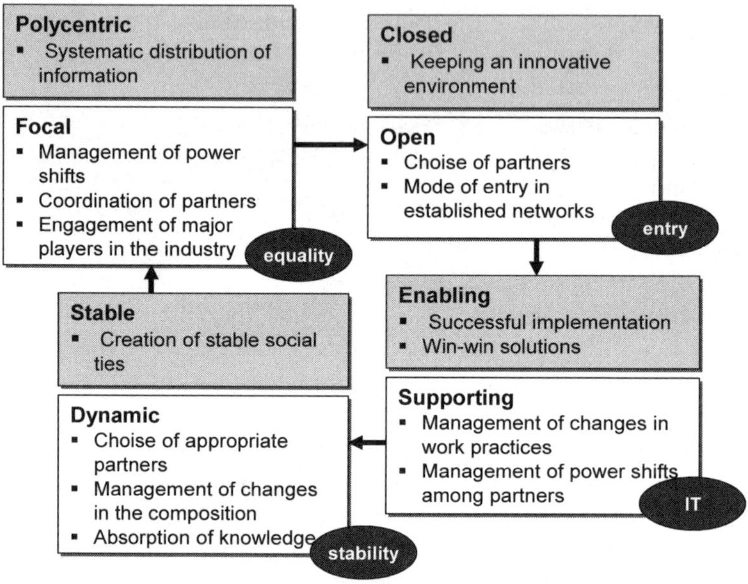

Figure 2. Overview of the major network management issues according to network characteristics

Polycentric vs. focal networks

Not all network members wield equal power and influence in a network, some network members have a much bigger say then others (Huxham and Beech, 2002). The strength of participating members influences the topology of the inter-firm arrangement (Nooteboom, 2004). As a consequence of the influence of one partner over the actions of the others, focal networks evolve (Ebers and Jarillo, 1998). If power is equally distributed among partners polycentric networks evolve.

Prasopoulou et al. in this book examine the case of a polycentric network. In eMaster, the primer issue that determined the network topology has been the nature of the participating members. Since all business schools were acknowledged authorities in the field of management and ICT, the structure of the network ought to respect their academic status. Should a more hierarchical structure have been adopted there would not be any incentives to form the network. Moreover, the *service* offered by the consortium, that is the MBA degree, demanded continuous collaboration and intensive information exchange among all contributing members, at least in the fist phase of its launch. Finally, the vast dispersion of the participating universities could not possibly allow a more hierarchical structure since systematic control is impossible. In the cases analyzed by Riemer in this volume on the other hand what led to polycentric arrangements was the difference in capabilities among partners (Chung, Singh, and Lee, 2000). For the FINANCE and TELCO networks to function properly all the participating members are indispensable and non substitutable. Therefore the power distribution among them could only be equal.

All the other inter-firm networks presented in this book are focal arrangements. There are many reasons that can explain such topologies. First of all, in traditional industries, networks are formatted around large companies that assume the role of the focal node. Such a case is presented by Corsten et al. where the network of suppliers emerged around the OEM. Moreover, the OEM itself triggered through specific actions the formation of the network and naturally assumed the role of the focal node. In this case the major issue that the focal node must address is the *management of the power shifts* that occur among its different tiers of suppliers in a way that will permit the focal node to preserve its position. Nodal network topologies emerge also in cases where a company creates a network of subcontractors for a specific project. In Dimer (Nikas and Poulymenakou, in this volume), a construction consortium, network partners are concentrated around the primer contractor. In such cases the node triggers the formation by assigning specific tasks to collaborating companies. The prime issue that any focal company needs to address is *the coordination of the partners*. Finally, focal topologies evolve also when large companies in some markets launch industry-wide initiatives that trigger the collaboration among the various players. This is the case of R-L that became the focal node in its network of suppliers through an ECR initiative. In such a network the basic issue is the *engagement of the major actors* of the industry in the initiative in order to gain acceptance and reinforce the position of the focal firm.

Stable vs. dynamic networks

Most inter-firm networks are characterized as medium to long-term purposeful arrangements however the longitudinal character of this organizational form does not mean that partners cannot enter or leave the network. There are many instances that prove that in inter-firm arrangements partners change according to the needs of the network.

There are networks that are stable throughout their life cycle like FINANCE and TELCO where the core of partners do not change. The major issues that managers have to address in this type of network is the *creation of stable social ties* among the responsible of each company in order to keep the network running. However, in most cases presented in this book, partners can join or leave the network at any time according to their strategic planning at the firm level. One typical instance of a dynamic network is the OEM network of suppliers presented by Corsten et al. (this volume). The composition of the network partners changes according to the components necessary for each new car model that the OEM launches in the market. There the major issue is the *choice of the appropriate suppliers* and the management of these changes in order to achieve a smooth transition. Networks like the OEM might be dynamic and constantly evolving however to the external observer they keep a unique, constant picture over time. There are other networks that are so dynamic and transient that even their outside picture is not the same over time. This is the case of the inter-firm collaborations presented by Nielsen and Mahnke, which have created a web of collaborating partners from which they can pick and choose according to their needs. Or the networks in the pharmaceutical industry discussed by Jørgensen and Vintergaard (this volume). There, the management issues that must be addressed concern the *absorption of the necessary knowledge* from each partner.

Open vs. closed network entry

The multitude of network types imposes yet another criterion against which managers need to map their inter-firm arrangements. This criterion concerns the entry barriers that each network imposes to potential partners. There are inter-firm arrangements that are open ended and permit entry to the companies that fulfill the criteria imposed by the network. There are also networks that once formed remain closed to companies interested to join in.

One of the closed networks investigated in this book is eMaster. Once the network reached the number of ten partners, it has been decided that no new member could join the arrangement. This decision can be primarily attributed to the concern of the existing members over the quality of the product they offer. Furthermore, pedagogical reasons regarding the number of students that could work together forced the universities to restrict the network to the number of ten partners. In this type of network the major issue is to *ensure innovation* in an environment that cannot be infused with novel ideas by the entry of new companies.

Inter-firm networks in mobile commerce, on the other hand, are open-ended. The focal firm has created a web of cooperations with different companies in the industry in to keep in pace with the innovation. In this type of inter-firm arrangement the major issues concern the *selection of appropriate partners*. However, another issue that managers who intend to enter open networks must also consider is the *mode of entry* in order not to disturb the ecology of the network and provoke the hostility of the existing partners.

Enabling or supporting role of IT

Information Technology is a powerful contributing factor of the business networking trend (Jarvenpaa and Ives, 1994). Most of the inter-firm arrangements presented in this book evolved out of the new capabilities of information management and communication systems. However, the influences of IT in business networks are not uniform (Fulk and DeSanctis, 1999) which means that managers need to have a clear picture of the role of IT in an inter-firm network (Monge and Fulk, 1999). This exercise will help them see clearly the degree of importance of IT in the collaboration among their partners. Most importantly, it will also help them overcome the usual optimistic voices about a unique and highly disruptive role of IT in the business environment (Ching, 1997).

IT can enable inter-firm networks (Fulk, 2001). This is the case of R-L (Papakiriakopoulos, this volume) that emerged out of the collaboration of retailers and suppliers in the implementation of a common electronic platform for the management of out-of-stock situations. Collaboration among retailers and suppliers existed even before. However, the emergence of an innovative firm, R-L, facilitated the creation of a stable network between these two groups of actors in the fast-moving consumer goods industry. More specifically, what triggered the formation of the network is precisely the technological solution that R-L offered to traditional players which indicates the enabling role of IT in this network. In this type of networks, managers need to deal with the *implementation of the IT solution* and the *creation of innovative offers* to the participants in order to gain their commitment.

IT can also support existing networks and endow existing practices with more up-to-date solutions. In the construction industry, as analyzed by Nikas and Poulymenakou in this volume, the undertaking of projects by inter-firm arrangements is a very old practice. In this case, the collaboration platform was implemented in the existing network of partners in order to facilitate the exchange of information and the overall coordination of the project. In such inter-organizational arrangements, managers need to explicitly *deal with the transition from one mode of work to another*. IT solutions may present great advantages nevertheless employees might resist their implementation and turn obsolete very innovative initiatives. To this end, managers need to deal with the *changes in work practices* and the *power shifts* real or imaginary that occur in the various members of the network.

4. Managing inter-firm networks: a life cycle approach

Inter-firm network management provides the concepts and methods that organizations engaged in inter-firm arrangements need in order to make sense of the more complex yet inherently more focused situation in which they are involved. As Dyer et al. (2001) claim, the role of network management is to "coordinate all [network] related activity within the organization". This means that network management encompasses a multitude of activities like partner selection, role structuring and establishment of governance mechanisms which are necessary to have the alliance rolling.

However, network management is not only about setting up the inter-firm arrangement. It is also about sustaining it over time. As Doz and Hamel (1998:vi) state "managing the [network] relationship over time is usually more important than crafting the initial formal design". Unlike what most managers think, once the deal is done the work is not over (Isabella, 2002). On the contrary, it is precisely at this point that network management is even more important since managers need to infuse a collaborative mindset on the partners in order to ensure success.

Table 2. Major stages of life cycle management framework

Stage	Context	Issues
Initiation	Initial contact and discussions with potential partners	Avoidance of opportunistic behavior Selection of partners Design of the initiative Value-adding proposition
Configuration	Set up of inter-firm relationship	Definition of tasks Structuring of an efficient interface Establishment of governance mechanisms
Implementation	Establishment of plans and decisions from previous stages	Management of information exchange Introducing the new working arrangements
Stabilization	Day to day management of the inter-firm network	Reinforcement of social ties Creation of a common identity Facilitate procedural alignment Create mechanism for environmental assessment
Transformation	Changes to accommodate new needs or new partners	Exploitation of inter-partner learning Adjustment of scope Assessment of partners Facilitate the entry of new partners
Dissolution	Decline of relationship	Allocation of common resources Detection of new opportunities for collaboration

In this section we analyze the managerial challenges at each stage of the management framework. The analysis responds to the challenges presented in chapter 2. Furthermore, we propose specific guidelines that managers need to take into account in their daily practice in the context of an inter-firm arrangement.

Initiation

The initiation stage inaugurates the formation of inter-firm networks. Initiation can occur in two opposite ways. First, initiation can be a *top-down process* where the decision-making authorities of each partner decide to establish inter-firm collaboration. In this case, the efforts of the participating firms are concentrated in the partner selection. More specifically, the issues to be tackled are the following:

- **Avoidance of opportunistic behavior:** participation in inter-organizational networks always entails the danger of opportunistic behaviour. Partners that intend to enter the alliance exploit the common resources and offer nothing in return must be traced at this initial stage and excluded from the arrangement.
- **Selection of partners:** Partners need to share common values and beliefs in order to achieve the necessary fit inside an inter-firm arrangement. Network participation is a risky investment and for this reason managers must have some cues on the attitude of their prospective partners. These cues can be usually found on the values of each company and on its overall behavior over time.

However, network initiation can also be a *bottom-up process* where the inter-firm arrangement evolves out of the initiatives undertaken by individuals within organizations. In these cases, the network has to ensure institutional support that will provide a steady flow of financial and human resources to the network and backup its operations in times of abrupt changes of market conditions. Therefore, the parameters that must be taken into account are the following:

- **Design of the initiative:** while designing their initiative, the individual incubators must make sure that they have identified and incorporated in the network activities all the relevant stakeholders and especially the ones deriving from the institutional environment.
- **Value-adding proposition:** in cases where network initiation is a bottom-up initiative, organizations tend to accept networking plans if they are innovative in terms of partners, operating scheme or product. Therefore, the value-adding proposition must concern a networking activity that will bring together major players within an industry. In the case where individuals bring together organizations that already collaborate

then the new network must held operations in a different but still profitable way. Finally, the product must be innovative in its market although solely an innovative product is considered a high-risk strategy and therefore the emerging network gains very difficult institutional support.

Whether the network evolves from a top-down or a bottom-up initiative, once the above-mentioned issues are successfully addressed by the managers the network enters the next stage of its life cycle, which is the configuration.

Configuration

In this stage, the network partners are selected and the major challenge that must be addressed by the members in order to officially launch the operation of the network is the definition of the scope of the network. To this end, the issues that have to be answered are the following:

- **Definition of tasks:** collaboration between companies entails great complexity that stems out of the different routines inherent in the practice of every organization. In a network environment the major challenge for managers is to achieve equilibrium among these routines and thus balance the actions that must be performed in the network level with the everyday routines at the firm level. This can only be achieved through the definition of specific tasks to be performed by each partner in order to provide a common ground for collaboration and contain conflict at these initial stages.
- **Structuring of an efficient interface:** another issue that needs careful design at the initial stages of the life cycle is the type of communication among partners. Managers need to assure that the persons involved with specific tasks of the network are also communicating. Furthermore, managers need also to establish frequent face-to-face meetings among these persons in order to facilitate the establishment of a common context of reference for all the involved parties and moreover reduce the equivocality generated by the use of electronic media for communication.
- **Establishment of governance mechanisms:** there are two major governance mechanisms to be deployed in an inter-firm arrangement, contractual collaboration or trust-based collaboration. Whatever type of collaboration they will choose; managers must first assess the pros and the cons and decide the one that best suits the scope and the strategic goals of the network.
- **Valuation of contributions:** in every inter-organizational network the contribution of partners may involve products, technologies, know-how, information or management practices. Whatever their nature these contributions are one of the most sensitive issues of network management since

they are tightly related to the perceptions of each partner regarding what it offers to the common effort and what it subsequently expects to receive.

Once the major building blocks of the inter-organizational networks are in place the partners are ready to launch its operation. However, there is an intermediary step that concerns mainly the introduction of technological solutions in an inter-firm environment. More specifically, this stage concerns the implementation of collaborative solutions that will facilitate interaction.

Implementation

This stage concerns existing networks that are reshaped by the adoption of new collaborative technologies like collaboration platforms. The technological solution implemented in a pre-existing inter-firm arrangement influences the status quo among partners. In order to stress the importance of explicit management of this transition, this process is presented as a separate stage. However, these issues can occur in newly founded networks as well when the technological solutions adopted at the network level are different from the ones that each partner uses at the firm level. Furthermore, the implementation stage deals also with the efforts of one important node to impose its technological platforms to the rest of the partners. The issues to be tackled in these situations are the following:

- **Management of information exchange:** pre-existing networks have their own way of exchanging information among the nodes, which is fixed by everyday practice. The introduction of new collaboration platforms usually rearranges the existing information flows and subsequently affects the power of the various nodes. But in new networks, as well, the mentality of information exchange (e.g. who reports to whom, in which format etc.) at the network level if different from the one at the firm level can also generate problems. This is why it must be explicitly managed in order to facilitate the transition to the new situation.
- **Introducing the new working arrangements:** with the introduction of a new technology the existing working practices of the network participants are bound to change drastically. To this end, managers need to help workers and staff to incorporate the new system in their practices. This type of assistance is crucial since a potential rejection of the system by its users will destabilize the network.

The need for stability introduces the next stage of the network, which is situated from a temporal perspective in the aftermath of the formation process. In this stage, the inter-organizational network has started its everyday operations and the major concern of the managers focuses on the stabilization of the arrangement.

Stabilization
This stage has mainly to do with people and expectations. Stabilization is an advanced stage in the network life cycle. This means that collaboration is not in its infancy anymore; partners have a more realistic picture of each other's capabilities and conflict can easily emerge and spread. This is why managers must elicit the expectations of each partner and help them transcend from an idealistic image of the network to the real one. To this end, the major themes that emerge at this stage are the following:

- **Reinforcement of social ties:** a very efficient mechanism that can bind the network together and help it endure the shocks of reality is the social network underneath the organizational one. The existence of social ties among network partners reinforces the sentiment of trust within the network and constitutes a fertile ground for trust to flourish.
- **Creation of a common identity:** the existence of a common identity that unites all partners under the vision of a common effort can fortify this stage of the inter-firm arrangement since it gives people something to look up to especially at this stage where there are not any external challenges that can act as a bonding mechanism.
- **Facilitate procedural alignment:** although the effort to establish common procedures has been explicit from the initial stages of the network life cycle, at the stabilization phase partners are in the position to have a more realistic outlook of the partnership and allocate more realistic tasks that will eventually lead to common processes.
- **Create mechanisms for environmental assessment:** the stabilization phase is a very misleading phase since it creates a sentiment of euphoria to the network members and therefore blinds them to the external environment. Managers, have to remember that the world is not static and therefore embed in the network a monitoring system in order to trace changes of the external environment. One such mechanism can be the creation of a network of social ties that reach out of the network to other industry members.

Once stabilization is achieved the network enters in a phase of unobstructed operation and hopefully prosperity and wealth. This stage can last longer then the previous one and has less clear boundaries then the ones before. However, in a fast changing environment, inter-firm arrangements cannot be unaffected by the external pressures and sooner or later they will be forced to change. This change is described in the following stage, which is named transformation.

Transformation

In this stage network partners face changing environmental conditions and realize the need to adjust in order to survive. Therefore, transformation reflects a laborious and frequently longitudinal effort to fine-tune the inter-firm arrangement to the demands of a changing market. During this process, inter-firm management gains center stage since the successful transformation depends entirely on its doings. At this stage the issues that must be addressed are the following:

- **Exploitation of inter-partner learning:** collaboration for a long period of time that usually precedes transformation permits a thorough evaluation of each partner's capabilities, strategic intent and general vision. Inter-firm partners by working together co-evolve and therefore they can learn from each other. Managers at this stage need to exploit this learning and use it for the benefit of the alliance.
- **Adjustment of scope:** to cope with a changing environment, managers need to adjust the scope of the network to reflect current needs. However, this process entails the repetition of the negotiation among partners that took place at the initial stages of the network formation.
- **Assessment of partners:** this managerial task is complementary to the first one of this stage. Managers must use the knowledge they possess and the experience they have after a significant time of collaboration in order to evaluate the contribution of each partner and remove some nodes if necessary.
- **Facilitate the entry of new partners:** very cohesive networks contain the risk to lose contact with the outside environment and therefore miss business opportunities. To this end, managers must always be alert and open to new opportunities and prospective partners in order to infuse the inter-firm arrangement with new innovative ideas that will prevent decline.

If transition to another more up-to-date model is successful then the inter-firm arrangement enters to a negotiation phase among old and new partners that resemble the initial stages of network life cycle. However, if the attempt to change fails then the network decline and finally dissolution follow.

Dissolution

This is the final stage of the network life cycle. It is usually the outcome of unsuccessful attempts to change. However, there are networks with a more precarious character like construction projects that dissolve after the completion of the common tasks. Dissolution may signal the end of collaboration but this does not mean that managers do not have to pay special attention to this stage as well. The major issues to deal with are the following:

- **Allocation of common resources:** when the dissolved inter-firm arrangements were strategic collaboration with specific investments for the creation of common resources an allocation of the common property is in order. This is a very critical point of the dissolution stage and managers must be very careful in its management.
- **Detection of new opportunities for collaboration:** it is not unlikely for new opportunities to flourish after the dissolution of old collaborations. Managers must be alert to detect these opportunities and even pursuit new inter-firm collaboration with partners that proved invaluable during the time of common pursuits. The decline of collaboration must be confronted graceful in order to avoid rivalries and fierce competition among old partners.

It is obvious from the issues analyzed above, that network managers need to address many issues, sometimes even conflicting, during the life cycle of an inter-organizational arrangement. Every stage has different problems that need to be solved for the network to operate smoothly.

5. Enabling an inter-firm network mindset: Managerial implications

Recent research in inter-firm network management has highlighted the need of an explicit alliance mindset that managers need to possess when involved in inter-firm arrangements (Spekman et al., 1998). The concept of inter-firm network mindset refers to the perspective or frame of reference through which managers view the world and translate events into managerial reality (Isabella, 2002). The existence of such a mindset is found by many scholars (e.g. Doz and Hamel, 1998; Ireland et al., 2002) to influence the way managers formulate their strategies and deal with the uncertainty inherent in their work. In the complex area of inter-firm management, developing such a mindset is very important for the future success of any inter-firm effort since it deepens managers' perceptions and makes them more alerted to their partners' needs (Spekman et al., 1996).

In this chapter, we have presented a comprehensive list of organizing principles which aim precisely at enabling a mindset appropriate for the management of inter-firm networks. The principles emerged out of the cases analyzed at the body of the book and group the most important issues and actions that must be taken into consideration during the formation and management of inter-firm networks. Complementary to these organizing principles there is a number of implications for managers in inter-firm networks. These implications stem also from the cases analyzed at the body of the book. Their purpose is to group in a short but concise list the most important issues that facilitate the creation of an inter-firm network mindset during the life cycle of multi-partner collaborations. These implications are the following:

- **Start simple:** inter-firm collaborations must start simple. Collaboration among different organizations should start from one specific area of business and then expand to large or more complex arrangements. This approach is advantageous in two ways. First, it helps to achieve quick wins and convince skeptical partners. Secondly, inter-firm network members can gradually learn to collaborate without causing problems on a wide range of business activities. Financially, this strategy is more beneficial since investment risks are minimized and the possibility of a fruitful collaboration is increased.
- **Find mutually attractive network configuration:** not every network arrangement is attractive or even beneficial for all organizations. In the early stages of network formation it is crucial to identify each partner's motives in order to understand the benefits acquired by participating in a certain network configuration. Knowing the partners' motives, the attractiveness of certain network configurations can be assessed and reasons for insufficient commitment or cooperation can be identified. The knowledge gained can be used in subsequent stages of the life cycle in order to reconfigure the components of the inter-firm network and rejuvenate the collaboration.
- **Facilitate social integration:** management, in practically every stage of the life cycle, has to take care of investments in social capital by bringing the relevant people together. It is necessary to give people time to meet with each other and to establish a common sense of the project and a joint understanding of the major issues. Furthermore, it is equally important to select the right people to work in the inter-firm context and to establish simple ground rules to guide the cooperative work. Investing in relationship building is quite important especially in occasions when information through official channels stalls. Then the existence of social ties can free its flow through nodes and enhance communication throughout the network.
- **Create specific mechanisms for information needs elicitation**: in inter-firm environments partners fulfill different roles and therefore have different information needs. Managers need to know the specific needs of each partner in order to foster a satisfactory information regime. The

most obvious way to elicit information needs stems from the tasks and processes defined at the configuration stage of the network lifecycle. These are the primary sources for the kind of information that each partner will need. However, since the actual operation of the network can create information needs that were not anticipated during configuration, managers need to elicit information needs through questionnaires, interviews and discussions with network participants at every level of hierarchy.

- **Create specific rules of communication:** since collaboration in complex environments like inter-firm arrangements entails significant uncertainty it is important to establish specific rules for communication among partners. These rules can be simple like carbon-copying the network e-mail list to every message or very sophisticated, like specific protocols of communication according to the rank and specialization of every member. The point of these rules is to make information flows transparent and facilitate information commonality. This means that although not everybody will be eligible to possess any kind of information, if the rules of communication are common and known then everybody will know what bits of information the other partners possess. Therefore, decision-making and communications at the network level will be facilitated and conflict among partners contained.
- **Monitor processes:** processes are the backbones of every business area. Therefore, processes can be an important indicator of the degree and the quality of collaboration among network nodes. Managers need to pay special attention to the operation of inter-firm processes. Although many inter-firm arrangements at the configuration and implementation stage tend to design inter-firm processes their actual operation depends entirely on the willingness and incentives of the various partners. Therefore, the successful operation of the designed inter-firm processes or the emergence of inter-firm processes in areas that were not anticipated is a good indication of a satisfactory collaboration. The opposite stands when inter-firm processes neither function nor emerge.
- **Foster a shared vocabulary:** an important issue often neglected by management literature is the important of a shared vocabulary among inter-firm network participants. Each organization develops over time its own distinctive way of naming processes and activities. This internal vocabulary is not always understood by outside collaborators causing some times serious problems and misunderstandings. Fostering a shared vocabulary is the basis for a common understanding of joint problems, the network mission and goals to arise. A shared vocabulary allows the network members to interpret and re-interpret their action, their tasks and the network mission to adapt to future changes.

- **Expectation management is important:** The acceptance of an inter-firm collaboration by employees of the participating partners determines its success. Therefore, the value proposition for the customer, expected benefits and changing roles and relationships must be communicated clearly. The expectations, requirements and restraints of customers should be taken into consideration. If possible, a participatory development approach should be applied.

6. Concluding remarks

The field of research on network management is characterized by a high degree of theoretical and conceptual plurality (Ebers, 1999). The organized principles and implications presented in this final chapter as well as the analyses in each chapter of this book testify to the multiple theoretical and conceptual lenses that can be used in the study of inter-firm networks. This plurality gives the impression of a field thoroughly analyzed by various scholars however it also covers the existence of some issues that need more careful consideration.

From a research perspective, a neglected yet important issue of research concerns the analysis of specific costs that come with inter-organizational networking (Ebers and Grandori, 1999). Current literature and research stress usually the advantages that specific forms of networking posses over other solutions (Ahuja, 2000). Yet business networking comes at a cost. The cases of this book highlight various instances of networking costs. Nevertheless, more comprehensive analyses of the internal and external costs of networking are still missing both in theory and in practice.

By internal costs for networking, we mean those costs that the parties to a network have to bear for establishing, maintaining and managing their inter-organizational relationships (Ebers and Grandori, 1999). These costs can include information costs, power shifts costs, costs for implementing new expensive technological solutions for collaboration or cost emanating by conflicts that arise between partners. Indications for these costs are in almost every chapter of this book however there is no explicit account of their impact on the propensity of firms to form networks or in the management practices in the aftermath of the formation. External costs of networking, on the other hand, are the threats that tight collaboration among firms poses to the normal operation of our economy. Networks can be considered as incubators of monopolistic situations and therefore they can be considered as harmful for the economy and society as a whole. However, the persistence of current theory and practice to consider business networking as a positive trend do not favor research on those issues that nevertheless need to be considered carefully. In this book these issues were not investigated mainly because of the type of research approach that most of the researchers chose (i.e. case study) but also because of the general stance of the academic and business community towards business networking.

References

Ahuja, G., 2000, The duality of collaboration: inducements and opportunities in the formation of interfirm linkages, *Strategic Management Journal.* **21**(3):317-343.

Anderson, P., and Tushman, M. L., 1990, Technological Discontinuities and Dominant Designs: A Cyclical Model of Technological Change, *Administrative Science Quarterly.* **35**(4):604-633.

Bensaou, M., and Venkatraman, N., 1995, Configurations of interorganizational relationships: A comparison between US and Japanese automakers, *Management Science.* **41**(9):1471-1492.

Boddy, D., Macbeth, D., and Wagner, B., 2000, Implementing collaboration between organizations: An empirical study of supply chain partnering, *Journal of Management Studies,* **37**(7):1003-1017.

Borys, B., and Jemison, D. B., 1989, Hybrid arrangements as strategic alliances: Theoretical issues in organizational combinations, *Academy of Management Review.* **14**(2):234-249.

Ching, C., 1997, Network organizations and information technology: Introduction to the special issue on the network organizations, *Journal of Organizational Computing & Electronic Commerce.* **7**(2/3):79-81.

Chung, S. A., Singh, H., and Lee, K., 2000, Complementarity, status similarity and social capital as drivers of alliance formation, *Strategic Management Journal.* **21**(1):1-22.

Das, T. K., and Teng, B.-S., 2003, Partner analysis and alliance performance, *Scandinavian Jounal of Management.* **19**(3):279-308.

D'Aunno, T. A., and Zuckerman, H. Z., 1987, A life-cycle model of organizational federations: The case of hospitals, *Academy of Management Review.* **12**(3):534-545.

De Rond, M., and Bouchikhi, H., 2004, On the dialectics of strategic alliances. *Organization Science.* **15**(1):56-69.

Doz, Y. L., 1996, The evolution of cooperation in strategic alliances: Initial conditions or learning processes?, *Strategic Management Journal.* **17**(7):55-83.

Doz, Y. L., and Hamel, G. (1998). *Alliance advantage: The art of creating value through partnering*: Harvard Business School Press.

Draulans, J., deMan, A.-P., and Volberda, H. W. (2003). Building alliance capability: Management techniques for superior alliance performance, *Long Range Planning.* **36**(2):151-166.

Dyer, J. H. (1997). Effective interfirm collaboration: How firms minimize transaction costs and maximize transaction value. *Strategic Management Journal, 18*(7), 535-556.

Dyer, J. H., Kale, P., and Singh, H., 2001, How to make strategic alliances work, *Sloan Management Review.* **42**(4):37-43.

Ebers, M. (1999). Explaining inter-organizational network formation. In M. Ebers (Ed.), *The formation of inter-organizational networks* (pp. 3-40). New York: Oxford University Press.

Ebers, M., and Grandori, A., 1999, The forms, costs, and development dynamics of inter-organizational networking, in: *The Formation of Inter-organizational Networks,* M. Ebers, ed., Oxford University Press, New York, pp. 265-286.

Ebers, M., and Jarillo, J. C., 1998, The construction, forms and consequences of industrial networks, *International Studies of Management & Organization.* **27**(4):3-21.

Elmuti, D., and Kathawala, Y., 2001, An overview of strategic alliances, *Management Decision.* **39**(3):205-217.

Fulk, J., 2001, Global network organizations: Emergence and future prospects. *Human Relations.* **54**(1):91-99.

Fulk, J., and DeSanctis, G., 1995, Electronic communication and changing organizational forms, *Organization Science.* **6**(4):337-349.

Fulk, J., and DeSanctis, G., 1999, Articulation of communication technology and organizational form, in: *Shaping organization form: Communication, connection and community,* G. DeSanctis and J. Fulk, eds., Sage Publications. Thousand Oaks, CA, pp. 5-32.

Garud, R., and Kumaraswamy, A., 1993, Changing competitive dynamics in network industries: An exploration of Sun Microsystems' open systems strategy, *Strategic Management Journal.* **14**(5):351-369.

George, V., and Farris, G., 1999, Performance of alliances: Formative stages and changing organizational and environmental influences, *R&D Management.* **29**(4):379-389.

Glaister, K. W., and Buckley, P. J., 1996, Strategic motives for international alliance formation, *Journal of Management Studies.* **33**(3):301-332.

Hitt, M. A., Dacin, M. T., Levitas, E., Arregle, J.-L., and Borza, A., 2000, Partner selection in emerging and developed market contexts: Resource-based and organizational learning perspectives, *Academy of Management Journal.* **43**(3):449-467.

Huxham, C., and Beech, N., 2002, *Points of power in interorganizational networks: Learning from a learning network*, in: Academy of Management Proceedings, pp. 6.

Ireland, R. D., Hitt, M. A., and Vaidyanath, D., 2002, Alliance management as a source of competitive advantage, *Journal of Management.* **28**(3):413-446.

Isabella, L. A., 2002, Managing an alliance is nothing like business as usual, *Organizational Dynamics.* **31**(1):47-59.

Jarvenpaa, S. L., and Ives, B., 1994, The global network organization of the future: Information management opportunities and challenges, *Journal of Management Information Systems.* **10**(4):25-57.

Kale, P., Dyer, J., and Singh, H., 2001, Value creation and success in strategic alliances: Alliancing skills and the role of alliance structure and systems, *European Management Journal.* **19**(5):463-471.

Kanter, R. M., 1994, Collaborative advantage: The art of alliances, *Harvard Business Review.* **72**(4):96-108.

Larson, A., 1992, Network dyads in entrepreneurial settings: A study of the governance of exchange relationships, *Administrative Science Quarterly.* **37**(1):76-104.

Lowndes, V., and Skelcher, C., 1998, The dynamics of multi-organizational partnerships: An analysis of changing modes of governance, *Public Administration.* **76**(2):313-333.

Madhavan, R., Koka, B. R., and Prescott, J. E., 1998, Networks in transition: How industry events (re)shape interfirm relationships, *Strategic Management Journal.* **19**(5):439-459.

Miles, R. E., and Snow, C. C., 1986, Organizations: New concepts for new forms, *California Management Review.* **28**(3):62-73.

Miles, R. E., and Snow, C. C. (1992). Causes of failure in network organizations. *California Management Review, 34*(4), 53-72.

Monge, P., and Fulk, J., 1999, Communication technology for global network organizations. in: *Shaping organization form: Communication, connection, and community*, G. DeSanctis and J. Fulk, eds., Sage Publications, Thousand Oaks, CA, pp. 71-100.

Nooteboom, B., 2004, *Inter-firm collaboration, learning and networks*, Routledge, New York.

Osborn, R. N., and Hagedoorn, J., 1997, The institutionalization and evolutionary dynamics of interorganizational alliances and networks, *Academy of Management Journal,* **40**(2):261-278.

Park, S. H., 1996, Managing an interorganizational network: A framework of the institutional mechanism for network control, *Organization Studies.* **17**(5):795-824.

Poulymenakou, A., and Prasopoulou, E., 2004, Adopting a life cycle perspective to explain the transition from technological innovation to alliance management, *Management Decision.* **42**(9):1115-1130.

Richardson, B., 1995, How to administrate the networked organization: tips from the theory and practice of management, *The Learning Organization.* **2**(4):4-13.

Ring, P. S., 2000, The three T's of alliance creation: Task, team and time, *European Management Journal.* **18**(2):152-163.

Ring, P. S., and Van de Ven, A. H., 1994, Developmental processes of cooperative interorganizational relationships, *Academy of Management Review.* **19**(1):90-118.

Salk, J. E., 2005, Often called for but rarely chosen: Alliance research that directly studies process, *European Management Review.* **2**(2):117-122.

Saxton, T., 1997, The effects of partner and relationship characteristics on alliance outcomes, *Academy of Management Journal.* **40**(2):443-461.

Spekman, R. E., Forbes III, T. M., Isabella, L. A., and MacAvoy, T. C., 1998, Alliance management: A view from the past and a look to the future, *Journal of Management Studies.* **35**(6):747-772.

Spekman, R. E., Isabella, L. A., MacAvoy, T. C., and Forbes III, T. M., 1996, Creating strategic alliances which endure, *Long Range Planning.* **29**(3):346-357.

Vervest, P., Preiss, K., van Heck, E., and Pau, L.-F., 2004, The emergence of smart business networks, *Journal of Information Technology.* **19**(4):228-233.

Vyas, N. M., Shelburn, W. L., and Rogers, D. C., 1995, An analysis of strategic alliances: Forms, functions and framework, *Journal of Business & Industrial Marketing.* **10**(3):47-60.

Printing and Binding: Strauss GmbH, Mörlenbach